The World Food Problem:
Consensus and Conflict

The World Food Problem:
Consensus and Conflict

Edited by
RADHA SINHA

PERGAMON PRESS

OXFORD · NEW YORK · TORONTO · SYDNEY · PARIS · FRANKFURT

U.K.	Pergamon Press Ltd., Headington Hill Hall, Oxford OX3 0BW, England
U.S.A.	Pergamon Press Inc., Maxwell House, Fairview Park, Elmsford, New York 10523, U.S.A.
CANADA	Pergamon of Canada Ltd., 75 The East Mall, Toronto, Ontario, Canada
AUSTRALIA	Pergamon Press (Aust.) Pty. Ltd., 19a Boundary Street, Rushcutters Bay, N.S.W. 2011, Australia
FRANCE	Pergamon Press SARL, 24 rue des Ecoles, 75240 Paris, Cedex 05, France
FEDERAL REPUBLIC OF GERMANY	Pergamon Press GmbH, 6242 Kronberg-Taunus, Pferdstrasse 1, Federal Republic of Germany

First edition 1978

British Library Cataloguing in Publication Data

The world food problem.
1. Food supply - Political aspects - Addresses,
essays, lectures
I. Sinha, Radha II. "World development"
338.1'9'08   HD9000.6   78-40673
ISBN 0-08-022229-3

First published as a special issue of the journal *World Development*

Volume 5, Numbers 5-7

Printed in Great Britain by A. Wheaton & Co. Ltd., Exeter

Contents

Contents

World Development, 1977, Vol. 5, Nos. 5–7, pp. 371–382. Pergamon Press. Printed in Great Britain.

The World Food Problem:
Consensus and Conflict
Editor's Introduction

RADHA SINHA

University of Glasgow

Not much has changed fundamentally since the World Food Conference met in November 1974 in Rome. Many blueprints are still on the drawing boards; many negotiations remain stalemated. World food security and the promised 'food-aid' target remain unattained. However, there have been some changes in a favourable direction.

Weather being kinder, recent harvests have been substantially larger. World cereal production in 1976 increased by nearly 9% over the previous year, i.e. by 110 million tons. Cereal production in developing market economies increased by 5% in 1976 following a 9% rise in the previous year. This improved performance in the last two years has pushed up the long-term growth rate of cereal production between 1961 and 1976 to 2.9% per annum.[1] At the national level several countries have improved their stocks, though in many stocks are still appreciably below the official targets. Improvements in the world supply situation for the main foodgrains and an absence of catastrophic famine conditions in any part of the world now provide an opportunity to discuss the probable line of action without the emotional atmosphere that surrounded the world population and food conference in 1974.

The prediction of alarming consequences stemming from the rise in oil prices and the much-publicized risk of the Arab take-over of 'Western' economic interests have not come true. Dreams of 'solidarity' on both sides — developing and developed — remain almost unrealized. The Third World countries have increasingly recognized that a policy of 'confrontation', in order to be something more than rhetoric, requires both internal as well as external sacrifices that many leaders will not be readily prepared to accept. All this has led both the developed and developing countries to adopt somewhat more realistic postures. The change in the US administration and its apparently more conciliatory attitude towards the Third World has helped in continuing the dialogue.

While such attitudinal changes have been taking place, there has been some though not substantial improvement in our understanding of the world food problem.

There is an emerging consensus, which is reflected in this collection, that alarming prognostications associated with the world's 'lifeboat' and 'triage' — the so-called tragedy of commons — are a flagrant denial of the technological possibilities for both increasing agricultural production and reducing family size. Many feel that hunger and malnutrition, the extent of which is still a debatable issue, are largely a product of maldistribution of world resources between the rich and the poor within and between countries and of misdirection of national as well as international priorities. It is therefore widely felt that while the need for ensuring expanded production to feed the growing population, together with a reasonably accelerated pace of population control — particularly in the areas of high density — cannot be minimized, it is the social reform within the countries and the restructuring of the world economic system towards a greater degree of international cooperation and fairness which must receive high priority. It is sometimes legitimately argued that without the latter, the former may not materialize, at least not as easily as is commonly believed.

In a world full of conflicting interests and ideologies, there are bound to be differences in the perception of problems and priorities, as well as in the methods of tackling them. The aim of this collection is not to gloss over such differences but to highlight both the consensus and the conflicts. It is only by appreciating these differences in their proper perspectives that realistic solutions can be formulated or implemented.

CURRENT FOOD AND POPULATION SITUATION

Before we delve deeper into some of the main economic and political issues it may be worthwhile having a brief look at the food and population situation both on the global and the regional levels. As Poleman stresses, because of the inadequacies of relevant information on production and consumption of food and its various determinants such as family size, levels and distribution of income, etc. and their interrelationships as well as the methodological problems of estimating nutritional requirements, the exact magnitude of hunger and malnutrition is difficult to estimate. No one doubts that there is a substantial number of underfed people all over the world, particularly among pregnant and lactating mothers, young children, the landless and the very poor both in the rural and the urban areas. Nevertheless, in the absence of detailed information on food distribution within families, the FAO estimate of 500 million inadequately fed people has to be treated as a rough approximation.

It is undeniable that, since World War II, the problem of hunger and malnutrition has been aggravated by unprecedented rates of population growth, resulting from momentus decline in mortality rates in most developing countries. In many of these food production kept pace with (or exceeded) population growth. As such, the existence of hunger and malnutrition cannot be solely explained in terms of the Malthusian phenomenon of population out-stripping food supply.

Besides, there are visible signs, as described by Mauldin, indicating that population growth is slowing down sharply in the developed countries and significantly in the developing countries. A few of the developed countries may even have negative rates of growth. In developing countries too, major decline in fertility has taken place, though it continues to be less marked than the decline in mortality. Changes in fertility have been dramatic in Asia (where the bulk of the world population lives) and the Pacific, and substantial in Central and South America. For lack of adequate statistics, the situation in Africa is uncertain, though in the three most populous African countries, Egypt, Tunisia and Mauritius, fertility has

declined appreciably in the last 25 years. All this suggests that there is a case for cautious optimism on the population front. However, even with the continuing trends of decline in growth rates, the total world population by the end of this century will be around 6.5 billion, nearly 5 billion of which will be in the developing countries. Obviously, such a large population, particularly in the developing countries, will raise issues not only of feeding the growing population at a decent level but also of providing basic amenities such as adequate living space, health and education. If political unrest, environmental catastrophies and resource depletion are to be avoided, more enlightened strategies of development, employment creation and redistributive justice have to be evolved. In so doing, attempts have to be made to learn from past mistakes of both the developed and developing countries.

NEED FOR REDISTRIBUTIVE JUSTICE

By now, there is a growing awareness that 'modernization' of agriculture and the resulting increase in output in itself will not cure the problems of poverty, inequality of income and malnutrition unless it goes hand in hand with a radical distributional strategy. Recent experiences with the 'Green Revolution' technology have clearly demonstrated that in spite of its 'scale neutrality', it is mainly the richer farmers who have benefited from it and the disparities of income between richer and poorer farmers have widened. Similarly, by the very input-intensive nature of the technology it can be used mainly in areas well-endowed with water and therefore income disparities between rain-fed and irrigated areas on the one hand and the dry areas on the other will be larger. This has implications for the arid zones of the world, of which Africa and the Near East have more than their fair share. Such inter-regional disparities can be reduced, as El-Sherbini argues, by special programmes directed towards the arid-zone farmers.

An equitable sharing of the benefits of new technology will ultimately depend on the 'ideology' of a country. As Etienne indicates, both China and India in the last 25 years had followed a broadly similar strategy with regard to agricultural technology; the overall rates of growth of agricultural outputs in both countries have been similar. However, in the absence of an egalitarian sharing of food the incidence of hunger and malnutrition in India continues to be high, while it is virtually eliminated in China. Recent emphasis by development economists as well as 'aid' agencies on employment creation and redirection of resources towards the rural poor may somewhat ameliorate the problems of poverty-related hunger in poorer countries. But unless there is a radical rethinking about the property relationships (land ownership in particular) and the institutional set-up through which such funds are channelled to the poor, and unless the machinery for political participation gives the poor an adequate voice in the determination of rural priorities, much of the funds diverted to the rural areas will once again fall into the hands of the richer rather than the poorer farmers. There is growing evidence that the resources of the cooperatives in many developing countries have been used by the richer farmers for their own ends while neglecting the interests of the poorer farmers. As long as property ownership remains the basis for political power, and the inequities of wealth and power continue, it is difficult to see how the rural poor will obtain their 'fair' share of the limited resources available for agricultural development in most developing countries.

The need for more egalitarian policies in relation to the sharing of economic resources as well as the power of political decision-making is important not only in the densely populated countries of Asia, but also in other parts of the world. For instance, the existence of high levels of under- and unemployment is explained by Barraclough in terms of the disproportionate share of resources going to the commercial sector to the detriment of the traditional smallholder sector. Production decisions in the former, controlled mainly by large national and multinational corporations (MNCs), are dictated essentially by financial considerations. With their considerable political influence, the MNCs may have monopoly power in national markets for specific commodities, and tend to restrict production with government collusion. In order to avoid labour problems, they often introduce agricultural machinery obtainable at highly subsidized prices, thus bringing about what Feder calls 'the elimination of Latin America's rural proletariat'. Both Barraclough and Feder suggest that the 'modernization' of agriculture together with the vertical integration of agricultural production, processing and marketing and their concentration in the hands of relatively few financial groups has benefited, as elsewhere, social classes with the most economic and political power. This includes foreign investors and the Latin American property-owning class, together with their allies and dependents

such as civil and military bureaucracies and a limited number of skilled and organized workers.

It is interesting to note that similar structural changes are taking place within developed countries as well. For instance, according to Sundquist, as a result of increased mechanization and specialization of commercial farms coupled with the dropping of numerous small and usually inefficient livestock enterprises, there has been a rapid decline in US farm employment which fell by nearly 38% between 1960 and 1975. There is also evidence of increasing penetration of agriculture through vertical integration and forward contact by multinationals (often non-agricultural ones). These tendencies, particularly the proletarianization of the US small peasantry, are causing increasing resentment within the US as well.[2] Even those small farmers who continue in farming are often at a disadvantage *vis-à-vis* the buyers, particularly in the cases of vertical integration through contract buying by big agribusiness. In such cases, as Rhodes suggests, group action, in the form of farmers' cooperatives, may provide an answer. Some of the preconditions for success of cooperatives are: (i) a long-term commitment of adequate capital and all of members' marketings; (ii) members must accept some sort of pool on average prices for the marketing period; (iii) the cooperatives, as strongly market-oriented firms, may specify varieties to produce and the extent of the output; and (iv) the cooperatives must integrate forward as far as possible. All this necessitates effective cooperative action, capable management, adequate capital and efficient administration. Since none of the above conditions can generally be met in developing countries, particularly with regard to poor farmers, state initiative and support is needed. In countries where bureaucracy is allegedly in league with agribusiness (national or foreign) interests, what chances do the poor peasants have of obtaining a fair price for their products?

The plight of the small farmers in the US is yet another reminder that, in the absence of countervailing economic and political power, the poor subsistence farmers in developing countries cannot be easily helped by conventional weapons such as guaranteed prices. Such guaranteed high prices, even though they may often lead to increased output (or marketed surplus), largely help the richer and middle peasants. In so far as the small and subsistence farmers are concerned, because of inadequate channels of marketing information and the inappropriate credit and marketing structure, the benefits of high prices rarely reach them. More often than not, the subsistence farmers have only a limited amount to sell, sometimes to their moneylenders with whom the crops are mortgaged in advance. It can also be argued that high prices of food may often increase the cost of living of the industrial workers and people working on the infrastructure projects. Such an increase in wage costs will not only reduce the competitiveness of manufactures in export markets, but also raise the cost of extension of infrastructure which may ultimately adversely affect the prospects of the agricultural sector itself. Besides, to the very poor both in the rural and urban areas who depend at least partially on bought food, increases in food prices will often be socially unjust, unless it can be conclusively shown that high prices do inevitably, by creating additional employment, raise the real income of the poor irrespective of the rise in prices.

It is also debatable whether 'paternalistic' programmes within the existing institutional set-up will be of much use to the poor. Experiences both in developing and developed countries are not very encouraging. For example, the small and marginal farmers' schemes in India which aim at raising the level of living of the poor through provision of credit and marketing facilities and crash programmes of employment creation have failed to benefit the poorest, while the relatively better off can be covered by them.[3] Similar has been the experience of the US Federal Food Stamp Programme aimed at subsidizing the food bill of the poor. Five years after President Nixon pledged to eradicate hunger in the United States a panel on nutrition and special groups contended that 'these efforts have been unresponsive to the needs of the poor. Even those who are receiving aid have been provided with inadequate relief in light of the inflationary price spiral.[4] The panel indicated that only 15 million of estimated 37 to 50 million eligible persons were taking advantage of the programme. Millions did not know they were eligible.[5] If this is the verdict of experts on the food and nutrition situation of the poor in the US, with all its wealth, grain surpluses and a very extensive and politically alert mass media, what hope can one have for the very poor in developing countries, who do not have any of the above advantages.

FUTURE TRENDS

Many developing countries, as Aziz indicates, are food deficit countries. Even though one has to accept long- or medium-term demand projections with some reservations, as both Aziz and Diwan warn, it is almost certain that with growing incomes, increasing urbanization and changing food habits, the gap between domestic demand and supply is likely to grow wider in coming years. The gap will probably be bigger even if egalitarian policies were more commonly adopted in the poorer countries. Whether such egalitarian policies, by improved productive efficiency and by increasing people's participation and involvement with development plans as has happened in China, will increase production and thereby reduce the eventual food deficits is difficult to surmise. However, it is almost certain that much of the increase in the projected demand in the developing countries has been, and will be met, by domestic increases in production. The relative self-sufficiency of most developing countries is much higher (and will remain so) than some of the food deficit developed countries such as Japan which has emerged as the largest grain importing country. The same is true of some of the Western European countries (such as West Germany or the United Kingdom) although there is a distinct possibility, as Bergman suggests, of the European Economic Community, as a 'whole', developing surpluses in some food products. Eastern Europe is not likely to fare much better. According to Nove the German Democratic Republic, much the same as its Western counterpart, will remain a substantial importer. Bulgaria, Czechoslovakia and Poland will continue to be grain deficit countries. The USSR in normal years is a grain exporting country. In spite of a considerable increase in grain yields during the last two decades, the USSR has to depend on substantial imports in years of crop failures caused by unfavourable weather conditions. However, in Nove's view, huge imports in recent years have been largely aimed at increasing highly subsidized meat production so as to enable the country to catch up with the excessive meat consumption standards of the West. Such a trend will most likely continue in the foreseeable future and it is highly likely that the 'vanguards of world revolution' by emulating 'capitalistic' standards of food consumption will continue to import significant quantities of grain, even though it may mean higher world prices which many developing countries can ill afford, and consequent misery and starvation in many developing countries.

Can the increasing deficits of food both in developing as well as developed countries be met by a similar increase in food production?

Technological potential

There is a growing consensus among technical experts that there is tremendous potential in the world to increase food production even within the limits of known technology. Buringh, after analyzing several studies, comes to the conclusion that enough food can be produced for a population that is more than 5 to 10 times the present number. Many experts feel that the world population growth will in a century and a half stabilize at 12,000 million people. Feeding them, if there is enough political will on the part of the governments, does not pose a problem. Besides, new technologies for greater photosynthetic efficiency, biological nitrogen fixation, and other new approaches to plant breeding and more efficient and non-polluting up-take of nutrients by plant roots are already within reach of plant scientists. Wittwer reports many such advances in the field of crop and animal sciences. There may be some cause for concern with regard to pest control, not only because many of the pesticides and insecticides cause serious environmental contamination but also because crop protection technology becomes obsolete at an alarming rate. Similarly, the experience with the control of soil erosion has not been very encouraging even in the US. In spite of 40 years of the US Department of Agriculture's efforts at promoting soil conservation practices through technical and financial assistance, education and persuasion, enormous losses of top soil from the best American lands are continuing. Thus, the question remains whether the transition from 'traditional' to 'modern' farming can be attained without creating ecological imbalances.

Similarly, there is a genuine risk of water depletion, particularly in Asia and Europe where water consumption may, by the year 2000, exceed the real water resources (the realistic proportion of run-off water can be used) by as much as 50%. In Sokolov's view, it is essential to change quite resolutely our view of rivers and lakes as the last link of the sewage systems. Proper planning in management and preservation of our water supply will not only require heavy investment in sewage treatment within national boundaries, but also international cooperation and participation in preventive inspection and enforcement against qualitative depletion of water.

Economic and political bottlenecks

Nevertheless, there are enough reasons for optimism on the scientific and technological front. However, the translating of the potentialities created by modern technology into reality will require tremendous resources, both financial and human, which most developing countries lack. It is doubtful whether sufficient international support can be mounted for this purpose. Recent experience with external assistance for food and agricultural development, according to Bhattacharjee, is rather disconcerting. The level of commitment, in real terms, remained at less than half of the requirements of assistance discussed by the World Food Conference; the actual flow was even lower. It is highly unlikely that the above trend will be reversed in the foreseeable future, at least not while the provision of aid, as Simantov suggests, continues to be a tool of foreign policy of the donor countries. Even if the foreign resources were made available, it is doubtful whether the developing countries would be able to raise domestically adequate complementary resources, let alone evolve appropriate institutions and value systems so as to ensure that the fruits of development are equitably shared between the rich and the poor, thus guaranteeing social justice to all sections of the community without unnecessarily impairing incentives.[6]

AREAS OF IMMEDIATE CONCERN

There are no easy solutions and the search for appropriate answers to some of the above problems will continue, for a long time, to tax the ingenuity of planners and political decision-makers both at the national and international levels. However, there are some areas of immediate concern which can be ignored only at the cost of jeopardizing developmental efforts and thereby aggravating human misery.

Supply of petrochemical inputs

One of the major problem areas, particularly for the developing countries, would be their vulnerability to shortages and high prices of petrochemical inputs (e.g., fertilizer, fuel and pesticides). According to Allen, in times of high prices as experienced in 1973 through 1975 they found it increasingly difficult to continue importing fertilizer on the scale to which they had become accustomed. The problem was further aggravated because the governments of most exporting developed countries ensured that their own farmers had preferential access to the available supply — even if in the process export contracts to the developing countries had to be broken. In many cases this probably resulted in a decline in agricultural output in those developing countries. In addition, it must have slowed down the adoption of modern agricultural technology. In Allen's view shortages may continue for the next two or three years and the situation may be further aggravated in the early 1980s. In spite of their own capacity expansion, the developing countries will continue to be critically dependent on imports. Ensuring a reasonable supply to developing countries in times of world shortages would not be easy, particularly if the major exporters behave as they did during the 1973—75 crisis. One way of mitigating the likely shortages is to increase investment in the fertilizer industry. Such investments — often cyclical in nature — are closely linked with fluctuations in world agricultural commodity prices. Therefore, any meaningful solution to the problems of fertilizer supply would require not only buffer-stocks in fertilizer together with a counter-cyclical investment incentive but also measures for reducing fluctuations in agricultural prices including a world grain reserve.

Instability in agricultural output

This brings us to the problems of instability in agricultural output, another area of concern requiring the immediate attention of world governments. By the very nature of the enterprise, agriculture is vulnerable to vagaries of climate. Droughts, storms, floods, etc. will continue to make the food supply position precarious, even in countries with satisfactory rates of growth in agricultural output *vis-à-vis* population (or demand). Such factors may cause a major drop in production over a wide area, adversely affecting national and international prices as well as levels of food consumption, particularly of low-income groups, especially in the developing countries. The effect of droughts in the developing countries on the very poor, i.e. subsistence farmers and the landless labour, is inordinately high. Subsistence farmers and their families faced with a shortfall in their own production are forced to eat less and evidence from drought-stricken areas in India suggests that calorie intake may in the short term fall to a little more than a quarter of the requirement.[7] On the large farms a reduction in the area under cultivation, due to climatic factors, leads to a reduction in the numbers employed on the farms, thus reducing the pur-

chasing power at the disposal of agricultural labour at a time when food prices are rising. Governments' efforts to deal with the problems caused by extensive crop failures lead to a major diversion of resources from development needs to emergency relief work and thus compromise economic growth and creation of employment.[8]

Any policy measures to eliminate or reduce the impact of fluctuations in domestic food production must aim at buying up surpluses in a favourable year and storing them for release in a deficit year. Normal trading activity may act in this direction, but in years with significant shortages, speculative hoarding of grain often aggravates the situation. What is true of private traders within national boundaries is equally true for individual countries in the international market. The interests of the producing and consuming countries do not always coincide. In times of widespread crop failures the surplus countries can force up world prices by withholding supplies from the market, while in times of abundant harvests they can dump their surpluses and thereby further depress world prices. In such a situation, an internationally-owned and operated stock can perform much the same functions on the world market as publicly-owned and operated stocks within a country.

The need for such a supra-national grain authority, in order to stabilize world grain prices, as well as to provide relief in emergencies, has been felt for a long time[9] but with no substantial progress to date. There is now a growing concern among climatologists, as reflected in the Bryson and Ross paper, that a new climatic pattern is emerging which may persist for several decades. Climate will become more variable than in recent decades and it is possible that food production systems will not be able to adjust easily to major crop failures. As a result, there is a great risk of massive suffering and starvation unless adequate grain reserves are created.

Nature of the world grain market

To appreciate the nature of the opposition to the idea of an internationally-owned and operated reserve, one has to look into the main characteristics of the world grain market. Two most important features of this market are: (a) the existence of various artificial barriers to production and trade and (b) the predominance of a small number of countries, particularly the developed ones, both on the demand and the supply side. As Labys indicates, grain exports to and from developed countries are restricted by trade barriers which include fixed import duties, *ad valorem* import duties, variable import levies, fixed import quotas and percentage import quotas. Grain production in the developed countries is protected by a combination of the above barriers and domestic price supports, acreage allotments and subsidies. This leads, as Schertz and Bernston suggest, to a continued insulation of internal markets from the effects of changes in food production in their own country or in other countries. Thus the present picture of agricultural production and trade is furthest from the conventional image of agriculture coming close to 'perfect competition'. Johnson also is critical of government policies and argues that the problems created during the early 1970s as a result of disappointing harvests would not have been as severe as they were, if the industrial nations, particularly the EEC, did not have such protective policies. To him, the miseries created at the time were the cost of the failure to liberalize world trade in grains. He, like Josling, feels that inflexible domestic farm and trade policies lie at the root of the world food problem.

If one goes by Bergman's assessment of the situation the prospects for any major removal of trade barriers in agricultural products are rather bleak. In his view, many European governments will not be able to cope with their employment problems, particularly in view of the structural changes taking place in European agriculture which might ultimately lead to impoverization and displacement of small farmers. One of their aims will be to keep as many people as possible on land even at the cost of farm surpluses. The Europeans feel that the social and political cost of agricultural *laissez faire* is rather high and therefore they would continue with their present state-managed system which in their view is not very different from the system used in the US.

On the other hand, even if it were possible to remove all the trade barriers the world would still be far away from 'free competition' in world grain trade because of the other feature of this market. As Labys points out, only a few countries account for most of the grain trade. The US, Canada and Australia account for 75% of wheat, 68% of barley and 58% of oats exports. The US and Canada supply 51% of total rye exports, while the US alone supplies 68% of the maize, 58% of sorghum and 25% of rice exports. Among the developing countries only Burma, Cambodia, Thailand and Argentina are grain exporters. On the demand side, major markets for wheat have been Japan and the EEC among the developed countries and India, Pakistan, Brazil and the United Arab Republic among the developing countries. More than 85% of wheat and 80% of the coarse grain entering world trade goes to the developed countries.

Thus the world market in grains is largely influenced by only a small number of exporting and importing countries. Within these countries international transactions often involve government agencies or their agents and are therefore, as Schertz and Bernston indicate, significantly affected by political decisions. Even in the case of the US where grain exports are mainly in the hands of private companies, export limitations have been imposed by political decisions, as in the case of soyabeans and oilseeds during July–September 1973, the cutbacks on USSR purchases in the last quarter of 1974 and the subsequent arrangements with the USSR for limits on their purchases.

Importing countries buy their grain through a central buying system, a commercial buying system or a combination of the two.[10] Most Communist countries have state agencies (e.g., Export Khleb of the USSR). Such agencies buy either directly from state selling agencies like the Canadian Wheat Board or from private trade.

Sometimes governments locate buying missions in exporting countries. Poland, Israel, Pakistan and India are countries which buy through such missions. Most North African and Middle Eastern countries (i.e. Algeria, Morocco, Tunisia) have official government purchasing organizations attached to one of their ministries (i.e. supply, commerce or agriculture). Countries in Western Europe, including the UK, obtain their grain imports through the activity of commercial buyers. The Japanese buy through a combination of government agency buying and private trading. The Japanese Food Agency has the monopoly of buying all wheat and barley requirements. It controls offers closely, allowing only Japanese importers to offer.[11]

Among the exporters, the Canadian Wheat Board, a government monopoly, is responsible for grain exports and for the 'Board' wheat sold in Canada. Coarse grain exports from the 'designated areas' are the responsibility of the Canadian Wheat Board. The Australian Wheat Board is the sole marketer of wheat within Australia and of wheat within Australia and of wheat and wheat flour for export. There is no national marketing authority for barley but grower-controlled statutory marketing boards operate in each state. The marketing of oats, maize and sorghum is undertaken by various state statutory marketing boards in most states of Australia.[12] In Argentina private traders handle all export trade but the National Grain Board (Junta National de Granos), a semi-autonomous government body has regulatory powers over all grain trading and can enter into export contracts.[13] In the US the marketing system is comparatively free from government controls with the Commodity Credit Corporation (CCC) being closest to the Canadian or Australian Wheat Boards. CCC, created in 1948 under a federal charter, is authorized to buy and sell, make agricultural loans, store, transport, and perform other necessary commodity activities.[14] However, the bulk of grain exporters from the US is handled by a small number of private companies. A recent report[15] suggests that five major grain export firms account for 85% of the US grain exports. In recent years this includes an estimated 93% of the wheat, 90% of the foodgrain, and 86% of soyabean exports. Sundquist suggests that the structure of the US grain export industry is highly efficient but at the same time highly oligopolistic.[16]

When only 4 or 5 companies control 95% of the world grain trade (it is suggested that between them Continental and Cargill control nearly half, i.e. around 50 million tons), the oligopolistic nature of the market is hardly open to doubt.[17] How this oligopoly power affects world prices or official policies is difficult to ascertain. Most grain oligopolies being private companies are not required by law to produce details of their profitability, which has sky-rocketed in the last few years, though in the course of Congressional investigations they have now done so. In recent years, there have been allegations that big companies and floor brokers had manipulated the futures market for their own advantage. Several of the largest companies have, in the last 2—3 years, been charged with and found guilty of malpractices relating to inspection, grading and other illegal practices.[18] A number of grain inspectors were also found guilty of corrupt practices. The Federal Government has now created a Grain Inspection Agency in the Department of Agriculture to replace the existing system, under which grain used to be inspected before export by private concerns, many of which were operated by boards of trade, chambers of commerce and commodity exchanges whose membership included grain company officials.[19]

While one can easily accept that such malpractices which received headlines in the press may often be exceptions rather than the rule, it is not easy to accept that an oligopolistic world market in grains, particularly when it is dominated by private companies, can be run in the interests of the world at large, however humanitarian such oligopolies may be. It is true, however, that in times of surplus such a market will remain competitive, but in times of scarcity who will stop them making huge 'monopoly' profits as they did in the early 1970s? Schertz and Bernston's statement, though aimed at the Soviet Union, applies equally to such oligopolies: 'without significant build-up of stocks of grain and effective rules of the game for monopoly traders such as the USSR in international markets, crisis conditions similar to those of 1974 and 1975 could return from time to time'.

International food reserve

It is this search for a countervailing power against the large grain oligopolies and to some extent against the major exporting countries which has led the developing countries to look for an internationally-owned and operated food reserve. An ideal international grain authority could take the form of an autonomous business enterprise created by, and responsible to, the UN General Assembly (or to the ECOSOC) with its own capital subscribed by member countries.[20] While the general policy guidance could be given by the General Assembly, the board of management could be left free to run the enterprise along established business lines. Such an international authority with its mandate to operate in the grain market could maintain reserves for price stabilization purposes, engage in future buying and selling arrangements with private grain dealers or governments, buy and sell on the futures markets, enter into long-term delivery contracts with grain-producing countries and handle emergency operations on behalf of member governments or the UN agencies. As Josling suggests, someone somewhere is profiting from holding such stocks, and this implies that the value over time of the world's grain harvests is enhanced by such arbitrage. Therefore, there is a reasonable chance of making such an international scheme economically viable. It is possible that on that part of the reserve which is kept for emergency purposes some losses are incurred. In such cases cross-subsidization has to be considered. The logistical problems such as determination of acquisition prices, price bands, levels of stock, storage and transport, management inefficiencies and above all political conflicts will inevitably have to be faced by the planners and managers of such a venture. Such difficulties would probably be no more than those under the alternative scheme of 'internationally coordinated national reserves' approved by the World Food Conference in 1974 under the title of International Undertaking on World Food Security (henceforth the Undertaking) and now being negotiated under the auspices of the International Wheat Council. The latter does not provide for anything more than inter-governmental consultations on stocks and stabilization policies. If the participation continues to be voluntary there can be no guarantee against unilateral violations. In the Undertaking, there are no safeguards, let alone sanctions, against the use of food as a political weapon. Above all, there is nothing in the Undertaking which tries to create a countervailing force to the oligopolistic powers of the major grain exporters — both the countries and the companies.[21]

On the other hand, it would be unrealistic to assume that an internationally-owned and operated reserve would provide the developing countries with a foolproof countervailing power against the major exporting countries. As Josling stresses, there is no world authority that can operate outside the constraints of major governments. It would be unduly simplistic to assume that such an agency could operate without the consent and cooperation of the major producing and consuming countries.

In any case, even an internationally-owned and operated scheme cannot meet all the needs of all developing countries. For instance, a country losing a substantial part of its export earnings as a result of the failure of crops, may not be able to buy foodgrains, even if available on the world market. In such a situation, Weckstein's proposals for an international grain-loan agency could come in handy. Such an agency could grant credit to member countries for financing commercial imports. The repayment, over reasonably long periods, could be financed out of export earnings in times of good harvests. Such a scheme would not interfere with the 'free' working of the market and as such would be acceptable to agribusiness. In fact, by creating additional purchasing power in times of food shortages, such a scheme will push up grain prices and therefore the profitability of grain trade. Besides, a fund does not suffer from the logistic problems of creating a buffer-stock, its storage and transport, fixing of price bands, etc. But the scheme would not be able to avoid the

managerial and political problems of cooperation between countries. However, its worst limitation is that the repayment capacity of the borrower developing countries will largely depend on the dismantling of trade barriers for which Weckstein himself is not very optimistic. In fact, an international food reserve and an international loan agency ought to be considered complementary rather than substitutes.

Let us be frank in acknowledging that whenever the question of a world food reserve has been discussed in an international context, it has not been rejected on grounds of technical feasibility or logistic difficulties. As Boerma, the last Director-General of the FAO in his Boyd Orr Memorial lecture said in relation to Boyd Orr's proposals of 1946 for a World Food Board:

> But it was clear in my mind that these practical difficulties were *not* the main reason why the proposals failed. Even at the time, I could see that they were by no means insuperable provided that the governments had sufficient political determination to accept the strategy of the World Food Board as a whole. And the sad fact of the matter is that they did not have it.[22]

Even after 30 years of continued misery of the millions of semi-starved peoples and millions of deaths in recurring famines, the 'political will' is still lacking. It is not that the idea of a food reserve is unacceptable; many intellectuals, legislators, farmers' unions, as well as grain companies even in the US, do advocate the creation of a food reserve. The conflict relates to who will own and operate it.[23]

The creation of a world food reserve is currently being negotiated in connection with a new international agreement on cereals, which is expected to replace the existing wheat convention of the International Wheat Agreement 1971, due to expire after three extensions by protocol on 30 June 1978. Although the basic elements of such an agreement are not yet finalized, according to Lamond, the establishment of an internationally-held stock has once again been ruled out and the discussions are proceeding on the assumption that any stocking operations under a new agreement would consist of internationally coordinated accumulation and release of nationally-held and controlled stocks. That too applies only to wheat. Lamond indicates that most members of the International Wheat Council are in favour of price provisions in a new agreement but the US is willing to support such provisions only if they are of a highly flexible nature. Under US insistence, there is a danger that we may be landed with another wheat agreement like the current one of which Senator Humphrey once said that 'without price provisions, the treaty' was a 'mere statement of good intentions' and a 'toothless agreement'.[24] The defence of a 'flexible' price range for wheat on the world market through the international coordination of nationally-owned and held stocks would require a sustained and complex effort in international cooperation. As Lamond stresses, in the absence of free trade in grains, there would be an obvious risk of conflict between such obligations as releasing from the buffer stock or building up such stocks by member countries regardless of the situation in their domestic market and national interests. Particularly in periods of shortages such conflicts could put the arrangement under considerable strain, especially when it is needed most.

It needs to be stressed, as Josling does, that management rules for the grain reserve will largely depend on the structure of the market which in turn is determined by national trading policies. Therefore, changes in the trading system and the rich country policies will have to be implemented before stocks can fulfill their main function. Josling feels that the domestic price stabilization policy objectives in the rich countries may have to be sacrificed in the interest of those who cannot afford at the moment to bear the cost of supply variability. The slow progress of negotiations under the auspices of the International Wheat Council, the World Food Council or UNCTAD do not provide any basis for optimism on this front.

It seems therefore that, in spite of the optimism on the technological front and cautious optimism on the population front, the pious hopes and dreams of the intellectuals and the 'moralists' will once again be sacrificed at the altar of 'pragmatism' of the politicians.

CONCLUSIONS

Nevertheless, the situation is not altogether hopeless. Apart from a more flexible attitude of the US administration, aid, labour and consumer lobbies are becoming much more critical of US agribusiness and its influence on the US agricultural policies. Besides, the Third World, though not yet interested in the overthrow of the existing system, is not going to remain satisfied with marginal changes in the volume of aid, or relaxation of trade barriers. After the repeated failures of the international negotiations under the UNCTAD and the North–South dialogue, the Third World has already begun to translate the concept of 'collective

self-reliance' into positive policy programmes. The failure of the recent UNCTAD negotiations on the Common Fund as well as the North–South Conference in Paris, has once again cast doubts in the minds of the Third World whether the 'promised' change of attitude of the US administration is real or ephemeral. Once they become convinced that it is a mere continuation of (or marginally better than) the previous administration, the Third World 'militancy' reflected in 'go-it-alone' policies will gather momentum. Aziz's sections on collective self-reliance provide suggestions for new policy directions. It is interesting to note that among the measures listed there is a suggestion for a 'collective system of food security' – a pooling of the national grain reserves of the developing countries in the event of richer countries failing to agree to an effective scheme of world food security.

It must be clearly recognized that the schemes for an international food reserve, international commodity agreements or for that matter UNCTAD's Integrated Scheme for Commodities or the Common Fund are not Marxist plots for the take-over of the capitalist world; they have been advocated by 'Western' thinkers like Keynes, Boyd Orr and Kaldor.[25] Such schemes are not fool-proof; the problems of logistics and conflict of interests would certainly arise. But they are workable and can be economically viable. After all, the World Bank and the IMF have been run largely on commercial principles. Why would an internationally-owned and operated reserve be necessarily different? And why should the developed countries be apprehensive that the new institutions created to run the food reserves or the Common Fund will largely be dominated by the Third World countries? On any criteria (e.g., GNP, main exporters, main importers, etc.) the North American and EEC countries and Japan have to be included in any board of management of such an international reserve and will have an effective voice on major issues. Under the circumstances, the opposition, particularly of Britain, Japan and West Germany (one of the largest importing countries), is difficult to understand.

In summing up it must be emphasized that whether it is the elimination of hunger and poverty, or the prevention of environmental pollution and ecological imbalances or the regulation and control of multinationals, there is a need for increasing international cooperation and participation. Many of these problems transcend national boundaries and can only be meaningfully resolved through effective international action. One of the most serious impediments in the way of collective international action is the prevailing mistrust among nations. The root cause of such mistrust is the unwarranted 'secrecy' which shrouds some of the international negotiations. A more open and public discussion of such major world issues will certainly strengthen international public opinion on matters where there is consensus and reduce tensions where there are conflicts. Old-style international diplomacy which thrives on secrecy is as out of date as the nation-state itself. In this respect one more point is worth noting. Particularly in view of the scarcity of both financial and human resources for world development, it is undesirable for international

fora to proliferate further. We already have too many — every new one not only creates 'demarcation problems' but also 'drains' the intellectual resources of poorer countries which have only a small trained bureaucracy or intelligentsia. We would make a strong plea that instead of creating new fora for discussions between the richer and poorer countries (i.e. North/South dialogue), an attempt should be made to confine discussion or negotiations to the auspices of the existing UN agencies. Special conferences are useful for creating favourable public opinion but they are wasteful of resources. If the secrecy shrouding international negotiations were reduced, there might be less need for big jamborees.

NOTES

1. FAO, *Assessment of the World Food Security Situation*, CFS 77/4 (February 1977), mimeo, p. 2.

2. For instance in a hearing of the Sub-Committee on Migratory Labour of the Senate Committee on Labour and Public Welfare held in November 1974, Adlai E. Stevenson III, the Chairman of the Sub-Committee, after citing figures on concentration of rural land ownership, was alarmed at the displacement of small farmers 'by newcomers to the farms with names like Tenneco, Gulf and Western, Goodyear, Monsanto, Union Carbide, Kaiser, Boeing and Dow Chemical, to name a few. Meanwhile one and a half million small farmers in America and a million migrant workers live in poverty'. (See *Congressional Quarterly Inc.*) (20 Nov. 1971), p. 2392.

3. Sen, A., *Employment, Technology and Development* (1975), p. 144.

4. *The Congressional Quarterly* (29 June 1974), p. 1695.

5. ibid., p. 1695.

6. Sinha, R., *Food and Poverty: The Political Economy of Confrontation* (1976), p. 24.

7. Casely, D. J., Simaika, J. B. and Sinha, R. P., 'Instability of production and its impact on stock requirements', *Monthly Bulletin of Agricultural Economics and Statistics*, Vol. 23, No. 5 (May 1974), pp. 1–8.

8. ibid., p. 1.

9. Lord Keynes had presented a proposal on the subject to H.M. Government in December 1942 as a secret document entitled *The International Regulations of Primary Products*. The proposal contemplated an authority, 'Control' which would establish an initial basic price and a price band of 10% above and below

the acquisition price. The price was to be maintained within these limits by adding to or reducing buffer stock. The General Council of the 'Control' was to consist of exporting, importing and independent countries. (Source: Annex II 'Background material in the field of trade, international monetary reform and development financing' prepared by L. Jayawardena for the UN, *A New United Nations Structure for Global Economic Cooperation: Report of the Group of Experts on the Structure of the United Nations System* (1975), mimeo. First major proposal for an international reserve was put forward by Lord Boyd Orr, the First Director General of the Food and Agricultural Organization of the UN in 1946.

10. Joseph, T., 'Major methods of buying grain', in *Grains and Oilseeds, Handling, Marketing, Processing* (Winnipeg: Canadian International Grain Institute, 1975).

11. ibid.

12. FAO, *National Grain Policies* (Rome: 1976).

13. USDA, *Contrasts in Marketing of Major Wheat Exporting Nations* (Economic Research Service, 1971), p. 2.

14. ibid., p. 2.

15. Thurston, Stanley P., Phillips, Michael J., Haskell, James E., and Volkin, D., *Improving the Export Capability of Grain Cooperatives* (USDA, Farmer Cooperative Service Research Report, 1976).

16. The attention of the American public was drawn to these grain companies by the activities of the Agribusiness Accountability Project – a public interest group whose publications are very critical of the working of these multinationals (see: Hamilton, Martha M., *The Great American Grain Robbery and Other Stories* (1972); also the background report on

the US–USSR wheat sale, 'Of the grain trade, by the grain trade, and for the grain trade' presented as an exhibit to the US Senate in 1972).

17. Whether there is collusion among these firms is not easy to prove. The Agribusiness Accountability Project group alleges that the companies have the opportunity to do so. It is argued that 'officers and directors of major grain trade corporations meet face-to face in a set of relationships built up over the years. Most join trade associations to promote mutual interests. They meet on boards and as officers of the Terminal Elevator Grain Merchant Association, the National Grain and Feed Association, .. the North American Export Grain Association, the US Feed Grain Council (and its International Trade Committee), the National Trade Council, the Board of Commodity Exchanges, and at symposiums and seminars around the country'. ibid. 'There are corporate relationships as well. Cargill, Peavy and ADM all move in the same milieu, Minneapolis's corporate elite, and have common interests in other Minneapolis companies. ... Grain trade officials from ADM, Peavy and Cargill all serve on the board of SOO Line Railroad Company. Officials of Peavy, ADM and Cargill have served on the board of North Western National Life Insurance.' Hamilton mentions several cases of interlocking directorships with banks. She concludes by saying: 'These elements – a concentrated market, lack of information outside the industry about what goes on inside the industry, diversification, interlocking directorates and easy access to capital – add up to market power. In the grain trade the six or seven largest corporations determine where the money goes.' ibid., pp. 47–49.

18. It was alleged in one of the cases that an officer of the company issued written instructions to an elevator employee to short-weight seven specific ocean-going vessels by amounts ranging from 1% to 3%. Such allegations indicated that the employees were instructed to short-weight ships as much as 1.5% if the cargoes were destined for Mediterranean, Middle East or South Asia ports. Later in 1970 instructions were given to increase the short-weighting to 3% for vessels going to Pakistan and India and other countries not having weighting facilities, *The Wall Street Journal* (7 May 1976).

19. *The Wall Street Journal* (13 Feb. 1976).

20. Sinha, R. P., 'The world food security', *Journal of Agricultural Economics*, Vol. 26, No. 1 (1976).

21. Such a grain authority could easily use the expertise and services (i.e. transport, storage, etc.) of the grain companies. After all, the Canadian and Australian Wheat Boards as well as the Export-Khleb use their services.

22. Boerma, A. H., 'The thirty years' war against world hunger', Inaugural lecture of the Boyd Orr Memorial Trust (10 April 1975), mimeo, p.11.

23. The agribusiness in the USA supports 'an American grain reserve to be administered by the US in its national interest' but they are opposed to 'programs . . . like commodity agreements'. (See Diercks, H. Roberts (the Vice-Chairman of the Board of Cargill), 'The role of government in the agricultural sector', Address to the Fifth International Commodities Conference (8–9 Dec. 1975), Chicago, mimeo, p. 13.) Similarly, the Chairman of the Continental Grain Company, Michael Fribourg, speaking at the annual dinner of the Grain and Feed Trade Association in April 1977 suggested that commodity reserves offered a far more satisfactory answer to world price and supply fluctuations than international commodity pricing agreements (see *The Times*, 3 May 1977).

It is interesting to note that National Farmers Organization (NFO) of America supports 'the negotiation of international agreements between exporters and importer nations that provides minimum and maximum prices that will sustain domestic prices equal to the cost of production plus a reasonable margin of profits'. (See National Farmers Organization, Resolution adopted at 1975 Convention).

24. *The Congressional Quarterly* (29 June 1974), p. 1712.

25. Lord Kaldor in his presidential address to the Royal Economic Society delivered on 22 July 1976, said: 'I remain convinced – as I have been for a long time – that the most promising line of action for introducing greater stability into the world economy would be to create international buffer stocks for all the main commodities. ... Assuming these buffer stocks cover a sufficiently wide range of commodities, their very existence could provide a powerful self-regulating mechanism for promoting growth and stability in the world economy'. (See Kaldor, N., 'Inflation and recession in the world economy', *The Economic Journal*, Vol. 86 (December 1976), p. 713).

26. There is a case for taking quicker decisions on the possible merging of the GATT and UNCTAD under the proposed International Trade Organization. Similarly, there may be a case for merging the International Wheat Council with the newly created World Food Council.

World Development, 1977, Vol. 5, Nos. 5–7, pp. 383–394. Pergamon Press. Printed in Great Britain.

World Food: Myth and Reality

THOMAS T. POLEMAN

Cornell University

Summary. – This introductory paper tries to dispel some of the myths surrounding the world food situation and to lay a foundation for further analyses of *real* problems. The author presents arguments to dispel three myths which have tended to obscure the real issues: (1) the myth of imminent global starvation; (2) the myth of the so-called 'Tragedy of the Commons'; (3) the myth of the food–population race. He sees the essence of the problem in terms of the income/employment dilemma. Prescribing increased economic participation – more and better paying jobs – i.e. development leading to widely shared benefits, he sets out possible guidelines to be followed by agencies concerned with food and agriculture.

The public has every reason to be confused about the food situation. Conflicting pronouncements abound. Depending on whose counsel is sought, it is possible to be informed that 'mankind has been led into a nutritional cul-de-sac from which there may be no escape',[1] or that 'world resources ... could feed, at maximum [American] standards, 47 billion people'.[2] Such discrepancies reflect, to be sure, the range of opinion to be found in any subjective evaluation. But above all they mirror the sorry state of our ability to measure those parameters which enter the food equation.

For the developing world, especially, accurate data on such basic components as levels of production and consumption are wanting, and causal linkages defy more than hesitant affirmation. Serious national food evaluations, in consequence, are characterized by great caution and circumspection. The trouble begins when regional or global sums are done. The student, groping in the half-light of imperfect evidence and flashes of perception, is reluctant to add up a series of caveats. Others are not so reticent. The circumstances are ideal for ensnaring the naive and tailor-made for those with a penchant for fitting the data to the thesis.

In such a situation, the function of an introductory paper becomes as much to deny what is not as to lay a foundation for subsequent in-depth analyses of very real problems.

I. THE MYTH OF IMMINENT GLOBAL STARVATION

It is important at the outset to put to rest the notion that the world is no longer able to feed itself and teeters uncontrollably on the brink of starvation. I have elsewhere discussed the failings of the analyses whereby pictures of massive global hunger may be conjured up,[3] but as so much devolves from it, repetition is not out of place. Unhappily it traces to the formative years of the Food and Agriculture Organization (FAO) of the United Nations, the agency which, together with the United States Department of Agriculture (USDA), has been responsible for most of the global food assessments carried out since World War II.

Within a year of its creation in 1945 the FAO issued the first in its series of *World Food Surveys*. The findings of this survey and its principal successors are summarized chronologically in Table 1. The analytical approach was simple in the extreme, and may be summarized by the equation:

$$\frac{\text{Food available for human consumption}}{365 \times \text{population}} - 15\% \text{ loss}$$

$$\leqslant \text{average daily recommended nutrient allowances}$$

To determine whether or not a country was experiencing a food problem, apparent *per capita* food availabilities, minus a 15% allowance for wastage, were set against estimates of *per capita* nutrient needs. Where and when availabilities exceeded requirements, all was presumed well; where they did not, the country or region's entire population was considered to be inadequately nourished. Never mind that the rich will eat differently than the poor, and one member of a family differently from another.

The limitations of this approach are many

Table 1. *Conclusions of major early postwar studies of the world food situation and selected recent pronouncements*

Year Published	Conclusions	Methodology
1946	*FAO – 'World Food Survey'** 'In areas containing over half the world's population [prewar] food supplies . . . were sufficient to furnish an average of less than 2250 calories . . . an average of more than 2750 calories . . . were available in areas [with] less than a third of the world's population . . . the remaining areas . . . had food supplies between these . . . levels' (pp. 6, 7).	National food balance sheet availabilities minus 15% wastage allowance compared with 2600 Kcal./caput/day allowance (p. 11).
1952	*FAO – 'Second World Food Survey'†* 'The average food supply per person over large areas of the world, five years after war was over, was still lower than before the war' (p. 2). '59.5% of population [lives in countries] with under 2200 [calories]' (p. 11).	National food balance sheet availabilities minus 15% wastage allowance compared with regional allowances (p. 22): Far East – 2230–2300 Kcal. Africa – 2400–2430 Kcal. Latin America – 2440–2600 Kcal.
1961	*USDA – 'World Food Budget, 1962 and 1966'‡* 'Diets are . . . adequate in the 30 industrialized nations . . . [where] more than 900 million people live . . . . For most of the 70 less-developed countries . . . diets are nutritionally inadequate, with shortages of proteins, fat and calories. These countries contain over 1.9 billion people. In most of them, population is growing rapidly, malnutrition is widespread and persistent, and there is no likelihood that the food problem soon will be solved' (p. 5).	Almost identical to 'Second World Food Survey'.
1963	*FAO – 'Third World Food Survey'§* [As of 1957–59, national food balance sheets and extrapolation of a limited number of budget surveys imply:] 'as a very conservative estimate some 20% of the people in the underdeveloped areas are undernourished and 60% are malnourished. Experience shows that the majority of the undernourished are also malnourished. It is believed therefore . . . some 60% of the people in the under-developed areas comprising some two-thirds of the world's population suffer from undernourishment or malnourishment or both'. [Since some people in developed countries don't eat well,] 'up to half of the peoples of the world are hungry or malnourished' (p. 51).	National food balance sheet availabilities with distribution around mean inferred from a few surveys in India and else-where compared after allowance for wastage with requirements calculated according to the 1957 FAO‖ system.
1964	*USDA – 'World Food Budget, 1970'¶* 'Two-thirds of the world's people live in countries with nutritionally inadequate national average diets' (p. iii). In 1971 an FAO/WHO Expert Panel reassessed energy and protein 'requirements' and dropped the protein figure for adults by about one-third.**	Little changed from 'World Food Budget, 1962 and 1966'.
1973	*FAO – 'Food Balance Sheets and World Food Supplies'††* [As of 1964–66, most national balance sheets] 'suggest a surplus of protein availability'. [However, other evidence] 'suggests a very uneven distribution of protein supplies . . . aggravated by seasonal imbalances . . . Furthermore, wherever calories are in short supply, proteins are diverted from their primary function of providing for growth and maintenance of tissues to the supply of energy for other vital functions. This explains the widespread incidence of protein/calorie malnutrition in spite of the apparent excess of protein supplies' (p. 19).	
1974	*UN World Food Conference – 'Assessment of The World Food Situation, Present and Future'#* 'Taking a conservative view, it would appear that out of 97 developing countries, 61 had a deficit in food energy supplies in 1970 . . . Altogether in the developing world . . . 460 million people [are affected]; a less conservative definition might give a much higher figure' (p. 5). 'The poorer segments of the population, and within these segments, the children in particular, will bear the brunt of an insufficient food supply' (p. 64).	National average availabilities with distri-bution by income inferred from a limi-ted number of surveys compared with energy cost of maintenance (1.5 × basal metabolic rate) minus 20%. 'It is the use of this very conservative level that leads to the estimate of over 400 million individuals . . .' (p. 72).

Sources:
* FAO, *World Food Survey* (Washington: 5 July 1946).

† FAO, *Second World Food Survey* (Rome: November 1952).

‡ USDA, ERS, *The World Food Budget, 1962 and 1966* (For. Agr. Econ. Report 4, October 1961).

§ FAO, *Third World Food Survey* (Freedom from Hunger Basic Study 11, 1963).

‖ FAO, *Calorie Requirements* (Nutritional Studies 15, 1957).

¶ USDA, ERS, *The World Food Budget, 1970* (For. Agr. Econ. Report 19, October 1964).

** FAO, *Energy and Protein Requirements* (Nutrition Meetings Report Series 52, 1973).

†† 'Food balance sheets and world food supplies', (FAO) *Nutrition Newsletter* (April–June 1973).

UN, World Food Conference, *Assessment of the World Food Situation, Present and Future* (Item 8 of the Provisional Agenda, November 1974).

and, when probed, obvious: in addition to the unrealistic assumption of dietary homogeneity, it presumes a sophisticated ability to quantify. To estimate food availabilities, one must construct a balance sheet, incorporating on the supply side measurements of production, trade, and stocks changes, and on the utilization side such items as seed and feed use and losses in storage. Availabilities for human consumption are derived as a residual and thus reflect the totality of error. The evidence is that these errors in statistically underdeveloped countries act in the direction of understatement; minor or exotic foods are often ignored and — because the government official is still equated with the tax collector — farmers tend to minimize production. Detailed evaluations of a number of Asian countries by Cornell students suggest underreporting of from 10 to 15%, and preliminary work on Africa points to an even greater margin of error.[4]

Compounding this tendency to undercount food availabilities have been the difficulties associated with estimating food needs. These have been overstated. Nutrition is still a young science and our ability to establish minimal or desirable levels of intake is not nearly so precise as we would like it to be. What in fact have been used as surrogates for minimal acceptable levels of intake in most food evaluations have been the recommended allowances prepared as guidelines for dieticians and other nutritional workers. To ensure that the substantial variations in food needs among individuals will be covered, these allowances consciously err on the side of caution. They are also periodically revised as new knowledge becomes available. The history of the FAO, the US Food and Nutrition Board, and other responsible organizations has been one of continual — and generally downward — modification. The energy allowances for the US 'reference man' — in his twenties, moderately active, weighing 70 kgs — now stand at 2,700 calories daily, 500 calories less than the 1953 recommendation.[5]

With the cards thus stacked, it is not surprising that the early FAO and USDA global food assessments were able to paint a gloomy picture of world hunger — a picture which has persisted despite appreciable changes in the method of analysis.

The first global study to break away from the assumption of dietary homogeneity and to recognize that the key determinant of an individual's (or country's) eating patterns is his level of income was the *Third World Food Survey* published in 1963. As such it marked an important milestone. It is obviously the poor

that suffer. Less obvious is how many and how. The *Third Survey* concluded that the problem was with malnourishment: that whereas their energy intake was generally adequate, at least 60% of the population of the developing world was too poor to afford the more costly foods which are the principal sources of protein and the essential vitamins and minerals. This conclusion was widely held during the 1960s; the food problem became a protein problem and in some quarters the technical advances which have come to be called the Green Revolution were decried because they emphasized crops which are principally energy suppliers.

But in 1971 there was a flip–flop. An expert panel was convened by the FAO and the World Health Organization to review the international dietary allowances and it revised the adult protein recommendations downward by about one-third. The effect was to convert the list of 'protein deficit' countries to ones of sufficiency. The footwork in Rome was fast and furious, almost comical. If the protein problem did not vanish overnight, at least its statistical underpinnings had been swept away.

The current consensus seems to be that the old notions of malnutrition (insufficient protein and other 'protective' foods) and undernutrition (inadequate energy intake) are no longer valid and nutritionists concerned with the LDCs (less developed countries) now speak of protein–calorie malnutrition. This sees a shortage of calories again as the prime problem and takes into account that an apparent adequacy of protein can be converted into a deficit should a portion of it be metabolized to compensate for insufficient energy intake. The Green Revolution is again acceptable.

The most recent estimate of the extent to which the poor of the Third World suffer from protein–calorie malnutrition was prepared by FAO for the November 1974 World Food Conference and is summarized by region in Table 2. It suggests the problem to be largely an Asian one — certainly true — and indicates that perhaps a quarter of the population of the Third World (excluding China), or in excess of 500 million people today, is inadequately fed. To be sure this is much less than the two thirds found by the *Third World Food Survey*, but none the less it represents an unconscionable segment of mankind.

It is difficult to evaluate this figure. Certainly the nutritional standards used today are far more reasonable than those employed 30 years ago. Food availabilities no doubt continue to be underestimated. But the real problem is

Table 2. *Number of people estimated by the FAO to have had an insufficient protein/energy supply in 1970, by region*

Region	Population (millions)	Percentage below lower limit	Number below lower limit (millions)
Developed	1074	3	28
Developing*	1751	25	434
Latin America	283	13	36
Far East*	1020	30	301
Near East	171	18	30
Africa	273	25	67
World*	2825	16	462

Source: UN, World Food Conference, *Assessment of the World Food Situation, Present and Future* (Item 8 of the Provisional Agenda, November 1974), p. 66. It is interesting to note that the preliminary version of this document included a similar table suggesting that 20% of the developing world's population fell below the minimal standard (Far East – 22%; Near East – 20%). No explanation of the change was given.

*Excluding centrally-planned countries.

knowing how available supplies are divided across the income range. It is a commonplace among serious pronouncements on the food situation that global supplies are sufficient to feed all. Would that our ignorance on matters of distribution were equally publicized. The survey data from which inferences about the effect income has on eating habits simply do not exist for most LDCs, and until there is a (modest) hue and cry for their generation I see no likelihood of the situation being corrected.

Figure 1, a summary of the effect income has on nutrient intake in Sri Lanka, illustrates some of the difficulties. The survey on which it is based is almost unique; to my knowledge only three or four surveys of equal coverage and integrity exist for the entire Third World. Yet, even with this survey, one can infer precious little about the extent of protein–calorie malnutrition. The dietary adjustment most commonly associated with rising income is a decline in the importance of the starchy staple foods – read rice in southern Asia – as sources of energy and a shift to the more expensive, flavorous foods such as meat, fish and vegetables. In Sri Lanka this tendency is observable among only the four uppermost income classes (20% of the population), and then, because of recent egalitarian measures, only weakly so. Between the lowest class (43% of the people) and the next lowest (37%), the sole change is quantitative. There is a difference

in apparent *per capita* daily availabilities of 200 calories and 10 grams of protein, but none in diet composition.

What are we to infer from this? Because FAO now (quite reasonably) reckons energy requirements in South Asia to average about 1900 calories per day, it could suggest either of two very different things. If the standard factor of 15% is applied to account for wastage between purchase and actual ingestion, the 200-calorie gap could be interpreted as implying enforced reduced activity among the poor or actual physical deterioration. But just as reasonably, one might postulate caloric adequacy among that element of society which is too poor to waste anything and which, given the very high rate of unemployment in Sri Lanka, leads a less active life and therefore has lower energy needs. Thus it is possible to have it either way: depending on your assumptions, you can prove beyond a statistical doubt that 43% of Ceylonese suffer protein-calorie malnutrition or none do.

Having been fortunate enough to have spent some time in Sri Lanka over the last decade and a half, my impression is that the optimistic interpretation more nearly approximates reality. Overt signs of inadequate feeding are few in Sri Lanka; and it is illogical for people who are short of calories not to satisfy this need from such cheap sources of energy as rice, sugar and coconut before spending on what to them are luxury items.

Indeed, an implicit presumption of such illogical behaviour underlies the whole notion of massive protein–calorie malnutrition, and I for one am skeptical. The more I study food behaviour in the developing world, the more impressed I am with the efficient and rational way in which most people allocate their resources so as to get by on what by the standards of the West is very little. There are exceptions, of course: the so-called vulnerable groups – pregnant and lactating women, the pre-school child – are truly vulnerable and need assistance. But the great majority of people neither look nor act malnourished, and quite possibly enjoy more healthful (though less tasty) diets than do many of their overweight and underexercised cousins in the West.

Thus, though I cannot prove it, there is no doubt in my mind that the picture of 500 million people struggling at the brink of starvation is a distortion. It is, as the title of this section suggests, a myth – a myth whose durability, given the history of the analyses upon which it rests, remains something of a marvel. It is tempting to see a conspiracy

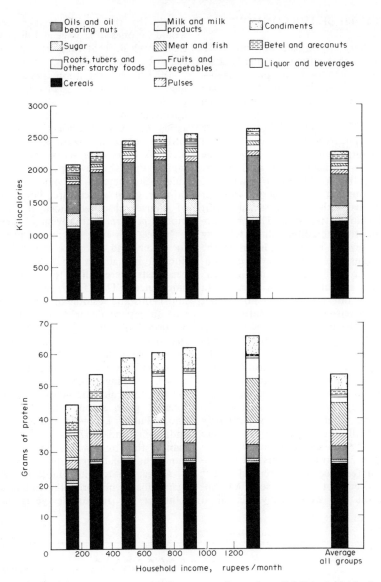

Figure 1. *Apparent per capita daily energy and protein availabilities in Sri Lanka (1969–70) by income class*

Source: T. T. Poleman, *Income and Food Consumption: Report to the Government of Sri Lanka* (Rome: FAO/UNDP, No. TA 3198, 1973), pp. 18–19.

between naive doomsayers eager to sell books and the vested interests of intrenched bureaucracies. In reality, though, I suspect it reflects nothing more than the persistence of honourable men attempting to dramatize their case through exaggeration. Surely it is not wrong to exaggerate the misery of the few by making it seem the plight of the many, if the result is to hasten remedial steps.

Unhappily, the best of intentions can go awry. Instead of galvanizing mankind to collective action, the hunger/starvation myth has rendered the global psyche vulnerable to further distortions and by so doing served to obscure the actual dilemmas of world food and population.

II. THE MYTH OF THE COMMONS

Of the corollary myths the one most flagrantly at odds with reality is popularly associated with the words 'lifeboat' and 'triage' — the so-called Tragedy of the Commons.[6] It sees an already hungry world plunged into even deeper misery as populations grow and agriculture stagnates. The developed countries are confronted with a heart-rending choice between diminishing resources and which among the LDCs to save — a decision to be made in the spirit of triage, the World War I practice of dividing the wounded according to whether they would survive without medical aid, profit from it, or die no matter what. The presumptions underlying this incredible call for lethargy are many, but revolve around a denial of the demographic transition and the eventual control of population growth it portends, and the presumption that agriculture in the Third World is operating flat out and can go no further without massive environmental disruption.

Nothing could be farther from the truth. As anyone who has spent much time in the developing world knows — and I suspect the doomsayers have ventured there hardly at all — the unrealized agricultural capabilities of most LDCs are still substantial. In Africa and Latin America, especially, great expanses of potentially productive land are but superficially exploited, if at all, and yields are everywhere far below what is obtained experimentally or in the West (Figure 2). To the doomsayer Bangladesh is the quintessence of a perennial basket case. Yet it need not be: its soils are uncommonly fertile and were rice yields raised simply to the world average her problems would be ones of storage and disposition rather than survival. That they are not reflects political, not technical, failings.

Indeed were the doomsayers to examine the record of agricultural change in the LDCs they would find much to give them cause for optimism. According to such generally used series of 'world' production as that of the USDA plotted in Figure 3, the LDCs over the past 20 years have expanded output no less rapidly than the developed countries, a remarkable achievement in view of the minimal priority given agriculture. Population growth, of course, absorbed most of the gains, but modest *per capita* improvement is evident.

Twice, however, the rate of progress seemed to falter and, as has been the case with doomsaying almost since Malthus' time, the pessimists were quick to stage their periodic emergence. The first pause came in the mid-1960s and resulted almost exclusively from two successive droughts in India. Indian production bulks so large in the LDC aggregate that major fluctuations in her output influence visibly the index for all developing countries. This fact, however, was lost on many commentators. Looking at the figures and hearing of massive food aid shipments — of the 30 million tons of grain shipped by the United States under Public Law 480 during the two years ending in June 1967, half went to India — the man in the street was receptive to forecasts of imminent global starvation.

A reaction set in almost immediately and again closely mirrored the Indian situation. A sequence of favourable years in terms of

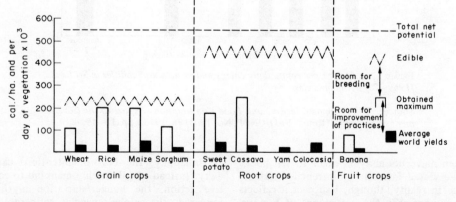

Figure 2. *Average world yields, maximum yields obtained in selected tropical experiment stations, and estimated potential yields to be reached through breeding and research*

Source: C. A. de Vries, J. D. Ferwerda, and M. Flach, 'Choice of food crops in relation to actual and potential production in the tropics' *The Netherlands Journal of Agricultural Science* (November 1967), p. 246.

weather was accompanied by introduction into the Punjab of high-yielding varieties of Mexican wheat. The result was that the index of production for all low-income countries rose steeply, as did *per capita* availabilities. The assessment was as extreme in the opposite direction as it had been in 1965 and 1966. These were the years when we first began to hear of the Green Revolution. The situation in Northwest India, together with the introduction of high-yielding, stiff-strawed, fertilizer-responsive rice in wetter portions of Asia, led many to believe that the situation had been fundamentally altered and that feeding the world's rapidly increasing population no longer posed problems. So pervasive was the optimism that the FAO even suggested in its *State of Food and Agriculture* for 1969 that the food problems of the future might well be ones of surplus rather than shortage.[7]

The factors underlying the second pause — the 'food crisis' so recently ended — were more complex and involved the developed as well as the developing countries. In brief, it resulted from an unhappy coincidence of four main influences: an intentional running down of stocks and a holding down of production in the United States; unprecedented prosperity and rising demand in Europe and Japan; unfavourable weather in the Soviet Union, India and the Sahelian zone of Africa; and a general relaxation of attention to agriculture in the LDCs. The last mentioned is difficult to quantify, but it is evident that the early Green Revolution

euphoria was accepted by many governments as justification for redirecting investment and pricing policies away from agriculture in favour of the politically more rewarding urban sector.

One is tempted to call the food crisis of the early 1970s the Soviet crisis, since the instabilities of that country's farming sector were responsible for the extreme volatility. Certainly it was triggered by the short crop of 1972 and prolonged by the failure of the 1975 harvest. But to term it such would be misleading. It was truly 'world' in that the price rises were general and in that it exposed the weaknesses of the international agricultural order. 'International' is the operative word: most affected were the countries trading in the world market. Least involved were the largely self-reliant economies of the Third World. They were mainly affected in that the surpluses of the West were no longer available to them in abundance on concessional terms.

This reduction in food-aid availabilities is central to the lifeboat thesis and hinges on the not unreasonable supposition that food aid is what the name implies — charity to those otherwise unable to feed themselves. In fact, about 80% of such shipments have moved from the United States under Public Law 480 and apart from the Indian bailout of the mid-1960s have been flagrantly political exercises in dumping; 'surplus disposal' rings better to the bureaucratic ear. South Korea, South Vietnam (until recently), and post-Allende Chile have been major recipients. True emergency relief, as

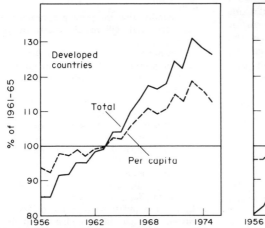
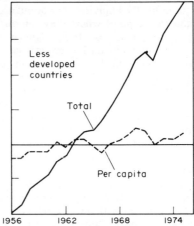

Figure 3. *World agricultural production, 1956–75.*

Source: USDA, *Handbook of Agricultural Charts, 1976* (Agriculture Handbook 504, October 1976), p. 53. Developed countries: North America, Europe, USSR, Japan, South Africa, Australia, and New Zealand; less developed countries: Latin America, Asia (except Japan and communist countries), and Africa (except South Africa).

to Bangladesh following hurricanes, Biafra after
its unsuccessful bid for independence, and more
recently to the Sahelian states, has amounted to
less than a tenth of the total.[8]

Most responsible commentators view this
sort of food aid with skepticism. About a fifth
of the US rice harvest now finds its way abroad
under concessional terms and the disruptive
effects this million tons can have on the world
rice market is well-known to the trade; I
travelled through Southeast Asia in early 1976
and heard about little else. But the principal
objections centre on the disincentives to
increased production in recipient countries. If
the farm sector in developed countries seems
possessed of political clout all out of proportion to the number of people involved, it is just
the opposite in the LDCs. There it is the urban
dweller who has the power to make or break,
and though their numbers may be small, the
politician is at pains to assure them cheap food.
What more painless way to do this than with
cut-rate imports from abroad? Thus it was the
politically articulate few who objected mightily
(and brought down the government in Thailand) when in the early 1970s the run-down of
surpluses in the West and signs of local agricultural stagnation caused many governments to
reverse their pricing policies and offer greater
incentives to farmers. And so it may be that
foundations for the next food crisis — of the
late 1970s? — may be laid by a clamour, now
that things no longer look so bad, that these
incentives are no longer necessary.

It does not follow, however, that all food aid
need be harmful. By implying that populations
will expand to the point where they run out of
food, the proponents of triage ignore the
evidence that rapid population growth can be
controlled rather quickly once certain preconditions have been achieved. Among the
most important of these preconditions is a
reduction in infant mortality, so that parents
need no longer plan on two live births in order to
feel reasonably assured that one child will reach
maturity. To this end there are no more
effective means than clinics which provide
supplemental food as well as medical services to
mother and child. Recent changes in Public
Law 480, requiring that 75% of concessional
sales go to countries with *per capita* GNPs of
less than $300, make support of such pro-
grammes a greater possibility. But whether the
recipient countries can muster the technical
expertise and administrative competence to
implement them — particularly at a level
commensurate to the 10 million tons of food
aid annually called for by the World Food

Council[9] — is open to question. It is a priority
matter which should be pursued with extreme
care.

III. THE MYTH OF THE
FOOD—POPULATION RACE

The doomsayers' silence on population control is symptomatic of the widespread acceptance of a second myth encouraged by the
hunger/starvation distortion: the old Malthusian one of a (losing) race between food and
mouths to feed. One calls it Malthusian with
reluctance, because it is impossible to believe
that Malthus, had he today's evidence on
matters about which he could only theorize
175 years ago, would have had much truck with
what is said in his name. Few have paid so high
a price for original thought.

Malthus wrote at a time when very little was
known about population trends. Censuses had
only begun to be taken and the good Reverend
seemed quite prepared to go along with
Bishop Ussher's timing of the Creation at 4004
B.C.[10] Evidence on food production was even
sketchier. None the less Malthus was bold
enough to perceive in them tendencies sufficiently strong to upset the then prevailing
notions of man's perfectability.

His theory was most succinctly stated in the
first edition of his famous *Essay*:[11]

> I think I may fairly make two postulata.
> First, that food is necessary to the existence of
> man.
> Secondly, that the passion between the sexes is
> necessary, and will remain nearly in its present
> state . . .
> Assuming then, my postulata as granted, I say,
> that the power of population is indefinitely greater
> than the power in the earth to produce subsistence
> for man.
> Population, when unchecked, increases in a
> geometrical ratio. Subsistence increases only in an
> arithmetical ratio. A slight acquaintance with
> numbers will show the immensity of the first
> power as compared with the second.
> By that law of our nature which makes food
> necessary to the life of man, the effects of these
> two unequal powers must be kept equal.
> This implies a strong and constantly operating
> check on population from the difficulty of sub-
> sistence . . . . The race of plants, and the race of
> animals shrink under this great restrictive law. And
> the race of man cannot, by any efforts of reason,
> escape from it. Among plants and animals its
> effects are waste of seed, sickness, and premature
> death. Among mankind, misery and vice. The
> former, misery, is an absolutely necessary con-
> sequence of it. Vice is a highly probable con-

sequence ... I see no way by which man can escape from the weight of this law which pervades all animated nature ...

Such was the (uncommon) wisdom of his youth. In later editions, as Malthus grappled with the question of how populations controlled their size, the argument expanded and became less tidy. As with most prolific writers and thinkers, he at one time or another seemed to be on most sides of most questions. But it was his original perception that first captured the world's attention and it is this perception which has been used by so many to dramatize the problems posed by the current spurt in population.

We are all familiar with drawings, such as the left-hand drawing in Figure 4, which indicate that the world's population remained essentially stable from biblical times to about 1650. Such drawings are valid in that they drive home the magnitude of the current explosion in numbers, some 80% of which is taking place in the LDCs, but they mislead in several important respects. The current upturn is not unique, and growth (and contraction) prior to 1650 took place not gradually but in spurts.

This is of fundamental importance and is perhaps most easily appreciated when visualized in terms of the right-hand drawing of Figure 4, a simplified graphing conceived by E. S. Deevey. The drawing, which is plotted on logarithmic scales to make great differences in time and magnitude manageable, summarizes much of what we have learned since Malthus' time. The present upsurge in numbers is not the first but the third in a sequence of bursts that have been associated with major breakthroughs in man's ability to cope with his environment. The first occurred several million years ago — Deevey plotted it at one million, although today he would no doubt move it back — and attended man's emergence from the primate line into a maker of tools able to hunt and

gather over a range of conditions. The second marked his domestication of plants and animals some 10,000 years ago and the beginnings of agriculture — the 'Neolithic Revolution'.

These breakthroughs, of course, did not take place simultaneously around the world, but were staggered in their impact. Just as the industrial and scientific revolution occurred first in Europe, food gatherers and hunters first became agriculturists in the Fertile Crescent and Southeast Asia. Still, the effect in a particular locality was rapid and profound. For example,[1 2]

> Twenty thousand people would probably be an extreme estimate of the population of hunter–gatherers the Egyptian section of the Nile valley could have supported at the end of palaeolithic times. The population of the Old Kingdom two thousand years later has been variously estimated at from three to six millions.

That such epochal technological breakthroughs would be accompanied by rapid population rises seems obvious. What is less obvious is the nature of the forces that ultimately acted to force a leveling off. Malthus' food supply, together with such other essentials as space, water and air, clearly set an upper limit, but one wonders how frequently an operative one. The long-term population equilibria of the past would seem to have been at levels below those associated with marginal starvation. Thus, 'a Paleolithic man who stuck to business should have found enough food on two square kilometers, instead of [the] 20 or 200' believed to have been available *per capita*, respectively, in the Upper and Lower Paleolithic ages.[1 3] And it is not weather but changed political circumstances that are most clearly linked to the great swings in China's population over the last two millennia.

If the parameters of the demographic transition associated with the Neolithic remain to be satisfactorily generalized, those associated with

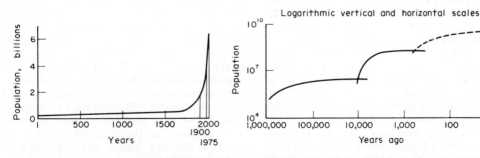

Figure 4. *Two views of world population growth*

Source: E. S. Deevey, Jr., 'The human population', *Scientific American* (September 1960), p. 198.

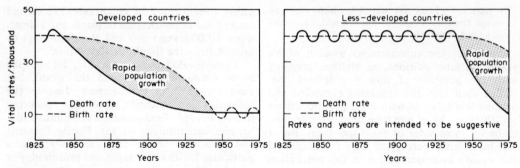

Figure 5. *The demographic transition schematized*

the third of the great upheavals, the industrial and scientific revolution, would seem fairly clear cut (Figure 5). Initial population stability is characterized by high birth and death rates. Then, as public health measures are introduced, the death rate drops. Birth rates, however, remain at their old level, and a period of population 'explosion' sets in. Then birth rates in their turn fall, and the population again approaches stability, but at a much higher level.

Most of the industrialized states of the West have passed through this transition and seem fairly near the new level of stability — 'zero population growth' in the idiom. For them the transition averaged between 50 and 100 years. Virtually all the LDCs have passed through the stage of declining death rates and are in the interval of maximum population growth. For them the 'population problem is essentially whether or not [they] will follow Europe and North America in reducing birth rates ...'.[14]

The evidence from some of the smaller, more prosperous LDCs (notably Singapore, Taiwan, Mauritius and Sri Lanka) is that they can reduce birth rates — and probably much more quickly — within 20 or 30 years. Contraceptives are becoming available at little or no cost to users in the Third World, and birth control information is widespread. However, for family planning to be rapidly introduced, people must consciously want fewer children and for this to happen there are certain preconditions. That one of these is a reduction in infant mortality we have already noted. Others revolve around a reduction in the economic attractiveness of large families, both as sources of labour and as old-age insurance, and the availability of opportunities for life styles involving more than just growing food and raising children. Expressed more positively, the preconditions imply access to health facilities, social security and education — all of which we tend to equate with 'improved living levels', 'urbanization' and 'development'.

Hence the quandary faced by the LDCs is best visualized not, as the doomsayers have it, in the sterile terms of race in which food and population push relentlessly toward some hypothetical saturation point. Rather it is a very malleable competition between population growth and economic participation on the one hand, and between economic participation and food on the other.

IV. THE REALITY OF THE INCOME/EMPLOYMENT DILEMMA

If increased economic participation — read more and better paying jobs — lies at the heart of both controlling population growth in the LDCs and transforming dietary patterns, the goal should obviously be to carry out development in such a way that its benefits will be widely shared. So far this has rarely happened. Progress in both the rural and urban sectors has tended to benefit only a portion of the population.

The equity problem in agriculture has its roots in the selectivity of the various breakthroughs of the Green Revolution. The high-yielding varieties in particular are not designed to be introduced alone, but require a host of complementary inputs: fertilizers, adequate water, and effective control of disease, insects and weeds to mention the more obvious. The 'miracle' rices, for instance, are highly responsive to fertilizer — as the *Indica* varieties they replace are not — and yield well only under irrigated conditions. To the degree that any of the new systems are suited to specific ecological conditions, benefits will obviously be restricted. Equally obvious is that participation will tend to be confined to those classes best able to command the new inputs: the larger farmers and landowners.

None of this is new. A similar selectivity characterized the innovations which transformed agriculture in Europe and North America during the 19th century. The difference lies in the cities and the opportunities they offer the displaced countryman. One has only to read Dickens to appreciate the misery that accompanied 19th century urbanization. But there was also promise: industry was growing and, since industry then had high labour requirements, virtually all who left the land found new jobs. Today the movement to town rests on less solid foundations. Though urbanization in the LDCs is proceeding at a breakneck pace — major centres are probably doubling in size every eight or ten years — most of the cities are 'cities that came too soon'.[15] To a remarkable degree they remain administrative and trading centres, built up to dispatch raw materials to the developed countries and to receive and distribute manufactures in exchange. That the bulk of what little industrialization is occurring is capital- not labour-intensive is apparently a necessity if foreign competition is to be warded off. Jobs are far fewer than the bodies in search of them.

The proportion of the population that finds itself either bypassed by rural development or without a job in town defies quantification. Governments in the Third World do not collect data on unemployment and underemployment, and if they did the findings would be too distasteful politically to permit release. World Bank officials speak of the 'lower 40%', and even if this figure is a very rough estimate, it is still a fair one. Somewhere between a quarter and half of the population is probably being excluded from the forward march of development.

If solutions to their plight are not obvious, we at least can take comfort from the fact that it is seen in responsible quarters as the central problem confronting the LDCs. With the World Bank and the US Agency for International Development in the van, the search has begun for investments that will benefit the poorest classes. 'Growth with equity' is the watchword, and a number of schemes for labour-intensive development have been launched. These focus on the rural disadvantaged, and though one sometimes suspects the true aim goes no further than keeping them down on the farm, the targets expressed are lofty. It is on 'eight-acre man', Barbara Ward writes, that 'the hopes of feeding most of mankind in the longer term depend';[16] and the Maoist model is widely proclaimed.

One can only hope there is an alternative. China has been able to reconcile today's revolution of rising expectations with what Marx termed 'the idiocy of rural life' only by repressing the individual's right to choose. Elsewhere the record of labour-intensive development has been so unimpressive that one is tempted to dismiss the theorizing in its behalf as an intellectual cop-out.[17] Yet the dilemma is very real. If the disadvantaged cannot somehow be persuaded to behave as if they were participating in the development process, there is the possibility that they will continue to breed as before.[18] The tragedy of our times is that the LDCs experienced the benefits of the scientific/industrial revolution before its causes.

V. CAN FOOD PLANNING BECOME A REALITY?

With the developing world seen as more hungry for jobs than food, what guidelines ought to be followed by the multiplicity of agencies concerned with food and agriculture? I venture to conclude with a few which may not be on everybody's list:

1. It would be helpful if the notion of a *world* food problem were played down. Problems there are aplenty, but the extent to which those of the West and the LDCs impinge on each other is minimal. In the industrialized nations they revolve around the perennial questions of managing reserve stocks, price maintenance, and in many capitalist countries, holding down production. In the developing world the need is to expand production quickly. That the requisites of the latter are pricing and investment decisions which may prove politically painful should be emphasized, something that the FAO and the World Food Council are only beginning to do. Just as the trumpeting of global disaster by Western doomsayers has misled, so many LDC politicians have for too long been allowed to ignore their country's food problems.

2. To the extent that food aid is pursued as a means of surplus disposal (or conscience assuagement), steps should be taken to minimize the effect on producer price incentives. An ideal mechanism for doing this, and simultaneously for improving nutritional well-being and the prospects for population control, would be to channel this aid through maternity and child health clinics.

3. The real aid from the West, however, should take the form of technical assistance to agricultural research institutes and credits to underwrite the capital works needed to complement the new varieties — irrigation systems, fertilizer plants and the like. To a maximum

degree these works should be designed to benefit the smaller farmers. But no matter should they not. Probably the best way the West can improve the lot of the disadvantaged of the LDCs is not — as seems the aim of recent modifications in the US aid legislation — to invest solely in projects oriented toward them. Rather it would be to reduce the incredibly high tariffs on processed and manufactured items which have prevented the LDCs from exploiting their one true comparative advantage in labour-intensive manufactures.

4. A final activity where minimal investment could bring high returns would be a crash programme for the generation of reliable statistics. Not until we are in a position to truly understand the situation of the LDCs can policy planning be confidently undertaken, and not until then, I fear, will we hear the last of the food myths.

NOTES

1. Anne and Paul Ehrlich, 'Starvation, 1975' *Penthouse* (July 1975), p. 136.

2. Colin Clark, *Population Growth and Land Use* (London: 1968), p. 153.

3. T. T. Poleman, 'World food: a perspective', *Science* (9 May 1975).

4. See the following sources: M. J. Purvis 'Evaluation and use of underdeveloped agricultural statistics: the food economy of Malaysia' (Cornell Univ., Ph.D. Dissertation, 1966); T. Jogaratnam and T. T. Poleman, *Food in the Economy of Ceylon* (Cornell Int. Agric. Bull. 11, 1969); T. T. Poleman, *National Food Accounting and Estimating Demand for Food in Tropical Africa* (Cornell Agric. Econ. Staff Paper 76–20, May 1976).

5. National Academy of Sciences, *Recommended Dietary Allowances* (8th Rev. Ed.; Washington, D.C.: 1974), following p. 128.

6. Most commonly equated with this sort of thinking are the many writings of Garrett Hardin, including: 'The Tragedy of the Commons', *Science* (13 December 1968); and 'Living on a lifeboat', *BioScience* (October 1974).

7. FAO, *The State of Food and Agriculture, 1969* (Rome: 1970), pp. 1–3.

8. USDA, ERS, *US Agricultural Exports Under Public Law 480* (Foreign 395, October 1974), pp. ii, v.

9. UN, World Food Council, *Food Aid Targets and Policies* (Report of the Executive Director, 22 April 1976), p. 2.

10. T. R. Malthus, *An Essay on the Principle of Population* (Parallel chapters from the 1st and 2nd eds.; London: 1906), p. 6.

11. Malthus, op. cit., pp. 6–8.

12. R. Oliver and J. D. Fage, *A Short History of Africa* (London: 1968), p. 26.

13. E. S. Deevey, 'The human population', *Scientific American* (September 1960), p. 198.

14. Dudley Kirk, 'Natality in the developing countries: recent trends and prospects', in S. J. Behrman, L. Corsa, and R. Freedman, eds., *Fertility and Family Planning: A World View* (Ann Arbor: 1969), p. 76.

15. Barbara Ward, 'The poor world's cities', *The Economist* (6 December 1969), p. 56.

16. Barbara Ward, 'Food', *The Economist* (2 November 1974), pp. 24–25.

17. An excellent disucssion of the limitations of the labour-intensive approach is to be found in W. C. Robinson, 'Some negative thoughts about labour-intensive development', *The Malayan Economic Review* (April 1975).

18. The experience of Sri Lanka and the neighbouring Indian state of Kerala suggest that it may in fact be possible to so persuade them. See F. C. Roche, *The Demographic Transition in Sri Lanka: Is Development Really a Prerequisite?* (Cornell Agric. Econ. Staff Paper 76–5, January 1976); and UN Dept. of Econ. Soc. Aff., *Poverty, Unemployment and Development Policy: A Case Study of Selected Issues with Reference to Kerala* (New York: 1975).

World Development, 1977, Vol. 5, Nos. 5–7, pp. 395–405. Pergamon Press. Printed in Great Britain.

World Population Situation:
Problems and Prospects

W. PARKER MAULDIN

Centre for Policy Studies,
The Population Council, New York

Summary. – This paper examines the possible implications of present and future trends in population size and rates of growth. It compares and contrasts the situation in different regions – both developed and developing – of the world. Following a discussion of various approaches to formulating population projections, the author considers the broader societal issues brought forth by population growth and the possible policy responses to them. The paper suggests that in order for population problems to be solved, the population programmes need to be developed and implemented within the framework of development plans.

INTRODUCTION

There is general agreement on the facts of population size and rates of growth in the world today, but there is lack of consensus on the implications of these numbers and on likely future trends. The population of the world is a little more than 4 billion [4×10^9], and the rate of growth is high, about 1.8–1.9% a year which adds 70,000,000–75,000,000 persons per year.

The rate of the world's population growth accelerated from less than 0.5% per year between 1750 and 1850 to 1.9% per year between 1950 and 1975. But these average figures mask sharply contrasting trends among the developed and the developing countries. From 1750 to 1850 the underdeveloped countries grew at an annual rate of 0.4% and the developed countries at a rate of 0.5%; from 1850 to 1950 the rates were reversed to 0.6 and 0.9%, respectively; and from 1950 to 1975 they were 2.3 and 1.1%. In recent years these rates of growth have slowed sharply in the developed countries and significantly among developing countries in Asia and Latin America.

POPULATION TRENDS 1950–75

The high rates of population growth during 1950–75 led to a population growth of about 1.5 billion, an increase of about 60%. What was the cause of this tremendous growth – and will it continue?

Life expectancy was just under 47 years in 1950, but has increased to a bit more than 56 years as of the present time. The difference between these two numbers reflects a momentous decline in mortality that is far from having run its course. Based on the mortality rates of 1950 and today's population of 4 billion, there would be some 75 million deaths per year; at current mortality rates, however, there will be about 50 million deaths a year.

What further reduction in mortality is likely? The World Population Conference of 1974 adopted a Plan of Action which, although it contained few specific goals and targets, did set targets for the reduction of mortality as follows:

It is a goal of this Plan of Action to reduce mortality levels, particularly infant and maternal mortality levels, to the maximum extent possible in all regions of the world and to reduce national and subnational differentials therein. The attainment of an average expectation of life of 62 years by 1985 and 74 years by the year 2000 for the world as a whole would require by the end of the century an increase of 11 years for Latin America, 17 years for Asia and 28 years for Africa.

Countries with the highest mortality levels should aim by 1985 to have an expectation of life at birth of at least 50 years and an infant mortality rate of less than 120 per 1000 live births.

If these ambitious goals are to be realized, there will be an even more dramatic reduction in mortality during the next than during the last 25 years. Mortality rates would be cut by a factor of 3 unless fertility were reduced very quickly and dramatically. Even the United

Nations' more conservative estimates of mortality reduction envisages a reduction of mortality by a factor of 2.

The crude birth rate of the world was about 36 births per 1000 population per year in 1950; it has been reduced by 17–18% in 25 years and is a little above 30 today. But the world is divided into high and low fertility countries, with the developing countries having both high fertility and the bulk of the population (72.5% or 2.9 billion persons). The more developed countries are far less populous, but even so contain more than 1.1 billion persons.

The more developed countries had moderately low fertility in 1950 (an average crude birth rate of about 23), but there has been a remarkable decline in fertility in almost all developed countries since then. The average decline has been more than one-quarter (28.7%), and the level of crude birth rates today is 16–17. A few of the developed countries have more deaths than births (both of the German states), and many have rates of reproduction that if continued would result in zero or negative growth. The average rate of population growth among these countries is well under 1% and is likely to decrease further during the next few decades. Thus, population growth among the more developed countries poses few problems in terms of maintenance of current levels of living, but there are many problems of urbanization and distribution.

The developing countries present a different picture. In 1950 their populations numbered 1.6 billion and death rates were high, more than 23. The revolution in mortality has reduced the crude death rate almost by half (45%) to 12 or 13. Fertility was high in 1950, about 42 per 1000. Thus, the rate of growth was slightly less than 2% per year in 1950. Major changes in fertility have also occured in many developing countries, though overall fertility changes have been less marked than the decline in mortality. The figures show a decline in the crude birth rate from 42 to 36 in 25 years – a decrease of 6 points, or almost 15%. Changes in fertility have been dramatic in Asia and the Pacific, substantial in Central and South America, and hardly noticeable in Africa. In Asia, where the bulk of the population lives, the crude birth rate declined almost 20%, from more than 41 to less than 34. In the Americas the decline was about 12%, from 44 to less than 39. The data for many African countries are woefully inadequate, and both levels and trends of rates may not be accurately reflected in the figures available, which suggest a crude birth rate of

about 48 in 1950, and perhaps dropping a couple of points to 46 in 1975. Only three countries in Africa – Egypt, Tunisia, and Mauritius – have had appreciable changes in fertility over the 25-year period.

POPULATION PROJECTIONS

Conventional population projections 'age' populations alive at the start of the projection period by estimating current age- and sex-specific mortality rates and estimating decreases in mortality over time. Typically, only one mortality assumption is made, but different assumptions about the rate of mortality decline are sometimes made. The future course of fertility is more problematic, but typically 3 or 4 variants are assumed, e.g. rapid, moderate, and no fertility decline within a specified time. Unfortunately, this is no sound theoretical base for estimating future fertility, and students of fertility trends mostly rely on various historical analogies either as to rate of decline or lower level of expected fertility. Most projections assume that the lowest fertility level will be a NRR of 1, a level that leads to a stationary population.

The UN has made a series of projections of the population of individual countries and regions of the world during the past 25 years, and these projections, although often criticized, are widely used by most students of population. A recent[1] set of projections gives figures between 5.8 and 6.6 billion for the year 2000, and the most quoted figure, the medium variant, is 6.3 billion. In 1976 the UN conducted the Third Population Inquiry among Governments' Population Policies in the Context of Development. Based on replies to that inquiry and using the high variant population projection for countries wishing to increase rates of population growth, the low variant for countries wishing to reduce rates of population growth, and the medium variant for all other countries, the projected population of the world is just under 6 billion[2] (5.972) for the year 2000.

Frejka[3] has used a different approach which generates the population of a country or region under 5 different assumptions as to when a NRR of 1 will be reached. Thus, the reader can compile his own projections by adding the component parts selected on the basis of an estimate of when a given country or set of countries will reach an NRR of 1. Frejka's results are as follows:

Projected date NRR of 1 would be reached	World population in 2000	2100
1970—75	4.7	5.7
1980—85	5.1	6.4
2000—05	5.9	8.4
2020—25	6.4	11.2
2040—45	6.7	15.1

Macura[4] has provided the framework for another approach to population projections, namely, taking into account expected or feasible alternative changes in economic and social factors and their interrelations with population structure and dynamics. In an article illustrating this approach, Macura presented projections for:

(a) total population by age, including assumptions on mortality and fertility, as projected by the United Nations;

(b) functional population groups, such as school-age population, working-age population, etc., computed from the same source;

(c) economically active population (the supply of labour) and non-active population, including age—sex economic activity ratios, projected by the International Labour Office (ILO);

(d) economically active population in primary, secondary and tertiary industries (the demand for labour), estimated partly by the Food and Agriculture Organization (FAO) and partly by the author;

(e) agricultural and non-agricultural population, estimated as in (d); and

(f) rural—urban population, projected by the United Nations.

Three alternative projections were considered:

(a) *Projections following present thinking*: these broadly correspond to extrapolations of what may be considered, according to current thinking, a continuation of observed demographic trends, and assumed steady but moderate economic progress in the less developed regions; both of these circumstances strongly influence world trends;

(b) *Projections of change in economic and urban—rural structures* of population, which assume rapid economic development in the less developed regions, but the same population growth trends as in (a); these projections explore a hypothetical situation in which fertility and population growth would not respond to changing economic and environmental conditions; and

(c) *Projections assuming change in both the structural and the dynamic aspects of population trends* as a consequence of rapid economic growth (as in (b)) which would tend to reduce fertility and to bring the population in

the year 2000 down to the number estimated according to the United Nations low variant; this would of course produce additional structural effects.

Macura used existing UN projections but explored the structural interrelationships under different assumptions. Several other writers have projected less rapid rates of population growth for a variety of reasons. Boyarsky[5] is optimistic about socio-economic development and projects a figure of 4,626,000,000± 410,000,000 in 2000. Bogue[6] feels that fertility will fall more rapidly than the low variant UN projection assumes, and projects a population of roughly 5.25 billion in 2000. Lester Brown states that the UN projections,

... do not examine the effect of these various population levels, supported at acceptable levels of consumption, amount of waste generated, the extent of pressure on ocean fisheries, the amount of energy this would require, the thermal pollution it would generate, the stress on food-producing ecosystems, or the level of unemployment. Stated another way, the ecological, economic, social and political stresses associated with these enormous projected increases ,in population are not taken into account. If these are considered, then even the 'low' projection of just under 10 billion people (for the year 2150) becomes unrealistic.[7]

Brown goes on to propose a population stabilization timetable that would produce 5.3 billion population in the year 2000 and 5.8 billion in the year 2015.

The more developed countries are growing at slightly less than 1% per year whereas developing countries are growing at about 2.3—2.4% per year. At the end of the century, according to a UN projection presented to the World Population Conference,[8] the population of the developed countries will number under 1.4 billion and that of developing countries 5.0 billion. By the year 2100, the figures will be less than 1.6 billion and 10.7 billion, respectively. The figures for different regions of the world are reproduced in Table 1.

ISSUES

Interest in population size, growth and distribution ranges through the continuum of pro-natalist to anti-natalist positions, with different views being based on economic, political, military, religious, ethical, human rights, genocide, status of women, and other social justice concerns.[9] This wide diversity in point of view has contributed more heat than light and more confusion than clarification, in many articles, speeches and discussions.

Table 1. *Long-range population projections for the world and major regions according to assumption of eventual stable equilibrium of fertility and mortality*

Region	Date of achievement of stated conditions (year)		Population (millions)		
	Net reproduction rate of 1.00	Annual percentage growth rate of zero	1970	2000	2100
World total	2070	2140	3621	6407	12,257
More developed regions ...	2020	2070	1084	1368	1570
Europe	2005	2065	459	540	589
USSR	2015	2085	243	321	399
Northern America	2000	2060	226	296	339
Oceania	2020	2085	19	33	52
Less developed regions ...	2070	2140	2537	5039	10,687
Africa	2070	2140	352	834	2435
East Asia	2010	2080	926	1373	1776
South Asia	2060	2120	1111	2384	5358
Latin America	2035	2105	284	625	1308

Source: Population projections available to the United Nations as of March 1974.

Berelson lists the following issues as arising because of concern about rates of population growth:

Economic Development: Will the developing countries be able to achieve substantial improvement in living standards with the current and anticipated levels of population growth?

Food and Nutrition: Will the world, or the critical countries, be able not only to feed the anticipated population of the next decades but also to improve nutrition sufficiently to provide a decent diet for every human being on earth?

Income Distribution: Would a lowered fertility rate and a reduced rate of population growth among the poor of the world contribute in an appreciable degree to the realization of 'distributive justice', or a more equitable distribution of wealth?

Employment: Will the rapidly growing countries, largely agricultural in character, be able to provide gainful and productive employment for the large numbers certain in the next decades?

Education and Literacy: Will the developing countries be able to extend the coverage and the quality of their systems of popular education so that every child has a decent chance of securing at least an elementary education, under the impact of rapid population growth?

Health: Will countries be able to extend the coverage and the quality of their health systems so that everyone has a decent chance at modern medical care, under the impact of rapid population growth?

Social Services: Will the world, and particularly the developing sector, be able to extend the coverage and the quality of other social services, like housing, transport, and social security, under the impact of rapid population growth?

Resources: Will the world, and particularly the developed sector, be able to support a high standard of living indefinitely into the future, with anticipated populations, without undue depletion of natural resources?

Environment: Will the world, and particularly the developed sector, be able to find ways to utilize such resources without undue environmental deterioration, given the anticipated populations?

Density: Does the ratio of people to space threaten psychological well-being, social stability, or aesthetic amenities?

Political Relations: Do current population trends, in growth or distribution or composition, present difficult political issues, either international or internal?

Women's Rights: Will current rates of fertility, continued into the indefinite future, unduly restrict the status of women and their options for individual fulfillment?

Child Development: Will current demographic trends limit the opportunities of the coming generations for productive lives and psychological well-being?

Human Rights: Are current demographic trends a threat to the preservation or extension of human rights with regard to population matters, and to what extent do they reflect limitations on human rights with regard to control over fertility and migration?[10]

On the other hand, Boserup[11] has reasoned that population pressure has in the course of history been a favourable and decisive element in the intensification of agriculture. Amin and Okediji[12] argue that the concerns about rapid rates of population growth are misplaced for the Third World where the ratio of population to resources varies widely, that an increase in population would be beneficial not only for the whole of tropical Africa and Latin America, 'but also for many regions of Asia (including many parts of the Indian sub-continent)'.[13] They also reason that 'stagnation in agriculture, slow industrial growth and the upward trend of unemployment in the Third World arise for reasons which have *nothing to do* with population growth',[14] and observe that many regions of Africa had a larger population in the remote past than they have today. Similar views are expressed by Okediji and Bahri,[15] who also argue that all meaningful scientific research necessarily involves the definition in advance of a certain epistemological approach, the admission of certain ideologies which guide our research, and the establishment of defined hypotheses which order the manner in which we search for and obtain our data. This view is shared by Pradervand.[16]

The most frequent policy response to population issues, as we shall see in the next section of this paper, has been the provision of family planning services, for the most part aimed at reducing rates of population growth. A number of writers have criticized family planning programmes on the ground that: they are failures;[17] they are inefficient;[18] they divert funds from other development programmes;[19] they distort fragile systems for the delivery of health care;[20] they diminish popular pressure toward social change by increasing the people's level of satisfaction and feeling of control;[21] they are devices to maintain the status quo;[22] their focus is misplaced in that they define population as the problem rather than the lack of development;[23] the motivations of the highly industrialized nations in pushing and financially supporting family planning programmes is questioned;[24] they are viewed as an attempt on the part of advanced nations to sell population control as a cheap means of achieving progress;[25] they are a form of genocide;[26] they hinder the proper development of maternal and child care, including nutrition;[27] they have potential effectiveness mainly at a certain (intermediate) stage of demographic development but not before or much after that stage.[28]

POPULATION POLICIES AND PROGRAMMES

Until the middle of this century there was either little interest in population growth or else growth was welcomed as a source of increasing military manpower or as a reflection of economic vigour. The welcome decline in mortality following World War II changed that perception in developing countries because of the increases in rates of population growth, in sheer population size, and in the astonishing growth of urban agglomerates. During the past two decades many governments have formulated policies on population, and this development has been reinforced by resolutions and funding from the United Nations, governments, and private sources.

In statements of population policy, the two most frequently articulated themes are the right of each couple to determine the number and spacing of their children, and the need to develop programmes designed to lower fertility and rates of natural increase. Among the most notable resolutions were those of the Economic and Social Council of the United Nations in July 1965: 'The rapid rate of population growth in many developing countries in relation to the growth of their national income calls for the most urgent action; the United Nations should provide advisory services and training on action programmes in the field of population to governments requesting assistance and should elevate population work to a position in the UN Secretariat corresponding to its importance'. This action was affirmed by the General Assembly in December 1966 in a resolution that also urged the further development and strengthening of national and regional and facilities for training, research, and information and advisory services in this field. Other important resolutions include the Teheran Proclamation on Human Rights which declares that couples have the right to 'determine freely and responsibly the number and spacing of their children', and the United Nations Declaration on Social Progress and Development which calls upon governments to make available to couples the 'knowledge and means necessary to enable them to exercise' this right. These themes are repeated in the World Population Plan of Action (paragraph 29) which recommended that all countries: '(a) Respect and ensure, regardless of their over-all demographic goals, the right of persons to determine, in a free, informed and responsible manner, the number and spacing of their children; (b) Encourage appropriate education concerning responsible parenthood and make available to persons who so desire advice and means of achieving it'.

A recent report from the United Nations[29] notes that of 114 developing countries, 81 have policies supporting unlimited access to modern methods of fertility control (71 by direct support and 10 by indirect support), 8 support limited access, and in 25 countries access is said to be unlimited, but without governmental support. 40 developing countries have adopted policies designed to decrease fertility; 10 seek to maintain fertility at current levels, 4 seek to increase fertility, and 60 have not formulated policies seeking to affect fertility. From the regional standpoint, and including developed countries, direct governmental support for access to modern methods of fertility control is given in 25 out of 30 countries in the ESCAP (Economic and Social Commission for Asia and the Pacific) region, 21 out of 27 in the ECLA (Latin America) region, 24 out of 39 in the ECE (Europe) region, 5 out of 12 in the ECWA (West Asia) region, and 22 out of 48 in the ECA (Africa) region.

Perhaps the most comprehensive and up-to-date assessment of the effectiveness of family planning programmes is given by Freedman and Berelson; it is briefly summarized below:

> Family planning programmes have been undertaken by a number of developing countries as the prime instrument of their policy of fertility reduction.
>
> Under realistic current conditions, such programmes have reached between 1–2% and 10–15% of the target per year, and achieved prevalence of up to 20–25%.
>
> Country performance is associated with both social setting and programme effort, in about a 7-to-1 ratio from the doubly favoured to the doubly deprived areas. The social setting also affects the quality of the programmatic infrastructure; still, the programme effort has a clear, substantial and independent effect upon performance.
>
> Programme effort appears to be associated along with social setting in both level and decline of birth rates, but for technical reasons definitive answers are not available, particularly with regard to the substitution effect – which is probably present to some unknown degree but unlikely to be of sufficient magnitude to account for the entire impact of moderately good programmes.
>
> To take 10 points off a birth rate around 40 in a decade requires sustained programme performance at about the current level of the best programmes; performance at about a third of that level will take off only about 4 points in that time.
>
> Two special cases are deserving of the most careful international attention: China, which may provide a test of fertility reduction in a country with little urbanization and relatively low living standards but with a combination of low mortality, intensive political commitment to fertility control permeating the local community and the structure of small groups, together with equity in what is available, and other institutional changes, for example, in status of women; and Indonesia, which may provide a test of the potential for programme effect under poor developmental levels and extreme population pressure but in the presence of strong political and organizational commitment.
>
> In the end, the proper appraisal is the comparative one: what alternative use of equivalent resources, under realistic conditions, would have achieved more impact toward fertility reduction?[30]

According to the UN report referred to earlier,[31] there appears to be more concern on the part of governments about spatial distribution of the population and of migration than about any other aspect of population dynamics. Of 156 countries surveyed, 78 regarded the spatial distribution of population as being largely unacceptable and an additional 59 countries viewed population distribution as being unacceptable to some degree. Only 19 countries consider the distribution of their population to be acceptable, and 13 of these are developed countries. The overwhelming concern is to slow down migration, with 100 countries expressing this view; of these, only 19 do not wish to change the structure of urban and rural areas, while 81 hope to change that structure. The views of developed and developing countries are not very different on this question: 25 of the 42 developed countries and 75 of the 114 developing countries have policies aimed at slowing down migration.

There is far less concern about immigration and emigration. Out of the 156 countries surveyed 139 perceived immigration to be satisfactory, and 115 of these also viewed the amount of immigration as being insignificant. The figures on emigration are almost as striking, with 130 countries viewing the level as satisfactory, and 102 of these perceiving the volume to be insignificant. Among developing countries, 8 view the level of immigration as being too low and 4 as being too high. The figures on emigration are similar: 5 developing countries perceive emigration as being too low, and 13 view it as being too high. Although few countries are concerned about immigration and emigration, these are important problems for several countries, and thus the subject is also of importance.

MORTALITY

In regard to government concern with mortality rates, the UN report concludes:

> No Government perceives the current levels achieved as completely satisfactory. Some, however, accept the situation , in view of the various

constraints weighing on the development of mortality. The acceptability of the situation depends to a large extent ... on the level of mortality observed in the various countries considered. But even in those countries which have a longer expectation of life at birth, there are still problems relating to differential mortality linked to such factors as age, sex, residence and occupation. Moreover, in some industrial countries where the levels of expectation of life at birth are among the highest in the world there has, during the past 10 years, been a reversal of the movement, evident for more than a century, towards a decline in mortality, particularly among men in certain age groups.

The Third Inquiry among Governments on Population Policies in the context of Development in 1976 included a question regarding the acceptability of current mortality levels .... the replies received and information collected from other governmental sources .... can be summarized as follows:

(a) In the developed countries (total 42), 32 consider the level acceptable and 10 consider it unacceptable;

(b) In the developing countries (total 114), 27 consider the level acceptable and 87 consider it unacceptable.

... the degree of acceptability varies according to the level of mortality expressed by expectation of life at birth. Of 54 countries with an expectation of life at birth of 50 years, none considered that level acceptable. On the other hand, of the 37 countries with an expectation of life at birth of 70 years and over, 31 considered that level acceptable.

A regional analysis ... shows that it is in the ECA region that the unacceptability of the current levels of mortality is most strongly felt: in 47 out of 48 countries. The other regions of the world are less uniform in their attitude of rejection since demographic situations are more varied than in Africa. In the ECWA region, 6 out of 12 countries consider the level unacceptable; in the ESCAP region, the proportion is 18 out of 30, and in the ECE region, 10 out of 39. Of the countries in the ECE region with that view, 6 have a life expectancy of over 70 years.[32]

BUCHAREST AND ITS AFTERMATH

In a sense, the heart of the World Population Conference was the World Population Plan of Action. Much controversy arose over the Draft Plan of Action, and more than 300 amendments were introduced to revise it. Many changes were made before the final version was adopted. The thrust of those changes was to emphasize that economic and social development were of overriding importance and that a new international economic order was fundamental not only to social and economic development but also to solving population problems. The Conference saw the politicization of population rather than treating it as a professional matter. In the process, population matters were viewed by many as having been downgraded. But this view was not shared by all. Leon Tabah, for example, wrote that the Conference was characterized by 'opening to the outside', 'expansion', and even 'breaking through'. 'The Conference enlarged the concept of population ....'.[33] What has happened in the two and a half years since the Conference?

Since that dramatic event, both the rhetoric and the position of governments, institutions and individuals have been (with very rare exception) that both development *and* population are important, that population programmes need to be developed and implemented within the framework of development plans. Funding has continued to increase, particularly in the United Nations Fund for Population Activities and on the part of a number of governments, additional countries have formulated population policies and programmes, and several countries have strengthened their efforts to reduce rates of growth. The United Nations summarizes developments as follows:

Between 1974 and 1976, a number of changes have affected the perceptions of countries with regard to their rates of increase and, consequently, their policies. To take, first, the case of the developing countries, Benin and Singapore no longer state that they believe a 'lower rate desirable', but consider the present rate 'satisfactory'. On the other hand, other countries such as Ethiopia, Honduras, Jordan, Nigeria and Surinam, while indicating that their current rate is 'satisfactory', appear to recognize the existence of problems habitually associated with high rates. In a group of six countries – Ecuador, Liberia, Madagascar, Nicaragua, Senegal and Sierra Leone – there are fairly clear indications that the Governments now consider a 'lower rate desirable', but have taken no policy measures. In another group of developing countries, the Governments have not only declared that a 'lower rate of increase is desirable', but have formulated policies to reduce the rate; these countries are Grenada, Lesotho, Seychelles, Papua New Guinea and Uganda. Lastly, countries such as India and Indonesia have reinforced their policies to bring about a decline in the rate of increase. In that connexion, India has adopted more vigorous measures.

In the developed countries, rates of natural increase have declined almost everywhere. However, some countries, such as Czechoslovakia and Hungary, have changed their perception of their rate of natural increase from 'higher rate desirable' to 'satisfactory', no doubt as a result of the success of their family planning policies. Other countries which formerly regarded a 'higher rate desirable' have reformulated their policies to check the decline in fertility. This applies to Argentina, France, the German Democratic Republic, Greece and Luxembourg. Two countries which, before 1974, had considered a 'higher rate desirable' but which had not formulated policies now seem concerned to do so: these are Finland and Uruguay. Some countries which formerly did not consider a 'higher rate desirable' have stated in 1976 that they now do: this applies to the Federal Republic of Germany, the Ukranian Soviet Socialist Republic and the Union of Soviet Socialist Republics. Switzerland has for the first time shown some concern at the decline in its rate of increase.

Lastly, other developed countries such as Portugal, which previously regarded a higher rate of natural increase desirable, now consider their rate 'satisfactory'. Chile, which formerly considered a 'lower rate desirable', now considers its rate 'satisfactory'. On the other hand, New Zealand, which formerly considered its rate 'satisfactory', now considers a 'lower rate desirable' although its rate has steadily declined.[34]

There are many other indications that interest in population has not lessened since Bucharest. The Arab League has provided substantial funding to UNFPA. Requests for assistance from UNFPA have grown so that available funds, although much increased, are far short of requests. The number of acceptors in family planning programmes has increased dramatically from an estimated 12.6 million in 1974 to 17.4 million in 1975. India has greatly strengthened its family planning efforts through a series of incentive and disincentive schemes and talk of compulsory sterilization. Indonesia's strong programme has continued, as have those of several other countries. Late in December 1976, Senegal announced that it will institute a national family planning programme. In summary, some observers say that population matters have become more respectable since Bucharest and there is less hesitancy on the part of governments to discuss population dynamics, always in the context of general economic and social needs, problems and plans.

CONCLUSIONS

The recent past has been a period of concern about the relatively slow rate of economic and social development, about a number of problems associated with population change, particularly rates of growth, increases in numbers, the large rural—urban migration flows, and emerging environmental problems. Food reserves have been reduced to uncomfortably low levels, partly because of climatic factors but more importantly because agricultural productivity has not increased sufficiently during the past 25 years. At the moment, two trends give some hope for a less dismal future. Those two trends are better weather and crops in much of the world, and the beginning of significant decreases in fertility in Asia and Latin America among the developing countries, and the attainment of quite low rates of reproduction in developed countries.

The key question is what of the future? What numbers must we prepare for by the year 2000? Will rural—urban migration continue its disorderly course? Will migration and investment policies exacerbate urbanization and other spatial distribution problems? Can immigration and emigration problems be reasonably managed? And what of resource shortages? And of environmental problems? Although hundreds of millions of couples will determine the numbers of population to come, their decisions (and failure to make decisions) will be influenced not only by economic and social factors, but also by governmental and other programmes designed to affect population dynamics. An important beginning has emerged during the past 25 years with reference to mortality, during the past 10—15 years with reference to fertility, and increasingly concern is expressed about migration flows and spatial distribution. The solutions are at hand for continued mortality reduction in developing countries and for at least appreciable fertility reduction; to reach those solutions, policies and programmes must receive somewhat more attention and resources than during the past two decades, but those factors are manageable. Problems of unemployment and underemployment will make solutions to migration flows very difficult. All the efforts toward economic and social development will affect those flows, but greater attention to causes of such movements and alternative policies to influence spatial distribution is required in order to meet the needs in this area.

Table 2. *Percent distribution of governments by type of attitude toward population*

Governments' views on:	Level of Development*			Regional Commission*				
	Total	MDC	LDC	ECE	ESCAP	ECLA	ECA	ECWA
Rate of population growth and achievement of economic and social objectives								
Contributes positively	21	35	14	37	10	13	12	43
Contributes to *and* constrains achievement	40	35	42	37	32	33	53	29
Constrains achievement	29	12	38	7	58	53	25	14
Present rate of population growth								
Satisfactory	29	47	20	50	10	27	16	57
Too low	11	29	1	27	–	13	3	–
Too high	39	3	56	3	74	60	47	14
Type of appropriate adjustment of population growth								
Economic and social factors only	2	–	3	–	–	–	6	–
Economic and social factors and minor adjustment of demographic factors	14	9	17	10	16	13	22	–
Economic, social and demographic factors	50	35	56	30	68	73	47	43
Government has formulated policy on adjustment of:								
Mortality	33	15	42	10	53	53	41	–
Nuptiality	12	9	13	7	32	7	9	–
Fertility	40	21	49	20	63	60	41	14
Internal distribution	39	29	36	20	42	53	38	14
Immigration	20	24	19	13	37	20	19	14
Emigration	18	9	23	7	37	20	19	14
Effects of age of women at marriage on family well-being								
Contributes positively	27	44	19	47	32	7	9	57
Contributes negatively too early	28	9	38	7	37	67	25	29
Population change in metropolitan region								
Contributing positively	14	24	9	30	10	–	3	29
Constraining development, change too fast	56	32	68	27	58	87	69	57
Population change in rural areas								
Contributing positively	15	24	10	30	5	7	9	14
Constraining development, change too slow	16	12	17	7	10	40	12	29
Constraining development, change too fast	31	29	32	23	37	33	34	29
Present level of immigration								
Satisfactory	18	24	14	27	5	–	22	29
Too low	4	9	1	–	5	13	–	14
Too high	5	9	3	7	16		–	–
Present level of emigration								
Satisfactory	8	5	9	7	10	–	9	14
Too low	4	–	6	3	10	–	3	–
Too high	14	15	13	10	10	40	6	14
Brain drain: % countries having a policy to reduce	21	12	26	10	37	40	12	29

Source: United Nations, Department of Economic and Social Affairs, *Preliminary Report on the Third Population Inquiry among Governments; Population Policies in the Context of Development in 1976,* E/CN.9 XIX/CPR.6, Population Commission, Nineteenth session (10–21 January 1977).

*MDC = more developed countries; LDC = less developed countries; ECE = Economic Commission for Europe; ESCAP = Economic and Social Commission for Asia and the Pacific; ECLA = Economic Commission for Latin America; ECA = Economic Commission for Africa; ECWA = Economic Commission for West Asia.

NOTES

1. United Nations, *Selected World Demographic Indicators by Countries, 1950–2000*, ESA/P/WP.55 (28 May 1975).

2. United Nations Economic and Social Council, *Concise Report on Monitoring of Population Policies*, E/CN.9/324 (19 November 1976).

3. Thomas Frejka, *The Future of Population Growth* (New York: Wiley, 1973).

4. Milos Macura, 'Demographic prospects for the next thirty years', International Population Conference, The International Union for Scientific Study of the Population (London: 1969).

5. United Nations, *World Population Conference* (1965), Vol. II: A. Boyarsky, 'A contribution to the problem of the world population in the year 2000', pp. 5–12.

6. Donald Bogue, Transcript of a CBS program, 'The 21st century: standing room only', CBS Television Network (7 May 1967), pp. 1–2.

7. Lester R. Brown, *In the Human Interest* (New York: Norton & Company, 1974), pp. 27, 157.

8. United Nations, *The Population Debate: Dimensions and Perspectives*, 'Recent trends and future prospects, report of the Secretary General', Vol. I (New York: 1975), pp. 3–44.

9. Teitelbaum lists 16 analytic positions on population policies. Michael S. Teitelbaum, 'Population and development: is a consensus possible?', *Foreign Affairs* (July 1974).

10. Bernard Berelson, 'World population: status report 1974', *Reports on Population/Family Planning*, No. 15 (January 1974), The Population Council, p. 16.

11. Ester Boserup, *The Condition of Agricultural Growth* (Chicago: Aldine Publishing, 1966).

12. Samir Amin and Francis O. Okediji, 'Land use, agriculture and food supply, and industrialization', *Population in African Development*, Vol. 2, ed. by Pierre Cantrelle (IUSSP, 1971).

13. ibid., p. 411.

14. ibid., p. 411. Their theses are developed further in footnote 6, p. 414.

15. F. O. Okediji and A. Bahri, 'A new approach to population research in Africa: ideologies, facts and policies', *Population in African Development*, op. cit., pp. 322ff.

16. Pierre Pradervand, 'The ideological premises of western research in the field of population', *Population in African Development*, op. cit., pp. 115ff.

17. Pierre Pradervand, 'The Malthusian man', *New Internationalist*, No. 15 (May 1974), p. 13; Bernardo M. Villegas, 'Innovation, not imitation', *CERES, FAO Review on Development, World Population Year* (1974), p. 51; Peter Adamson, 'A population policy and a development policy are one and the same thing', *New Internationalist*, No. 15 (May 1974), p. 7; Amin and Okediji, 'Land use . . .', op. cit., p. 418.

18. Mahl, 'The super gadget', *New Internationalist*, No. 15 (May 1974); Villegas, op. cit., p. 51.

19. USSR Country Statement, World Population Conference (1974); Paul Singer, 'Population growth: the role of the developing world', paper presented at the World Population Conference, Bucharest (August 1974), IUSSP Lecture Series on Population, p. 13.

20. Maurice H. King, 'The debate in Africa', *International Journal of Health Services*, Vol. 3, No. 4 (Fall 1973), p. 747.

21. M. Francoise Hall, 'Population control: Latin America and the United States', *International Journal of Health Services*, Vol. 3., No. 4 (Fall 1973), p. 727.

22. Kamla Bhasin, 'A socio-economic perspective of population problems, programmes and policies', Background documentation, International Youth Population Conference (Bucharest: 10–15 August 1974), p. 3; Rene Dumont (as quoted by Bhasin) pp. 4–5; Amin and Okediji, op. cit., p. 419.

23. Okediji and Bahri, op. cit., p. 321ff.; Amin and Okediji, op. cit., p. 419; Samir Amin, *Accumulation on a World Scale, A Critique of the Theory of Underdevelopment*, Vol. 2, translated by Brian Pearce (Monthly Review Press, 1974), pp. 593–4; National Academy of Sciences, *In Search of Population Policy; Views from the Developing World* (1974), p. 59.

24. Francis O. Okediji, 'Socio-political implications of family planning as an aspect of population policies and development planning in Africa', *Third Bellagio Conference on Population* (New York: The Rockefeller Foundation), p. 17; People's Republic of China, Head of the Delegation, speech delivered at the World Population Conference (Bucharest, 1974), p. 7 (mimeo); Report of the African Regional Seminar held at Nkrumah Hall, University of Dar-es-Salaam, Tanzania (2–6 May 1974), 'The relation between population growth and economic development', World University Service (1974), p. 68.

25. Mercedes B. Concepcion, 'Emerging issues on population policy and population programme assistance', *Third Bellagio Conference on Population,* op. cit., p. 28.

26. Steve Weisman, 'Why the population bomb is a Rockefeller baby', *Ramparts,* Vol. 8, (May 1970), pp. 42–47.

27. United Nations Children's Fund, Executive Board 1976 Session, 'Programme developments in the South Central Asia region', E/ICEF/L.1351 (6 February 1976), pp. 23,24,26.

28. Riad Tabbarah, 'Birth control and population policy', *Population Studies* (November 1964); 'Toward a theory of demographic development', *Economic Development and Cultural Change* (January 1971); and 'Population education as a component of development policy', *Studies in Family Planning,* Vol. 7, No. 7 (July 1976).

29. United Nations Economic and Social Council, *Concise Report,* op. cit.

30. Ronald Freedman and Bernard Berelson, 'The record of family planning programmes', *Studies in Family Planning* Vol. 7, No. 1 (January 1976).

31. United Nations, *Concise Report,* op. cit., pp. 25–28.

32. United Nations, *Concise Report,* op. cit.

33. Leon Tabah, 'New emphases in demographic research after Bucharest', United Nations Fund for Population Activities, UNFPA/WPPA/12 (September 1975).

34. United Nations, *Concise Report,* op. cit., pp. 13–15.

World Development, 1977, Vol. 5, Nos. 5–7, pp. 407–415. Pergamon Press. Printed in Great Britain.

Agricultural Policies in the EEC and their External Implications

DENIS BERGMANN

*Institut National de la Recherche
Agronomique, Paris*

Summary. — In reviewing the major trends in agricultural production and food consumption in the EEC countries, the author assesses the role of the Common Agricultural Policy and compares its effect with that of other economic forces in bringing about the dynamism in EEC agriculture. He then discusses the major current policy choices facing the EEC and their potential external effects: hidden productivity reserves; agricultural expansion versus farm unrest; outlook for exports. The essential point in his argument is that, in the short to medium term, it is not desirable to slow down the rate of expansion of agricultural production in the EEC.

INTRODUCTION

In view of the high levels of food consumption of most of the 260 million inhabitants of the European Economic Community (EEC), it is by far the world's largest food importer despite intensive farming of much of its 95 million agricultural hectares. It absorbs about 35% of the agricultural commodities entering international trade. The evolution of EEC agriculture and the policies pertaining to this sector are therefore an important part of any analysis of the world food situation.

The first objective of this paper is to review major trends in agricultural production and food consumption in the EEC countries, and to show how, under the influence of very strong economic forces and with the help of policies which have been rather favourable to producers, agriculture in Western Europe has grown increasingly efficient. Two conclusions, which are of course open to question, will be drawn from this analysis of past tendencies: firstly, that the agricultural policies, though helpful, were not the most important factor of change, and secondly, that the momentum of the whole food and agriculture sector will be difficult to slow down.

Since a great production potential has thus been unleashed and self sufficiency reached or even exceeded for many commodities, several policy issues arise — and our second objective is to attempt to present and clarify them. Should policies continue to be production orientated,

or has the time come for supply control? What internal conflicts loom in the background to this general decision on the suitable rate of production increases? What is the situation with regard to the different commodities? How do the various EEC interests conflict with those of major low-cost food exporters? Can the EEC agricultural policies help poor countries?

I. A DYNAMIC AND RELATIVELY STRONG AGRICULTURE

Growth and change

In most countries of north-western Europe — which roughly coincides with the EEC as it now stands — the agricultural sector has experienced almost continuous growth and extensive transformation for the past 30 years.

For the nine EEC members, the annual growth rate of production for the period from 1963 (three-year average centred on that year) to 1973 (similar three-year average) was 2.9% for grain, 3.1% for sugar beet, 1.5% for milk and for beef, 3.2% for pork and 6.6% for poultry.[1] For overall agricultural production the annual rate of growth of the six original members was 3% per year (1963–73). For the Nine and for 1968–73 (three-year averages) the corresponding figure is 2%. Since purchased inputs increased to more than double that rate (6% in the case of France), value added increased 1% per year. Labour input decreased by 4.4% per year — which means that gross labour productivity grew very rapidly.

These creditable performances do not however appear to have been accompanied by significant changes in the size of farms. For the Six, their average size increased by no more than three hectares (ha) from 1958 to 1973, reaching only 13.3 ha at that date. These figures are however rather misleading for several reasons.

The definition of a farm used by European statisticians is very broad and the average is thus reduced by a mass of micro-units which are often retirement farms for old farmers or enlarged weekend gardens. Part-time farms are also very numerous and their economic problems are not the same as those of full-time commercial units. Also, there is a significant trend towards specialization of farms which enables some units to attain reasonable efficiency even with rather small acreages.

The convergence of these factors explains that a growing share of the commodities marketed originates from a relatively small number of farms which attain a reasonable size and can use most modern inputs efficiently. Thus in the course of only 15 years, the share of French farms marketing more than 100 tons of wheat increased from 20 to 50% of the total marketed. 2% of the pig fatteners in France produce half the output, and 11% of sugar-beet producers grow half the beet acreage, while for vineyards, the 50% mark is reached by 8% of the farmers marketing wine.[2]

These figures imply of course that a large number of small farmers with little to sell are in a very difficult situation. From the point of view of the EEC's competitive position with regard to the various commodities, it is the upper bracket which is important. It thus appears that agriculture in north-western Europe is not only increasing its production but also its efficiency. To explain this a more detailed examination of growth sources seems necessary.

Farm policies have helped but other forces predominate

The very deep-seated changes which European agriculture has experienced over the past 30 years can probably be explained by the convergence of three sets of forces.

The rapid and almost continuous rate of economic growth — at least until 1973 — is the first major factor.[3] It helped absorb a large share of the excess population in agriculture.

This is particularly the case for Italy and France where industrialization was less developed. In Italy, farm population decrease reached 5.2% per year in 1961—71, probably the highest rate in the EEC. Economic growth and the rise it ensured in consumer's real incomes explain why the demand for food was sufficiently buoyant to absorb a fair share of production increases.

The second major element relates to technology and skills. Particularly in the more backward areas like most of France, Ireland and Italy, the rate of adoption of new agricultural methods had been very slow during the inter-war period. The abundant supply of cheap labour, the depressed prices, the low status of agricultural research, the poor educational level of farmers, the underdevelopment of input industries and of their sales outlets all combined to induce stagnation. After 1945, these conditions began to change. Labour became less abundant and eventually scarce, the lengthening of compulsory education and improvement of agricultural schools and advisory services slowly became noticeable.[4] Progress in the input industries has been spectacular and the use of fertilizers, pesticides, weedkillers and machinery has reached very high levels. Even if price ratios were to change significantly — and they deteriorated in 1973—74 — it would still pay many farmers to use more variable inputs. In fact their purchases tend to be more closely linked to the overall farm income situation than to specific price ratios. Lastly agricultural research has made great progress in Europe and provides farmers with a rather satisfactory flow of innovations.

Agricultural policies constitute the third major element which explains the dynamic nature of EEC agriculture. This factor is intentionally given third place although numerous aspects of farm policy such as the provision of funds for research mentioned in the previous paragraph naturally had some kind of side effects on production and productivity. Two elements are essential: price policies and investment policies.

Under national policies and later under EEC rules, an overwhelming part of farm production has benefited from price interventions preventing any major price decline (but less effective in curbing price increases). For many commodities including grain, sugar beet, oil seeds, ordinary wine, milk and beef — which are the backbone of European agriculture — prices have not only been stabilized but supported above equilibrium levels. Elementary theory and concrete observation show clearly how this unusual degree of price certainty encouraged farmers to invest, expand, modernize.

Simultaneously, a complex set of national subsidies, low-cost credit and favourable institutional arrangements (like mutual guarantee funds within farm credit banks) were combined with a few EEC measures (like low-cost credit for development plans) to feed an important flow of funds into the agricultural sector. Modernization not only became technically possible and economically paying, but financially attainable.

Has the Common Agricultural Policy (CAP) been important?

Although this is a tricky question which a wise economist would probably have evaded, it seems of interest to suggest a few ideas that may shed some light on basic policy options which will soon have to be decided upon.

As already mentioned, there is no doubt that the generally dynamic character of the economies of the Six during the 1960s was very favourable to their agricultural sectors. Agricultural adjustment to rapid technological change is always difficult. If unemployment is high and demand faltering it becomes impossible — or at least unbearable in terms of social costs. Since it seems certain that economic integration was a positive factor (though not the only one) in keeping national economies buoyant during that period, it may be safely assumed that on the whole, the setting up of the Common Market had a beneficial effect on the agricultural sector.

The more direct effects of economic integration on agriculture are difficult to interpret. What would have happened to the agriculture of the Six or Nine if there had been no Common Market? What are the real effects of the CAP on the achievements mentioned above? To answer these questions it seems necessary to discuss briefly the real nature of the CAP both from the point of view of its basic principles and with regard to the effects of integration on the location of agricultural production.

Basic principles of the CAP

The first basic principle of the CAP is *free movement* of agricultural products within the whole community. This is unfortunately not achieved for two series of reasons.

In order to prevent guaranteed farm prices from falling in re-evaluating countries, they are protected from imports by a kind of duty: the monetary compensatory amounts (MCAs). Conversely, devaluating countries, which should pay their imports at a higher price (in their currency) after devaluation are exempted from that increase in the case of farm commodities coming under CAP regulations. Community funds (MCAs again) are given to the importing country so that it should not bear the added cost of imported food. This lowering of import prices is favourable to consumers in the importing member country and contrary to the interests of its farmers.

The most valid justification of MCAs is that they prevent food price increases in countries with weak currencies. It is in the essence of an economic community that members who are better off should help partners in difficulty.

There is little doubt however that major differences in the rate of productivity increases, production efficiency, structural changes and financial management — all leading to changes in the exchange rates — must be solved by instruments of global economic policy and general measures of mutual assistance among partners, not by agricultural price manipulations. Until these more satisfactory instruments are applied, we may have to accept MCAs but they should be of a temporary nature as recommended by John Marsh (1975).

The second reason for the failure to achieve intra-community free movement of goods is linked with various so-called technical barriers to trade concerning, for instance, labelling, food additives, veterinary regulation. This is, however, a matter which does not raise problems of great interest to economists.

The second major principle of the CAP — and indeed, like free internal movements of goods, it is a general rather than a specifically agricultural principle — is that *competition should not be distorted,* whether between countries, regions, farms or firms. One example of the infringement of this principle concerns taxes on petroleum products, which are not harmonized. Another aspect concerns railroad fare structure which may be biased in favour of domestic producers.

More important still are the numerous national agricultural subsidies and other types of aids which are more favourable to some countries than to others. The EEC Commission has been attempting to determine what is acceptable in that complex field. Awarding a red ribbon and maybe even a cash prize to the owner of the best bull may not be very significant, but subsidizing the entire system of artificial insemination might be considered as unfair. Where should the line be drawn? What about direct income payments to help low-income farmers? Are they an income support intended essentially to prevent poverty, which means the sums involved will be used for household consumption, or will they be used by eager beneficiaries for investment, in which case they can rightly be criticized as distorting competition?

The third major principle of the CAP is that there should be a common external tariff (import duties are the same whether goods come in through Rotterdam or Genoa) and that this tariff wall should be high enough to encourage EEC sellers compared to external ones. This *community preference* is essential for the surplus areas and countries of the EEC. Without it they could not expect to withstand competition from low-cost 'new' countries.

The fourth major principle of the CAP is that the *financing* of the costs incurred to implement it – essentially the costs of the price support measures it entails – should be considered the *joint responsibility* of all member countries and divided among them on some fair basis linked to their prosperity (rather than to the actual distribution among members of price support expenses).

Contrary to most authors we do not consider that uniform prices are a basic principle of the CAP. Since distances between the various regions are not very great and transportation systems are highly developed, the effect of the above-mentioned principle of free trade will be a fairly uniform spatial price pattern throughout the EEC. Such a pattern is thus a *consequence* of a basic principle rather than being one in itself. However, this is not accepted in Brussels and the official view among experts there is that prices fixed under CAP rules should be almost the same throughout the Community.

The EEC has not induced great changes in the location of agricultural production

It is amusing to remember the fears which had been expressed by the farmers' organizations when the Common Market was set up or even enlarged. The French – to mention the case we know best – said the Dutch or Danes were dangerously efficient and thrifty, the British had the most powerful processing industries, etc.... Of course it is a well-known fact that farmers seldom express satisfaction about their situation and their pessimistic warnings were rightly discounted by politicians.

Now, after 15 years of integration it appears that no member country saw its agriculture decline globally through the effect of competition. Some segments did however suffer.

On the whole, there was little change in location for major commodities like milk, meat, grain and sugar beet. From Brest to Lübeck or Helsingor, farm production is based on grain, pasture and dairy cows. The product mix may vary slightly, but the end products are milk, meat and wheat and no large area in north-west Europe has ever been very far from being at least self-sufficient in those commodities (with however a rather wide range of degrees of reliance on imported feed). This striking similarity in the types of farming practised and the limited differences in natural conditions were of course not conducive to extensive development of East–West trade.

From North to South the situation is quite different. Natural conditions differ greatly. Mediterranean areas are at a disadvantage for cattle raising compared to areas where grass grows fairly abundantly for at least half the year. Conversely they are well suited to fruit, wine and vegetable production. The opening of the frontiers has thus, for instance, clearly created difficulties for fruit and vegetable growers in Southern Germany. They were the early producers for their compatriots. Mediterranean competition which comes much earlier still than theirs has skimmed off their profits and even put some of them out of business. (Happily this took place in a period when consumption of these commodities increased.)

This is not only a matter of climatic conditions. The crops concerned are labour-intensive and Italy has lower wages which gives it another type of locational advantage.

As we shall see in the second part of this paper, the North–South types of competition will probably gain in importance in coming years. So far, the development of economic integration has not on the whole brought about great shifts in the location of agricultural production. On account of the general similarity in natural conditions and significant rigidity and nationalism in consumption habits, the various EEC countries have not become dangerously dependent on imports for the basic elements in their diets. This is fortunate because they would probably not have accepted high levels of food imports.

Partial conclusion

The rigid economist can rightly criticize

both the agricultural policies of EEC countries and the CAP. They are very costly for tax-payers and consumers (price supports are mostly implemented through purchases on the market by some intervention agency, which may spend modest sums by Treasury standards but whose actions raise the price for all consumers). For instance, the cumulated amounts of national and EEC public expenditure in favour of agriculture amounted to some 11.5 billion units of account (UA) both in 1973 and 1974.[5] This should be compared to a global value of production of 64 billion UA for 1974 and a value added of 35 billion UA. The United States taxpayer pays a slightly larger amount per dollar of agricultural production but much more per farmer since the number of farmers in the US is about half that of the EEC.

The second major criticism is that European agricultural policies have failed to reduce income disparities between farmers and regions. In France farm income per farm or per full-time family farm worker varies from one to ten between the best and the poorest 'departments'. Clearly, since these great differences in farm incomes are linked to a widely dispersed distribution of factor endowments, they could only be reduced by radical land reform – which very few people in north-western Europe want – or by slow structural and institutional change. One cannot expect the EEC, in its short life span, to have produced great improvements in that field.[6] It is true however that price supports, the CAP's main policy instrument, do not correct income inequalities. The recent development of direct transfer payments to farmers either on a per person or per farm basis, or per cow owned (with a ceiling), is however an important move in the right direction.

These major economic weaknesses of European agricultural policies – not to mention several minor ones[7] – should not overshadow the great achievements in agricultural development and change outlined at the beginning of this paper. The emphasis on *economic* performances must also be questioned. After all, for the politicians, the problem was how to manage, in the most orderly fashion, the contraction of an overpopulated and obsolete agricultural sector without being voted out of office! Although there has been some dissatisfaction and even unrest (French farmers in particular have developed some quite effective techniques of nuisance making . . .), the farm sector has, on the whole, remained alien to revolutionary or extremist tendencies. This is no small achievement considering the rapid process of change it went through.

The political aspects will probably continue to carry great weight in future decisions. As P.C. van den Noort (1976) has emphasized, most governments in Europe remain in power with very small majorities. They cannot therefore afford too much agricultural discontent – even if the farm vote is continuously shrinking. Keeping this idea in mind, we can turn now to a more forward-looking analysis.

II. MAJOR CURRENT CHOICES AND THEIR EXTERNAL EFFECTS

Our view is that the EEC, though still a major net importer of agricultural commodities, could within a few years, become an exporter of several products and cause a great deal of trouble on world markets. This opinion is clearly supported by a recent OECD study (OECD, 1975) which states (our translation from the French text):

> For temperate zone agricultural commodities, the import requirements of Western Europe from North America and Oceania (as well as certain regions in South America) could globally shrink; however certain import flows for specific products should be maintained. Western Europe could increase its role as permanent supplier of certain commodities to other regions of the world, particularly developing countries . . .

It would be pointless to rewrite here the results of this well-documented study or of similar surveys by large research teams with access to many varied sources of information. The single researcher's analysis relies to a greater extent on intuition.

Hidden productivity reserves

In spite of the great changes of the past 30 years, there is little doubt that EEC agriculture still contains what Marxist authors would call hidden productive forces. These are mostly located in France – which has 35% of the agricultural land in the EEC – but also in Ireland and Italy, where, as mentioned earlier, agriculture was also rather stagnant during the inter-war period. However, in recent years, Dutch farmers have succeeded in obtaining growth rates in production even higher than the French ones, which shows that hidden reserves are present throughout most of the EEC.

The first major factor explaining why production increases will continue concerns education and science. The level of farmers' education and technical knowledge has risen considerably and many of them have the ability to master any new technique launched on the market with a very short time lag. This is a kind of cumulative process which can hardly retrogress. The importance of the scientific establishment of Western European agriculture is also very significant. There are thousands of eager researchers, hundreds of well-equipped laboratories and a solid array of input industries eager to develop and market any innovation originating from these institutions. A large share of this establishment is more or less directly production-oriented and cannot concern itself entirely with golf greens or ecology ... Its impulse will be felt for many years to come.

The second factor explaining drive and what J. K. Galbraith has called the vested interest in output is the existence of a big population potential on European farms. Farm advisors throughout Europe tell their farmers that the best way to improve their incomes is to intensify. The hidden productive forces in the form of underemployed manpower and equipment are still very considerable and eager to be put to work. (Incidentally it should be noted that the situation is different in the United States. Farm population there has decreased to the point where it is a limiting factor in any major agricultural expansion.) Microeconomically, therefore, European farmers know and are told that their interest lies in producing more to spread the fixed costs of their machinery and increase the residual returns to their own labour. *Ex post* and when it is so generally practised that it has macro effects, this reasoning might prove rather ineffective — but to ignore it would make things still worse. (This is the famous treadmill image of W. W. Cochrane, 1958.)

Rather than listing various other technical hidden reserves like under-utilized pasture lands, we may now turn to more economic and even political components of the agricultural production 'lobby'.

Agricultural expansion vs farm unrest

Any slowing down in the rate of increase of farm labour productivity would have unacceptable negative effects on farm incomes. This productivity increase must be accounted for by a combination of increases in the volume of production and reductions in the labour input. If one wishes to slow down the population decrease, one will have to find outlets for the corresponding production increases.

Our view is that, in coming years, many governments will prefer the costs of farm surpluses to the worries of added unemployment. In other words, since European economies will not be able to cope with their employment problem, one of their aims will be to keep as many people as possible on the land. Since they will tend to be fairly productive there, outlets will have to be found for their production.

Another component of the intrinsic output-oriented tendencies is the export value of agrcultural surpluses. For obvious reasons connected with lack of raw materials — particularly oil — the trade balances of most European countries will show chronic tendencies towards deficits. Exporting grain and even meat may be one of the few ways of alleviating foreign trade difficulties.

The effects of these expansionist policies on world markets should however be considered.

The outlook for exports

In recent years, the EEC (the Nine) has reached or exceeded self-sufficiency for sugar beet, potatoes, wine, milk, butter, cheese, beef and veal, pork, poultry and eggs. For all grain it reached 91% self-sufficiency, for fresh vegetables 94%. If tropical crops are excluded, the main deficits concern vegetable fats and oils (the Six import three-quarters of their needs) and protein concentrates (80% imported).

There is little doubt that the continuation of normal trends in yields combined with one or two years of favourable weather will cause the community to accumulate surpluses for its major products — grain, milk and meat. This stems from the fact that internal demand has reached the point where expansion is very slow. Population increases are significantly below 1% per year. *Per capita* consumption is nearly saturated and hardly responds to real income increases (which are not as striking as they were in the 1960s). Thus the French planning commission estimated that, for 1976—80, domestic food consumption would only increase by 1.7% per year against 2.8% for the previous plan period (1971—75).[8]

The conclusions of OECD quoted above therefore seem unassailable: the EEC will, in coming years, be more and more present as an exporter on world markets. This in turn leads to several comments.

The CAP provides for export restitutions to help clear the stocks of surplus commodities accumulated. This can be called dumping — by those who do not mind undiplomatic language. In spite of such restitutions, however, the whole organization of the CAP is not really export-oriented. Experts in the practical aspects of international trade (a qualification which does not apply to the author of this paper) say that several changes in the administration of the CAP and even in its outlook will be needed in order to improve the effectiveness of Europe as an exporter of agricultural commodities.

The fact that the EEC will soon emerge as a significant exporter of grain (and not only wheat as in recent years) will certainly not be welcomed by the United States. They should easily understand that EEC farm policies are not so different from their own — as explained for instance in a recent book by W. W. Cochrane and Mary E. Ryan (1976). In both cases there is the same pressure of irresistible technology on an inelastic demand. Like Europe, the United States decided that the social and political cost of agricultural *laissez faire* was too high. They supported prices, subsidized exports and gave food away.

It is true that low-cost exporters can complain about the *level* of price supports and export subsidies for CAP regulated commodities. This criticism, however, is much less justified now than in the 1960s. EEC grain prices were then about double the so-called world price. Now they are often only 10 to 30% above it. The accusation of inefficiency levelled at EEC farmers is less and less valid as we have attempted to show in the first part of this paper. It seems quite probable that the EEC will be compelled in the future to adopt, with due slowness, a policy of lowered prices (in real terms) and reduced protection which will deprive its critics of their arguments.

Incidentally, until now, the United States cannot complain about the volume of its exports to the EEC. In 1975, the EEC purchased 5.6 million dollars' worth of US agricultural commodities (and only sold for 1.1 billion dollars' worth of the same commodities to the US). This is nearly three times the value of 1968 exports, hardly a sign of brutal protection. At the same time, EEC exporters of dairy products to the US suffered from strict quantitative restrictions. ... Those arguments, presented by Community authorities (Lardinois, 1976), relate, however, to the past. If the reasoning on which this paper rests is correct, EEC imports of temperate commodities and particularly grain should cease fairly soon.

This implies that the EEC will have to enter into agreements with major grain exporters to stabilize the markets, finance and manage reserves, regulate food aid, prevent wasteful competition, etc. ... These questions will be examined in other papers.

Similarly it does not seem possible, within the framework of this paper, to discuss extensively the relationships between the EEC and developing countries. Only a few remarks can be made here.

With regard to temperate commodities like grain one can argue about the wisdom of food aid from the EEC to poor countries. As a disaster relief operation when people are dying it is essential. As a permanent feature of international trade it is probably debatable. Each major part of the world should no doubt count on its own forces.

For hot climate commodities, the essential point concerns the Lomé Convention signed in 1975 between the EEC and 46 countries of Africa, the Caribbean and the Pacific. The EEC has agreed to import without duties or quantitative restrictions commodities which represent 96% of the agricultural exports of those countries. The main exceptions are competing products like maize, rice, sugar (which, however, benefits from a special scheme) and beef. Possibly more important is the *Stabex* scheme under which the EEC guarantees a minimum level of export income for 29 commodities (including cocoa, coffee, tea, cotton, groundnuts and several other oil plants).

The details of this very important agreement cannot be studied here. Its principles seem to be original and relatively generous. Some African countries would like to obtain physical quotas in addition to Stabex. The Community may, at some later date, move further in that direction.

European and particularly Southern European farmers are, however, diffident with regard to this policy or even opposed to it. As explained in the first part of this paper, East—West trade in high technology and low labour input commodities is no great danger. European producers of those goods are efficient enough to cope with competition. North—South trade in commodities with a high labour component is a different matter.

This is not only a question of the Lomé Convention, though several of the items concerned are sensitive to European farmers, it extends to the whole matter of 'Mediterranean enlargement'. French farm organizations have forcefully expressed their opposition to the entry of Greece or Spain into the EEC because they feel the North—South agricultural trade it would involve would have unbearable effects on wine, fruit and vegetable producers in southern

France. It is difficult to say whether sectoral oppositions of this kind will carry much weight in the face of the political wish to enlarge the Community southwards. They may be reinforced by other critics like trade unions who will argue that integration with countries where wages are much lower than in the rest of the Community is premature.

CONCLUSION

This paper has probably covered too much ground and has had to remain very general. The essential thrust of the reasoning is that it is, in the short to medium term, not desirable to slow down the rate of expansion of agricultural production in the EEC. Agricultural expansion is wise as a means of raising farm incomes, employing as many people as possible, and paying for imports. In fact, technological forces and the natural tendencies of millions of eager and better educated farmers are such that, even if one wished to stabilize the volume of production, it would be very difficult to do so.

EEC temperate farm imports will therefore fall and exports will increase. The need for an understanding with other major exporters, and maybe importers, on the management of this potential is clear.

However if short-term pressures favour expansion, its whole logic must be questioned in the longer run. Will there in the future be many countries willing to rely on imported grain for a significant share of their food supply? Some time or other a reversal of the expansionist tendencies recommended in this paper will probably have to occur.

In the meantime, the management of national agricultural policies and the CAP will continue to be very tricky. Expansion will have to take place but reducing costs is essential. This implies structural policies to increase labour productivity, hardly an appealing programme in times of high unemployment. To find the optimal path within these contradictions and conflicts of interest will require a highly diversified set of policy instruments.

The level of price supports should probably be lowered and the loss of income resulting from this move should be corrected by direct income payments, subsidization of rural public services and special regional measures for poor areas. This may well reduce the importance of the CAP compared to national policies which will have to be better coordinated. The endless and innumerable Brussels meetings are easy to laugh at but they will be an increasingly necessary feature of an irresistible integration which in our opinion is not now likely to break up.

NOTES

1. Except when noted, all figures quoted are based on official national or EEC statistics — particularly those published in the 1975 report on 'The situation of agriculture in the Community' (Brussels: March 1976).

2. Commissariat Général du Plan, *Préparation du 7ème Plan, Rapport de la Commission Agriculture et Alimentation* (Paris: 1976).

3. Of course, in the later years of the period examined, economic integration has been a positive factor encouraging growth.

4. This does not imply that there is no remaining knowledge gap between the northern and southern parts of the EEC.

5. It is important to note however that the scope of 'agricultural' expenses is quite broad and variable among countries. Nearly one-third of the cumulated budget is devoted to social measures which concern mostly old farmers. They could be rightly handled by a 'Ministry of Social Justice' rather than by the

Ministry of Agriculture... Many 'agricultural' expenses concern facilities for a 'rural' population which is less and less composed of farm producers.

6. The statistical evidence concerning income distribution has only recently improved. Comparisons over time are therefore mostly based on impressions. Very few large 'capitalist' farms have developed and many of the poorest ones have disappeared. It may well be that income differences have decreased though poor farmers may suffer more than in the past about their situation.

7. See for instance, MacKerron and Rush (1976) for a rather overcritical view of the CAP.

8. Of course this global analysis about food consumption is, like all this paper, dangerously oversimplified. Within a general setting of saturation, some commodities might gain at the expense of others. Even if *per capita* consumption of wine in Denmark were to reach an index of 200, the problem of wine surpluses in France and Italy would not be solved.

REFERENCES

Barbero, Giuseppe, 'Agricultural development and regional economic integration', Paper presented at the 16th International Conference of Agricultural Economists (Nairobi: 1976).

Bergmann, Denis, *Matériaux et Réflexions pour une Réorientation de la Politique Agricole* (Paris: INRA-Economie, 1975).

Cochrane, Willard W., *Farm Prices: Myth and reality* (Minneapolis: University of Minnesota Press, 1958).

Cochrane, Willard W. and Ryan, Mary E., *American Farm Policy 1948–73* (Minneapolis: University of Minnesota Press, 1976).

Lardinois, Pierre, 'Speech to National Soyabean Processors Association' (Monterey, California: 24 August 1976).

MacKerron, Gordon and Rush, Howard J., 'Agriculture in the EEC – taking stock', *Food Policy*, Vol. 1, No. 4 (August 1976), pp. 286–300.

Marsh, John S., rapporteur, 'European agriculture in an uncertain world', *The Atlantic Papers* (1975) (1).

Noort, P. C. van den, 'Integrated rural development projects: decision-making on the regional level'. Paper presented at the 16th International Conference of Agricultural Economists (Nairobi: 1976).

OECD, *Etude des Tendances de l'Offre et de la Demande Mondiales des Principaux Produits Agricoles* (Paris: OECD, 21 November 1975) (Document C (75) 157).

World Development, 1977, Vol. 5, Nos. 5–7, pp. 417–424. Pergamon Press. Printed in Great Britain.

Can Eastern Europe Feed Itself?

ALEC NOVE

Glasgow University

Summary. – This paper examines the proposition that the USSR and the other East European countries are, and will remain, a burden on the world grain market because of the inability of their system to function effectively in agriculture. The proposition has two parts: that consumption does and will exceed production and that this is due to state and collective farming. The author eliminates East Germany, Bulgaria, Romania, Czechoslovakia and Hungary from the discussion except for a brief comment on each, explaining that their situations are quite clear. Therefore, the paper centres on the more complex situations of Poland and the USSR, especially the latter. The paper concludes that neither country is likely to find a rapid solution to its problems and neither, therefore, is likely to meet its domestic grain production requirements and/or targets by 1980.

The object of this paper is to examine the proposition that the USSR and her European allies are, and will remain, a burden on the world grain market because of the inability of their system to function effectively in agriculture. Obviously this proposition has two parts: that consumption does and will exceed production, *and* that this is due to state and collective farming, implying that some alternative way of organizing agricultural production would be more effective.

Let me begin by eliminating certain countries from the discussion, because, in my view, their situation is clear and requires no expenditure of time and ink beyond the paragraphs that follow.

The *GDR* is by any standards à country of intensive and reasonably high-yielding agriculture (see Tables 1 to 5). It is clear that the reason for her substantial dependence on imports of grain is the same as Britain's: lack of suitable soil in a densely populated and largely industrial country. Dependence on imports has slowly declined with a steady rise in grain yields.

Bulgarian agriculture has been doing reasonably well, with steep rises in output of grain and meat. Tractor hp per 1000 ha now actually exceeds that of the USSR and Hungary (though, as might be expected, it is only half of that of the GDR).[1] Only an unusually poor harvest in 1974 led, exceptionally, to a net import of grain.

Romania is a net exporter of both grain and meat, and has shown a particularly large rise in meat production. Though yields have improved,

there seems to be scope for still better results if fertilizer utilization reaches even Bulgarian, let alone Polish, levels (see Table 5).

Czechoslovakia is second only to the GDR in the intensity of its agriculture (i.e. second both in fertilizer application and in tractor-power per unit of land). She imports little meat, but inevitably has a grain deficiency, though the import trend is slightly downwards.

Hungary has done well. Except after bad weather in 1970 she has been a sizeable grain and meat exporter, while producing more meat *per capita* than any other of the countries of Eastern Europe. Yields are high by historic Hungarian and indeed international standards. Livestock exports to the West have been impeded by the Common Agricultural Policy of the EEC, which has also adversely affected Poland.

This brings one to the special case of *Poland*, which requires a more detailed comment.

Poland, alone of the countries analyzed here, has predominantly a private smallholder agriculture. This private sector is still comparatively little mechanized, and so Poland in 1974 still had 2,264,000 horses (against only 76,000 in the GDR and 163,000 in Hungary). Horses eat grain. This helps to explain Poland's grain deficit, which, as Table 6 shows, is astonishingly large and continues to grow. Compare production *per capita* figures in Table 4: Poland has more grain than the GDR, yet its imports have risen above those of the GDR. Poland has 31.4% of its population engaged in 'agriculture and forestry', the GDR only 11.5%.[2] Poland also has nearly three times as much sown area as the GDR. It is true that Poland has been expanding meat exports, but domestic consumption has risen faster, indeed demand has risen faster than supply, causing highly embarrassing shortages.

These shortages are due (as also in some other Eastern countries) to a price policy explicable only by politics, and not by economic common sense. Polish money wages have risen in the period 1968–75 by over 60%. Prices of livestock products have been frozen. Attempts to increase them, in December 1970 and June 1976, have been frustrated by mass protest. Income elasticity of demand for meat is high. Evidently, such a price policy as this guarantees trouble. Poland's output of meat has in fact risen impressively. (The most popular meat is pork, which doubtless helps to explain the huge *per capita* production of potatoes shown in Table 4 — pigs eat potatoes). Yet demand outpaces supply; it is a very heavily subsidized demand. Relatively to other things, it could be said that meat sells at a price which in contemporary British terms would be of the order of 30 pence a pound, or about a third to a quarter of the price of meat in the West.[3] The subsidy required to keep food prices at these unreal levels reached 100,000 million zloty, according to official statements at the time of the abortive price rise of June 1976, representing a heavy burden on the budget. To feed the expanded livestock herds requires still more grain imports.

Therefore Poland, with a high proportion of its people still on the land and a relatively modest population density, finds herself a large net grain importer because people eat too much meat (relatively to the general level of economic development) and there are too many horses. Looking at Table 4, one also gets the impression that animals must be eating some sizeable share of the bread-grains (since wheat and rye output *per capita* is second only to Hungary, and Hungary is a net *exporter* of grain).

What remedies are there? The traditional nature of smallholder agriculture is a brake upon efficiency. As any visitor to Poland can see, fields are small, many peasant households have 5 ha of land or less, which is scarcely conducive to mechanization, and I saw myself literally dozens of peasants sowing by throwing seed into the wind by hand. Productivity *per capita* cannot be other than low, and it is arguable that further gains in yields are improbable without some major structural changes. Against this, Polish peasants clearly detest collectivization, and the government wisely

does not use coercion to solve the smallholder problem. Furthermore, the government has itself contributed to technological backwardness by refusing (until 1970) to sell tractors to peasant households, or to make small mechanical tools available, preferring to concentrate tractors and combines in the so-called agricultural circles (*kolki*). Japanese experience points to the very considerable potential of small-scale privately-owned farms worked intensively. By reaching grain yields equal to those in Hungary or Czechoslovakia, Poland could be self-sufficient in grain, even with the continuing subsidization of meat prices (and the resultant high demand for fodder-grains). Progress is likely to be both slow and costly. So, for the next quinquennium Poland will probably continue to be a net importer, though, if only on balance-of-payments grounds, the government will clearly do its best to lessen dependence on imported grain and to stimulate exports of meat, subject to the constraints imposed by its fears of the consequences of large and unpopular price rises.

The *USSR*, however, is the key to the entire problem, not only because she has been in some recent years the world's largest importer of grain, but because of her role as a supplier to the grain-deficient East European countries. Thus in 1974 Soviet exports of grain included the following:[4]

	(000 tons)
GDR	1425
Poland	1898
Czechoslovakia	669

Consequently we must examine in some detail the performance and potential of Soviet agriculture. A whole book can easily be devoted to this theme. What follows is therefore a necessarily abbreviated summary of the principal factors involved.

In the first place, a glance at Tables 1 and 5 shows the USSR at the bottom of the 'league table' both in yields and in fertilizer supplies. This has, of course, multiple causes. Thus the USSR (like Canada) has a more extensive form of agriculture than Central Europe, and in wide areas the problem is not one of fertilizer so much as of rainfall: a good crop can be obtained (e.g. in North Kazakhstan or the southern Ukraine) if there is no drought. *Climate* is a serious handicap. Thus in the years 1963 and 1975 the weather was outstandingly bad, and most problems would disappear if only the favourable years 1973 and 1976 were to recur regularly. It is also only proper to note that grain yields were far lower 10 or 20 years ago, that progress has undoubtedly been made, though at heavy cost to the rest of the economy (thus investments in agriculture more than doubled between 1966 and 1974).

None the less, there is no doubt that the northern and western areas of the USSR, where moisture is sufficient and soils not naturally fertile, do require *more fertilizer* (and also lime), and there are numerous Soviet official statements to that effect. This, then, represents one remediable cause of low yields, a cause which it is planned to remedy, since fertilizer production is planned to continue its rapid rise. (It is important to recall that in 1960, say, mineral fertilizer was scarcely available at all except for a few priority crops, such as cotton).

There remain many problems connected with the utilization of fertilizer. Packaging, transportation, storage are all deficient, and there is sharp criticism of the imbalance between deliveries of fertilizer and the production and supply of machines to spread it. No doubt this can be remedied in time.

Another factor adversely affecting agricultural performance is the *size of farms*. It is perhaps not always realized that they are at once too big and much too small, mechanized (though inadequately) and totally unmechanized, at one and the same time. This requires some words of explanation. *State farms* average 19,000 ha of agricultural land (6,000 ha arable), and *collective farms (kolkhozy)* 6,300 and 3,400 ha respectively. They employ an average of 500–700 persons. The level of specialization is low. Only recently a correspondent in *Pravda* was complaining that *all* the farms of his region were given compulsory plan targets for a wide range of vegetables. Farms usually cultivate a variety of crops, keep most kinds of livestock, and are difficult to administer. There is evidence of diseconomies of scale. These are accentuated by plan-orders from bureaucrats and regional party officials, who also launch annual campaigns to fulfil plans for ploughing, sowing, harvesting. This, as will be shown, has unfortunate effects also on the peasant's sense of responsibility and his material incentives.

Side by side with these farms are the *private allotments and animals* of peasants (and of suburban townspeople). These are usually cultivated by spade and hoe, and are often a quarter of a hectare or so in size. These little holdings cannot be disregarded: they produced at least 26% of total agricultural output in 1973 (cal-culated from figures in the 1973 *Statistical Annual*, pp. 456, 469). Individuals own 35% of the cows, produce 32% of meat and milk, 41% of the eggs, 64% of potatoes and negligible quantities of grain. Time is spent on these unmechanized operations, and also in taking produce to the free market in the city. In recent years the pay for collective and state work has substantially improved, and so proportionately less attention is being paid to the private plot and to sales in the market. However, the output of this private sector is still slowly rising, and, owing to the very inadequate system of rural food shops, these plots and animals still play a vital part in providing for the needs of peasant families.

This leads one to discuss *labour* problems. As in many other countries, the bright lights of the city beckon, and there is a grave shortage of skilled labour which affects the quality of maintenance and repair of equipment. Despite the apparently very large size of the total rural labour force, there are the most acute shortages of labour at peak periods, necessitating a massive 'import' of workers from the towns plus the help of the army at harvest time. This is due partly to the lack of interest in extra effort of the peasants on the huge impersonal farms and partly to the inadequacies in mechanization (of which more in a moment). Lack of effective incentives are ascribed by Soviet commentators to the piecework system on these large farms: thus a tractor driver is paid by the area he ploughs, and finds it easiest to plough shallow. He feels no personal responsibility, moral or material, for the outcome. 'Who does not watch the work of the ploughman: the accountant, the supervisor, the brigadier, the representative of the People's Control, the rural Soviet, the agronomist, the agitator–political-organizer, and even a volunteer quality-controller. Yet what sort of peasant is it, if it is necessary to follow him about to ensure that he ploughs and harrows properly'.[5]

Machinery is often of poor quality, and provided in a 'non-complex' and bureaucratic manner. That is to say, farms often fail to obtain what they ask for, and are allocated what they do not need. Gaps in mechanization create bottlenecks which contribute to labour problems.[6] Livestock raising, vegetable cultivation, loading and materials handling are poorly mechanized. Spare parts and essential replacements fail to arrive, so that many tractors and combines are out of commission. Very poor roads shorten the lives of lorries.

Distribution of food is inadequate, so that many items are not marketed or are lost.

Storage space is very scarce. Until a recent drive to build many more grain elevators it was true even of grain. It remains the case for vegetables, fruit, milk: lack of handling equipment, lack of packaging materials, bad roads, insufficient retail outlets and no incentive for the trade network to handle perishables, etc. (see, for example, the series on vegetable shortage which was printed in *Pravda* during February 1977).

The specific problems of agriculture are 'concerned with live organisms, affected by a variety of natural including biological factors, as well as by organizational–economic and social conditions.'[7] For reasons given above, the system of state and collective farms and of basically centralized planning and party control have given rise to inefficiencies, and have made progress very costly. We have been informed by Glushkov, the head of the state prices committee, that subsidies required to cover the losses on the livestock products sector now reach 19 milliard roubles, or the fantastic sum of 25 milliard (billion) dollars! This is *additional* to an investment expenditure which, if one includes investments in industries serving agriculture, takes a third of the total amount invested in the USSR.

It must be stated that output *has* grown, as a glance at Table 1 will confirm. There are very substantial fluctuations due to weather (one has only to compare the official grain harvest for 1975, 138 million tons, with the record year 1976, 224 million tons), but the trend is upwards. Indeed, there is a problem that must be explained: how is it that the USSR imported hardly any grain in (say) the period 1956–62, when production hovered around 120 million tons, and has become a major importer even when harvests are on average some 60% higher.

This, as in Poland, brings one to questions of price policy in general, prices of livestock products in particular.

In the early 1960s Khrushchev gave publicity to a campaign to 'overtake the United States in the production of meat and milk'. At that time, Soviet meat output was barely a third of that of the United States. Given the calorie-consciousness of the Americans and the cholesterol scare, it has been possible to reach the (falling) American levels in the consumption of milk products (though fresh milk is often unavailable, owing to lack of means of keeping it fresh and getting it to the customer). It is quite another matter in the case of meat.

American meat production absorbs (or rather the animals absorb) a high proportion of total US production of grains. Maize is especially widely used as a fodder, and this so impressed Khrushchev that he launched a 'maize campaign', insisting on a vast increase in maize-growing. Unfortunately, most of the USSR is not well suited to maize, and the effort to grow it for silage in areas in which it could not ripen was a disaster at first, because it was done to order, regardless of availability of labour, machines, fertilizer or experience. Maize silage has become an important contributor to the Soviet fodder balance, but ripe grain, root crops, concentrates, and particularly hay, are chronically short, especially in years of drought. Yields, as well as the level of mechanization, are low or appallingly low, as the figures below demonstrate, taking the fairly normal year 1974 (see table below).[8]

Meadows and pastures are notoriously in poor conditon. Consequently, livestock is often poorly fed, and the diet is unbalanced, with insufficient protein. All this is well-known in the Soviet Union, and decrees have been issued designed to improve matters.

Livestock herds have been built up to the limit of available fodder supplies. A bad harvest can cause a sharp drop in numbers, especially of pigs. Thus the 1963 drought led to a decline (January 1963 to January 1964) from a total of over 70 million head to 41 million. Numbers reached 72 million by January 1975, but the disastrous weather of that year caused another cutback, this time to 45.7 millions. Numbers of cows have been, as a rule, preserved in the bad years, but their numbers rise slowly: thus the increase from 1965 to 1976 was only 7%, or

(quintals per hectare)

	USSR	Hungary	GDR	Poland	Czechoslovakia
Fodder root crops	240	420	472	315	523
Maize for silage and green fodder	138	186	346	420	282
Hay (annual grasses)	22	27	74	38	34
Hay (perennial grasses)	23	42	77	63	58

less than the increase in human population, though milk yields per cow rose by over 20%.

Livestock has, on average, been better fed,[9] and the output of meat has risen faster than the numbers of head — though inevitably the slaughter that followed the 1975 harvest led to a decline in meat output, as the following figures show:[10]

1965	1974	1975	1976
	(million tons)		
10.0	14.6	14.0	13.3

Obviously the 1977 figures will be better, following the record harvest of 1976.

The essential point, then, is that the effort to increase meat production and to build up livestock numbers has literally eaten up the grain supplies. The demand for meat is, as we have seen, heavily subsidized. Glushkov, whom we have already quoted, gave the following information: the price of beef in the shops is 2 roubles per kilogram; the total cost to the state per kilogram is 3.50 roubles. Butter is sold at 3.60 roubles; the cost is 5.00 roubles. The last increase in prices of meat, butter and milk occurred in 1962 (and led to some disturbances). Since that date, money wages have risen by over 55%. As in Poland, the income-elasticity of demand for meat is much greater than unity. Therefore shortages are inevitable. Endeavours to provide enough meat run repeatedly up against the fodder supply barrier.

This is why the question of the estimated size of the actual or future Soviet grain deficit is, in a real sense, unanswerable. If measured against the declared intention to reach American levels of meat consumption, or to satisfy demand at the present heavily-subsidized price, grain supplies are inadequate even in the most favourable years. One way of roughly calculating the 'deficit' in this sense is to take as a basis the American level of consumption: this calls for roughly one ton of grain per inhabitant per year. (Of course in the United States much less of it is eaten as bread than in the Soviet Union, and much more of it is for livestock.) By this standard, the USSR in 1980 will 'need' something of the order of 265 million tons of grain. Its own declared objective for 1980 (i.e. the five-year plan target for the 'end of the quinquennium') is 235 million tons. This is likely to be reached only if the weather is very kind, and suggests a continued dependence on imports, though not at the very high rates (such as 25 million tons) of some recent years.

Of course the livestock population will be limited by available supplies of grain, and also of the currency to buy it abroad. So it is within the power of the Soviet authorities to reduce import dependence by reducing the pressure to increase livestock numbers and meat supplies. However, this will mean a continued shortage of meat in the shops, unless prices are raised.

To put the point another way, since demand for livestock products exceeds by a substantial factor the means available to feed the livestock, the projected level of Soviet imports of grain (or, for that matter, meat) in an average-weather year can be as high as deliberate policy, or ability to pay, determine it.

However, this view could be based on an over-pessimistic view of the potential for improvement in the performance of Soviet agriculture. So let us look at the factors which might lead to higher yields, beginning with the Soviet policies which are designed to achieve the planned goal of 235 million tons by the end of the present decade.

Steps actually being taken include large expenditures on 'melioration' (drainage, improvement of pastures, irrigation), more fertilizer, more and better machinery, a large road-building programme. Experts urge much greater attention to seeds, one of them arguing that good seed selection in the USSR and Eastern Europe as a whole would by itself raise yields by 50%.[11] Improvements are needed and are possible in livestock breeds, and the same amount of grain can be used for fodder much more efficiently in a more balanced diet (several experts have pointed out that the Soviet use of grain is relatively greater per unit of fattened livestock, than the American); this could follow from a much-needed increase in Soviet yields of hay, the development of chemical fodder additives, and similar planned measures. Also the diet of the people can be improved by increasing the very inadequate provision of vegetables, canned foods, etc., thereby perhaps reducing the pressure on meat supplies. (Oddly enough, the USSR appears 'statistically' to consume large quantities of fish, but it is by no means easy to obtain in the shops.)

The point is: the poorer the performance of agriculture is in relation to its possibilities, the greater the *potential* for improvement. Having listed so many evidently remediable deficiencies, have I not in fact argued in favour of the proposition that 235 or even 270 million tons of grain is possible if the correct action is taken? After all, the area sown to grain is around 125 million ha — it is unlikely to be possible to increase this substantially, given the soil and climate. A steady average yield of 20 quintals per ha equals 250 million tons. As Table 1 shows, this would still leave the USSR with the lowest yields in Eastern Europe. Why is this impossible? If it *were* possible, then the pessimistic prognostications are baseless. They *can* feed themselves, or rather they *will* be able so to do.

However, this would be, in my view, an unwarranted conclusion. Given (to repeat) the fact that a steady improvement in yields is both possible and probable, there are major obstacles to overcome. One is climatic: no Soviet or Russian government can eliminate drought risk, and irrigation can only help marginally (too much land in relation to the available rivers and underground sources of water).

The other is organizational. The Soviet leadership understands the importance of this aspect, but is locked into the state-farm–collective-farm system. So far its efforts have been in the direction of adapting it by a combination of specialization and merger: farms are being urged to undertake joint activities, forming in many cases an agro-industrial complex (e.g. for processing and canning foods, and also for producing building materials, electricity, etc.). Specialized livestock enterprises, based upon modern technique, are being developed. Strong criticism is being directed at inflexible bureaucratic planning.

However, this observer at least is doubtful if the cure might not be worse than the disease. If diseconomies of scale beset the large and clumsy state and collective farms, they will cause trouble also for the merged and joint activities. Perhaps the way out is the one which, so far, has been rejected, and which is in the opposite direction: decomposing some at least of the farms' activities into small autonomous groups, free to arrange their own work schedules and responsible for an entire complex of operations on the particular plot of land, or crop, or animals. In Hungary, this method is intelligently combined with large-scale mecha-

nized cultivation (e.g. of wheat) where technical and soil conditions favour this method. 'Small-scale' care for cows, onions, grapes, may have substantial advantages, and can also utilize the considerable number of unskilled peasants, many of them older women. In addition there is the problem of adapting the clumsy system of supply of machinery and spare parts to the needs of an increasingly complex and more mechanized and specialized agriculture. After all, it has hardly been a secret all these years that tractors need spare parts, workshops and mechanics, and yet articles and cartoons appear which continue to denounce the chronic shortage of all these necessities of mechanized life.

The party's policy seems still to be to approach agriculture as if it were an industrial-manufacturing activity, its problems to be solved by better technique and more intelligent planning. Ideology favours this approach: the 'elimination of differences between town and country', turning peasants into workers, farms into agricultural factories. Of course 'factory-farming' does exist — there is ample scope for modern techniques in agriculture. But the best Western models are small-scale with respect to the number of human beings employed, which makes for a sense of responsibility and/or the possibility of effective supervision.

So, finally, my estimate remains: that the Soviet Union will continue its slow advance in output, at very high cost to the rest of the economy, but will not reach the target set for 1980 in the yields of grain and fodder crops, and that consequently the USSR herself, and therefore Eastern Europe as a totality, will be net importers of grain and probably also of meat, for the next ten years. After that — well, the world may not last that long, and, even if it does, forecasts purporting to predict the world in 1990 cannot, by their nature, be worth much more than the paper they are written on.

NOTES

1. *Comecon Statistical Annual* (1975), p. 214.

2. *Comecon Statistical Annual* (1975), pp. 393, 394.

3. Multiple exchange rates make any precise comparison impossible.

4. *Soviet Foreign Trade Statistics* (1975).

5. P. Rebrin, *Novyi mir*, No. 4 (1969), p. 156.

6. Most forthright criticisms of this state of affairs may be found in G. Dobrynin's article, in *Voprosy ekonomiki*, No. 11 (1974). See also *Pravda*, 9 January 1975 and many other sources.

7. Dobrynin, op. cit.

8. *Comecon Statistical Annual* (1975).

9. Supplies of concentrates have almost doubled between 1965 and 1974 (*Statistical Annual* (1974), p. 420).

10. Source for 1975 and 1976: *Pravda*, 23 January 1977.

11. Yu. Kormnov, in *Voprosy ekonomika*, No. 1 (1977), p. 90 ('Kormnov' literally means 'Fodderman'!).

Table 1. *Grain output and yields*
All grains, including pulses
(000 tons, and quintals per ha respectively)

	1961–5 average		1966–70 average		1971–4 average	
	output	yield	output	yield	output	yield
Bulgaria	4863	19.0	6454	27.4	7386	33.0
Hungary	6905	20.3	8400	25.4	11 317	34.2
GDR	5969	25.3	6991	29.4	8703	35.9
Poland	15 427	17.0	17 367	19.8	21 598	25.2
Romania	11 101	15.9	12 948	19.3	14 873	24.0
Czechoslovakia	5658	21.8	7111	26.6	9439	34.0
USSR	130 335	10.2	167 562	13.7	191 913	15.6

Source for Tables 1–5: *Comecon Statistical Annual for 1975.*

Table 2. *Potatoes: output and yields*

	1961–5 average		1966–70 average		1971–4 average	
	output	yield	output	yield	output	yield
Bulgaria	400	85	380	114	365	122
Hungary	1998	79	2044	105	1523	115
GDR	12 066	166	12 283	185	11 589	179
Poland	43 682	154	47 906	176	47 275	177
Romania	2600	85	2874	93	3555	120
Czechoslovakia	5635	114	5676	151	4822	156
USSR	81 628	94	94 813	115	90 052	113

Table 3. *Meat*
(selected years, 000 tons)

	1960	1965	1970	1974
Bulgaria	307	464	476	562
Hungary	816	929	1040	1361
GDR	1021	1126	1271	1598
Poland	1751	2012	2182	3066
Romania	561	657	857	1207
Czechoslovakia	802	978	1098	1307
USSR	8681	9956	12 278	14 535

Table 4. *Production* per capita, *1974*
(kgs)

	Grain	of which wheat & rye	Potatoes	Meat	Milk
Bulgaria	774	338	39.7	65	205
Hungary	1204	491	152	117*	177
GDR	578	302	792	94	442
Poland	692	424	1444	91	499
Romania	651	240	196	62	213
Czechoslovakia	712	390	308	89	383
USSR	776	393	321	58	364

Note: *1973

Table 5. *Deliveries of mineral fertilizer per ha of arable land*
(kgs of nutrient content)

	1960	1965	1970	1974
Bulgaria	36.1	85.5	159	140
Hungary	29.4	63.3	150	243
GDR	188	267	319	376
Poland	48.6	73.1	162	228
Romania	7.9	28.9	66.7	88.2
Czechoslovakia	94.6	167	230	275
USSR	12.2	28.5	47.0	60.9

Table 6. *Foreign trade in grain, 1970–74*
(000 tons)

		1970	1971	1972	1973	1974
Bulgaria	(export)	462	558	833	367	149
	(import)	158	195	—	136	637
Hungary	(export)	810	112	505	1732	1830
	(import)	181	808	789	265	390
GDR	(import)	3424	3066	3845	2990	2770
Poland	(export)	200	111	208	410	262
	(import)	2484	2950	3108	3263	4091
Romania	(export)*	370	702	900	1026	711
Czechoslovakia						
	(import)	1439	2033	1550	1552	1038
USSR	(export)	5700	8600	4560	4853	7029 §
	(import)	2200	3500	15 500	23 900	7131 ‡

Source: *Foreign Trade Annuals;*
Notes: *Wheat plus maize only.
‡1975 figure was 15 909
§1975 figure was 3578

Table 7. *Foreign trade in meat*
(000 tons)

		1970	1971	1972	1973	1974
Bulgaria	(exports)	65	67	74	65	61
Hungary	(exports)	123	163	163	134	201
	(imports)	61	16	13	77	25
GDR	(imports)	85	56	47	42	24
Poland	(exports)	157	174	173	194	234
	(imports)	44	153	65	55	6
Romania	(exports)	55	55	69	100	133
Czechoslovakia						
	(imports)	121	76	45	22	40
USSR	(imports)	165	225	131	129	515

Source: *Foreign Trade Annuals.*

World Development, 1977, Vol. 5, Nos. 5–7, pp. 425–440. Pergamon Press. Printed in Great Britain.

Foodgrain Production and Population in Asia: China, India and Bangladesh

GILBERT ETIENNE

*Graduate Institute of International Studies
and Institute of Development Studies, Geneva*

Summary. – On the basis of the present trends of population growth in China, India and Bangladesh, one can reasonably expect a gradual decline in the growth rates, thanks to family planning.

In spite of wide political differences, the three countries have entered a phase of complex agricultural development, requiring more new inputs and better planning at the national and local levels. While becoming less vulnerable to natural calamities, especially China and India, all three countries become more vulnerable to human shortcomings and deficient planning.

Although increasing efforts are needed in agricultural research, water management, chemical fertilizers and pest control, it should be possible to increase foodgrain production faster than population.

South Asia, especially India and Bangladesh, has a bad name among model-makers who try to assess the future of the world's food and population. The gloomy scenarios of M. Mesarovic and E. Pestel in *Mankind at the Turning Point*[1] find roughly similar echos in other studies. South Asia appears as a huge black spot where millions of people may die of hunger unless enormous amounts of aid are poured into the area.

Too often, in this type of study, it is puzzling to see the deep difference of views between several model-makers on the one hand and people, both Asians and others, having considerable field experience and a practical knowledge of what is going on in Asia. According to them it is by no means inconceivable to see the food production curve rise faster than population.

These three countries – China, India and Bangladesh – have a number of common features as far as technical issues and economic planning are concerned, regardless of their political differences. We have tried to underline them, but this does not mean that we are *comparing* them, especially China and India. The level of available information on these two countries is so different that real comparisons are hardly possible except on a few broad points.[2]

I. POPULATION ISSUES

All three countries are increasingly aware of the need to curb population growth, but while India and China already have a fairly long experience behind them, Bangladesh is only beginning to propagate family planning after a limited start during the Pakistani regime in the 1960s.

China

First and ticklish question: the actual number of people. Here is a country which is particularly well organized to know the figure of its population each year. In the rural communes, people are counted each year, once or twice, in order to allocate grain rations. During my last visit in 1972,[3] I could obtain in some districts the actual figure of the population, based on such records, often for the whole past decade. In Hupeh and Kwangtung I also got provincial figures based on such records. In other provinces (Hopei, Honan, Hunan) I got only very rough data with no precise year reference.

As to the urban population (around 15% of total population) it could be known through the grain and cotton textile rationing system.

Yet such data does not seem to be available.

Several recent official statements mention by now a total population of 800 million, with an average growth rate up to now of 2% per year. Such a rate is most likely not under-estimated, when considering that countries like India or Bangladesh are above 2% with a lower standard of living, nutrition and public health.

What is more disturbing is the figure of 800 million. The only full census of the People's Republic took place in 1953, which gave 582 million for the mainland of China. On the whole, at that time, neither the Chinese nor the foreign demographers contested the overall result of the census. Starting from that figure, with a yearly growth rate of 2%, one arrives at 900 million in 1975. Now, for unexplained reasons, Chinese officials have stopped for many years to take the Census as base year. They mention instead an estimate of about 500 million for 1949, which should be very rough.

It seems also that some uncertainty prevails in Peking. In an often quoted interview to an Egyptian journalist, Li Hsien-nien, then Vice-Premier (1971), declared that they had no precise data. Estimates from different ministries ranged between 750 and 830 million.[4]

We are thus left with two estimates of 800 and 900 million!

Last but not least, the impact of family planning should be considered. The first campaign started in 1957. The year after, one could still see exhibitions, as I remember, in Canton and other cities, but the propaganda was being swept away by the Great Leap Forward and its emphasis on manpower.

In 1961, from conversations with Marshall Chen Yi, one could guess that the Chinese were again concerned with the problem. In the following year a full-fledged campaign started, which, apart from some interruptions during the cultural revolution, is still going on today.

Abortion is free, even without the agreement of the husband; late marriage (25—27 years) is strongly recommended. People are induced to have no more than two children. All available contraceptives are encouraged: condom, sterilization of males or females, loop, pill, etc.

It is quite clear that in cities, especially the big ones, the birth rate is falling rather fast. In factories and offices cadres can control the population rather easily. Besides health facilities are more easily available.

In the countryside progress is much more uneven as Chinese officials admit very frankly. Local customs sometimes hinder propaganda, especially for late marriages, and the organization and distribution of contraceptives repre-sents a difficult task, when one must reach the five million production teams, often away from roads or railway lines.[5] All these reports, to which could be added several statements by the late Chou en-Lai and Mao Tse-Tung, give us a different and more accurate picture than the naive statements of some foreign travellers who claim that China has brought her population under control! Finally the best summing up comes from *Pekin Information*: 'Family planning is now widespread in towns and gradually introduced in the countryside' (11 November 1974).

With such a lack of data, it is very difficult to make any forecast. Simply, we can assume that within the next 25 years, population may rise by no less than 40% or slightly below that.

India

Family planning was already widely dis-cussed in India before independence. Some concrete steps appear already in the *First Five-Year Plan 1951—56,* but one must wait until the mid-1960s for a more energetic policy. By that time propaganda gathered momentum in favour of sterilization, the loop and the condom. As to abortion — it has been legalized. Success is uneven, some States are doing pretty well (Maharashtra, Gujerat, Tamilnadu, Kerala, Punjab) while others proceed much more slowly (Uttar Pradesh, Bihar, Madhya Pradesh).

In spite of such differences, the idea of family planning is definitely progressing, not only in towns (20% of the population) but also in villages, as I could observe between 1963/64 and 1975. In addition, effective implemen-tation of birth control is increasing. One comes across the usual difficulties of both a traditional and practical nature, but the latter appears more important. Often it is striking to see how illiterate women have, already for a long time, been anxious to get rid of so many preg-nancies.[6]

The birth rate may have fallen from $41.7^\circ/_{oo}$ in 1960/61 to $35.4^\circ/_{oo}$ in 1973/74. By 1975/76, 16.3 million out of 102 million couples in the reproductive age (15—45 years) were brought under family planning through sterilization, loops, condoms, etc.[7]

Since the beginning of the emergency (June 1975) propaganda measures have considerably increased. Several States (Maharashtra, Har-yana, Punjab) wanted to make sterilization com-pulsory by law after three children. In prac-tically all States more energetic efforts are being made. For instance, between April and

September 1976, 3.4 million people had been sterilized.[8]

Even if the excesses committed during the Emergency may temporarily slow down family planning, the new Janata government has re-affirmed the need to curb population growth.

However, for at least another decade, it would be dangerous to expect a drastic reduction in the demographic rate of increase. A growing number of young people are reaching marriage age, and it looks doubtful that raising the marriage age by as many years as in China could be implemented, although it is slowly rising.[9] Besides, the death rate is still high especially in the countryside: $16.4°/oo$ in rural areas (80% of the population): $9.7°/oo$ in urban areas[10] which gives an All-India average death rate of $15°/oo$.

Starting from a yearly increase of 2% now (600 million in 1975) one could assume a global population increase of at least 45–50% within the next 25 years, assuming a fall in the death rate from 15 to $10°/oo$ and of the birth rate from 35 to $25°/oo$, the latter target, being perhaps on the optimistic side.

Bangladesh

The first census of Bangladesh gave a total population of 71.5 million (March 1974). However under-enumeration may have been important; that is why census officials emphasize that population could have been close to 76.2 million.[11]

Estimates of crude birth and death rates range respectively between $45.6–47°/oo$ and $14.2–17°/oo$.

M. Hossain has presented other estimates of a birth rate falling from $46.9°/oo$ in 1961 to $45.7°/oo$ in 1975 and a death rate declining from $20°/oo$ to $17.2°/oo$. This gives for 1975 a yearly increase of 2.85% per year.[13] These data, especially the death rate, seem more plausible than the other ones, because considering the low standard of living of Bangladesh compared to India, one should also assume a higher death rate, even perhaps more than $17°/oo$.

Family planning has been hardly felt so far: less than 5% of eligible couples practice any type of birth control.[14] Besides, only 9% of the population live in towns and are thus more easily reached by propaganda than rural people.

Taking all these facts into consideration, one could assume that population control may not proceed faster than in India; it could, in fact, be somewhat slower, although more energetic measures are now being taken.

Summing up

In all these countries, one can reasonably expect a slowing down of population increase. However, for the next 25 years, the pressure is bound to remain heavy, unless new birth control devices are soon introduced. Both in China and India research is going on. In the latter, Dr. G. P. Talwar and his colleagues of the All India Institute of Medical Science are, at present, experimenting with a vaccine on some groups of women. If it proves satisfactory, it could have a rapid impact on the birth rate, since it would be much easier to carry out birth control programmes through an injection once or twice a year.

II. AGRARIAN REFORMS

In recent years land reforms have again become topical in developing countries as well as in academic circles or international organizations.

All three countries fall in the same category. Over several decades, the land–man ratio has become so skewed that any redistribution of land through a ceiling on landownership would have but a limited social impact. There are simply too many people (landless labourers, small owners) who claim for land or more land. We should also remember that a landlord in old China had an average of 10–11 ha. In India today, the local landlord has very often not more than 10–15 ha. Very rare are situations as in North Bihar where fairly often one comes across landlords owning 50–100 ha. In Bangladesh, where population pressure is even more acute than in China and India, landlords have frequently no more than three ha.

Under such conditions, a rational solution is the Chinese one, i.e. collectivization of land. Yet such a drastic remedy cannot be imagined in India or Bangladesh for political reasons: the dominant forces have never considered such a step, and it seems doubtful that political changes could lead to such a solution, unless some very unexpected events occur. It would really be no mean achievement if the present ceiling laws in India were thoroughly implemented: in several States prescribing a limit of seven ha of irrigated land. The strong drive for such an implementation which took place in 1975 and 1976 released, as surplus land, 350,000 ha in the whole country.[15]

The very uneven distribution of land creates obvious and serious social problems, but as far as production is concerned, the effects are much less adverse than assumed. By far the bulk of the cultivated area is divided into economic holdings or holdings which could be as follows: in good alluvial soil areas, with at least some irrigation, it may be around 1.5–2 ha, or even 1–1.5 ha in good rice areas. It rises to 3–5 ha in dry lands and poor soils of the Deccan.

Types of holdings should also be considered. Various types of tenancy (fixed rent, share-cropping) are found in South Asia, as they existed in old China. Such arrangements present obvious social defects. They may also have a negative effect on production, especially in cases where a large owner takes hardly any interest in his land and does not provide any inputs. However, owners renting their land are not all big landlords. Not infrequently does one come across very small landowners who prefer to rent their land to a larger owner in order to work outside the village.

Finally, tenancy plays a relatively limited role. In both countries, by far the largest part of the land depends on cultivating owners (see Appendix).

While recognizing many social defects in the present land tenure system of both countries, one must admit that such systems do not block agricultural production.

III. FOOD PRODUCTION AND ITS PROSPECTS

In all three countries, some broadly similar trends can be observed. In both China and India substantial increases in foodgrain production occurred in the 1950s; in the former, thanks to restoration of law and order, rural works, greater use of organic manure and traditional irrigation, and some land reclamation also took place. In India, the bulk of the increase was due to land reclamation and some more traditional irrigation. In Bangladesh, little progress was achieved until the early 1960s and the Second Five-Year Plan of Pakistan 1960–65.

The improvement of the situation in China and India was confirmed by the trends of imports and/or exports of grain. The former not only became self-sufficient, but could export around half a million t (tons) of rice per year. The latter was able to substantially reduce its imports in the mid-1950s. In Bangladesh, on the contrary, the deterioration of the food–population ratio crept in gradually in the 1950s. At the time of independence, East Pakistan was self-sufficient in foodgrain. After a decade, it had to import cereals (see Appendix).

Towards the beginning of the 1960s, in all three countries it became obvious that traditional techniques were reaching their limits. Production was levelling off. In India and Bangladesh imports were rising. As to China, it became a substantial net importer in cereals.

By that time only the large-scale intro-duction of new inputs could lead agriculture to a new phase of growth. Such a policy in India and Bangladesh took the name of package programme. The early emphasis was on new techniques of water management and chemical fertilizers. Later on the new seeds and pest control were added. In China we come across similar trends.

Agricultural development is thus becoming much more sophisticated than in the past, or even in the last few decades. National and local planning, technical constraints and foreign trade, become much more important, regardless of the ideological framework.

China

As can be seen in the Appendix, foodgrain output started moving upwards again after the difficulties of the Great Leap Forward, very severe natural calamities, as well as the sudden withdrawal of Soviet technicians in 1960.

Total cultivated area has hardly increased since the end of the first five-year plan 1953–57. Due to urbanization it may even have decreased to 106 million ha (112 million in 1957). Therefore most progress was due to increased yields.[16]

Considerable achievements appear in the field of major and minor hydraulic works. What is striking is the very sound combination of traditional and new technologies. Especially in the Northern Plain, several flood control and drainage schemes against water-logging and salinity have been carried out between the mid- or late 1960s and today.

Until the Great Leap Forward included (1958–60) such schemes, relying nearly exclu-sively on manpower, pick and shovel in the old traditional way could not successfully win the battle against floods. Today one comes across sophisticated works, using masses of farmers during the lean winter season and relying on fine engineering, heavy equipment, concrete, steel gates for sluices, etc. For instance, one of the junctions regulating the Taching River (Hai Ho Basin) involves two barrages with sluices, a lock for navigation and dykes. Total invest-ment: five million Y out of which 20% was spent on manpower,[17] 80% for machinery, concrete and steel.

Elsewhere one comes across large pumping stations for drainage. At Lu Hsin Ho, ten pumps (each of 280 kw) improve 17,000 ha of arable land (Hai Ho Basin).

For irrigation, one uses surface water through canals fed by reservoirs constructed at the foot of the hills, but the number of tube-wells keeps on increasing. Usually they are of 1½–2 cusec; 1.7 million tube-wells installed so far are in the Northern Plain.[18]

Irrigation requirements are less acute in Central and Southern China which enjoy a better and less erratic rainfall. Yet, very often, irrigation also plays a crucial role, in case rains are delayed or insufficient. Besides, irrigation facilitates double or sometimes as in the South, triple cropping in one year. Here also pumps play an increasing role with pumping sets on river banks or near to reservoirs, pumps and rubber pipes used to irrigate at least part of the terraced fields.

In the advanced district of Hsinchow (Hupeh), the Tatu commune has installed 31 pumping sets and 19 tube-wells to improve several hundred hectares. That type of mechanized irrigation can be found more and more widespread in other provinces. In the commune of Kao Tang Ling (District of Changsha, Hunan, 50 km from the town) six pumping stations (1300 kw total) are installed near the river. Other pumps irrigate terraced fields. The total investments have reached 300,000 Y, half from a State grant, half paid by the commune, its brigades and teams. The maintenance and operations cost comes to about 5,000–6,000 Y per year and 20,000 Y for power.[19]

Thanks to all these efforts, irrigation has increased from 34.6 million ha in 1957 to 45–50 million in 1975. Power used for irrigation and/or drainage has increased from six million HP in 1964 to 40 million in 1975. Nowadays around 34 million ha are classified as enjoying safe yields, whereby the danger of drought or floods has been eliminated.[20]

Progress is no less striking in the field of fertilizers. For hundreds of years, if not more, Chinese farmers have shown an amazing talent in collecting and using organic manure. Besides being mostly located in the temperate zone, China gets a much greater profit from farm manure than tropical countries like India and Bangladesh. Today, it is quite common to find applications of 15–30 t/ha of organic manure. However, chemical fertilizers are badly needed to boost yields further.

After a rather slow progression until 1957, by which time annual consumption reached 427,000 t (in terms of nutrients), production and imports increased to 4.26 million in 1970. For 1975–76 (July–June) we would propose the following estimates:

	Production	Imports
N:	2.75 million t	1.30
P_2O_5:	1.45 million t	0.40
K_2O:	0.50 million t	0.06
	4.70	1.76

This expansion must be qualified: around 60% of nitrogen fertilizers produced in China come from the small indigenous factories[21] producing mostly ammonium bicarbonate (16–17% of N) or aqua ammonia (14% of N), both fertilizers which are not as good as other nitrogen fertilizers. The former cakes and/or evaporates rapidly, while aqua ammonia is very bulky to transport. These defects partly explain the order of 13 ammonia–urea production plants from some Japanese and French firms as well as from Kellogg Continental. When completed, probably not before 1980, they will produce 3.5 million t in terms of N, thus making it possible to gradually give up the small factories.

No less typical is the emphasis on mechanization: tractors and power tillers. Especially in Central and South China, there has been for many decades a serious shortage of draught animals for ploughing and more so for transportation, hence the use of men and women pulling carts or carrying big loads on a bicycle.

Tractors are thus relieving farmers of a very tiring job. They may also make multiple cropping easier thanks to rapid ploughing. All over China, but particularly in the Northern Plain, tractors are no more a rare sight, as they were until the 1960s. In 1975, according to rough estimates, there may be 500,000 tractors in use and perhaps 150,000 power tillers.[22] During the National Conference on Agriculture (September/October 1975) the aim announced for 1980 was to have 70% of field activities (irrigation, ploughing, threshing, etc.) mechanized.

In the present expansion of new inputs, the weak link appears in the field of long-term genetic research on new high yield varieties (HYV). This is due to the relative scientific isolation from world currents in the 1960s and to disturbed conditions during the cultural revolution, and possibly after.

The impression I gathered during my field trip in 1972, has been amply confirmed by several American scientists much more competent than I am.[23]

One comes across some new dwarf or semi-dwarf HYV for rice in different provinces, often giving good results. Hybrid corn is fairly widespread in parts of Manchuria and near Peking. There is also some hybrid sorgho. As to wheat, progress has been particularly slow, with the exception of a few new varieties.[24] Often, instead of HYV, one finds improved varieties selected through traditional techniques. They increase yields by 20–50%, unlike the much higher increases of dwarf varieties responding well to heavier doses of chemical fertilizers.

Recent improvements in the field of research may have taken place, but, as one knows, the breeding of new seeds is a long process. As to the import of new seeds, it has not proved very successful. In several parts of China (though not in the South) Mexican wheat proved ill-suited to local conditions. The same happened with the well-known IR8, paddy variety from the International Rice Research Institute in the Philippines.

Production prospects. From 1952, the final year of the reconstruction period, until 1975 foodgrain production has overtaken population growth:

Population + 65 or 75%*

Foodgrain + 80%† (round figure)

* depending on the figure of 800 or 900 million for 1975, † both years enjoyed good weather conditions.

The investments in hydraulic works and chemical fertilizers have led to some acceleration of growth during the last five years (see Appendix).

Two series of estimates are at our disposal: in the first columns are the latest figures of the US Department of Agriculture; in the second columns the figures gathered by Ben Stavis:

Starting from the USDA data, one can make the following assumptions. Net cultivated area would increase only by a few million hectares but gross cultivated area could rise by 10–20 million ha thanks to irrigation. Average yield of paddy would reach 4,500–5,000 kg/ha, of wheat 2,000 kg/ha or above. Other grain (maize, sorghum) would increase by 50% and tubers by around 10%. Another hypothesis would be to take a slightly lower average yield for paddy per crop, which would be compensated by a larger increase in cultivated area, through major land reclamation in Manchuria, Sinkiang, and perhaps inner Mongolia which might push wheat.

In both cases, it seems possible to get 100 to 150 million t or slightly more of additional foodgrains within the next 20–25 years, a 40–65% increase roughly equivalent to the population increase or ahead of it.

Both hypotheses imply a further sizeable expansion of irrigation, for which untapped potential is still important in the Northern Plain, in the Yang Tse Basin and further south.

The larger quantity and better quality of fertilizers should begin to be felt after 1980 thanks to the new urea plants. Several more based also on oil or gas could be further developed. Untapped phosphate reserves so far appear at least fair, and potash, needed in smaller quantities, should be imported.

We can also expect further progress in pest control, where serious damage still occurs.

Last but not least, we must add the so-called side-lines activities, private and/or collective: vegetables, fish, pigs, poultry, where there is still large scope for improvement.

The Chinese authorities are well aware of the needs to improve and strengthen the whole economy. Industries supporting agriculture (fertilizers, pumps, tractors and other machinery, cement) are bound to carry an increasing

	paddy		wheat		coarse grain		tubers	
Gross area (including multi-cropping, million ha)	33.6	39.1	26.7	27.5	58.3	60.4	14.0	10.5
Production (million t)	115.14	118	35.3	45	76.0	72	27.5	22
Yield (kg/ha)	3,434	3,000	1,322	1,600	1,304	1,400	1,964	2,100

Total gross area: 132.6 million ha – 138 million ha
Total production: 256 million t – 257 million t

Source: Ben Stavis, 'A preliminary note for grain production in 1974', *The China Quarterly,* No. 65 (March 1976).
Note: The USDA takes average data for 1971–75, whereas Ben Stavis takes it for 1974 only. Stavis uses early estimates which were revised later on. See Appendix.

weight. No less urgent is infrastructure. Power supply through both large and small local stations keeps on increasing. Already 60,000 of the latter have been installed mostly in rural areas. In Kwangtung there are more than 12,000 producing 1.7 billion KWh. Today around 90% of the communes' village head-quarters have electricity.[25] A more recent source of power comes from the use of methane derived from the fermentation of manure pits. In Shantung alone, 10,000 cadres have been trained in this new device.[26] Even more badly needed is the expansion of secondary roads within districts and more vehicles in order to accelerate the circulation of goods.

All these tasks involve more planning between provinces and within districts. Hua Kuo-feng, at the National Conference on agriculture (Sept.–Oct. 1975) particularly emphasized the role of district cadres in all these tasks, the improvement in their efficiency as well as their ideological work. Such a process is bound to increase the role of district and commune authorities, and increase the dependence of production teams, although they remain the basic unit of production. Following the Conference, a number of radio broadcasts underlined the need in particular for a better co-ordination of activities and a greater co-operation between the different departments at work in the districts. See for instance Kweiyang Radio of 12 February 1976 (FBIS, 13 February 1976).

India[27]

In the 1960s, and more precisely towards the end of the decade, modern inputs began to play an increasing role, while land reclamation reached more or less its limits.

Data on irrigation need qualifications. On the one hand, several areas classified as irrigated

are often poorly irrigated. On the other hand, this defect has been partly corrected by the rapid increase in tube-wells and pumping sets.

	1965/66	1973/74
Private tube-wells	100,000	820,000
State tube-wells	12,400	20,000
Pumping sets	513,000	2,000,000

Private tube-well (often similar to the ones used in China) command area 3–20 ha; State tube-well, 100–200 ha; pumping set, 1–3 ha.

Such progress is interconnected with the expansion of new high-yield varieties of cereals (HYV) which appeared in the mid-1960s and require more water and chemical fertilizers than local varieties.[28]

The propagation of HYVs has been very uneven. Mexican wheat proved well adapted to wheat areas. Besides North-West India (Punjab, Haryana, West Uttar Pradesh) was already at a fairly advanced stage of development thanks to irrigation canals and excellent agricultural castes. For all these reasons progress was really spectacular: total wheat production increased from 12 million t in 1964/65 to 26 million t in 1971/72. The North-West has absorbed a large part of new inputs, especially tube-wells and chemical fertilizers. In 1973/74, for instance, the consumption of nitrogen fertilizers (in terms of nutrients) was 56 kg/ha in Punjab, compared to 4.5 kg in Bihar or 6.5 kg in Maharashtra.

Progress for rice, the main cereal, was much more modest. The early new varieties (IR8 among others) proved to be ill-adapted to local conditions in most rice areas. Besides, the impact of pests (insects and diseases) is heavier on monsoon crops like rice than on wheat which is grown in the dry season.

The introduction of new rice varieties is also made more complex than wheat varieties

	1950/51	1960/61	1970/71	1974/75
Net cultivated area (million ha)	118	135	139–141†	n.a.
Net*irrigated area (million ha)	20.9	24.7	31.2	35
Consumption of fertilizers (in terms of nutrients in t)	62,000	288,000	1,688,000	2,573,000

* Net, i.e. without multi-cropping. † The Surveyor General of India gave 139.4 million ha for 1971/72, *Economic and Political Weekly*, 9 October 1976

because of the greater diversity of micro-climates and other conditions under which paddy is cultivated: rain-fed, irrigated, etc. For all these reasons rice production has grown from 39 million t in 1964/65 to 43 million t in 1971/72.

As to other cereals (millet, maize) they have been little affected by new inputs. Production has fluctuated according to good or poor monsoons. New hybrid varieties of jowar (sorghum) or bajra (pearl millet) have not made much headway. They require more water and fertilizers, but since such cereals are usually grown in non-irrigated areas with a low and erratic rainfall (mostly in the Deccan) farmers can not take the risk of using new seeds and chemical fertilizers. As to pulses, for which research only started towards the end of the 1960s, one does not notice any definite upward trend during the last twenty years.

All these factors combined explain the following progress:

	1949/50	1964/65	1970/71
Foodgrain output * (million t)	60	89	108
	1971/72	1975/76	
	105	121	

* Includes cereals (clean rice *and not paddy as for China*) and pulses. (See appendix for details.) All reference years were very good years from the weather point of view, except 1971/72 which was fair.

Population +72%; Foodgrain production +100% (1950—1976).

The average growth rate between 1964/65 and 1970/71 was 3.28% per year, against 2.55% for the period 1949/50—1964/65. Later on production fluctuated below the 1970/71 figure. In 1974/75 it fell to 100 million t. Two monsoons (1972 and 1974) were exceptionally bad. Then the winter crops (rabi) of 1974/75 were affected by very cold weather. Besides, wheat production levelled off in the North-West for several reasons: the new seeds were not renewed every four or five years as they should have been, hence the seeds began to lose their qualities. They also became more vulnerable to rust which hit the crops in 1972/73 and 1973/74. Power shortages affected irrigation especially in the North-West where one finds the highest concentration of electrical tube-wells.[29]

Finally, consumption of chemical fertilizers began to slow down. Between 1973/74 and 1974/75 it even declined by 300,000 t. Production did not proceed as scheduled. As for imported fertilizers (659,000 t versus a production of 1.7 million t in 1973/74), their prices sharply increased. In 1974/75, the supply position improved, but the prices were so high that farmers reduced their purchases. Consumption rose again in 1975/76, but remained 3% below the figure for 1973/74.

Production increased again in 1975/76 (121 million t) but this was mostly due to very good weather for both the kharif and rahi. As to the monsoon of 1976, it looks good also.

What can be the future of agriculture? The scope for new land is very small,[30] maybe a few more million ha, but much remains to be done in improving yields per crop and having more multi-cropping. As in China, water management plays a central role through irrigation and flood control. According to rough estimates, it should be possible to reach a maximum net irrigated area of 70 million ha, which, with multi-cropping, could be raised to a gross area of 107 million ha. Out of the latter, 72 million ha would be covered through surface water, and the balance through ground water.[31]

As far as fertilizers are concerned, even in advanced wheat areas, average use of chemical fertilizers amounts to about half the recommended doses. Elsewhere, from the figures quoted above, the margin of progress is still more considerable. India has reserves of rock phosphate which they have begun to develop. As to nitrogen fertilizers, unlike China, the industry is hindered by the lack of oil or gas. Discussions are going on concerning expanding nitrogen fertilizers production based on coal. At least for the immediate future, India will have to rely on imports of oil for producing fertilizers and/or on imports of fertilizers.

It is difficult to assess possible increased use of farm manure. As mentioned earlier, such organic matters have a much briefer effect on tropical soils than on temperate ones. As to the recent expansion of biogas plants, it is mostly useful as a source of power in villages, because fermented manure released has a very low nutrient content: 8% N, 5% P_2O_5; 7—8% K_2O.

In the field of seeds, a very serious effort has started in order to strengthen both research and seeds industry and multiplication, in order to avoid the troubles faced recently with wheat. New varieties, as in Europe and North America, must be continuously bred and multiplied in a satisfactory way.

Wheat yield averages above 2,000 kg/ha are now widespread in North-West India, but elsewhere wheat remains around 1,200 kg/ha as in Varanasi or even less in non-irrigated zones. There is still some possible increase in advanced areas, and considerably more in central and lower parts of the Ganges Basin.

Although a decisive breakthrough has still not occurred in rice, there is no reason that it could not take place. Already now some progress begins to be noticed.

Much work could be done for maize, which, with a few exceptions, has done poorly so far. There are wide areas of irrigated maize, which during the monsoon in North-West India could achieve much better yields than now, either through hybrids, or at least, improved varieties.

The future of jowar and bajra appears much less bright; wide areas of the Deccan cannot be irrigated and rains are poor.

Finally, it is conceivable that gradually research will bring out better varieties of pulses responding well to chemical fertilizers.

Double cropping, so far less advanced than in China, amounts to 24—25 million ha and could be raised to around 60 million ha (cash crops included). Already now in the lower Ganges Basin, the expansion of irrigation enables farmers to grow wheat in the dry season after monsoon paddy. In Bihar wheat production has expanded from 913,000 t in 1967/68 to 2 million t in 1974/75, in West Bengal from 71,000 t to 836,000 t. In the latter State, average yield has attained 2,030 kg/ha, a figure not far from the yield in Punjab (2,250 kg/ha).[32]

In the same areas, as well as in Eastern Uttar Pradesh, the scope for progress is no less with regards to paddy which nowadays is around 1,000—1,500 kg/ha.

Good land and possible irrigation are no less striking in a very slow-moving State like Orissa. As to the fine deltas of Andhra and Tamilnadu, they often already achieve 3,000 kg/ha or more of paddy (2,000 kg clean rice) per crop. This can be raised further and, in a number of areas, more double-cropping could be achieved, especially thanks to ground water.[33]

Some broad assumptions can be made. Irrigated area devoted to cereals could reach 55 million ha out of which 37 million would bear two crops a year: wheat and rice; wheat and maize; rice and rice. Taking as average yield 2,000 kg/ha of clean rice or of the other cereals, one arrives at 184 million t of grain.

Unirrigated areas devoted to cereals and pulses (often jowar and bajra) would cover a total area of at least 60 million ha:

40 million ha	yield	500 kg/ha	20 million t
10 million ha	yield	1,000 kg/ha	10 million t
10 million ha	yield	1,500 kg/ha	15 million t
			45 million t

In round figures it makes 230 million t or nearly double the bumper crops of 1975/76.

To be on the safe side, one could modify such data to around 200 million t because we should also consider human factors. The attitudes and behaviour of farmers towards agricultural work are much more diverse in India than in China. A number of agricultural castes — for instance the Jats in the North-West, the Kammas and Reddis in Andhra, the Pattidars in Gujerat . . . are very hard-working and enterprising farmers. The same cannot be said of a number of landowner castes in areas such as Eastern Uttar Pradesh or Bihar or parts of Orissa. Such factors, as well as the present low level of development of these regions may slow down increases in production.[34] We must also remember that advanced areas like the North-West and several deltas of South India started moving ahead fairly fast, already since the end of the 19th century thanks to canal irrigation, which also stimulated non-agricultural activities, urban markets, roads, later on electricity.

In conclusion, a target of 200—230 million t by the year 2000 would enable India to free itself from its grain deficit and also to improve the overall level of nutrition in the country. In recent years, there has been a growing concern for agriculture. The overall agricultural policy, the importance given to practical tasks, rural infrastructure[35] (power, roads) have improved. The nature of these activities is not basically different from what has been mentioned about China.

Bangladesh

No Asian country is as exposed as Bangladesh to so large a scale of natural calamities. At the same time, the average population density is around 500 per km^2 including rivers and 550 without rivers. (Total area 141,000 km^2.) With the exception of the Chittagang Hills Tracts, the whole country is covered by the delta of the Ganges—Brahmaputra—Meghna mostly consisting of rich alluvial soils. All three rivers together can reach a peak discharge of 5.3 million cusec, which is more than double the maximum flow of the Mississippi. Besides, the country is so flat that floods take a long time to be drained away.[36]

Unlike the Tonkin or China, which have a

centuries' long tradition of flood control, the relatively low population density did not make flood controls very necessary. Today, practically every plot of land is under cultivation, even in low-lying areas exposed to floods.

From the sea side, Bangladesh is exposed to very severe cyclones. Finally, land is attacked by sea water infiltration during high tides.

To solve all these problems is extremely complicated and costly. Some work was done during the Pakistan period 1947—71 (sea embankments, dykes) but much more remains to be done.

Even in normal years, low-lying areas cannot be cultivated during the monsoon and, when floods are severe, up to 40,000 km^2 (around one-third of the delta) can be under water for several weeks. Finally, the frequency of major calamities is high: between 1954 and 1976, one counts nine very bad years with between half a million t and over one million t of rice destroyed per year.

Other handicaps should be considered. The eastern part of Bengal was particularly underdeveloped during colonial rule in terms of modern elites, infrastructure, urbanization, industries. From 1947 until 1958, the pace of development was very slow. Rice, by far the main food crop, did not show a real upward trend.

The situation improved with the second Five-Year Plan 1960—65: average rice production which had remained around 7.5 million t (1950—60) increased to 9.7 million t (yearly average 1960—65). Irrigation essential for dry season crops began to appear thanks to low-lift pumps and chemical fertilizers. Towards the end of the 1960s HYV of paddy were introduced. They do not give good results under monsoon conditions, but are successful in the dry season on the very small irrigated areas.

These more dynamic trends are soon hindered by the growing political disturbances and the war of liberation against Pakistan. Then, from 1972 to 1975, the situation hardly improves: political instability, lack of serious planning, damages due to the war, violent inflation, severe calamities (drought in 1972, floods in 1974). Finally, in the latter years, famine broke out with at least 30,000—50,000 death casualties. Grain imports kept on increasing from an average of 1.13 million t (1965—70) to 2.26 million t in 1974/75.

For all these reasons, Bangladesh is often considered as a hopeless case, which, in fact, it is not, provided the country continues to enjoy a minimum of law and order, peace and stability.

Growth prospects. For a number of decades it will be difficult to check river floods or typhoons, but other means can lead to fairly rapid agricultural growth. Rice, by far the main foodgrain, is cultivated as follows:

	aus	aman	boro
Area (million ha)	3	5.8	0.8
Yield (clean rice) (kg/ha)	930	1165	2100
Total output (million t)	2.9	6.7	2

average per year for the period 1965—70, except for boro 1969/70.

aus broadcast: March—May to July—September
aman broadcast: March—April to November—January
aman transplanted: July—Sept. to November—January
boro transplanted: November—February to March—May

The other main crop is jute (800,000 ha). Then come some pulses, sugar cane, oilseeds, fruit and vegetables. The total net cultivated area is around 9 million ha. Cropping intensity had reached 146 in 1969/70 but fell back to 130—135 in later years.

Most crops depend on the pre-monsoon rain[37] starting in April and on the monsoon from June to October, with the result that land is empty during the dry season for lack of irrigation facilities. Only one million ha have been irrigated mainly through low-lift pumps using the rivers and through some tube-wells pumping ground water and with traditional means.

Rivers flow in the dry season and ground water could provide enough water for irrigating four million ha of land, mostly through minor irrigation works: pumps for surface water and tube-wells. Such a target, following World Bank estimates, could be reached in the 1990s. In the meantime and later on, major work combining flood control and irrigation could be gradually constructed.

This development strategy offers several advantages. First of all, one does not start from zero. Farmers are beginning to get used to pumps; boro HYV varieties have given good results; the consumption of chemical fertilizers,[38] though still low, is increasing. Also irrigated crops during the dry season are much less exposed to pest than monsoon crops. Finally, there is practically no risk of natural calamities during that part of the year.

One could envisage different arrangements: boro followed by irrigated and transplanted irrigated aus, or transplanted aman followed by boro. Another solution is to push wheat instead of boro rice, since it requires less water. One must also consider that during the monsoon, 25% of the cultivated area is deep flooded (above one meter of water) even in normal years. Such areas can bear only low-yielding floating rice varieties.

To sum up, four million ha double-cropped could give 20 million t of rice and wheat (average yield 2,500 kg/ha of clean rice or wheat). Then around three million ha of aman rice are fit for HYV. This could give six million t of rice. Areas of low yield (broadcast aus and aman) could give around four million t. The total would be 30 million t, i.e. more than double the present production level of 13 million t in 1975/76 (an excellent year due to the weather), and imports of 1.6 million t. Population increase, in the meantime, may be of 60—70%.

Finally, one must emphasize another set of factors, some positive, some negative. Bengali farmers have been used for a long time to sophisticated agriculture, with their clever system of three rice seasons. They are hard-working and by no means closed to innovations. In the last few years they started using hand pumps for irrigating paddy, an ideal device for very small landowners. Wheat has spread in many areas in 1975/76 in spite of very poor extension services. Yields of boro rice are already quite high.

On the other hand, farmers face severe handicaps. Rural infrastructure — access roads, electricity, repair workshops and mechanics — is much behind all the fairly advanced parts of India. In addition, the average size of holdings of medium and upper farmers is quite low, thus reducing their margin of savings and investments. All these factors make the foreign inflow of loans or grants more crucial than in India.

IV. FOOD CONSUMPTION AND INEQUALITIES

The most striking contrast between China on the one hand, and India and Bangladesh on the other, lies in differences in standard of living, particularly nutrition. One can assume, in spite of the limitations of direct enquiries, that acute misery has disappeared from China. Not only is production per head higher than in South Asia (an old trend of China's agriculture) but distribution is much less unequal. However, disparities are fairly important in China, between rich and poor areas, and even within the same commune or brigade. In my survey of 1972 (op. cit.) I came across a wide range of values for the ten points working day: from 0.32Y (1 dollar = 1.90—2Y) in a team of Pai Ho commune (Honan, Loyang) to 1.36Y in some teams of Kwang Li commune (district of Kao Yao, Kwangtung).

Differences are smaller between grain rations. In the above teams of Pai Ho, the average was 155 kg of grain per head per year versus 260 kg in the affluent brigade of Liu Chuang in the famous commune of Chi Li Ying (Hsinhsiang district, Honan). Other differences can be found in the number of private pigs and poultry, which on the whole are more numerous in Central and Southern China compared to the Northern Plain.[39]

As far as towns are concerned, the grain ration is considered normal: 13—15 kg per month for non-manual workers (clerks, etc.) and 15—26 kg for industrial workers. In several cities (though not in Peking) pork and eggs are still rationed. The cooking oil ration is a quarter of a kilo per head per month. Cotton textile is available on ration: 6m per head per year. (Personal observations made in 1972 and *Current Scene*, No. 5—6 (1975).)

Food deficiencies in India and Bangladesh are well known as is the greater inequality in food consumption. What is less clear is the extent of deficiencies is spite of a large number of studies in particular about India.

Let us first mention the differences between data supplied by the Ministry of Agriculture (quoted throughout in this paper) and the estimates of the National Sample Survey. For 1952, 1958/59 and 1964/65, the NSS arrived at figures higher than the Ministry by 20 to 30%.[40]

One should also mention the well-known study, *Poverty in India*,[41] by V. N. Dandekar and N. Rath. Using the National Sample Survey data and enquiries, they reach the conclusion that 40% of the rural population and 50% of the urban population are below the 'poverty line', i.e. the minimum standard of living. P. G. K. Panikar points out that in Kerala, the data proposed by V. N. Dandekar and N. Rath for a minimum acceptable diet should, in fact, be reduced by one-third.[42]

Last, but not least, come the warnings of the well-known anthropologist M. N. Srinivas. After drawing attention to different sources of food for poor people never mentioned in nutritional surveys, such as rats, water snakes, field crabs, roasted insects, recovering paddy stored by rats, he adds: 'Our dieticians and nutritionists who sit in the cool of their urban offices must get out to the fields and study the diet of ordinary people' instead of relying on 'this kind of study . . . left to the tip and run method of an inferior class of investigators'.[43]

Even when taking into account all these

reservations, it is obvious that a sizeable proportion of people are undernourished in India and Bangladesh so that massive efforts are needed to boost production.

Now comes another major question: will the poor benefit from the growth policies outlined in this paper? In spite of all the slogans on 'the poor getting poorer and the rich richer', a number of studies clearly demonstrate that a wide process of growth does not favour *only* upper farmers. In advanced areas in India, a number of small landowners are using new seeds and chemical fertilizers, and buying water from their less poor neighbours who own a tube-well. Although such farmers cannot afford the same amount of inputs as upper farmers, they do increase their yields. As for landless labourers, their wages increase in real terms along with their opportunities to find more employment. It is also striking that money-lenders' rates are lower in advanced areas than in others.

All these trends are the result of a wide process of growth visible in the North-West of India or in the rich deltas of Andhra for instance. Foodgrains do not grow in isolation. Their growth provokes a whole process of development and chain reactions. It may lead to more cash crops bringing higher income per hectare and in certain cases more employment. Secondary activities (vegetables, fruit, poultry, etc.) do not remain static either. The expansion of roads boosts the production of commodities which require a quick delivery system. Power, when properly encouraged, opens the way to repair workshops and small-scale industries. Trade from the towns to the villages also increases. Such a global process of rural development has both an economic and social value.[44]

For all these reasons, one can expect some improvement in diet to reach the poorer classes of the society, even if during the first stages of growth the gap between the rich and the poor increases.[45]

SUMMING UP

In all three countries modern factors of growth are playing an increasing role. In a way they make agriculture less vulnerable to natural calamities and uncertainties of the weather, especially in China and India. At the same time, agriculture becomes more vulnerable to human errors, shortcomings in planning and poor implementation of development policies. It becomes also more exposed to external factors, e.g. world prices of inputs like fertilizers.

The pattern of agricultural development is not just a copy of Western or Soviet models. It involves new technologies absolutely unavoidable like research and seeds, water management, fertilizers and pest control. On the other hand, several old techniques need not be replaced, or at least not so soon and not thoroughly for such activities as ploughing, sowing, weeding, harvesting, threshing. For all these operations, there is room for various combinations of the 'new' and the 'old'. A tractor or a mechanical thresher may be needed under certain conditions and not in others.

The future of these countries is by no means desperate, but the magnitude and complexity of the tasks hardly need to be emphasized. Agriculture requires closer links with the other sectors, e.g. industries supporting agriculture, rural infrastructure especially better transportation and power.

Although we have dealt mostly with foodgrain, one should not forget cash crops and sidelines as well as new agricultural activities in rural areas — what we have called the global process of rural development. By widening this process, production is bound to increase and there are reasonable chances that acute poverty will retreat.

NOTES

1. (New York: E. P. Dutton, 1974). For critical comments see my article, 'Le Club de Rome et l'Asie: mort ou survie', *Esprit*, No. 2 (Paris: 1975).

2. See the very pertinent remarks of R. P. Sinha, 'Chinese agriculture: a quantitative look', *The Journal of Development Studies* (April 1975).

3. G. Etienne, *La Voie Chinoise, La Longue Marche de l'Economie 1949—1974* (Paris: Presses Universitaire de France, Coll. IEDES, 1974); also ed. by G. Etienne,

China: Men, Grain and Machines (Geneva: Graduate Institute of International Studies, Asian Centre, 1977.

4. Joint Economic Committee, Congress of the US, *People's Republic of China, An Economic Assessment* (Washington: US Govt. Printing Office, 1972), p. 317 (article by J. S. Aird).

5. See the excellent book of Jack Chen, *A Year in Upper Felicity, Life in a Chinese Village during the*

Cultural Revolution (New York: Macmillan, 1973). Periodically, radio broadcasts emphasize the difficulties encountered: Canton, Kweiyang, Nanning, Hofei, Chengchow Tsinan (US Department of Commerce, Foreign Broadcast Information Service (cited hereafter as FBIS), 1975: 21 January; 3, 10, 11 February; 5 March; 2, 3 April).

6. G. Etienne, *Studies in Indian Agriculture, the Art of the Possible* (Berkeley: University of California Press, 1968).

7. Figures released by the Ministry of Health and Family Planning, *Overseas Hindustan Times* (8 July 1976).

8. *Overseas Hindustan Times* (21 October 1976).

9. In April 1976, it was decided to raise the marriage age to 18 for girls and 21 for boys (until now, 15 and 18).

10. Estimates from the Census 1971, quoted in *Yojana* (15 July 1974).

11. *Bangladesh Population Census 1974*, Bulletin No. 2 (Dacca: Census Commission, 1975).

12. The first figures are World Bank estimates, the latter come from G. T. Curlin, L. C. Chen and B. Hossain, *Demographic Crises, the Impact of Civil War on Births and Deaths in Rural Areas* (Dacca: Ford Foundation, 1975), mimeo.

13. Quoted by L. C. Chen and R. H. Chowdhury, *Demographic Change and Trends of Food Production and Availabilities in Bangladesh (1960–1974)* (Dacca: Ford Foundation, 1975), p. 12.

14. L. C. Chen, R. H. Chowdhury, op. cit., p. 2.

15. Ministry of Agriculture, *Report 1975–76* (New Delhi: 1976), p. 71.

16. The 106 million ha often given by Chinese authorities in recent years looks low. One wonders whether land reclaimed within the commune's activities has always been reported. I would feel inclined to take a figure of 110–115 million ha.

17. Farmers are fed and sheltered by the State and they receive their labour points from their respective production teams.

18. Peking Radio, 18 February 1976 (FBIS, 19 February 1976) out of which one million in the last three years in Hopei, Honan, Shantung.

19. Field observations, see *La Voie Chinoise*.

20. For all these data, see L. T. C. Kuo, *The Technical Transformation of Agriculture in China* (New York: Praeger, 1972), p. 81–82. *Peking Information* (12 July 1974); Peking Radio (18 February 1976. FBIS, 19 February 1976).

21. US Department of Agriculture, Economic Research Service, *The Agricultural Situation in the People's Republic of China: Review of 1975 and Outlook for 1976* (Washington: August 1976), p. 31.

22. S. S. Halford, 'Mechanization in the P.R.C.', *Current Scene*, No. 5 (1976).

23. See in particular, Plant Studies Delegation to the PRC, *Trip Report* (New York: Rockefeller Foundation, 1975); also Joint Economic Committee, *1975 Report*, p. 339–340.

24. Ed. by G. Etienne, *China's Agricultural Development* (Geneva: Asian Centre, 1974).

25. Peking Radio (3 June 1976: FBIS, 7 June 1976).

26. Tsinan Radio (21 February 1976: FBIS, 1 March 1976).

27. Unless otherwise mentioned, data come from *Economic Survey*, yearly publication of the Govt. of India and *Report 1975/76* (Ministry of Food and Agriculture, 1976).

28. Tractors' use has also expanded, mostly in Punjab and Haryana.

29. This was due to lack of hydro-power, as a consequence of drought, and also to various shortcomings in the electrification programmes.

30. See B. H. Farmer, *Agricultural Colonisation in India since Independence* (London: Oxford University Press, 1974).

31. Ministry of Agriculture and Irrigation, Dept. of Irrigation, *Report 1975–76* (New Delhi: 1976), p. 25.

32. In both cases, average for the years 1968–73, *Overseas Hindustan Times* (25 September 1976).

33. The present canal irrigation systems do not deliver enough water for the dry season.

34. It is, however, striking to see changes occurring also in such areas, as I could do when resurveying after eleven years some parts of the Varanasi District. See G. Etienne 'Some Indian villages and districts resurveyed 1963/64–1975', in *Community Development and Panchayati Raj Digest* (Hyderabad: July 1976).

35. Roads network is more developed in India, but rural electrification could be more advanced in China, especially due to a large number of small local power stations.

36. Most of the delta is no more than 30m high above sea level. The Sylhet area, 250 km from the sea, is at 7m. See P. Gourou, *L'Asie* (Paris: Hachette, 1971), p. 473–476.

37. Pre-monsoon rains are very uncertain which explains the low yield of aus.

38. Total consumption 150,000 t in terms of nutrients 1975/76.

39. For further details see G. Etienne, *La Voie Chinoise,* op. cit., Chapters 12 and 13.

40. National Sample Survey, First Survey 1952; Report No. 73 and D. N. Basu, *A Long Range Perspective for India* (Baroda: Operations Research Group, January 1975).

41. V. N. Dandekar and N. Rath (Poona: Indian School of Political Economy, 1971).

42. P. G. K. Panikar, 'Economics of nutrition', *Economic and Political Weekly* (Annual number, February 1972).

43. *Economic and Political Weekly* (Bombay: 5 June 1976).

44. These different trends come out from a large number of studies, such as Hanumantha Rao, *Technological Change and Distribution of Gains in India* (Delhi: Macmillan, 1975); B. Sen, *The Green Revolution in India* (New York: John Wiley, 1974).

45. Such a conclusion should certainly not be taken as too 'optimistic'. In fact, I wonder whether I have not been too conservative. In a much more detailed study than this one, Kirit S. Parikh arrives at the conclusion that it should be possible for India to produce at least 261 million t of foodgrains in 2001. 'India in 2001' in *Economic Factors in Population Growth,* ed. by A. J. Coale (London: Macmillan, 1976).

APPENDIX

LAND TENURE

China
Collective farming consisted of about 50,000 rural people's communes divided into brigades and production teams. Around 5 million teams. Usually the team is the basic unit of production, responsible for its profits and losses. A team has 10–50 families.

Private farming. Around 5% of the cultivated area is divided into private plots for vegetables, pigs, poultry, etc., part of which is sold. Private income is equivalent to 20–35% of collective income.

India.

Agricultural holdings
(round figures)

	National Sample Survey (NSS) 1971/72		Agricult. Census 1970/71	
	No. of holdings	Operated areas	No. of holdings	Operated areas
0.002–1 ha	27.4 million	12 million ha	35.7	14.5
1–2 ha	13.09	19.06	13.4	19.3
2–4 ha	10.4	29.2	10.7	30.0
4–10 ha	6.5	39.5	7.9	48.2
10 and above	1.8	30.3	2.7	50.1
Total	59.19	130.06	70.4	162.1

Source: H. Laxminarayan and S. S. Tyagi, 'Some aspects of size distribution', *Economic and Political Weekly* (6 October 1976).
Notes: Part of the differences between the two sets of data is due to the fact that NSS does not take into account non-household land, i.e. land owned by government, public and private institutions. In 1961, around 75% of the holdings (85% of the cultivated area) was dependent on cultivating owners. 16% of landowners cultivated part of their land and leased another part. 8% of the owners leased all their land. Even if such estimates may be too low, many field observations confirm the broad trends. See P. S. Sharma, 'A study of the structural and tenurial aspects of rural economy in the light of the 1961 Census', *Indian Journal of Agricultural Economics,* No. 4 (1965).

Bangladesh.

	% of farms	% of land
Below 2.50 acres	51.6	16.3
2.50–7.50	37.7	45.7
7.50–12.50	7.2	19.1
Over 12.50	3.5	18.9

Total No. of Farms: 6,139,000   Cultivated Area: 8.8 million ha

	Owner-operated farms	Total	Owner-share-cropped Farms		Tenants
			Owner	Share-cropped	
% of total land	54	45	29	16	1
% of total no. of farms	61	38	–	–	2

Source: *1960 Pakistan Census of Agriculture:* data are rather rough estimates.

FOODGRAIN PRODUCTION, IMPORTS, EXPORTS

China.

	Foodgrain production*	Weather
1952 (base year)	154 million t	good weather
1957	185	–
1958	200	good weather
1970	240	–
1971	250	good weather
1972	240	bad weather
1973	255	
1974	265	good weather
1975	270–275	good weather
1976	≈ 267	–

* Includes cereals and tubers; rice accounted in terms of paddy; tubers (mostly sweet potatoes) taken at one-fourth of their gross weight. Grain reserves 45–60 million t.

China.

Imports of cereals (mostly wheat)		Exports of rice*	
1934–38	around 1.5 million t per year	1934–38	17,000 t per year
1951–60	no imports	1955–57	600,000 t per year
1961–66	5.9 million per year	1968	886,000 t
1967–70	4.3 million per year	1970	885,000 t
July 1971– June 1972	3.4 million per year	1972	890,000 t
1973/74	7.7 million per year	1973	2 million t
1974/75	5.5 million per year	1974	1.9 million t
1975/76	3.5 million per year	1975	1.4 million t
1976/77	2.2 million per year	1976	1.0 million t
1977 (calendar year)	6 million t (provisional)	1977	0.9 million t

*excluding exports to North Korea and Vietnam

440

India.

	Foodgrain production*	Weather
1949/50 (base year)	60 million t	good
1960/61	82	good
1964/65	89	good
1970/71	108	very good
1971/72	105	fair
1972/73	97	bad
1973/74	105	–
1974/75	101	bad
1975/76	121	very good
1976/77	110–114	preliminary estimate

* Includes cereals and pulses, rice in terms of clean rice. If we convert rice into paddy and add tubers for one-fourth of their gross weight, for 1976/76 one gets around 142 million t.

Grain imports
(million t per year (average))

1935–40	1.4
1948–50	2.9
1952–57	1.7
1958–62	3.8
1963–67	7.4
1968–72	2.9
1973–75	5.3

Sources: Government of India, *Economic Survey 1965–66 to 1975–76.*
In 1976/77 there should be no imports thanks to the bumper crops of 1975/76. Government grain reserves reached 19 million t in Spring 1977.

Bangladesh.

Foodgrain production (mostly rice)

1950–1960	7.5	million t, average per year
1960–1965	9.7	
1966–1970	10.9	
July 1969–June 1970	11.8	
1971/72	9.8	
1972/73	9.9	drought
1973/74	11.7	
1974/75	11.1	severe floods
1975/76	12.8	very good year
1976/77	12.4	preliminary estimate

One should add 300,000 t of wheat, around 200,000–300,000 t of pulses, around 700,000 t of vegetables, 900,000 to of fish, 750,000–850,000 t of potatoes.

Imports of cereals (wheat and rice)
average per year – tons

1955–1960	503,000
1961–1965	774,000
1966–1970	1,130,000
1971–1976	1,980,000
July 1975–June 1976	1,420,000

Source: Ministry of Agriculture. *Bangladesh Agriculture in Statistics,* 1973 and information collected in Dacca in 1976.

World Development, 1977, Vol. 5, Nos. 5−7, pp. 441−446. Pergamon Press. Printed in Great Britain.

Problems of Arid Agriculture in West Asia

A. A. EL-SHERBINI*

UN ECWA, Amman

Summary. − The problems of resource depletion in arid zones are discussed here in relation to agricultural production in West Asia. Discrepancies between domestic demand and supply of food in the countries treated (i.e. Iraq, Jordan, Lebanon, Syria) are said to have serious policy implications. The future prospects of food production, especially of key food commodities, are estimated, taking into consideration such factors as rainfall, fertilizer use, irrigation, use of HYV crops, weeds, etc. Price policy measures including subsidies are suggested as producer incentives to promote modernization in agriculture.

INTRODUCTION

In recent years there has been a marked increase in interest in the arid regions of the world. This concern is largely the result of the disastrous consequences suffered by both humans and animals during serious droughts and famines (e.g. Sahelian zone disaster) in various parts of the world. Another, and perhaps a more important reason, has been the growing recognition that ecological and environmental imbalances are often man-made. The problems of resource depletion or degradation are far more serious in arid zones because in such areas 'soils, plants, and landscape exist in a state of precarious equilibrium'.[1] The physical and biological environment is so fragile and unstable that any perturbations, however small (e.g. protracted drought, or destruction of the plant or soil cover by a heavy vehicle), may cause permanent damage to the soil productivity. The recovery from such damages tends to be slow.[2]

In this context the regions selected in this paper, though not covering West Asia comprehensively, have special significance. Much of the area under study coincides with Sumer, 'the land between the twin rivers, the Tigris and the Euphrates'.[3] Although most of the territory of Sumer today is part of the modern state of Iraq, it was between the Syrian Desert on the west to the mountains of Persia − the Zagros Mountains − on the east, where the Sumerian civilization came into existence in the second half of the fourth millennium B.C.[4] The Sumerian's was an urban culture 'based on a flourishing agriculture; barley was the main crop, but wheat, emmer, millet and sesame were also grown, and, of course the date palm ..... There were. fruits and vegetables, and domesticated cattle and sheep'.[5] According to the archaeologists it was 'a well organized agriculture with a complex system of irrigation canals. Irrigation and drainage involved complicated and cooperative efforts requiring control, organization, and a centralized society'.[6] It must be remembered that the plains watered by the Tigris and Euphrates continue to be rich farming land but their productivity was much higher before extensive salinization took place.[7] It has been estimated that the yield of wheat in southern Iraq in 2400 B.C. could compare favourably with that of the best modern Canadian wheat yields.[8] Irrigated agriculture 'experienced alternating periods of prosperity and adversity over thousands of years due to wars, droughts and floods. The final disruption came about when salinization of soils became a greater problem than people were able to control.... Seven hundred years ago, Mongols invaded Mesopotamia [Greek name for the land between two rivers] and completed the destruction of the society that had already become weak. Today, Iraq is still trying to recover from the effects of soil destruction that occurred a millennium ago'.[9]

---

* Mr El-Sherbini is the chief of Economic Commission of West Asia/Food and Agricultural Organisation (ECWA/FAO) Joint Agricultural Division. The views expressed in the paper do not necessarily represent the views of the organisations to which he belongs.

CURRENT FOOD SITUATION

It is a sad commentary on human follies that the very same area which gave birth to flourishing agriculture, today cannot even feed itself adequately. As is clear from Table 1, during the two decades between 1952 and 1972, food production in Iraq, Jordan and the Syrian Arab Republic has failed to keep pace both with population growth and domestic demand for food.

As in the case of other developing countries, because of the reduction in mortality rates, population – the largest component of food demand – grew at rates higher than most countries in Asia. In countries with already low levels of nutrition (see Table 2), the growing gap between domestic demand and supply may have serious policy implications.

It must be remembered that the average deficit level does not necessarily indicate the actual incidence of malnutrition. For lack of information on the distribution of food among families (or people) it is not easy to assess the incidence of under- or malnutrition in the region. However, according to the UN estimates for the Near East as a whole, nearly a fifth of the total population suffer from protein—calorie malnutrition (PCM).[10]

According to a Joint FAO/WHO Expert Committee Report, 24% of hospital cases in Jordan were suffering from Kwashiorkor and 15% from Marasmus.[11] Protein—calorie malnutrition was responsible for nearly a third of pediatric admissions in Iraq.[12] Using weight deficit as the main criterion of PCM, Rao suggests that from half to two-thirds of pre-school children weighed between 60 and 90% of standard weight, which indicates that they were suffering from mild to moderate malnutrition.[13] In the Middle East 25 to 70% children and about 20 to 25% of pregnant women have been found to be anaemic.[14]

FUTURE PROSPECTS

Although the countries being considered in this paper as a group are food-deficit countries, the magnitude of deficit differs widely between

Table 1. *Population, food supply and demand for food in selected countries of West Asia*
(Annual percentage rates of growth)

Country	Population	Food production	Domestic food demand†	Population Total in millions	Density per hectare
Iraq	3.3	2.8	5.2	11.07	1.3
Jordan	3.2	1.8	6.6	2.69	1.7
Lebanon	2.8	5.0	3.1	2.90	8.4
Syrian A.R.	3.0	1.8	4.6	7.26	1.0

Source: United Nations World Food Conference, *Assessment of World Food Situation, Present and Future* (5–16 November 1974), (E/Cont. 65/3), p. 51–54.
Notes: *Food component of crop and livestock production only.
†Source FAO, *Population, Food Supply and Agricultural Development* (Rome: 1975), Table 1–A and 1–D.

Table 2. *Per capita food availability (1969–71)*

	Kilocalories per day		Proteins
	Total	Percentage of requirement	Grammes per day
Iraq	2160	90	60
Jordan	2430	99	65
Lebanon	2280	92	63
Syrian A.R.	2650	107	75

Source: FAO, *Population, Food Supply and Agricultural Development* (Rome: 1975) Tables 1–A and 1–B.

countries. For instance, for wheat the deficit in Iraq and the Syrian Republic is less than 15%, while it is between 46 and 60% for Jordan and more than 80% for Lebanon. For rice the deficit in Iraq is between 31 and 45% while for the other three countries it is more than 80%; for sugar the deficit is over 60% for all the four countries. In vegetable oils and red meat Syria has a surplus while the deficit in vegetable oils in Iraq is more than 80%.[15] On the whole it is mainly Jordan and Lebanon which have serious deficits. Iraq and Syria, because of their factor endowment, low density per hectare, availability of irrigation and extensive pasture have a relative self-sufficiency in wheat and red meat, the two main items of food. Rice and sugar may present problems for all four countries because of inadequacies of topography and climate.

Most governments are conscious of the seriousness of the situation. Although the details of the 1976–80 development plans are not yet available, broad indications of the order of magnitude and direction of the plans suggest that by 1980 Syria will have a surplus in wheat, sugar, vegetable oil and red meat. Iraq will have a surplus of wheat, while the deficit of rice will be reduced to less than 15%. The deficit of sugar and vegetable oil may be slightly reduced but the deficit in red meat will increase. In the case of Jordan and Lebanon the food deficit will continue to be much the same as in 1975 and will have to rely heavily on imports of key food commodities in 1980, despite the efforts to increase agricultural production.[16]

PRODUCTION POTENTIAL

The fulfilment of the plan targets will, of course, depend on certain conditions being met. It is well-known that in arid regions of the world, apart from raising cropping intensity on good rain-fed lands, there are severe limitations on expansion of land under cultivation, at least in the short run. Rainfall is not only deficient but uncertain. For instance, in Jordan, very poor or poor early rainfall occurs in 30% of the cases and in only 11.3% the total rainfall is average or above.[17] Intensive use of chemical fertilizer becomes meaningful only in those areas which receive a minimum of 300 mm of rainfall. In the countries in question, it is only the zones receiving 300 to 500 mm of rainfall (semi-arid) which are the most important wheat growing areas. It is this inadequacy and uncertainty of rainfall or lack of irrigation facilities which has led to a rather slow expansion of areas under high-yielding varieties (HYV) wheat in Iraq and Syria. At present the use of improved seeds in both countries covers only a small proportion of irrigated and high rainfall areas.[18]

Experiments in Iraq have shown that grain yields can be increased several times (Table 3) by the introduction of HYVs.

It is felt that the other major constraint to the extension of area under HYVs would be the multiplication and distribution of the hybrids. Similarly, experiments on fertilizer use in Iraq, Syria and Lebanon have shown promising results. For instance in areas of good rainfall

Table 3. *Recent results of yield performance in Greater Musayib Project, Iraq*

	Yield Index	
	Low level of technology	High level of technology
Wheat		
(a) local variety	100	337
(b) Mexi pak·	—	600
Sorghum grain		
(a) local variety	100	357
(b) Bran's (hybrid)	—	1,185
Sorghum forage		
(a) local variety	100	200
(b) NK 376 (hybrid)	—	650
Coarse grain		
(a) local (loltin)	100	416
(b) ASC (hybrid)	—	1,333

Source: El-Husseni, K., *Crop Production Investigations in Greater Musayib Project Area* FAO/UNDP (1975), Draft.

(average of 500 mm or more) dressing of 150 to 180 kg N and 100 kg P2O5, results in yield gains over one metric ton of amber rice (a local variety) per hectare and is profitable, even at prevailing high prices of fertilizers. Even in low rainfall zones under a wheat—vetch—forage rotation, application of reasonably heavy doses of fertilizer can still prove profitable even if one assumes two crop failures out of ten. But even in the case of fertilizer use, much would depend on promotion and demonstration programmes as well as timely distribution of fertilizers.

An extremely serious problem facing agriculture in this region is weed infestation. Infestation of wheat and other cereals is reported to reduce yields by up to 70%, while in the case of sugarbeet and groundnuts crop losses amount to nearly 20 to 25%. It is felt that the use of herbicides, even though quite beneficial, may have adverse ecological consequences. Besides, in the absence of an extensive network of extension services and demonstration facilities it may require skills which the traditional farmers in the region do not possess. It is possible, however, to reduce the incidence of weed infestation by pre-sowing irrigation of the lands. Such irrigation helps to germinate the weed seeds in the upper soil surface, which can then be destroyed by one run of a disc-harrow. In fact some experiments have shown that this method is more effective than the use of the best available herbicide.[19] Increased intensity of cropping with forage crops (e.g. berseem) in the rotation may in itself reduce the weed-infestation. Besides, such forage crops will provide fodder for the cattle and thereby assist the development of livestock products which the region badly needs.

Other farm management practices, such as early sowing, use of seed drills, more dense planting, etc., are also helpful in increasing agricultural production.

It must, however, be emphasized that modern agricultural technology (HYV type) is often more labour-intensive than traditional technology and it is possible that Iraq and Syria, with their heavy investments in non-agricultural sectors, may develop labour shortages at least in the seasonal peaks. This has been anticipated by the two governments which are now aiming to achieve a high level of mechanization in the next few years. In doing so there is a need for taking cautious steps, not only because the topography and soil conditions of arid and semi-arid zones can be easily damaged by excessive use of heavy agricultural machinery but also because the effective use of agricultural machinery depends on the support-

ing repair and maintenance services. Therefore, efforts should be simultaneously directed towards importing or developing appropriate machinery as well as training skilled personnel for repairs and maintenance.

OTHER POLICY MEASURES

It goes without saying that modernization of agriculture requires an appropriate system of incentives, the most important being the price incentive for the producers. In all the four countries, the government is involved with price intervention. The degree of such intervention is lower in Jordan and Lebanon than in Iraq and Syria. However, the governments in all four countries now aim at giving incentive prices to producers while subsidizing the prices of basic commodities (wheat, rice, bread, vegetable oils, sugar and red meat) for the consumers.

In Iraq from 1973 a price-support programme for agricultural commodities and farm inputs has been introduced; a special fund was established for this purpose. In 1974 the Central Price Organization was established to analyze the price situation and to submit proposals for price changes which would be finally approved by the Council or Trade Regulations.

With a view to stabilizing prices (and/or incomes) the Iraqi Grain Board was created in 1973 and has a monopoly of domestic and foreign grain trading. By 1976, the Grain Board has been given the powers of centralized marketing of maize, sesame, linseed, lentils, millets, green grain, oats, cotton and cotton seed.

The subsidies on basic foodstuffs and agricultural inputs vary between 30 and 75% of the market price. Subsidies on improved seeds, fertilizers and compound feeds are around 30%; plant protection and the use of combine harvesters receive 50% and other combine machinery use nearly 75%.

In Jordan, a Joint Committee of the two Ministries of Agriculture, Supply and Economy fixes the minimum price of wheat. But only a small proportion of total domestic supply is delivered to the Governments, the bulk of trade in grains is in private hands. The Ministry of Supply determines and administers the prices of main food items including flour. Sugar prices are subsidized but rice and imported meat are sold at prices reflecting import prices.

In Lebanon the Minister of National Economy fixes annually guaranteed minimum prices for major cereals, sugarbeet, and sunflower seed. The Cereal and Sugarbeet Office, a government department, in competition with private traders, buys the above crops. It receives nearly 50% of the wheat crop; however, it has the monopoly of foreign trade in cereals and sugar, owns grain silos and is responsible for distribution of wheat flour.

In Syria, prices are fixed by the Ministerial Committee for Economic Affairs on the recommendation of a Joint Committee of Ministerial Representatives after detailed studies carried out by the Ministries of Agriculture and Supply. The Government has made frequent use of incentive prices for promoting a particular crop or for changing the crop-mix.

While state intervention in agricultural markets on social as well as economic considerations has proved necessary even in developed countries, there is always a risk of price-distortion between crops and between regions. There is also the risk of bureaucratic delays in adjusting the prices according to changing circumstances. Fine tuning of the system requires highly trained personnel in the Ministries involved with administering prices and most countries have an acute shortage of such people.

Fixing prices also requires adequate information on costs of production as well as likely trends of demand and supply. Data on almost all these are either inadequate or non-existent. Under the circumstances fixing prices of one or more commodities often becomes arbitrary and may even become counter-productive.

It must also be remembered that any price stabilization policy requires an adequate buffer stock which in its own turn requires storage and transport facilities and distribution networks for the management of buffer stock. It is only in recent years that the building of adequate storage facilities has received priority.

There is also a need for caution with regard to subsidies for agricultural inputs, particularly agricultural machinery. This may encourage the use of inappropriate machinery, and particularly in labour surplus economies may lead to displacement of labour. In any case, small farmers, particularly those in arid zones, are generally not able to take advantage of such subsidies. Either they are too poor to buy such inputs or the regions have poor factor endowments, therefore, subsidised use of inputs may often create further income inequalities between rich and poor farmers, as well as richer and poorer regions. In such cases there may be a need for an allocative mechanism that promotes both equity and efficiency so as to overcome the biases associated with traditional forms of subsidy. A discriminating pricing of inputs (e.g. water or credit) between people and regions, can be of some value. Both on grounds of equity as well as efficiency dryland farmers may require additional financial incentive, particularly in the form of crop insurance to compensate for crop losses in years of drought. If this is not done, they would hesitate to modernize their agricultural methods because they stand to lose a much greater investment under modern farming than under traditional, i.e. from a total failure of their crop due to a serious drought.

CONCLUSIONS

In summing up, it needs to be stressed that in adopting modern technology in arid zones extra care needs to be taken in adopting appropriate technology and crop systems in order to safeguard the precarious ecological balance. This requires a great deal of research effort, which many developing countries cannot afford themselves. It is important, therefore, that the UN system (particularly the newly created International Fund for Agricultural Development (IFAD)) gives greater attention to the problems of arid-zone agriculture than it has so far given. It is advisable that countries with substantial arid and semi-arid zones pool their resources for such research efforts. It is only on the basis of much more knowledge about topographical and ecological conditions and their interaction with agricultural systems and dry farming techniques, that we can prevent the repetition of the experience of Sumer and save our scarce land resources for posterity.

NOTES

1. Dregne, H. E., *Soils of Arid Regions* (Amsterdam: Elsevier, 1976), p. 4.

2. ibid., p. 4.

3. Daniel, G., *The First Civilizations: The Archaeology of Their Origins* (London: Book Club Associates, 1974), p. 37.

4. ibid., p. 37.

5. ibid., p. 70.

6. ibid., p. 70.

7. ibid., p. 70.

8. ibid., p. 37.

9. Dregne (1976), op. cit, pp. 2–3.

10. UN, *Preliminary Assessment of World Food Situation,* (Rome: 1974).

11. WHO, *FAO/WHO Expert Committee on Nutrition, Eighth Report* (Geneva: 1971), quoted in Bengoa, J. M., 'The state of world nutrition' in Recticigl, M. (ed.), *Man, Food and Nutrition* (Ohio: CRC Press, 1973), p. 8.

12. Rao, S. K., 'Malnutrition in the Eastern Mediterranean region', *WHO Chronicle,* Vol. 28, No. 172 (1974).

13. ibid.

14. Bengoa (1973), op. cit, p. 8.

15. ECWA, *Short-Term Possibilities for Increasing Food Production in Selected Countries of the ECWA Region* (1977), mimeo, p. 8.

16. ibid., p. 16.

17. Simaika, J. B., *On the Problem of Food Security, A Case Study: Wheat in Jordan* (Amman: ECWA, 1976), (preliminary draft), p. 9.

18. ECWA (1977), op. cit., p. 29.

19. ibid., p. 32.

World Development, 1977, Vol. 5, Nos. 5–7, pp. 447–457. Pergamon Press. Printed in Great Britain.

Africa: A Continent in Transition

EMIL RADO and RADHA SINHA

University of Glasgow

Summary. – The African continent is attempting to telescope into decades the process of agricultural development that spread over centuries in Asia and Europe. This paper highlights some of the potential problems of this rapid process, discussing the factor endowments of the continent, the food and nutrition situation, the population situation, import requirements and finally, the prospects and conditions for success in increasing agricultural production.

Most developing countries, in the process of 'modernization', are undergoing a profound transformation in their social, economic and political life, but nowhere is the pace of change so pronounced as on the continent of Africa. Whether it is agricultural technology, or intensity of farming or the forms of land ownership, Africa presents a curious mix of the earliest to the most modern. In Africa, 'the rural populations are at all stages of economic development, ranging from the Babinga, or Pygmies, who live in the dense forest by gathering fruits, hunting, and fishing, to the modern farmers of the North-African Coast and the high plateaux of East Africa'.[1] In many parts of Africa 'the basic farm implement remains the simple hoe, with which the soil is turned after the land has been cleared, or the digging-stick, with the pointed end of which small holes are made in the ground, into which the seed is then dropped'.[2] Yet in others modern agricultural machinery is being widely used. While shifting cultivation is characteristic of a great deal of Sub-Saharan Africa,[3] very intensive agriculture is practised in the United Arab Republic and in parts of the Sudan, Kenya, etc. Similar comments apply to irrigation as well. While almost the entire arable area in the UAR and a large part of the Sudan are under irrigation, in Sub-Saharan Africa (except Madagascar) irrigation is either negligible or virtually non-existent. Land tenure systems also vary greatly – the traditional mingles with the most modern. In many parts of Africa the man–land relationship is still determined by the time-honoured institutions of tribal society, in which 'land belongs to a vast family of which many are dead, few are living and countless members are still unborn'.[4] At the other extreme are the system of individual peasant proprietorship in Kenya, several variants of partnerships between the peasants and the State as in the case of Gezira in Sudan, nucleus plantations in Nigeria, the *paysannat* in the Congo and collectives in Dahomey and Tanzania. Thus both in the field of agricultural technology as well as in the related socio-economic relationships, the continent of Africa (perhaps with the exception of the UAR which has a long agricultural history of her own) is attempting to telescope into decades the entire process of agricultural development that spread over centuries on the continents of Asia and Europe. Such rapid change, while full of promise, has its problems and hazards. The aim of this paper is to highlight some of these in the hope that the discussion might help other agrarian societies in transition to avoid similar pitfalls.

FACTOR ENDOWMENT IN AFRICA

The size of the continent and wide variety of topographical and climatic conditions as well as differences in cultural traditions make it almost impossible to make generalized statements about the food and agricultural situation in Africa. It is well-endowed with land, in relation to its size of population, containing nearly 23% of the world's land area and about 14% of its agricultural area, with only about 10% of the world population. But it suffers from excessive droughts. Around 59% of the continent falls into the arid zone against only 33% for Asia and less than 7% for Europe (Table 1 *overleaf*). Only small parts of West Africa and the interior of the Congo have really high annual precipitation, with rainfall dropping off very quickly both northward and southward. In West Africa only

a comparatively narrow coastal zone has sufficient rainfall, while there is practically no rain
at any time in central Sahara. Much of East
Africa is quite dry.[5] In Southern Africa the
rainfall is rather low, between 150mm and
500mm per annum. Broadly two types of
rainfall distribution are found in Africa:[6] (1)
wet winters and dry summers along the
Mediterranean Coast and in Southern Africa,
and (2) dry winters and a short wet summer
covering most of the sub-Saharan region.

Table 1. *Distribution of arid-region soils by
continents
(excluding polar regions)*

| Continents | Arid-region Soils | |
	area (Km^2) (in millions)	Percentage of the continent
Africa	17.66	59.2
Asia	14.41	33.0
Australia	6.25	82.1
Europe	0.64	6.6
North America	4.36	18.0
South America	2.84	16.2
Total	46.15	

Source: Dregne, H. E., *Soils of Arid Regions* (1976),
p. 39.

In the case of winter rainfall, evaporation rates
are low and water penetrates to greater depths
in the soil. As a result the soils are leached
more, and are less calcareous than the soil in
the other regions. Since the winter rains are
gentler than summer thunderstorms, the regions
do not suffer from serious rain erosion. In the
case of summer rain, hot tropical sun evaporates the rainwater faster thereby reducing the
soil moisture available for plant growth. Therefore a 'mean rainfall of 400mm in North Africa,
spread out over several winter months, is
adequate to produce a good wheat crop,
whereas 400mm falling in July in Mali may be
only marginally adequate for a moderate sorghum crop'.[7] High variability of rainfall is one of
the main reasons for high instability in agricultural production. For instance, in the savanna
areas, especially towards the steppe margins,
there may be excessive rainfall one year and an
almost negligible amount the next. Both conditions are unsuitable for cultivation, particularly
of cereals. In the wetter and warmer parts of
the continent, root crops such as yams, cassava
and sweet potatoes are the main staples, while
in some areas of the Congo and of Uganda, the
climate is too humid for growing cereals; as a

result the banana is the staple food.[8] Apart
from Mediterranean Africa, it is mainly in the
Savanna and Steppe regions and on the
highveld of South Africa that grains predominate.[9]

African soils, largely tropical, are heavily
leached of nutrients and often are not able to
sustain annual cropping. In some parts of
Africa, particularly the West African savanna-
steppe, East Africa and the plateau of South
Africa, pastoral activities supplement farming,
although some African peoples, such as the
Masai in East Africa and herders in Somalia
depend entirely on cattle. As a result of scanty
and uncertain rainfall these cattle herders move
from one region to another in search of
pastures. Apart from the lack of reasonable
pastures, improvement in the quality of cattle is
inhibited by the infestation of tsetse fly.

In spite of low densities of population and
the relative abundance of land, earlier forms of
farming[10] (i.e. forest and bush fallows) and the
slow growth of alternative employment opportunities have resulted in very low farm incomes
and significant underutilization of labour in
most African countries. Topographical and
ecological as well as economic constraints have
resulted in slow growth of agricultural output
and in low levels of nutrition in this part of the
world. These remarks apply particularly to food
crops for domestic consumption. In parts of
Africa whose climate and topology are favourable, African peasant farmers have shown
themselves capable of developing and sustaining
major agricultural cash crop exports, e.g. cocoa
in Ghana, Nigeria and the Ivory Coast, palm oil
all over West Africa, coffee in East Africa and
the Ivory Coast, tea and pyrethrum in Kenya,
cotton in Uganda, etc. There have also been
successful collaborations of peasant farmers
with the state or with private capital, e.g. the
Gezira (cotton) scheme in the Sudan[11] and
'outgrowers' schemes for tobacco, sugar and tea
in East Africa.

FOOD SITUATION

The indices for population growth, agricultural and food production by countries are
given in Appendix Table 1. It appears that out
of 45 countries for which statistics are available
— in many cases only at a rudimentary level —
in 27 food production has failed to keep pace
with population growth. In at least 12 countries
per capita food production has declined by 15%
or more. In 33 countries the *per capita* energy
(calorie) intake is below the minimum nutri-

tional requirement as recommended by the FAO and WHO. In at least 12 of these countries the energy deficit is greater than 10%. However, except in the case of Zaire, average protein intake seems to be adequate (see Appendix Table 2). One cannot read too much into the adequacy of protein in an average diet. In cases where a diet suffers from inadequate energy, the protein in the diet is partly diverted from its primary function to the provision of energy. This is the case in large parts of West Africa as well as in parts of Eastern and Southern Africa, where 'quashiorkov' or protein—calorie malnutrition (PCM) is one of the most common and deadly conditions affecting the recently weaned child (nutritional marasmus being another form of PCM).[12]

Community surveys conducted between 1963 and 1973 in 16 African communities, covering 34,000 children mostly 5 years of age, indicate that between 7% and 73% of children surveyed were suffering from PCM. Between 1–10% of those children were said to be suffering from severe forms of PCM.[13] Nutritionists estimate that as many as 2.5 million children may be suffering from some form of PCM.[14]

Other types of nutritional deficiencies point in a similar direction. For instance, among children up to the age of 15, the incidence of nutritional anemia is between 30 and 60% while it is much higher for children below the age of 7.[15] Nutrition surveys in Egypt, Nigeria and South Africa indicate some prevalence of rickets. However, in a recent WHO survey in North Africa, 45 to 60% of the children examined showed signs of rickets. The proportion of children suffering from severe rickets ranged between 3 and 18%.[16] As a result of malnutrition, infection and vulnerability to diseases infantile mortality rates are very high in Africa (Table 2).

These figures probably underestimate the actual infant mortality rates, because the deaths of one-day-old infants are often not reported. Similarly, the deaths in the scattered rural population are also underestimated.

THE POPULATION SITUATION

Because of the spread of modern medicine etc., the overall (crude) death rate is declining all over Africa. In the absence of compulsory registration of births and deaths all figures cited are rough estimates, but the orders of magnitude are likely to be reliable. This applies equally to the population statistics quoted

Table 2. *Infantile mortality rate in selected countries*

(Deaths of infants of less than 1 year per 1000 born alive)

Country	Rate
Zambia	259
Gabon	229
Guinea	216
Niger	200
Central African Rep.	190
Mauritania	187
Upper Volta	182
Tanzania	160–165
Uganda	160
Chad	160
Liberia	159
Burundi	150
Morocco	149
Ivory Coast	138
Cameroon	137
Rwanda	132
Togo	123
Southern Rhodesia	122
Mali	120
Dahomey	110
India	139
Brazil	85–95
Sweden*	12
U.S.A.*	19

Sources: UN, Dept. of ESA, Statistical Office (1974), 'Population and vital statistics report', Data available as of 1 January 1974. Quoted in Toro, J., 'Food and nutrition policy' in *Priorities in Child Nutrition*, Vol. II, (Harvard University School of Public Health, 1974), p. 12.
*Mayer, J., 'The dimension of human hunger', in *Scientific American* (Sept. 1976), p. 41.

below from the UN sources. In some countries such as Ethiopia and Upper Volta the overall death rate is estimated to be as high as 25 per thousand. In Egypt, Libya, Algeria, Morocco and Southern Rhodesia, it is thought to have come down to 13 per thousand; in Mauritius it is estimated to be only 6.5. The average death rate for the continent as a whole works out at 16 per thousand. The birth rate in most African countries, with the exception of Mauritius, Reunion, Equatorial Guinea, Gabon and Egypt, continues to be over 40; in Togo and Niger it exceeds 50 per thousand. The average for the continent is around 46. As a result the current population growth rate for Africa as a whole is around 2.8% per annum. According to the UN medium-variant population growth estimates, there is a likelihood of this growth rate steadily accelerating to about 2.9% per annum in late 1980s, when the growth rate may begin to slow down. By the late 1990s it may come down once more to 2.8%. The high variant places the population growth at around 3% in the 1980s rising to 3.1% in 1990s.[17] Thus if current trends in the growth in food production continue during the next decade or two, domestic food production will barely keep pace with (or even lag behind) population growth. With normal patterns of economic development and a continuing rapid rate of urbanization, many African countries will have to depend increasingly on imports of food.

IMPORT REQUIREMENTS

Already Africa imports a significant quantity of cereals and other foodstuffs. In 1974 the net import of cereals into Africa was around 7 million tons, which amounts to roughly 12% of the total consumption of grains for the whole continent. On a *per capita* basis Africa imports much more on average than India, also more than China. In fact, except for South Africa, which is a major exporter of cereals, and Kenya and Malawi which are more or less self-sufficient, most other African countries are net importers. The United Arab Republic is by far the largest importer of cereals, followed by Algeria and Morocco. Other countries which import significant quantities are Senegal, Tanzania, Libya, Zaire, Nigeria and Tunisia.

Assuming that the growth in *per capita* incomes in Africa between 1970 and 2000 maintains an annual rate of 3%,[18] and that population grows by 2.9% per annum (UN medium variant), the demand for cereals in African developing countries in the year 2000 AD is estimated by Aziz in this collection[19] at 156 million tons. The average annual output of cereals in Africa for the three years 1973−75 was nearly 66 million tons. Thus, to match the likely growth of demand, the production of cereals would have to increase by 136% (or by 3.5% per annum) during the last quarter of this century as against 2.5% during the last 25 years.

Similarly, in many African countries the demand for meat and dairy products, fruits and vegetables, and sugar will increase substantially. Unless the domestic production of such items increases correspondingly, there will be a substantial increase in the import bill for most African countries, which are already net importers of all these products. Thus the African countries are not only facing the problem of accelerating the rate of growth of cereal production, but also that of diversifying their agriculture. It should be emphasized that increasing production alone will not solve the problem of hunger and malnutrition. Measures for ensuring a more meaningful employment to provide adequate purchasing power and a more equitable distribution of income and wealth have to be adopted. In addition, strengthening of nutrition education and improved maternity and child care would also be imperative.

PROSPECTS FOR INCREASING PRODUCTION

In the long run the physical potential for increasing agricultural output in Africa is immense. According to our estimates, so far only about 22% of the potentially cultivable land[20] has been brought under cultivation. While to readers familiar with Africa this estimate may appear unduly low, even if one multiplied it by factor of 2 there would still be a significant amount of potentially cultivable land not in economic use. Even the arable land has a low cropping intensity.[21] For Sub-Saharan Africa the cropping intensity is as low as 42%; in North Africa it is somewhat higher at 56%. This broadly indicates that arable lands in Africa produce an average of one crop in two years.[22]

Low intensity of agriculture is mainly caused by the lack of an assured water supply either by rain or through irrigation. In 1967 the total' area under irrigation in Sub-Saharan Africa is only about 1 m ha or less than 1% of the total arable land.[23] It is possible to increase agricultural output substantially both by bringing new land under cultivation and by increasing the intensity of cropping through the extension of irrigation facilities.

However, it must be remembered that all regions of Africa do not possess the same potential. For instance North-west Africa is very close to reaching its full arable land potential. This may also be true of the Sudan.[24] In Sub-Saharan Africa, although there is much unutilized potential in the forest (even after making allowance for the needs of timber production, wildlife protection and preservation of forest for climatic reasons), the prohibitive cost of clearing forests, the presence of tsetse, the lack of manpower and the absence of infrastructure inhibit the rapid expansion of modern agriculture.[25] It is easier to expand the area under cultivation in the Savanna Zone and to combine agriculture with animal husbandry; but once again the eradication of tsetse flies from the northern edge of the forest belt would be a necessary precondition.

The scope for the extension of irrigation is rather limited in North-west Africa, where irrigation is already well-developed. But there is considerable scope for expanding irrigation in Sub-Saharan Africa. However, in addition to irrigation, the provision of drainage and flood control together with land levelling and other farm-level improvements would also be necessary to make optimal use of the available water. All these would require substantial investments. According to the FAO's Indicative World Plan for Agricultural Development (IWP), the average cost of bringing 1 ha of arable land under irrigation in Sub-Saharan Africa would come to roughly $1000. After allowing for the recent inflationary rise in prices, the cost must be much higher now. Besides, this did not include the cost of land clearing because it was assumed that much of this would be done by the subsistence farmers.[26]

In the areas which have a reasonable water supply, chemical fertilizers are the quickest means of increasing agricultural output. Total consumption of fertilizers[27] per hectare of arable land including land under permanent crops in Africa in 1974 was under 10 Kg. against a world average of 54 Kg. Among the African countries, Mauritius has the highest rate of fertilizer use at 254 Kg. per hectare per annum, followed by Reunion at 205 Kg.; UAR at 151 Kg.; Rhodesia, South Africa and Swaziland have consumption levels between 50 and 62 Kg. per annum; the other countries have either a much smaller or negligible consumption of chemical fertilizers. As a result of the rapid increase in the price of fertilizers in the last 3–4 years, there has been a decline in consumption levels in several African countries (e.g. Algeria, Angola, Congo, Lesotho, Liberia, Madagascar, Malawi and Mozambique). There must now be some doubt whether African countries – and LDCs in general for that matter – will in the foreseeable future be able to attain rates of fertilizer usage that now exist in developed countries.

Although the need for better quality seeds is clearly recognized in Africa, and in fact, North Africa has well-equipped seed centres, in most of Sub-Saharan Africa, except Kenya, seed development programmes are still embryonic.[28]

Besides increasing crop yields by irrigation and modern methods of farming, the supply of food can also be substantially increased by improved crop protection methods. It is estimated that almost 42% of the potential value of crops is lost in Africa because of plant diseases and pests prior to the harvest; losses from

diseases are estimated at nearly 13% each, while the loss from weeds is estimated roughly at 16%. The total value of lost output in recent years has been estimated at $8000 million per annum (at 1965 prices).[29] Severe losses also occur in storage. It is estimated that in West Africa 25% of the food produced is lost after harvest at various stages between the producers and the consumers.[30]

Despite the need for the effective prevention of pre- and post-harvest losses from diseases and pests etc. the rate of use of pesticides in Africa per hectare of arable land in value terms in the early 1960s was as low as 11 US cents (at 1962–64 prices) against 30 cents for the average for all developing countries.[31]

Thus it seems plausible to argue that modernization of African agriculture may go a long way torwards meeting the increasing demand for food and other agricultural products. Since modernization of agriculture, in any developing region – and Africa is no exception – requires fundamental changes in the outlook, values and motivation of farmers, certain social and economic preconditions have to be met if one is to place any hopes on such modernization taking place.

CONDITIONS FOR SUCCESS

Reforms of land ownership

One of the most important of these preconditions is the creation of an appropriate system of land ownership and management. It is commonly argued that the traditional tenure systems (tribal ownership), though they guarantee a high measure of social security to an individual, often function as a bulwark against any changes in the customary standards of life and work and therefore are a hindrance to modernization of agriculture.[32] In the traditional system farming is often under the direction of the head of the extended family or the village headman, thus concentrating the main economic power in the hands of the older people.[33] Such persons are often deeply suspicious of the social upheavals that normally accompany rapid economic change – sometimes with good reason. Colonial administrations, with their European backgrounds, have tried in many countries to introduce individual ownership of land but it has now been recognized that:

> individual ownership being such a new concept to the majority of Africans, it was desirable in the early stages to give Divisional Boards a very wide

discretion which will enable them to forbid, for instance, if they so wish, the alienation of land outside the tribe, clan or family group, and also to exercise some restraint over the newly emancipated landowner who wishes to sell his land to the detriment of his family. It has been proven in many countries that the surest way to deprive a peasant of his land is to give him a secure title and make it freely negotiable, and we do not think that anybody will seriously challenge the need for control in the early stages.[34]

In fact, the fears expressed in the above passage have come true in many parts of Africa. Dumont in his book *False Start in Africa* gives several examples, particularly of French Africa (e.g. Ivory Coast and the Cameroon) where the individual ownership of land was encouraged and the tribal chiefs made enormous profits by handing over unutilized communally-owned forest lands to Europeans. The breakdown of the traditional tenure system and the attempted individualization of land ownership have meant that land is now being concentrated in the hands of those with money.

According to Dumont, businessmen and civil servants in the capitals Tananarive, Abidjan, Dakar, Bamako and Freetown are buying up suburban land for weekend cottages.[35] The African governments are conscious of this problem and they realize that neither purely traditional forms of land tenure nor totally uncontrolled forms of private land ownership are the sensible answers to their peasant needs. Many of them have therefore experimented with forms of land ownership which combine in varying proportions private decision-making by the cultivator with a residual state control over crops, cultivation methods, quality control, etc. For instance in Kenya in the post-independence period increasing numbers of European estates were parcelled out to African settlers particularly in Kikuyu areas. To guarantee an economic living the size of farms on the high-density schemes in fertile areas has been kept at 10 acres while in low-density schemes on poorer soils or steep slopes the size of farms is 30 acres.[36] These schemes are reasonably well-supported by a credit and extension network, and have shown substantial increases in output.[37] But there is some official supervision and control regarding the selection of settlers, quality of inputs and crops, etc. Similarly, peasant proprietorships have been tried out in Uganda where the settlement was supported by considerable government investment in land clearing, subsidized inputs and other technical services. While the farming is done individually, cooperative marketing of products was encour-

aged.[38] Given the low man–land ratio in Sub-Saharan Africa, there is no reason why peasant proprietorship cannot be viable, assuming of course that supporting services, credit, marketing, storage, transport, research and extension are adequately provided. In land-poor countries of North Africa, where employment opportunities in non-agricultural sectors are rather limited, surplus rural population will have to be retained on the land. Dividing land equitably among the entire rural population may create farm sizes too small to be economical. In such cases some form of cooperative or collective organization may provide the answer. There are several cases of such experiments in Africa. One of the best known examples is the *Ujamaa* village. Similarly, the Cameroon and the Ivory Coast have organized cooperatives for the cultivation and marketing of certain plantation crops. Dahomey has introduced compulsory cooperatives with self-management by farmers and landless labour with some official representatives on the board. In such cooperative and collective ventures, in addition to the absence of local leadership, lack of capital and managerial skills have continued to be the major bottlenecks.

While peasant proprietorships do provide much more individual incentive than communal forms of production, voluntary or otherwise, they have to be supported by complementary services, many of which can be provided largely by credit and marketing cooperatives. Lack of capital, managerial ability and leadership plague these cooperatives as much as a farming cooperative or a collective.

In any case, as stated earlier, many African countries are experimenting with several types of rural agricultural organization; in fact several forms could be fruitfully tried in the same country. In a decade or two it would be possible to judge their relative performance — in fact some forms such as the Gezira plantation have proved their worth already —and then it would be easier for other African countries (or for that matter for other developing countries) to adopt such options. In the meantime, the hasty adoption of one system of land ownership and cultivation may prove prejudicial to the interest of agriculture as well as the rural population.

Price stabilization

Apart from the reforms of land ownership and the provision of supplementary services, the stabilization of agricultural prices is one of the necessary preconditions for ensuring sufficient incentives for agricultural modernization. We have already argued that instability of agricultural output resulting from the vicissitudes of climate is rather high in Africa. Such uncertainties are not conducive to modernization of agriculture, since the investment in modern farming is both much greater and riskier than under traditional methods – a crop failure hits a modern farmer harder than traditional cultivators.

Besides, many of the African countries depend only on one or two major crops for most of their export earnings; hence wide fluctuations in their prices may play havoc with development expenditures in such countries as their amplitude is impossible to predict. Therefore stabilization of prices (or of export earnings) has received special attention in many African countries, where statutory marketing boards have been given a monopoly of exports of primary products. However, there is little evidence to show that in most African countries such boards have stabilized (or even attempted to stabilize) either prices or incomes. They have generally operated as instruments of agricultural taxation. While they have, no doubt, increased the proportion of the 'surplus' that accrues to the state and is therefore available for capital formation, it is far from clear that their net impact has been to promote or accelerate development, either in their own industry or in the economy in general.

Fixing the producer price of a product by the marketing boards does not guarantee that small producers will not continue to be exploited by local buyers, sub-agents and quality inspectors from the marketing boards, especially if the marketing board also runs a monopolistic buying organization.[39] Some of these malpractices might be reduced by permitting cooperative societies to operate (and to compete) as agents for the marketing boards, to handle the local purchases and collection of crops. Until such time as a cadre of trained, efficient and honest personnel develops, it may be worthwhile creating parallel channels of marketing. If private traders are operating in competition with cooperatives, then this competition alone will probably ensure that small producers actually receive the fixed price. If the administrative and political machinery is inefficient and corrupt 'a marketing board scheme may still prove completely ineffective when, for instance, the required reliable higher calibre staff or financial reserves are lacking, or when the board is hampered in the elaboration and implementation of its price and marketing

policy by political and/or sectional pressures'.[40]

Need for caution

Finally, if resource depletion and ecological imbalances have to be avoided, the pace of technical modernization itself has to be governed by availability of knowledge about the interaction between agricultural technology, topography, environment and ecology. Much of agricultural technology so far has been developed largely for temperate climates, and it cannot be easily transplanted into Africa, particularly into arid zones without adequate adaptive research. Apart from the infamous 'Groundnuts Scheme' in the Tanganyika Savanna there are many disastrous examples of hasty modernization of African agriculture.[41] Even with regard to irrigation, which is an essential factor in African agricultural development, there is a need for taking some precautions. In the absence of drainage facilities, which in some areas results from inadequate levelling (e.g. cultivation of cotton by *Office du Niger*) and in others from difficulties in the run-off of excess water, problems of water-logging and salinity can arise (e.g. in Nile Delta and lower Chêlif in Algeria).[42] Inadequacy of anti-erosion measures in the catchment areas of large dams can result in the silting up of reservoirs (e.g. some Algerian dams). In the case of the Ksob dam in Algeria it took only 10 years for the reservoir to be silted up.[43] The use of heavy agricultural machinery on unstable soils can accelerate soil erosion. The example of the French peanut project in Casamance in Senegal is a good example of misuse of heavy tractors. Dumont stresses that the 'Use of tractors has been uneconomical everywhere: in Boulel-Kaffrine, the centre of mechanized peanut cultivation in Senegal where they still scrape off the topsoil when they fell trees; at Loudima in the Congo; on the rice plantations in the Niger Valley (Guinea, Mali, Niger) and Logone Valley (Chad and the Cameroon) and at the CRAM in Madagascar'.[44] All these mistakes point to the need for research and experiments in modern methods of farming under African conditions before they are widely adopted.

CONCLUSION

In conclusion, it needs to be stressed that Africa has immense potentialities for agricultural development even though the topography and climate in many parts are not the most suited for agriculture. African farmers have already shown their ability to respond vigorously to price incentives in developing a wide variety of export crops some of which (e.g. coffee and tea) were long thought to be beyond their technical capacity. If the production of foodgrains and animal products is lagging, we believe the responsibility must lie to a large extent with the incentive structure that confronts the African farmer and therefore, with the agricultural price policies of the African governments. The implementation of appropriately adapted technology, along with improved infrastructure and increased expertise on the part of the farmers and technical advisers, will hopefully be able to surmount the remaining difficulties posed by natural factor endowments or the lack of them.

NOTES

1. Dumont, R., *African Agricultural Development: Reflections on the Major Lines of Advance and the Barriers to Progress* (UN Economic Commission for Africa, 1966), p. 35.

2. De Blij, Harm J., *Geography: Regions and Concepts* (New York: John Wiley & Sons, 1971), p. 327.

3. FAO, *Provisional Indicative World Plan for Agricultural Development* (Henceforth IWP), (1970), p. 44.

4. Jacoby, Eric H. and Jacoby, Charlotte F., *Man and Land: The Fundamental Issue in Development* (Andre Deutsch, 1971), p. 89 and 319.

5. De Blij, op. cit., p. 326.

6. Dregne, H. E., *Soils of Arid Regions* (Amsterdam: Elsevier Scientific Publishing Company, 1976), p. 54.

7. ibid., p. 54.

8. De Blij, op. cit., p. 327.

9. ibid., p. 327.

10. Researchers suggest that the man-days required under the system of forest-fallow does not exceed 230 man-days per hectare for all operations with complete clearing of real forest. (See: Forde, C. Daryll and Scott, R., *The Native Economies of Nigeria* (1946) p. 92.) Forde and Scott suggest that for summary clearing in preparation of yam production in Ibadan is as low as 50–60 man-days (p. 91). Labour time required under the system of bush fallow is much the same. (See: de Schlippe, P., *Shifting Cultivation in Africa* (1956), p. 121.

11. For a more critical and pessimistic view of the Gezira scheme, see Barnett, Tony, *The Gezira Scheme – An Illusion of Development* (London: Frank Cass, 1977).

12. Bengoa, J. M., 'The state of world nutrition' in Rechcigl (JR), M. (ed.), *Man, Food and Nutrition* (Ohio: CRC Press, 1976), p. 3.

13. ibid., p. 6.

14. ibid., p. 7.

15. ibid., p. 8. Among the adults 6 to 17% of men and 15 to 50% of women (except the Bantu women in South Africa) suffer from iron deficiency (p. 8).

16. WHO, Joint FAO/WHO Expert Committee on Nutrition, Seventh Report, WHO Tech. Rep. Series No. 377 (1967) quoted in Bengoa, op. cit., p. 10.

17. UN Population Division, Department of Economic and Social Affairs, *Selected World Demographic Indicators by Countries, 1950–2000* (mimeo), ESA/P/WP 55 (28 May 1975).

18. This is consistent with the 'trend' assumption of UN World Population Conference, *Assessment of the World Food Situation: Present and Future (1974)*, p. 105.

19. See Aziz, Sartaj, 'The world food situation and collective self-reliance', in this volume.

20. The White House, *The World Food Problem: A Report of the President's Science Advisory Committee* (1967), Tables 7–9, p. 434. See also Buringh, P., 'Food production potential of the world', in this volume.

21. Cropping intensity is calculated by dividing the harvested area by arable area and expressing it as a percentage.

22. IWP, op. cit., pp. 43–44.

23. ibid., p. 46.

24. ibid., p. 48.

25. ibid., p. 49.

26. ibid., p. 62.

27. FAO, *Annual Fertilizer Review, 1975* (1976), Table 11.

28. IWP, op. cit., p. 185.

29. ibid., p. 207.

30. MIT, *Policies for Promoting Agricultural Development* (Centre for International Studies 1965), p. 64, quoted in IWP, pp. 208–209.

31. IWP, p. 210.

32. Jacoby, op. cit., pp. 319–320.

33: Dumont, *African Agricultural Development.*

34. *Report of the Working Party on African Land Tenure, 1957–58* (Nairobi), p. 45, quoted in Jacoby, op. cit., pp. 322–323.

35. Dumont, R., *False Start in Africa* (1966), pp. 127–128.

36. Jacoby, op. cit., pp. 327–328.

37. Whetham, E., 'Land reform and resettlement in Kenya', *East African Journal of Rural Development,* Vol. 1, No. 1 (1968).

38. Jacoby, op. cit., p. 328. See also Belshaw, D. G. R., *An Outline of Research in Uganda, 1945–63* (Kampala: 1963).

39. Abott, J. C. and Creupelandt, H. C., *Agricultural Marketing Boards, Their Establishment and Operation* (1966), pp. 190–191.

40. ibid., p. 188.

41. One of the examples is given by René Dumont of the experiments by Belgian agricultural scientists at Yangambi which ended in failure and the experiment had to be given up. (See Dumont, R., *Types of Rural Economy: Studies in World Agriculture* (1957), pp. 36–37.) See also the experience of high cost irrigation and mechanized rice cultivation at Molodo by Niger Office. (See Dumont, R., *False Start in Africa*, p. 53.)

42. Dumont, *African Agricultural Development*, op. cit., p. 27.

43. ibid., p. 27.

44. Dumont, *False Start In Africa*, p. 58.

Appendix Table 1. *Indices of population, agricultural and food production in selected African countries in 1975* (1961–65 = 100)

	Population	Food production	Agricultural production	Food production *per capita*
Algeria	148	94	96	63
Angola	128	92	93	72
Benin	136	145	148	107
Botswana	129	185	183	143
Burundi	122	237	238	195
Cameroon	124	154	153	124
Central African Republic	128	115	117	89
Chad	127	79	88	62
Congo	131	101	102	77
Egypt	134	139	131	103
Ethiopia	131	103	105	79
Gabon	114	135	135	119
Gambia	124	124	124	100
Ghana	134	123	123	92
Guinea	131	119	119	91
Ivory Coast	133	161	165	121
Kenya	148	140	137	95
Lesotho	124	121	114	97
Liberia	129	122	140	95
Libyan Republic	150	215	210	144
Madagascar	139	128	129	92
Malawi	132	151	155	114
Mali	131	83	87	64
Mauritania	127	83	83	65
Morocco	140	130	130	93
Mozambique	131	118	115	90
Namibia	154	167	163	108
Niger	141	103	103	73
Nigeria	136	113	113	83
Reunion	135	111	111	82
Rhodesia	154	141	132	91
Rwanda	140	153	153	109
Senegal	133	128	131	96
Sierra Leone	131	132	132	101
Somalia	133	136	135	102
South Africa	142	156	149	110
Sudan	143	181	178	127
Swaziland	136	192	194	141
Tanzania	141	137	128	97
Togo	141	118	119	84
Tunisia	129	189	188	147
Uganda	139	126	123	91
Upper Volta	129	109	111	84
Zaire	139	123	123	88
Zambia	144	139	137	97
Total of Africa	137	131	130	96

Source: FAO (1976), *Production Year Book, 1975,* Tables 5, and 7 to 10.

Appendix Table 2. *Average per capita and protein supplies for selected African countries 1969–71*

Countries	Energy (kilocalories)	Protein (grams)	Energy as a percentage of requirement	Protein/energy ratio
Algeria	1710	44.7	71	10.4
Angola	1910	39.9	81	8.3
Botswana	2040	65.1	87	12.7
Burundi	2330	61.0	100	10.4
Cameroon	2230	58.9	96	10.5
Central African Republic	2170	47.5	96	8.7
Chad	2060	72.8	86	14.1
Congo	2160	39.8	97	7.3
Egypt	2360	66.1	94	11.2
Ethiopia	2150	68.6	92	12.7
Gabon	2210	55.7	94	10.0
Gambia	2370	62.6	100	10.5
Ghana	2200	46.3	96	8.4
Guinea	2040	43.9	88	8.6
Ivory Coast	2490	60.3	108	9.6
Kenya	2350	70.9	101	12.0
Liberia	2040	36.1	88	7.0
Libya	2540	61.3	108	9.6
Madagascar	2350	52.9	104	9.0
Malawi	2150	54.4	93	10.1
Mali	2170	68.9	92	12.7
Mauritania	2060	75.0	89	14.5
Morocco	2400	63.6	99	10.6
Mozambique	2190	41.0	94	7.4
Niger	2180	72.2	93	13.2
Nigeria	2290	59.9	97	10.4
Rhodesia	2550	73.2	107	11.4
Rwanda	2160	61.5	93	11.3
Senegal	2300	64.0	97	11.1
Sierra Leone	2240	49.0	97	8.7
Somalia	1770	56.9	77	12.8
Sudan	2130	63.2	91	11.8
Tanzania	1700	42.5	73	10.0
Togo	2160	51.4	94	9.5
Tunisia	2060	53.6	86	10.4
Uganda	2230	55.3	96	9.9
Upper Volta	1940	65.9	82	13.5
Zaire	2040	32.7	92	6.4
Zambia	2040	63.6	88	12.4

Source: FAO (1975), *Population, Food Supply and Agricultural Development*, Table 1 – C.

World Development, 1977, Vol. 5, Nos. 5–7, pp. 459–476. Pergamon Press. Printed in Great Britain.

Agricultural Production Prospects in Latin America

SOLON BARRACLOUGH

Adjunct Professor of Agricultural Economics,
Cornell University

Summary. – This article argues that there are excellent possibilities for Latin America to increase substantially both its agricultural production and *per capita* food consumption, and therefore to reduce general levels of poverty. This requires more rational use of the region's relatively abundant resources and of modern technologies. However, there are strong social and political constraints operating both at the national and international levels against the implementation of necessary structural reforms. The author acknowledges the influences on agricultural growth and human nutrition of population expansion, national income growth, foreign markets, education, values, public policies, investment, technologies, etc. but stresses that the parameters of Latin American agricultural growth are in fact defined by the social context, i.e. a rigidly elitist and highly stratified society extremely dependent upon the US and other industrialized nations. The author also emphasizes the diversities within the region – among countries, but mainly among social classes.

INTRODUCTION

Latin America's most visible food and agricultural problems are well-known to all of us. They are, with important regional peculiarities, the same as those found in other under-developed regions. Moreover, they illustrate dramatically many of the contradictions associated with dependent capitalist economic growth found throughout the so-called 'Third World'.

Food production in the region has been increasing at about the same rate as population (about 3%) for the past several years and the FAO expects this trend to continue for at least the next decade.[1] In many Latin American countries *per capita* food production has apparently even been declining.[2] Large numbers of Latin Americans remain poor and malnourished, while a great many others eat far less than they would like to. While estimates vary wildly, there seems to be a wide consensus that between at least one-sixth to nearly one-half of the region's residents are seriously underfed by internationally adopted standards.[3] Food imports to the region have been growing much faster than have agricultural exports from it – some 60% faster since the early 1960s – both in volume and value. Urbanization has been proceeding rapidly,

leaving only about 40% of the region's workers in agriculture. None the less, the worst poverty and lowest living levels are still concentrated in rural areas. Unemployment and under-employment, both rural and urban, are wide-spread and have been increasing rapidly.[4] Idle and under-utilized potentially good farm land in the region is plentiful. To a lesser extent, so is idle and under-utilized plant capacity and other physical capital in agriculture. Agricultural and livestock technology in the region is for the most part backwards. Agricultural investment lags. Agrarian unrest is endemic and frequently violent. While the traditional *latifundia–minifundia* complexes are slowly disappearing, they are being replaced by dual agricultural systems (no less pernicious in their socio-economic effects) of large commercial farms and dependent smallholdings associated with rapidly growing numbers of landless rural labourers.[5]

This familiar vulgar liturgy of the under-development and poverty of nations has been repeated about Latin America in hundreds of official reports, books, articles, speeches and 'development plans'. Unfortunately, it contributes little to our understanding of the region's food and agrarian problems. It is even less helpful in identifying the policy issues involved in seeking solutions.

The argument of this article is that there are excellent possibilities for Latin America to increase substantially both its agricultural production and *per capita* food consumption, while at the same time greatly reducing poverty during the remaining decades of this century. More rational use of the region's relatively abundant resources and of already well-known technologies would enable it to increase food production greatly. Presently inadequate nutritional levels could be significantly improved and agricultural exports augmented even if current high rates of population growth were to continue. The obstacles are primarily social and political, not technical.

Assuming no major devastating disasters such as catastrophic climatic changes or nuclear holocaust, realization of these rosy possibilities depends, above all, upon world economic and political developments and upon profound institutional reforms taking place within Latin America itself. Of course, the two are so closely related as to be practically different sides of the same coin. Unfortunately for those who want to improve food production and human nutrition rapidly in the region, neither the state of the world nor domestic social structure is an 'independent variable' which can easily be manipulated by men of good will or by governments.

Now, in the late 1970s, it should not be necessary to take seriously the myth promulgated by 'establishment' interests in the rich countries that the poor nations' poverty and malnutrition is a direct result of their rapid population growth and the persistence of traditional agricultural technologies.[6] This implies that if population increase were to be checked and the modern 'green revolution' technologies widely adopted, the problem would go away. Several scholarly and popular analyses have been published during the last decade amply refuting this simplistic and self-serving ideology both on the basis of well-documented recent evidence and logic.[7] None the less, the population-explosion—backward-technology syndrome as an explanation of sluggish agriculture and hunger in the 'Third World' continues to be widely accepted. It is commonly used to rationalize many irrelevant and sometimes anti-development policies (from the viewpoint of the poor) of national governments, international agencies and private institutions.

In any event, the evidence in Latin America hardly supports this conventional wisdom about agricultural development or any other sanguine easy generalizations for that matter. On the contrary, there appears to be absolutely no simple relationship between rates of population growth and the availability of modern agricultural technology, on the one hand, and rates of growth of food production *per capita* and the improvement of nutrition, on the other.

The subject is much too complex to analyse in detail here. Cynthia Hewitt de Alcántara has attempted to do so for the case of Mexico and her conclusions support my own hypothesis that the primary obstacles for the region's agricultural development are social and political.[8] Other Latin American examples are also highly edifying in this respect.

In Chile, the rate of population increase has been slowing down for several years associated with rapid urbanization and higher incomes. Successive governments since the 1950s have actively promoted modern agricultural technology. Educational levels are relatively high. Agricultural technical assistance and research have been good by Latin American standards. Credit and price policies have been designed to encourage farm production and agricultural investment. During most of the period, investment by progressive transnational agro-industrial companies has been vigorously encouraged, especially since 1973. None the less, food production on average scarcely kept up with population growth. Within the past four years, agricultural production has plunged to the lowest *per capita* levels in recent decades. Nutrition of the lower income half of the population had improved markedly from 1964 to 1973 but is now by all reports disastrously worse than it has been since the great depression of the late 1930s.

The Puerto Rican experience is even more thought provoking. Population has been nearly stable for two decades because of out-migration to the United States. Educational levels and health services are among the best in Latin America. There have been excellent agricultural extension and research programmes since the late 1940s. Modern agricultural technologies have been available for many years at about the same costs as in the United States. Numerous modern US based agro-industries have invested in the island, drawn by low wages and liberal tax benefits. The island's industrial production has been increasing rapidly. Personal incomes have been rising from new job opportunities, remittances from the mainland and US-financed welfare payments. A large influx of tourists has provided for a further potential expansion of the domestic market. A significant land reform was carried out during the 1950s. None the less, agricultural production has been declining since the late 1930s and falling at an accelerated rate since 1960. Within only the five years from 1964–69 the value of all farm products sold fell by 18% and the area harvested by 38%.[9] In 1976, over half the population was benefiting directly from the US food stamps programme because their incomes were below US poverty standards.

Of course, Chile is a special case and Puerto Rico a very special one (every country is a special case, for that matter). The failure of their agricultures to respond vigorously to the availability of modern technologies and to the growing food needs of their populations can be explained in economic and political terms. But these examples should caution us against facile generalizations.

This is not to minimize the influence on agricultural growth and human nutrition conventionally assigned to population expansion, national income growth, foreign markets, education, values, public policies, investment, technologies and the like. These factors, however, must be analysed within their broader social context. Rigidly elitist and highly stratified Latin American societies that are extremely dependent upon the United States and other rich industrialized nations define the parameters of Latin American agricultural growth. Within these limits marginal improvements in government policies, markets and prices, seem to have little effect upon the region's pervasive historical patterns of poverty. On the contrary, without profound structural change, effective demand for food will probably continue to increase only slightly faster than population, production costs will remain relatively high, producer's incentives will be too low to spark major new investment or efforts, income concentration will probably continue to increase and under-utilized resources and unfilled bellies will become even more abundant.

These generalities about the region, however, cover up the immense diversities within it. Each nation, sub-region and community has its own peculiar history, institutional complex and resource endowment. A global examination of Latin America's agriculture can at best point to some apparently common problems. It can never lead directly to recipes for their solution.

For example, Argentina and Uruguay still can boast of having among the highest average consumption of food *per capita* in the world. In addition, they are large exporters of agricultural products. On the other hand, Haiti and Bolivia have food supplies *per capita* comparable to those of such famine-prone areas in

Southeast Asia and Central Africa as Bangladesh or Mauritania.[10] Agricultural exports constitute over three-fourths of all exports in many Latin American countries such as Ecuador until the mid-1960s, Honduras, Argentina, Brazil and the Dominican Republic but are relatively insignificant for others such as Chile, Bolivia and Venezuela.[11] All the Latin American countries import significant quantities of their food but some like Argentina, Ecuador, Mexico and Brazil are also large net food exporters or practically self-sufficient. Others, such as several in the Caribbean and Central America, Chile and Venezuela, are importing from one-third to more than half of their foodgrain requirements.[12] The availabilities of agricultural land per person, degrees of urbanization and industrialization, *per capita* national income and educational levels in the region, show similarly wide diversities among countries. Moreover, while overall agricultural growth has been relatively slow in relation to population, there have been spectacular increases in the production of certain crops from time to time in given countries, such as soybeans and wheat in Brazil during the last decade. These inter-country differences dramatize the pitfalls of generalizing about the region as a whole.

The differences among countries, however, are overshadowed by those among social classes. The well-to-do have plenty to eat and can purchase better food more cheaply than most of their counterparts elsewhere in the world. The poor, both rural and urban, must confront problems of chronic malnutrition, periodic physical hunger and occasionally near-starvation. While the relative and absolute numbers of poor and the degrees of their poverty also vary greatly from place to place, the problem is almost universal throughout the region. The mere production at national levels of sufficient foodstuffs for everyone to enjoy a decent diet does not solve this dilemma in the least, nor does the absence of sufficient national production necessarily exacerbate it.

For example, Mexico, Brazil and Cuba all can boast of average *per capita* availabilities of food energy and proteins about 10% above the minimum required for health and hardwork according to FAO estimates.[13] Brazil's populous Northeast is still subject to periodic drought-triggered famines most severely affecting the rural population.[14] Nationally, there are probably some 30 million Brazilians with insufficient incomes to consume regularly minimum internationally accepted food energy requirements.[15] Mexico's National Scientific and Technological Council estimated in 1976 that the poorest 30% of the population consumed only about 6% of the value of that nation's food supplies, while the richest 15% consumed nearly half. Of the approximately two million Mexican babies born annually, 100,000 die during their first years of causes associated with malnutrition, while over one million enter later life with nutritionally-caused physical or mental defects.[16] In Cuba, on the other hand, there has been an extremely equalitarian distribution of real income and especially of basic necessities since the early 1960s. As a result, hunger and malnutrition have practically been eliminated in Cuba even though the average *per capita* level of food availability has been about the same as in Brazil and Mexico.

Food production, nutrition and income distribution statistics are notoriously poor for underdeveloped countries and Latin America is no exception. Even so, they are probably indicative of gross trends and major differences. To the extent one can trust these data, except in Cuba, Puerto Rico and temporarily in Chile during the Frei and Allende administrations, there does not appear to have been any significant improvement in nutritional levels of the lower income one-third to one-half of the population during the last two decades in any Latin American country. Average *per capita* food production, however, apparently has increased most rapidly in recent years in Venezuela, Costa Rica, Bolivia and up until the mid-1960s, in Mexico. All these countries have high rates of population growth and Bolivia, at least, has had very limited access to modern technology. Barbados, on the other hand, with relatively easy access to technology and a stable population has apparently suffered an 18% drop in *per capita* food production since the early 1960s.[17]

Climatic factors are usually most explanatory of short-term variations in food production. One must obviously look beyond climate, population growth, technology and even capricious government policies, however, to understand the longer-term trends in food consumption, distribution and production.

To interpret these data and to support the affirmations and hypotheses presented above, I should provide a geat deal more hard evidence. Unfortunately, there is no space for this in a short article. Much of the information that would be required is not available anyhow. What I propose to do in the following few paragraphs is merely to suggest some of the lines of research that could help us to understand better the region's agricultural problems.

Where possible, I present some of the fragmentary data available. First, we will look at agricultural production structures and resources. Then, we will turn our attention to the structure of demand and Latin American 'food systems'. Finally, I will speculate about agricultural prospects for the region during the remainder of the 20th century.

I used to work as a professional forester. One of the numerous advantages of that calling was that I would be long gone and forgotten before the gross errors of my long-term management projections became evident. With this experience and secure in the knowledge that none of my readers will remember or care about what I said in 1977 when the year 2000 arrives, I will not shirk a little futurology. Moreover, I take added courage after having read several recent exercises in crystal-ball gazing by some of my 'social science' colleagues. They provide me with ample margins within which to intrude my own. The Club of Rome has already projected both global breakdown through asphyxiation in our own pollution and exhaustion of just about everything from food to energy, and in a second report, salvation through enlightened paternalistic planning and aid by the industrialized nations.[18] Herman Kahn's Hudson Institute is confident of an ever expanding world economy benevolently managed by liberal technocrats.[19] The American Academy of Sciences published the results of a high-level academic conference sponsored by the Carnegie Foundation and it sees a bigger and better Western industrial civilization wrestling ever more successfully with the same old problems of the 1960s.[20] The Dag Hammarskjold Foundation proposes measures to create an almost 'automobile-less' Scandinavian-type social utopia.[21] In any event, I can hardly be more mistaken than were top-level social scientists advising the Pentagon in the early 1960s on how to 'pacify' Vietnam or than was Professor Daniel Bell when he wrote his obituary to ideology two decades ago.

AGRICULTURAL RESOURCES AND PRODUCTION STRUCTURE

Latin America is about as well-endowed with basic resources of labour, land, water and sunlight in proportions suitable for productive agriculture and animal husbandry as are the world's other inhabited continental areas. To be sure, the spatial distribution of these resources within Latin America is less than ideal from an economic viewpoint. Moreover, the region's physical geography presents some major barriers to efficient internal transportation. But one can hardly maintain that the absence of sufficient agricultural resources is either a primary cause of low agricultural growth or of the relatively inadequate food consumption by many Latin Americans.

The region's population was estimated in 1976 to be already well over 300 millions. It is projected to increase to about 500 millions by the end of the century. Nearly half this population still lives in rural areas and some 40% of the total active work force is dependent upon agriculture for employment, estimated as 38 million workers in 1976. Depending on whose estimate one takes and the criteria employed, from one-fifth to one-half of this agricultural work force can be considered unemployed or seriously under-employed. There is no reason to believe that this human resource is on the average any better or worse endowed biologically than is any other major population group in the world, although the effects of generations of deprivation may have handicapped many members of today's labour force.

The region's resources of agricultural land, rainfall and irrigation potential are also comparatively adequate. Again according to whose estimate one takes, there are now nearly 120 million hectares under cultivation in South America, Central America, Mexico and the Caribbean. This means there are about 0.4 hectares *per capita*.[22] This is a more favourable cropland–man ratio than in Europe, one-third greater than that of Asia, excluding the USSR, and slightly above the world average.

Estimates of the potentially cropped area differ wildly depending on the economic and technical criteria used and the analyst's optimism. After all, with enough investment in labour, capital and technology, almost any piece of land that is not vertical rock or subject to year-round below-freezing temperatures is potentially arable. Revelle estimates that in South America alone the slightly more than 80 million hectares of cultivated area in 1970 could be expanded to 715 million – an increase of nearly 900%.[23] Much of this potential is in the humid tropics where soil management is difficult and costly investments in clearing and drainage would be required; or they are in semi-arid areas requiring large investment in irrigation. While Revelle's technological and economic assumptions are unclear, we know from numerous detailed studies in all parts of Latin America that the potentials for expansion of cultivated area are very great and could be

economic in many places even with approximately present price relationships. Detailed studies with which the author is associated of pilot areas in Mexico's humid tropics indicate that at least two or three million hectares in the Gulf Region, now in extensive pasture and forest, could be made suitable for relatively intensive cropping and livestock-raising with what appear to be costable investments in infrastructure such as roads, drainage and supplementary irrigation. In Chile's Central Valley, over 40% of the already irrigated land was used extensively in natural pasture in the 1960s. Many thousands of hectares of cropland could be obtained in Northeastern Brazil merely by completing irrigation systems that have already been built. Much of the vast Amazon Basin is believed to be technically suitable for development for crops and pastures, although the longer-run ecological effects of removing the rain forest are at best questionable.

One does not have to imagine five- to ten-fold increases in cropland, however, to envisage Latin America's immediate agricultural potential. More intensive use of presently cropped areas with chemical fertilizers, better seeds and other improved management practices, plus a very modest increase in cultivated areas could easily double production with minimal new investment. Energy requirements have been cited as a limiting factor for developing a high fertilizer-use agriculture globally.[24] Energy is certainly going to be more costly but it may be less of a bottleneck in Latin America than in Asia. In much of the region, untapped water power abounds and new petroleum fields have been recently found in several areas of the humid tropics. Experiences could be cited from nearly every Latin American country showing how, in limited areas, agricultural production has recently more than doubled. Even in the inhospitable terrain and climates of the densely settled Andean and Mexican Altiplanos there are large potentials for increased production. After all, the Incas and Aztecs and their predecessors demonstrated, centuries ago, that these lands could produce much more on a sustained basis than they do now.

What then is the problem? Why are many countries importing nearly half their food consumption and why do they import from the United States and Canada instead of other Latin American countries with good agricultural resources? 'Comparative advantage' can explain some of this but by no means all. In fact, the classical doctrine of comparative advantage is much more useful for rationalizing the *status quo* than in explaining trading patterns between parties whose bargaining powers are very unequal.[25]

If we focus narrowly on the production, processing and marketing system, the simple answer must be that costs are frequently too high and incentives too low to stimulate new investment. For the same reasons, many Latin American food products cannot compete with imports even in domestic markets. This conclusion, while essentially true, often serves to cover-up the structural problems behind the paradox. To pose the problem merely in terms of higher prices for farm products diverts attention from the reasons why costs are high and prices at the producers' level are too low. Also, it suggests a solution of higher relative food prices. This in itself would leave Latin American agriculture even less competitive internationally and would price many domestic consumers out of the market altogether. On the other hand, to pose the problem as being one of inadequate production technologies ignores the fact that available efficient technologies are often not used. Moreover, new technologies based largely upon high capital investment and manufactured inputs will necessarily be completely beyond the reach of most Latin American farmers until the region becomes much more highly industrialized. To the extent that these technologies are labour-saving with respect to output and that there is not an adequate compensating increase in total production, their adoption within present social structures would cause rural unemployment and poverty to increase disastrously.

Throughout Latin America the most outstanding characteristic of agrarian structure is its dualism.[26] There is a modernizing commercial sector of mostly large farmers that includes the best lands, has relatively easy access to national and international markets, to credit, new technology, services, manufactured inputs and consumption goods. This sector accounts for the bulk of marketed production. On the other hand, there is a traditional mostly smallholder sector in which the bulk of the rural population resides, but which controls relatively little and usually poorer land. This sector is largely without credit, modern technology or services and produces primarily for family consumption and local markets. While there is a floating population of landless labourers and there are many landless labourers permanently attached to the commercial sector, most of the 'so-called landless', who make up close to half of the region's agricultural work force, reside in the traditional sector and draw a part of their livelihood from it.

This situation is greatly complicated by the fact that many large *haciendas,* especially in the Andean Highlands of Ecuador, Colombia and Central America, are still very traditional and can more accurately be described as quasi-feudal communities of small producers and serfs with labour obligations to the estate owners, than as commercial farm units; also, there are numerous smallholders, such as many coffee growers in Colombia, who are fully integrated into commercial agricultural systems. Successive 20th-century land reforms in Mexico, Puerto Rico, Venezuela, Bolivia, Chile, Peru, Honduras and, to a lesser extent, in other countries, have greatly accelerated the disintegration of traditional estates into larger commercial farms and poor traditional smallholding communities.[27]

The commercial modernizing sector has been steadily expanding at the expense of traditional agriculture. I would guess that it now accounts for about 50% of the region's gross agricultural production, 30% of the cultivated area and 20% of the labour force. Yields per hectare of cultivated land are higher in this sector (but not of potentially arable land as land-use is much more intensive in most traditional smallholding communities). Productivity *per capita* fully employed averages about five times higher in the modern sector than in traditional agriculture. Unemployment and under-employment are concentrated in the traditional sector which would make this productivity gap per worker appear even greater. Actually, many of these workers have part-time jobs in other activities or in commercial agriculture which partly compensates for the superficially extremely high rate of rural unemployment.[28]

If one projects present trends, the situation would become much more dramatic by the early 1980s. The modernizing sector would account for well over half of gross agricultural product but would be employing only the same number of workers as at present (about 17% of an expanded total labour force) because of its higher productivity associated with modern technologies. The traditional sector, however, would include over 70% of the labour force. Under-employment would have increased markedly and the gap between average productivities per worker in the two sectors would have greatly increased.[29]

Production decisions in the modernizing sectors are dictated essentially by financial profitability considerations similar to those in capitalist commercial agriculture anywhere. But the enterpreneurs and resource owners in this sector are likely to be large operators, often national or multinational corporations. These managers and owners have many alternative opportunities for employment and investment, both nationally and internationally. They require relatively secure and high rates-of-return before expanding their production. Moreover, as they often wield considerable political influence and monopoly power in national markets for specific commodities, they are prone to restrict production with government collusion in situations where this appears profitable for the individual capitalist. If he is a 'multinational', he might be more interested in the effects of his production on prices in the United States, Japan or Europe than in maximizing his returns only in Latin America. Often he is able to buy modern technology at highly subsidized prices. This, plus his wish to avoid labour problems, impells him to go in for highly mechanized operations. Also, as land ownership still carries with it considerable prestige and power in Latin American societies, even some commercial farm owners may invest disproportionately in land at the expense of improvements and operating capital, although this tendency has been waning in recent years. All in all, the structure of incentives in the modernizing sector is such as to reduce its potential competitive advantages derived from the ready availability of cheap labour.

The decisions of small producers in the traditional sectors are better understood within the context of the peasant economy analysed by Chayonov than within that of modern business accounting.[30] Family subsistence and risk avoidance are necessarily first priority considerations for survival. Also, the small peasant farmer is practically powerless nationally. He can offer little security and implies high costs for lenders. His small surplus is usually appropriated by landlords, middlemen, government officials and other more powerful groups. As a result, he has little access to modern inputs, and if he can obtain them, he must pay a relatively high cost. He is seldom in a position to benefit directly from higher food prices and expanding markets. His principal resource is his own and his family's labour. As population and commercial agriculture expand, more and more of his surplus is skimmed off. He must continuously work harder only to survive. Much of the steady increase in food production in Latin America comes from this traditional sector and can be explained by these dynamics. Low income, high costs of purchased inputs and capital, limited land, low prices and low incentives for commercial production, all militate against the traditional peasant producer

taking advantage of expanding urban markets.[31] The problem is made more difficult by the rapidly increasing social stratification in peasant communities as commercial farming expands.[32] This, together with the well-known difficulties associated with geographic dispersion, makes cohesive group action by the peasant almost impossible.[33]

Landless labourers are for the most part still partially integrated into this traditional peasant economy. They both sell their labour to other sectors (which is a crucial factor in explaining the remarkable survival power of peasant communities in the region) and are themselves peasant producers part of the time. Capitalist agriculture continues to penetrate traditional areas but the landless proletariat employed in commercial agriculture is not growing very fast, if at all. The numbers of this semi-proletarian and under-employed group of very poor rural residents in traditional agriculture, however, are increasing extremely rapidly.

Another way of looking at the agrarian structure nationally is by commodity system.[34] The marketing, processing and production of agricultural products entering national and international trade is becoming increasingly integrated vertically. The control of sugar, wheat, meat, feed grains, cotton, bananas, dairy products, fruits, etc., that are sold in the large cities or abroad is generally concentrated in the hands of relatively few financial groups.[35] These oligarchies work hand in hand with the multinationals and other foreign investors and with national and local government officials. They usually have great influence over government bureaucracies, either directly by furthering bureaucrats' and politicians' self-interests or indirectly through their own considerable political power. The net result is to reinforce the structural dualism in agriculture and to accentuate the structures of high costs and low incentives described above.

In summary, traditional agriculture has been continuously squeezed. The peasants have few resources while landlords, merchants and others extract whatever surplus they are able to generate. Costs are high and incentives low. The same is true for modern commercial farming, but for reasons having more to do with high opportunity costs and monopoly power than lack of resources or the absence of normal capitalist incentives.

DEMAND STRUCTURE AND 'FOOD SYSTEMS'

Elementary economics tells us that effective

demand and product prices are at least as important as are resources, technology and costs in determining capitalists' production decisions. Curiously, little more than perfunctory attention is paid to demand questions in most analyses of agricultural development in the 'Third World'. Neo-classical economists and agricultural entrepreneurs usually content themselves with calling for more favourable relative prices to stimulate production and for the promotion of export markets. They then settle on projecting past consumption trends as a function of population growth and gross national product. It seems stupid, or at least perverse and contradictory, to argue that inadequate effective demand is a major factor in distorting and limiting Latin American agricultural growth. After all, the world is supposedly entering a period of increasing food shortages. Hunger and malnutrition are major regional problems. Many Latin American countries are already importing an important part of their food consumption.

Paradoxically, 'over-production' causing disastrous declines in agricultural prices is even more common in Latin America than in most countries where food production is not considered to be a serious problem. In Chile, in 1974 many fruits and vegetables, and in 1975 potatoes, rotted in the fields because the price would not cover out-of-pocket harvesting and transport costs at a time when diets of the urban poor were sinking to all-time lows. In 1975 the Mexican government had to aid producers market 'surplus' beans (frijoles) abroad in order to maintain official prices, although many Mexicans could not buy the beans they needed. Mexican strawberry growers in 1975 found their US markets inadequate to absorb their installed production capacity and had to cut back drastically. Frequently, fresh fruit rots in Mexican States distant from urban centres such as Chiapas, when prices fall in local markets, even when there are national shortages. Latin American sugar exporters in 1976 faced a drop in world market prices to only about one-fifth of the 1974 highs leaving some producers, such as Gulf and Western in the Dominican Republic, threatening to withhold their production from the market. On the other hand, coffee prices reached an all time high in early 1977, while Mexican tomato growers will probably get a similar windfall following destruction by frost of the 1977 Florida winter crops. The tremendous expansion in Brazil in soybean production after 1960 was in direct response to unfilled effective demand primarily from Europe, especially West Germany, and now in 1977 this threatens to taper off.[36]

Demand prospects obviously affect producers' decisions. Often they are determinant. The surge and decline of the Ecuadorian cocoa industry after World War I, of Ecuadorian bananas after World War II, of Brazilian rubber during the 1940s and the 'over-investment' in sugar in many countries in the early 1970s are but a few more of countless examples that might be cited.

The structure of effective demand for food in the region is in many ways a mirror image of the dualistic agricultural production structure described above. Structural dualism is not limited to agriculture but permeates the whole society.[37] The poor have little opportunity to increase their economic productivity and even less to improve their incomes. Low-income groups would use most of any additional income they could get for food and other basic necessities, but they seldom have a chance to do so. The wealthy, on the other hand, already consume about all the food and other basic necessities they want. Additional income accruing to them is spent on other things, most often goods and services with a high import component, and if they are good capitalists, on investments promising to provide a high return.

The Mexican and Brazilian data cited earlier on food consumption by income strata are not atypical. In Chile, a 1968 survey showed the families in the lower-income majority of the population spending on the average less than one-third as much for foodstuffs as those in the upper-income decile. Food energy consumption per capita of the poor was only 60% of that of the upper-income group and protein consumption was less than half. Per capita consumption of such high value products as red meat, dairy products, chicken, fruits and the like were only about one-fourth as much in the majority lower-income group.[38] Without doubt, these data would be much more dramatic for 1976.

Detailed food consumption studies in Lima, Peru, show similar income and expenditure patterns. In fact, families in the lowest income group in the sample (approximately one-fifth of the total) spent 78% of their incomes on food with an average per capita daily consumption of about 1,700 calories — mostly cereals, tubers and sugar — while those in the highest income group (about 16% of the total number of cases) spent only 13% of their incomes on food and consumed nearly 3,400 calories per capita, over half of which were in the form of high-value fruits, vegetables, meat, fish, dairy products, eggs, fats, oils and drinks.[39]

The situation in the Dominican Repbulic appears to be equally dramatic. The lowest income majority of the population spent about half their income on food (also mostly sugar, tubers and cereals) while higher income groups ate much better and spent only 15% of their incomes on food and drink. The lowest income half of the population was consuming less than 1,500 calories and 29 grams of food energy and protein *per capita* per day in 1976. The upper income 6% of the population consumed over 3,100 calories and 85 grams of protein daily, or more than twice as much *per capita*.[40]

In view of these data it is a small wonder that domestic demand for food in Latin America corresponds closely with population growth plus a slight additional component attributable to increased incomes. Biological needs and psychic wants have nothing to contribute to effective demand. But this does not explain why so many countries in the region are importing more and more of their domestic food consumption. The answer is also closely related to the region's production and demand structures.

There are two fundamental and closely connected reasons why imports are increasing in many Latin American countries at the expense of domestic production. The first is the high-cost and low-incentive structures in agriculture analysed above. This is greatly accentuated by the rapid growth of capitalist commercial farming at the expense of resources (especially good land) available for the traditional sector. Capitalist entrepreneurs' greatest profits are to be made producing for export and for the narrow domestic market provided by higher income groups. The second reason is to be found in the interaction of Latin American and international political, financial and economic institutions. This frequently results in an 'effective' demand for food imports superior in quality and quantity to that for domestic production of similar products even when their costs and prices in real terms for the Latin American nations could be more than competitive.

Evidence supporting the first of these assertions is straightforward and abundant. Export agriculture on the average is highly profitable, especially for foreign investors who also control processing, marketing and transport. So are domestic markets among high-income groups who are able and willing to pay relatively high prices for food produced, processed, packaged and marketed using modern imported technologies. As would be expected, commercial farmers expand their business to take advantage of these profit opportunities.

Today's patterns of agricultural growth and consumption in the region began to take shape nearly five centuries ago following the European conquest. Commercial plantations were established on the best and most accessible agricultural lands to produce the exports necessary to help finance the colonial enterprise. The proceeds from these exports were used to pay for imports, to amortize loans and repatriate interests and profits, to pay fees and taxes to home country governments and to accumulate personal fortunes. These plantations were worked by forced labour — imported slaves and vanquished natives.

At the same time tribute in the form of food, gold and other valuables was extracted from the Indian communities. In addition to the plantations, large landed estates were formed to produce other agricultural products such as hides for export and to supply the conquerors' food needs in their towns, mines and plantations. Marketable surpluses were extracted from the Indian peasants residing in these *encomiendas* and later *latifundia* through imposition of various neo-feudal institutions whereby commercially valuable products were delivered as 'rent' or tribute to the *latifundistas* by the native communities. Food was also produced on lands (usually the best) directly farmed by these estate owners using non-paid labour that the natives were obligated to provide.

Thus, very early in modern Latin American history, distinct 'food systems' began to evolve for different social groups.[41] From the beginning imports of some luxury foods had a role in the diets of the ruling conquerors in the larger towns and the owners and managers of the *latifundia* when they were residing on their estates and plantations. Imports of basic food necessities also were frequently important for the urban colonists and their servants and workers, both in the towns and in their mines and plantations, when there were sufficient funds to pay for them and when local cheap food supplies were inadequate. This was facilitated by low-cost transport as the ships carrying bulky primary products extracted from Latin America to Europe and North America often returned with excess capacity. New England cod-fish and New York State beans were crucial staples in the Caribbean workers' diet for centuries as a result. Finally, the residual native population maintained its traditional food system almost wholly dependent on locally produced products.

These same food systems with important modifications persist today throughout most of Latin America. There are still significant differences in the 'food systems' of the well-to-do, of the urban poor, the workers in commercial farms and mines and the provincial towns and, finally, those of the peasant communities. In the peasant economy, food production, distribution and consumption have been and continue to be more an integral part of their way of life than a commercial activity of commodity exchange governed by the 'laws' of capitalist markets. To be sure, the peasant is a highly rational farm manager but the parameters within which he makes his decisions are not those of the commercial farmer. Only in Argentina and Uruguay have 'food systems' based on traditional peasant economies been insignificant, while they are becoming so in Cuba. In Argentina and Uruguay there were no large groups of vanquished natives or imported slaves. In Cuba peasant food systems are now being rapidly integrated into a national system of socialist agriculture and food distribution.

The best located and physically suited agricultural lands everywhere in the region are usually incorporated into capitalist agriculture as soon as it becomes profitable to do so. One needs only to visit Jamaica, the Dominican Republic or nearly any other country in the region to see the smallholdings dotted on steep mountainsides and the extensive sugar plantations and cattle ranches in the coastal plains and fertile valleys. In the Caribbean, for example, for decades the production of most subsistence crops has been increasing much more slowly than the population while the production of sugar, meat and other high-value export products has been relatively responsive to international markets and prices and to the internal demands of the well-to-do.

In Mexico, the sustained rapid growth in agricultural production after 1940 until about 1965 was in part made possible by the introduction of new high-yielding varieties of wheat, sorghum and other commercial crops. The new varieties were complemented by huge government and private investments in irrigation, transportation, processing, fertilizer production, farm credits and technical assistance to commercial farmers. But it was also made possible by the rapid expansion of domestic markets accompanying the surge in industrialization and urbanization beginning with World War II and following the massive land redistributions in the late 1930s. Significantly, the most impressive production gains were shown for wheat, sorghum and other crops primarily consumed directly by high-income groups or crops that are consumed by livestock and poultry which in turn are sold mostly to high-income consumers. Maize production increased much less rapidly, although it remains the most important single item in the diet of some two-thirds of the Mexican people. Maize and beans are grown primarily in the traditional sector and even in these areas during the last two decades sorghum replaced maize as a cash crop on many of the better lands. During recent years the Mexican government has frequently had to import maize, and to a lesser extent beans, to meet the needs of the poor. The slowing down of Mexican agricultural growth after the mid-1960s can be explained by the exhaustion of the most attractive new production opportunities derived from the new technologies and by the unavailability of new lands for traditional agriculture. It can also be explained by the contraction in the growth of effective demand for the most profitable commercially produced products.

Parallel developments have been taking place throughout the region. There has been rapid expansion in the production of Brazilian wheat, meat, sugar, coffee and soya, of Argentine wheat (almost entirely a function of export markets), of Venezuelan livestock, fruits and vegetables, of Colombian sugar and sorghum, of Guatemalan cotton and coffe, and of Honduran meat and bananas. But nearly everywhere the production of basic food staples that are consumed primarily by low-income groups has been disappointing. The better lands available for the peasants producing them have shrunk except where important agrarian reforms temporarily increased peasant lands as in Bolivia and Mexico.

How Latin American and international institutions interact to create effective demands for food imports that frequently are not accompanied by the same kind and quality of demand for domestic production is more complex. It is a result of deeply embedded dependency relationships reflected in economic, financial and political structures.

We have seen how during the colonial period receipts from produced and plundered exports were used to finance imports of many goods and services consumed by the conquerors but not available locally. Some of this income was also used to import necessary inputs to keep these exports flowing (especially arms, slaves, manufactured capital goods and supplementary food for the workers) and to repatriate personal fortunes and other profits from the colonial enterprise to the home country. Incomes from abroad (whether it comes from exports, investments, credits or grants) represent claims on the economy in which this income originates. In one way or another these claims are eventually collected (or defaulted) at their source. The Latin American colonies were highly dependent on their home countries and the social-economic structures that evolved reflected this dependency. Formal political independence in the 19th and 20th centuries did not change the situation. Instead it reflected new lines of dependency to other European countries and to the increasingly powerful United States.

The sophisticated balance-of-payments accounts maintained by Latin American governments spurred and supervised by international financial institutions bear contemporary witness to this elementary rule of business accounting that income claims originating abroad must be settled there sooner or later. A crucial question from the standpoint of our analysis is why part of these claims are so frequently used to import food instead of importing capital goods and services required to increase domestic agricultural production. Again the superficial answer is simple — it is more expedient and profitable to those who make the decisions. In order to understand why, one must discover who benefits, how the decisions are made and how the mechanisms of implementing them work in practice.

There is no question that historically those social classes with the most economic and political power have been the primary beneficiaries of Latin American governments' decisions. This, of course, is true anywhere, but in Latin America where the peasantry and workers have had little or no effective organization or real political influence, except for brief periods in a few countries, this has reinforced the dualistic social structures prevailing since the European conquest in the face of increasing industrialization, urbanization and exposure to more progressive values about society. The principal beneficiaries have been foreign investors and the Latin American property owning class, together with their allies and dependents such as the civil and military bureaucracies and various professional and other 'middle class' groups in addition to limited numbers of skilled and organized workers. The poorer classes of peasants, unorganized workers and unemployed are relatively, and in many cases absolutely, as badly off now as they were several decades or even centuries ago. There is no reason to expect that decisions affecting agricultural imports and production would not follow this same pattern. They do.

The typical government, or private importer for that matter, first becomes aware of a probable shortfall in domestic supplies of wheat or some other basic food product after a drought or other misfortune causes a partial crop failure. Pressures on prices become evident and speculation begins. The government then must either import supplies rapidly or face the social consequences of sharply increased costs of living. This brings the probability of strikes and higher wages. Food is a vital input for industry and services. Costs of manufactured goods would rise. Both workers and employers pressure the government to keep food prices down. The political opposition stands ready to capitalize on popular discontent. The government naturally chooses to import.

If the amount is not too large and the foreign exchange situation permits this will often be done through normal private trade and financial channels with the government subsidizing any gap between costs and sale prices of the imported food. If the situation is more critical, however, the government itself may have to negotiate credits facilitated by private exporters, foreign banks, the governments of exporting countries or international institutions. Governments of countries with exportable surpluses are usually anxious to dispose of their excess agricultural production even on concessionary terms (practically the equivalent of 'dumping') as was the case with the United States and several other nations during most of the 1950s and 1960s. If the food supplying country can in return obtain claims to some of the importing countries resources or exports on favourable terms or increase its political and economic leverage through control of local currency, so much the better.

The importing country has no immediate choice but to accept. In any case, it would not want to do otherwise even if it could, as the profits from handling food imports go not only to the exporting country but also to many of the importing governments' friends and allies and in some cases to government officials. The actual operation is usually handled by a large efficient transnational agricultural trading company (there are only a handful) that can guarantee prompt delivery of a standard quality product at reasonable cost. Some commercial farmers in the importing country may protest against the dampening effects of potential price hikes of domestic agricultural products but even they realize it would be several years before higher prices could result in a permanently expanded production base. Meanwhile, the hungry must be fed at reasonable prices or the whole system would not only appear inhuman but its very stability would be threatened. Important pressure groups on all sides have been pleased. The food imports have a humanitarian purpose. Without question, low-income groups benefit in comparison to what would have been their immediate situation without the imports.

Production may improve the next year if the weather does. But soon the importing country has to recognize that its food deficit will continue for a long time. Plans are made to stimulate production through research, technical assistance, investments in irrigation, subsidies on inputs, etc. A few new lands are opened up at high public costs. International development institutions provide loans and 'experts' for agriculture and the government initiates various 'rural development' programmes. But past trends continue in spite of all this. The best lands are still used for the most profitable lines of production destined for foreign markets and high-income domestic groups. Production of the basic foods of low-income consumers continues to lag. Imports continue to climb.

At this point one asks why capitalist entrepreneurs in the importing countries do not divert their production to fill this demand and make new investments for this purpose; or why they do not contract production with peasant producers. Of course, some do in a limited way. However, the problem is not so simple. Unless relative product prices and costs are changed drastically it remains more profitable for capitalists to expand production of the already more profitable crops. The peasants do not usually have the incentives or resources of land and capital to expand. But if the government attempts to change relative prices in favour of the basic food staples it must embark on a costly programme of subsidies and storage for which it has neither the resources nor the organization. Increased taxes usually are politically out of the question. The opportunities for corruption in price subsidy programmes are multiple, the bureaucracy is inefficient and public funds needed are not available.

In any case the larger, more influential capitalist producers would be the ones who could take most advantage of price and input subsidies. To the extent that they divert their production to basic foods there are negative repercussions on their profits from high-income markets. The effect on the balance of payments from reduced food exports might be more negative than that of importing food. To the extent that they develop capitalist farming in lands previously used by the peasant sector (or new capitalist entrepreneurs arise among the peasants) the process of pauperization, polarization and capitalist penetration accelerates with

its attendant political and social problems. Moreover, as the capitalist entrepreneurs will usually employ modern technology that must be imported, at least until more domestic manufacturing capacity is installed, there will be a further drain on foreign exchange. To the extent that the price subsidies are financed by credit and monetary expansion, inflation accelerates.

All in all, it is much easier for the government to continue negotiating imports on a year-to-year basis. Moreover, imports can be reduced at will providing insurance against sharp price declines in agricultural prices because of 'over-production'.[42] One must remember that political planning horizons are notoriously short and the decision-makers must give a much greater weight to what happens this year in order to conserve their jobs and power than to what might happen a decade hence. In any event, effective political power is held by the propertied classes and their allies. The transnational corporations, for example, wield power at all levels. As noted above, they can usually arrange for a coincidence of their interests in expansion and profits with the personal interest of government bureaucrats, politicians and local businessmen. They represent the most efficient and 'progressive' elements in the economy. It is difficult to argue against 'progress' and 'efficiency'.

Following this line of reasoning, many analysts have concluded that the only available solution is more employment and effective income redistribution. In fact, this is being proposed with varying degrees of seriousness by the World Bank, by most government development plans and by populist demagogues. But this course has seriously fatal flaws too. Politically it is almost impossible within existing structures. The rich usually have sufficient power to block policies that would fundamentally alter their privileged position. If they do not, they can mobilize additional help from abroad. If a reformist government meets some measure of success in income redistribution, not only do direct internal and external political pressures upon it mount, but the whole dependent capitalist system malfunctions disastrously. Foreign credit and investment dries up. Domestic private investment stagnates. The reformist government must soon retrocede or fall unless it is able to install a genuinely planned 'socialist' economy. This it probably does not want. It could usually neither install it nor manage it if it did because of the class interests supporting the reformist administration.

One must keep in mind as well that 'effective' demand implies that in the final analysis the consumer can exchange for his food the goods and services that the producer wants. Obviously, the mere printing of money to enable low-income consumers to purchase food simply results in more inflation. Not so obviously, redistributing money incomes by creating new jobs and expanding welfare programmes financed by sound fiscal measures such as taxes on the rich, even if by some political miracle this were to be possible, would have many of the same inflationary effects. The poor would choose to spend most of this extra income on food and other basic necessities. If other products are not available, they would spend nearly all their increased incomes on food if possible. The economy's production structure and its mix of goods and services available for consumption would have to change simultaneously. But production structures are never changed overnight. This is one of the major reasons why income redistribution in Chile during 1971–73 resulted in hyperinflation once idle installed capacity was exhausted.[43] It is why Cuba and other countries embarking upon effective and rapid income redistribution programmes have invariably had to resort to *per capita* rationing of basic necessities for prolonged periods. It is why highly necessary and potentially productive public works programmes designed to provide widespread employment in Mexico and various other countries soon have had to be scaled down or abandoned because of inflationary pressures on food supplies. If the poor receive additional money incomes but have to compete in the market place with the rich for a limited supply of food and other basic necessities, their prices skyrocket.

No matter what politically feasible courses Latin American governments take, they fail to solve the problem of producing sufficient food to feed the poor adequately within their means or of providing them with sufficient productive employment so that they are no longer poor. Many of the urban poor are unemployed and make up a highly visible and often vocal labour reserve. The rural poor – the peasantry and under-employed workers in the traditional sector – constitute an additional vast potential 'reserve army of the unemployed'. Their immediate future appears about as bleak today as it has been during the nearly five centuries since the European conquest. Escape from the traps of under-employment and poverty in non-industrialized weak countries is not simple. On the contrary, it is nearly impossible for

Latin American nations as long as the present international order and internal social structures work together to block the way.

In summary, demand structures in Latin America, the same as production structures, present crucial bottlenecks for increasing food production. 'Food systems' of the rural poor depend primarily on local production. Effective demand in peasant communities increases more or less in proportion to population while their lands and other capital resources are stagnant or shrinking. Effective demand by the urban poor for basic food staples also increases only in proportion to population because of low incomes. Traditional agriculture lacks sufficient resources and incentives to fill this demand with the result that it must be met by commercial farmers or by imports. Commercial farmers, however, find it most profitable to produce for export or for high-income domestic markets. Governments find it more expedient and economically advantageous for the governing classes to import food in order to cover deficits in the production of staples consumed primarily by the poor than to make the necessary investments and take the political risks required to increase domestic production of these staples and to redistribute real incomes in favour of the poor. Because of embedded structural dependency relationships these government decisions are reinforced by a coincidence of interests of the local elite with those of foreign investors and of international financial institutions.

PROSPECTS

Our conclusions indeed confirm that economics is the 'dismal science'. Fortunately, pessimistic forecasts of the future are belied by history about as frequently as are optimistic ones. The prudent course for Latin American peasants would be to expect the worst and hope for the best.

Serious projections of Latin American agricultural growth during the next decade or two all assume a continuation of recent trends with minor modifications. As the World Bank, FAO, the World Food Council, the USDA and the International Food Policy Research Institute all work with the same basic data, similar methodologies, similar premises and interchangeable personnel it could hardly be otherwise.

Their studies all indicate food production in Latin America will, in the future, increase only slightly faster than population growth. On the assumption that world markets for agricultural exports will be stronger, however, these specialists expect the rate of the region's agricultural growth to accelerate slightly. Better relative prices for agricultural exports would stimulate investment, production and research in the capitalist farming sector. Ironically, the pressure of expanding capitalist agriculture on the peasant sector's scarce land resources would also increase at the very same time that higher prices of food imports should make greater peasant production all the more imperative. Since neither relative nor absolute poverty are assumed to decrease, the projections do not allow for either a major change in production organization or in demand structures.

The sad truth is that these projections and assumptions are very probably the most realistic ones. The only thing one can fault these agencies for is in not emphasizing the human tragedy and the lost opportunities behind their statistics concerning the patterns and quantities of food production and consumption and for a superficial analysis of the reasons behind the trends they project.

The political implications of a continuation of past agricultural trends in the region are even more shocking than are the economic ones. The peasantry would continue to diminish in relative importance but not in absolute size. There is now no place for the peasants to go. There are no large-scale new sources of urban employment, few new lands available for them to colonize, no chance to move in large numbers to new opportunities in the United States, Canada, Australia or even Latin America as did Western Europe's peasantry after the commercial and industrial revolutions there. Industrialization and urbanization would proceed, however. So would the expansion of capitalist agriculture in the region. Class contradictions would undoubtedly become more acute. They would be sharpened not only by changing class structures and relations but also by modern electronic communications and the examples of how other peoples have at least partially solved similar problems.

As a consequence of growing class conflict, the continuation of past trends implies ever increasing repression in the Latin American countries. The Brazilian 'miracle' and Pinochet's Chile appear to foreshadow the future as much as they also represent a continuation of Latin America's militaristic past. In this way the industrialized capitalist countries could be assured of their continued access to the region's resources and markets on favourable terms. What Trotsky called the 'bonapartism of

dependent capitalism' appears to be the almost ubiquitous solution in Latin America during the coming few years.

Behind these projections of agricultural growth lurks considerable state planning of the economy for the benefit of the large national and transnational corporations backed by efficient military repression. The 'custodial state' of dependent state capitalism with a veneer of Bismarkian welfare measures — not liberal capitalist democracy or democratic socialism — would be on the Latin American menu for the remainder of this century.

There are, however, countervailing trends that also must be taken into account. One is the growing gap in wealth and power between the rich countries and the poor ones so eloquently expounded by Mr. McNamara in his speach to the World Bank's Governors in Manila last year. By his estimates, this gap in *per capita* incomes between rich industrialized 'developed' countries and the poorest countries will increase from a ratio of roughly 31:1 in 1975 to 37:1 by 1985, while the gap between the rich and the medium income 'Third World' countries (which include nearly all of Latin America) will increase from 5.7:1 to over 6:1 in the same decade.[44] The implications of these data for Latin America are that more complete integration into the United States economy, for at least some Latin American countries, might eventually prove more feasible than mere dependency. The Puerto Rican 'model' might become more generalized. This is not probable. The United States' working population would hardly accept massive immigration that could lower its own living standards in order to help its large corporations expand their power and productive capacities more rapidly. But possibly greater integration with the United States economy of some Caribbean islands — Panama, Venezuela, Central America or Mexico — would become plausible. A deduction of this kind from the World Bank's projections is not out of the question.

The Puerto Rican experience implies improved incomes and nutrition for the poor and more rapid growth of capitalist industry and agro-industry. The peasantry would decline in absolute numbers because of more rapid outmigration to the metropolis. With trade and immigration barriers eliminated or greatly eased, marginal agricultural lands now intensively cultivated would be abandoned. In compensation, highly mechanized farming would incorporate some areas of now relatively unused pasture, jungle and desert into the North American agricultural system. The extended 'welfare state' would modify somewhat traditional food systems and demand structures.

But this model also carries with it the threat of growing repression and violence. Recent events in Northern Ireland, Uruguay and Argentina hardly augur well for the political harmony that an extended welfare state might bring to unwilling beneficiaries.

The other countervailing trend is towards some kind of planned 'socialist' economies in Latin America with varying degrees of democratic participation. We have already mentioned the changing class structures and growing class contradictions in the region sharpened by modern communications. Given the fact that there is no visible solution for the poverty and employment problems within the dependent capitalist framework, the pressures for a radical 'socialist' solution are going to increase. Unless real income for the individual is somehow separated from property ownership and from his 'average' and 'marginal' productivities at the micro-level, the introduction of efficient labour-saving technologies will often be slowed even when cost—output and capital—output considerations are favourable. At the same time, 'irrationally' high capital—output technologies ('irrational' from the standpoint of both national social-welfare criteria and national economic criteria but not from that of profits for the individual firm) will continue to be introduced by the multinationals and other large capitalist entrepreneurs causing increasing unemployment, pauperization and polarization. Moreover, the region's resources will continue to be exploited primarily for the benefit of the industrialized nations and a relatively small group of their Latin American colleagues. There will be increasing pressures to form governments whose political power base lies with the workers and peasants and that can challenge private corporate (national and transnational) interests. These governments will inevitably be labelled 'socialist' or 'communist' no matter how much they may differ from standard stereotypes.

The potential impact of the Cuban experience should not be minimized in this respect. Cuba confronted all the classic problems of dependent capitalism in Latin America before the revolution. With the emergence of a planned 'socialist' economy (with strong economic and political support from the USSR) it was able rapidly to solve its worst poverty, employment, nutritional, educational and public health problems. To be sure it is taking considerably more time to change production structures and raise average productivities. But with the highest rate of investment in Latin America during the last two decades these problems promise to diminish rapidly in the future. This is true even if part of the investment turns out to have been relatively inefficient. Unemployment was simply defined away. Sufficient real income to cover basic needs was made a right for everyone independent of the individual's direct contribution to commodity production. The positive results in terms of social welfare for the poorer majority are undeniably clear even to the Cuban regime's most obdurate ideological critics. Economic results, while still much more ambiguous, are already impressive and promise to become more so within the next decade. This experience will undoubtedly have an increasingly powerful impact in the rest of the region.

The experience with 'revolutionary socialist' governments in other regions of dependent capitalist underdevelopment certainly provides no grounds for optimism concerning a rapid transition to any classless utopia, or even to democratic participatory socialism of the kind apparently dreamed of by Marx and Engels. But that reasonably rapid economic growth has taken place and distributional inequalities lessened in many 'socialist' countries seems to be an incontrovertible fact. Moreover, recent history in China, Cuba, Poland, Yugoslavia and many other 'socialist' nations certainly shows that large portions of peasantry do not have to be brutally sacrificed by farm collectivization being imposed overnight, as it was in the USSR in the late 1920s and early 1930s, in order for these economies to function and grow. For many of the Latin American poor, even 'bureaucratic socialism' with its autocratic privileges and prerogatives for a 'new class' might appear infinitely preferable to their present situation. Several Latin American intellectuals argue that there is no inherent reason why future 'socialist' governments in the region could not be considerably more democratic and participatory with a much greater degree of independence in their relations with both super-powers than was even possible in Cuba.

While this may represent utopian dreaming, it also represents a real political force. Just possibly the global balance of power might be modified enough to permit a considerably wider range of political options in Latin America. The growing relative economic weights in the region of Japan, Western Europe and the 'Eastern Block' countries, possible internal modifications of power structures within the United States and the Soviet Union, the probable coming to power of communist and socialist parties in Italy and France, the continued growing influence of China, the realignment of power among nations because of the 'energy crisis', etc., all might create opportunities within which planned 'socialist' economies might become the trend for the future in the region. Moreover, even the United States might recognize that an independent prosperous Latin America in which poverty has been largely eliminated, even if it is 'socialist', could be more harmonious with the United States' real long-term interests than would a continuation of present trends. This is not probable before year 2000 but it remains a possiblity. The Allende government's tragic collapse in Chile, however, should leave no illusions that 'democratic socialism' is the inevitable road for the immediate future.

If 'socialist' planning were to become widespread, its impact on agricultural growth patterns could be very significant. Both production structures and internal demand structures would be radically changed. There would be strong pressures to increase production of basic foodstuffs. Nevertheless, the need for foreign exchange would continue and there would also be many pressures to increase agricultural exports, as has been the case with Cuban sugar. One would expect more investment to be directed into the agricultural sector and particularly into what is now traditional peasant agriculture. One might anticipate that towards the end of the century there would be a rate of agricultural growth averaging slightly better than those now optimistically projected by the international agencies for the next couple of decades. The patterns of agricultural and industrial growth would radically change, however. The poor, both rural and urban, would be much better fed and the mix of goods and services produced would have to take into account their needs.

This is idle speculation. With countervailing pressures there will probably be mixed solutions — a little bit of everything in various countries. Possibly even the transnationals and ruling local elites might devise a viable democratic solution for poverty and unemployment in the region within a liberal capitalist framework. But it appears highly unlikely. No one

can see the future clearly. Fortunately.

This pessimistic analysis does not imply there is nothing that those interested in the welfare of Latin America's peasantry and other poor can do. The broad strategy of 'men of good will' seems clear. In the first place, efforts to increase the region's productive capacities and incomes, especially those of poorer groups such as the peasants are worthy of support, although one should have no illusions about their immediate impact on the region's food supplies or nutritional levels. New technologies must be developed and existing ones adapted to local conditions, meeting as much as possible the region's need for more productive jobs. Secondly, the contradictions inherent in the region's pattern of growth must be analysed, sharpened and brought home to all social groups both within the region and within the rich developed countries. This is what this article is attempting to do in a modest way for a small group of interested readers. Thirdly, all efforts should be supported to encourage the poor (the numerous groups of workers, small tradesmen, artisans and peasants) in the region to organize themselves democratically, to analyse realistically their situation and problems, to educate themselves and to act collectively in their own longer-term interests. Without informed organized pressures and democratic participation from below there will be no viable solutions even if the existing world order and domestic social structures were to crumble or be modified sufficiently to permit deep social changes.

The repressive 'custodial state' guiding semi-planned dependent capitalist economies in Latin America in filling their growing contributions to the powerful industrial nations' needs for more and more natural resources, and for better markets for their high-technology agricultural and industrial surpluses, appears the most probable trend. This is regrettable. Perhaps it will not come to pass. The resources and technologies are available in Latin America for the region to develop rapidly and to feed all of its population well. It could happen. But I take seriously my own advice to the Latin American peasants. I expect the worst and hope for the best.

NOTES

1. FAO, *Población, Suministro de Alimentos y Desarrollo Agrícola,* Cuadro 20 (Rome: FAO, 1975). There are minor differences among FAO base data and projections and those of other United Nations agencies, the World Bank, the US Department of Agriculture, the World Food Board and the International Food Policy Research Institute. The general conclusions (and data sources at the national level) are essentially the same, however.

2. FAO, *The State of Food and Agriculture – 1975* (Rome: FAO, 1976).

3. FAO estimates 36 millions in Latin America with serious malnutrition (FAO, *Población,* etc. op. cit.), the World Bank speaks of 55 millions of 'absolute poor' in Latin America (Robert S. McNamara, *Address to the Board of Governors* (Manila, Phillipines: 4 Oct. 1976)), while the ILO estimates 118 millions of Latin Americans as 'seriously poor' and 73 millions as 'destitute' (ILO, *Employment, Growth and Basic Needs* (Geneva: ILO, 1976)).

4. ILO, op. cit.

5. S. Barraclough, *Agrarian Structure in Latin America* (Lexington, Mass.: Lexington Heath and Co., 1974).

6. Since the 1972–75 'world food crisis', the emphasis in the conventional wisdom about development has shifted somewhat from agricultural modernization to population control but both are still widely posited as being fundamental causal variables. See, for example, Lester Brown, *Seeds of Change* (N.Y.: Praeger, 1970) and the same author's *In the Human Interest* (N.Y.: North & Co., 1974). Much more sophisticated statements of the same basic propositions can be found in numerous other recent publications, e.g. The World Bank, *Assault on World Poverty* (Baltimore: Johns Hopkins University Press, 1975) and *Scientific American,* 'A Special Issue on Food and Agriculture' (September 1976).

7. See, for example, UNRISD, *The Social and Economic Implications of Large-Scale Introduction of New Varieties of Food Grain – Summary of Conclusions,* (Geneva: 1974); Andrew Pearse, *Social and Economic Implications of Large-Scale Introduction of New Varieties of Food Grain* (review mimeo)(Geneva: UNRISD, 1976); Keith Griffin, *The Political Economy of Agrarian Change* (London: Macmillan, 1976); Susan George, *How the Other Half Dies* (London: Penguin, 1976).

8. Cynthia Hewitt de Alcántara, *The Social and Economic Implications of Large-Scale Introduction of New Varieties of Food Grains in Mexico* (mimeo) (Geneva: UNRISD, 1974).

9. *US Census of Agriculture,* 'Puerto Rico', (Washington, D.C.: 1970).

10. FAO, *State of Food and Agriculture – 1975,* op. cit.

11. ERS, *Agricultural Trade of the Western Hemisphere* (Washington, D.C.: USDA, 1972).

12. Sandra Hadler, *Developing Country Foodgrain Projections for 1985,* World Bank Staff Working Paper, No. 247 (World Bank, Nov. 1976).

13. FAO, *Población, Suministro de Alimentos y Desarrollo Agrícola,* op. cit.

14. UNRISD, *Famine–Risk and Prevention in the Modern World* (Geneva: UNRISD, 1976) (mimeo).

15. FAO, ibid. See especially Cuadro 1-D.

16. CONACYT, *Política Nacional de Ciencia y Tecnología: Estrategia, Lineamientos y Metas* (Mexico: 1976).

17. FAO, *State of Food and Agriculture,* op. cit.

18. Meadows *et al., The Limits of Growth* (the First Report to the Club of Rome), 1972; Mesarovic and Pestel, *Mankind at the Turning Point* (the Second Report to the Club of Rome), 1974.

19. Herman Kahn and Anthony Weiner, *The Year 2000* (New York: The Hudson Institute, 1967).

20. 'Towards the year 2000', *Daedalus,* American Academy of Science, Vol. 96, No. 3 (1967).

21. *What Now?,* The 1975 Dag Hammarskjold Report (Motala, Sweden: 1975).

22. See: *FAO Production Year Book – 1971* (Rome: 1972), and Roger Revelle, 'The resources available for agriculture', *Scientific American,* op. cit.

23. Revelle, *Scientific American,* op. cit.

24. P. Pimental *et al., Science,* 182, 443 (1973); John Steinhart and Carol E. Steinhart, *Science,* 184, 307 (1974).

25. See: J. Vanek, *The Absurdity of the Richman's Trade Doctrine and Institutions for the Present Day World Economy,* Department of Economics Paper No. 125 (Cornell University, 1976).

26. I use the term dualism in the literal sense of 'having or composed of two parts' and I do not wish to imply any endorsement of the basically reactionary theories of economic dualism so frequently put forth in neo-classical 'development' literature.

27. For detailed analysis of this structure in seven countries see: S. L. Barraclough, *Agrarian Structure in Latin America,* op. cit. For similar analysis of Mexico,

see: Sergio Reyes, R. Stavenhagen, *et al.*, *Estructura Agraria y Desarrollo Agrícola en Mexico* (Mexico, D.F.: Fondo de Cultura, 1974).

28. See: S. Barraclough and Jacobo Schatan, 'Technological policy and agricultural development', *Land Economics,* Vol. XLIX, No. 2 (May 1973).

29. S. Barraclough and J. Schatan, op. cit.

30. A. V. Chayonov, *The Theory of Peasant Economy* (American Economic Association, 1966).

31. For a good economic analysis of these agrarian structural problems see: Keith Griffin, *The Political Economy of Agrarian Change,* op. cit.

32. Andrew Pearse, *The Latin American Peasant*(London: Frank Cass and Co., 1976).

33. See for example, SRA–FAO–PNUD, *Investigación de Tres Ejidos del Oriente de Morelos; La Torre y La Galera; Estudios en la Mixteca Alta* (Mexico: Programa Nacional de Capacitación Agraria, 1976).

34. For a highly suggestive analysis of this structure in Mexico, see: Arthur Domike, *Agro-industries en México: Estructuras de los Sistemas y Oportunidades para Empresas Campesinas* (Mexico, D.F.: CIDE, 1976), (mimeo).

35. See for example, Ernest Feder, 'El imperialismo fresa, *Revista del México Agrario* (México, D.F.: 1977).

36. *Latin American Commodity Report,* Vol. 10, No. 3 (17 December 1976).

37. There is no space to develop this argument here and numerous studies have dealt with it. For summary of official data relating to this problem, see: Raul Prebisch, *Change and Development* (Santiago, Chile: IDB, 1970).

38. Flavio Machicado, *et al. Estudios del Consumo de Alimentos Esenciales por Estratos de Ingreso* (Santiago, Chile: ODEPLAN, ODEPA, ICIRA, October 1973).

39. Marco A. Fenoni, *The Impact of Urbanization on Nutrition in Latin America,* Graduate thesis, Cornell University (Ithaca, N.Y.: August 1974) (mimeo).

40. PLANDES, *Posibilidades del Desarrollo Económico-Social* (Santo Domingo: Oficina Nacional de Planificación Educativa Dominicana, 1976).

41. The concept of food system . . . refers to the complex of actions and interactions within a country concerned with the production–exchange–and–consumption of food. The concept 'system' is appropriate because of the actual existence of articulate circuits along which food passes – with varying degrees of storage and processing on the way – from its origin in the earth to its final consumption, whether or not it passes through the market place. In passing through the market, food tends to become a commodity like any other and to reach the table for final consumption on the basis of 'effective' demand (rather than biological need). UNRISD, *Famine Risk and Famine Prevention in the Modern World,* op. cit.

42. I have on various occasions in several countries listened to well-documented 'briefs' presented by representatives of commercial farmers to government officials arguing against increasing production capacity for various basic food crops because of the danger of engendering market 'gluts'.

43. S. Barraclough and José Antonio Fernández, *Diagnóstico de la Reforma Agraria Chilena* (Mexico, D.F.: Siglo XXI, 1975).

44. Robert S. McNamara, *Address to the Board of Governors* (Manila, Phillipines: 4 Oct. 1976).

World Development, 1977, Vol. 5, Nos. 5–7, pp. 477–485. Pergamon Press. Printed in Great Britain.

Food Production Potential of the World

P. BURINGH

Agricultural University,
Wageningen, The Netherlands

Summary. – This paper provides a critique of some recent studies of food production potential. The author briefly analyzes the different approaches taken in various studies. The discussion which follows attempts to draw the implications of these studies together in order to discuss some general observations on the question of limits to world food production potential and on what procedures should be adopted by countries towards achieving increased production levels. Given the right social, political and economic conditions, the author takes a relatively optimistic view of world food production potential.

1. INTRODUCTION

Hunger is nothing new on our planet. There have been many periods in history when people were hungry for various reasons, e.g. crop failure often as a result of abnormal climatic conditions, destruction of land and crops during wars and uprisings, overpopulation, decreasing fertility of soils, destruction of soils by erosion, floods or salinization. The related hunger problems which had a limited, regional character were always followed by a better balanced relation between population and available food. Since the advent of modern means of transportation and communication, a global society has developed and the food problem has become a real world problem that attracts more and more attention. It is therefore studied now by various specialists and discussed in several international meetings.

Nearly 80 years ago, in 1898, Sir William Crooks, president of the British Association for the Advancement of Science (Baade, 1960), stated that there was almost no suitable land left that could be reclaimed for food production. He foresaw hunger on global scale in 1930 because of the population growth if it were not possible to increase the production of nitrogen fertilizers on a commercial basis. This became possible after World War I, and a disaster of world-wide hunger was prevented.

Baker (1923) has studied some geographical and demographic aspects of the land utilization problem in the United States of America, concluding that the US could feed and cloth some 200 m people, the number that he estimated were living in the US by 1950. He expected at that time that food from the tropical countries would soon invade the US markets in increasing amounts. It turned out to be the other way around. At present the USA is even the greatest exporter of food products, and according to Heady (1976), exports by the year 2000 could be much greater if all possibilities would be used.

In the 1950s and 1960s some books and articles on the food problem were published. As an example, reference is made to Baade (1960), who estimated for the year 2000 a population of 6,500 m people that could easily be fed, because the area of cultivated land could be increased to two and if necessary to three times the 1950 area. Applying the possibilities that were known in 1960, production of 3 to 4 tons, probably 5 tons per ha of cereal grains should be possible. This means that, according to Baade, some 30,000 m people could have enough food.

Although it would be interesting to continue with a review of various authors' work on potentials of food production published during the last decades, this will not be done because I prefer to concentrate on results of more recent research work. Readers who are interested in reviews on the general problems are advised to study the books of Brown and Eckholm (1974), Gruhl (1975), Garbutt *et al.* (1976) and Eckholm (1976), who also give the most important references. Some of the studies referred to below are computer simulated models of world food supply, food demand and nutrition (models of Meadows, Mesarović and Pestel, MOIRA). These models and an unpublished Latin American model are reviewed by Clark and Cole (1976) and by Garbutt, Linnemann, *et al.* (1976). Reference is also made to the September issue of *Scientific American*.

2. THE US WHITE HOUSE STUDY (1967)

In 1967 a report (US Report, 1967) on the world food problem was published by the US President's Science Advisory Committee. This committee studied various aspects of the problem including the potential of land for food production. Potentially arable land was defined as land including soils considered to be cultivable and acceptably productive of food crops adapted to the environment. In order to compute the potentially arable land of the world, specialists studied maps indicating 33 types of climate from five climate zones, that were grouped in 17 agroclimate regions. A world soil map (scale 1:15 m), prepared by the US Soil Conservation Service, showed 13 broad geographical groups. The climatic map was superimposed on the soil map and some 200 combinations of soil—climate conditions were studied. With some additional information a computation was made of land that is (1) potentially arable, (2) non-arable, but with grazing potential, and (3) non-arable and without grazing potential. The area of cultivated land is rather well-known from FAO publications. The land actually harvested in a particular year is approximately 2/3 of the total cultivated land area. The question of how much land could be irrigated was also dealt with. The results of this important investigation are presented in the tables. For each broad soil group the potentially arable land is given in percentages for each continent and the USSR. For more details reference is made to the original report (US Report, 1967) and to articles by Kellogg and Orvedal (1969) and by Simonson (1967). Tables 1 and 2 are taken from the latter publication.

From these tables it is learned that 10.6% of the total land area of the world is cultivated at present (1,406 m ha) and that 24.2% of the total land area (3,190 m ha) is considered to be potentially arable land. That means that there is even more land available to be reclaimed in the future than is cultivated at the present time. In making these estimations the authors had in mind an average level of agricultural technology used in the USA. It will be clear that various assumptions had to be made, e.g. that the reclamation costs of the land would not be excessive in relation to the anticipated returns. These data confirm more or less what was said by some agronomists and economists before; however, in my knowledge it was the first time that a reliable investigation was made. Later on these results have been used in some studies related to the world food problem, e.g. by Meadows (1972), who wrote the well-known book *Limits to Growth*. Unfortunately his detailed and complete study has not been published.

3. THE STUDY BY MEADOWS (1972)

In their study, Meadows *et al.* estimated the agricultural land needed to feed the growing world population (0.4 ha per person). As there is only 3.2 m ha of land available for cultivation and as this figure will decrease as a consequence of increasing non-agricultural use of land, Meadows' study concludes there will be a desperate shortage of land before the year 2000. This can be delayed by some decades if the productivity of the agricultural land is doubled or quadrupled. Besides land the availability of fresh water is a very important factor. Meadows concludes that in some areas the limit of available water will be reached long before the land limit becomes apparent. This study considers the whole world as one unit and calculations are made on a global scale. Although I believe that some of the conclusions of Meadows are wrong, as will be shown later, this study is extremely important as it was a first attempt to show the interaction of various crucial factors. Up to 1972 not much attention was given to such an integrated approach.

4. SOME OTHER STUDIES

Firstly, reference is made to various studies of the FAO concerning countries and special regions and in particular to the studies carried out in setting up a *Provisional Indicative World Plan for Agricultural Development* (FAO, 1969), which, I believe, is well-known to the readers. The conclusion is that 3,200 m ha of land are potentially fit for farming.

Mückenhausen (1973) deals with the productivity of the various great soil groups of the world as presented in the US Report (1967). He also concludes that the potentialities of the world are many times the present production. He expects much of new crop varieties to be obtained by plant breeding. Finally, he states that the world could definitely feed ten times

Table 1. *Total land area and arable land by continents*

Continents	Total land area*	Cultivated land*	% of land area cultivated	Potential arable land*	Ratio of cultivated to potential arable land %
Africa	3010	158	5.2	734	22
Asia	2740	519	18.9	627	83
Australia and New Zealand	820	32	3.9	153	21
Europe	480	154	32.1	174	88
North America	2110	239	11.3	465	51
South America	1750	77	4.4	681	11
USSR	2240	227	10.6	356	64
Total	13,150	1,406	10.6	3,190	44

Source: Adapted from Table 7–9, p. 434, of *The World Food Problem, A Report of the President's Science Advisory Committee*, Vol. II, Report of the Panel on the World Food Supply (USA).
*Areas are given in millions of hectares.

Table 2. *Estimated total land area and potential arable land by broad soil groups*

Broad soil groups	Total area*	Potential arable land*	Potential arable as % of total area	Potential arable as % of group total	Included orders, 7th Approx.**
Tundra soils	517	0	0	0	4, 1
Desert soils	2180	430	3.3	20.7	3
Chernozems and Brunizems	822	450	3.5	54.5	5-
Noncalcic Brown soils	291	110	0.8	37.8	7
Podzols	1920	300	2.4	15.6	6, 7
Red-Yellow Podzolic soils	388	130	1.0	34.2	8
Latosolic soils	2500	1050	8.1	42.0	4, 9, 8
Grumusols and Terra Rossas	325	180	1.3	55.4	2, 7
Brown Forest soils and Rendzinas	101	30	0.2	3.0	4, 5
Ando soils	24	10	0.1	41.7	4
Lithosols	2722	80	0.6	2.9	1, 4, *et al.*
Regosols	763	70	0.5	9.2	1, 4
Alluvial soils	595	350	2.4	58.8	1, 4
Total	13,150	3,190	24.2	–	–

Source: Adapted from Table 7–1, p. 423, of *The World Food Problem, A Report of the President's Science Advisory Committee*, Vol. II, Report of the Panel on the World Food Supply (USA).
*Areas are given in millions of hectares.
**Orders are identified by numbers as follows: 1-Entisols; 2-Vertisols; 3-Aridisols; 4-Inceptisols; 5-Mollisols; 6-Spodosols; 7-Alfisols; 8-Ultisols; 9-Oxisols.

the present world population, a conclusion already drawn by some other scientists. Mostly, however, it is not clear how they came to such a conclusion.

Some more attention will be given to the results of the investigations of Mesarović and Pestel (1974), who have made some classical mistakes in estimating the agricultural productivity of soils in the tropics. Their computations are based on the assumption that the maximum area of land that can be cultivated is 2,425 m ha. They conclude that only North America and to a lesser extent Australia have important reserves of cultivable land. The authors do not expect much of tropical Africa and Latin America, in particular of the Congo and Amazon basins, because it is believed that the biologically poor tropical soil will harden as soon as the forest is removed. Those soils therefore will become unsuitable for agricultural purposes. Mesarović and Pestel believe that the humid tropics are unimportant from the point of view of food production and the situation in the savanna regions is not very favourable. They conclude that the possibilities of increasing the area of cultivated land are very limited.

Similar wrong conclusions can be found in various articles and books (e.g. Gruhl. 1975). They are based on the old story of laterite and laterization, a specific phenomenon of tropical soils. Recently, Sanchez and Buol (1975) have written once more about various misunderstandings on tropical soils and their agricultural potential, in particular on 'the laterite exaggeration' and the organic matter in those soils. They conclude that laterite may be found only in approximately 7% of the soils in the tropics! I will not refer to the various studies of soils in the tropics that clearly show the possibilities of various soils for food production. Especially during the last decade much progress has been made by French, British, Belgian, Dutch and American soil scientists and agronomists on all continents since it is realized that many tropical soils have characteristics different from those of temperate regions as described in textbooks and handbooks and as taught in the colleges and universities. Moreover it also is proven that in semi-arid regions precipitation is not the limiting factor for crop production in normal years and that the production of the natural grass vegetation in such areas can be increased considerably (van Keulen, 1975). From the point of view of tropical soil science I cannot agree with various results obtained by Mesarović and Pestel. Important reserves of cultivable land are not found in North America and Australia, but in Latin America and Africa (see part 5).

Of the Russian authors only Kovda (1974) shall be mentioned, because he also has reviewed the Russian literature. He suggests that more accurate estimations of the potential land resources of the earth should be made on the basis of new world soil maps. He believes that the cultivated land area could be increased by more than three times up to 5,000 m ha. In this interesting book Kovda also deals with the various problems of soil destruction.

5. THE MOIRA STUDY

A group of Dutch specialists (often referred to as the Linnemann group) has made a study called the *Model of International Relations in Agriculture* (Linnemann and Keyzer (eds.), in press). The second chapter of this study has been published separately (Buringh, van Heemst and Staring, 1975), whereas De Hoogh (1976) and Garbut and Linnemann (1976) have given a review of some results. Here we shall deal mainly with the results of Chapter Two in which a computation was made of the absolute maximum food production of the world. The results provide basic material for other specialists (economists, agronomists, sociologists, etc.) when studying the world food problem. The readers of that chapter are first warned not to misuse the results, because there are several assumptions made, there is a high level of generalization and the yields calculated can hardly be obtained in practice.

In order to know the area of potentially arable land the soil conditions were studied on the new soil map of the world, scale 1:5 m (FAO/UNESCO, 1971–76), and finally grouped into 222 broad soil regions. For each of these broad soil regions the details of soils, vegetation, topography and climate were studied. The possibilities of irrigation were studied by Moen and Beek (1974) from the available literature. Taking into account these factors, the following was determined for each region: the area of potential arable land, the average soil productivity, the average water availability, the possible area to be irrigated, the maximum production per ha and the total maximum production, both expressed in grain equivalents of a standard cereal crop.

The computation of this theoretical potential production is based on the assumption that the standard cereal crop is healthy, green, closed, well-supplied with nutrients, oxygen, water and foodhold and therefore the production is only limited by the daily photosynthetic rate, that depends on the state of the sky, the latitude and the date. In order to compute the absolute maximum production for each unit, factors for deficiencies in climate, soil conditions and/or water availability were introduced; for more details reference is made to the original publication.

The result of the study is that in total 3,419 m ha or 25% of all land of the world is potentially arable land, which is almost equal to the 3,190 m ha (24.2%) in the White House study (1967) (see part 2). An important difference is that the data are not only given in tables, but are also shown on small-scale maps indicating the 222 regions, which give a general idea of the regional distribution of the potential arable land of the world (see Figure 1 as an example of the six maps of the continents).

The absolute maximum food production (expressed in grain equivalents of a standard cereal crop) for the whole world was computed

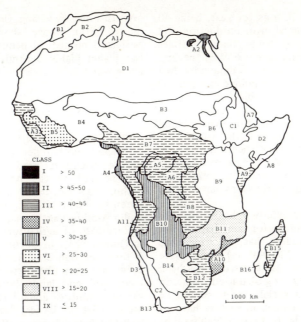

Fig. 1. *Classification of the relative importance of potential agricultural land in the broad soil regions of Africa.*
Note: The classes I to IX indicate in percentages of the areas concerned the land area potentially suitable for cultivation expressed in equivalent land with potential production, including irrigation.

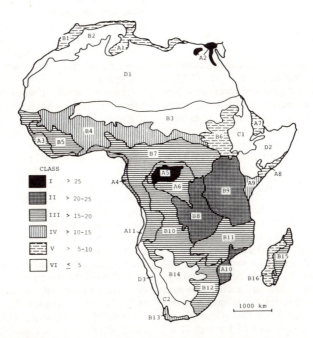

Fig. 2. *Land productivity classes for the potential agricultural land in Africa.*
Note: The classes I to IV indicate the computed maximum production of grain equivalents in 1000 kg per hectare.

to be almost 50,000 m tons per year, being 40 times the present cereal crop production and 32,390 m tons per year, being almost 30 times the present cereal production if 65% of the land would be used for cereals as it is done now. In a second series of six maps (example in Figure 2) the productivity classes are indicated.

The authors compare some results with wheat and rice yields obtained on experimental stations in various parts of the world and conclude that the results of their computation are realistic. One year later I have to conclude that they probably are somewhat pessimistic, and for some regions corrections have to be made.

The approach in this study indicates that the results are not suitable for newspapers nor should it be concluded that 30 times the present population (120,000 m) could have food and clothing, because this study has been made as a basic study for global food studies in which economic and social aspects should be incorporated. Many reduction factors have to be introduced, in order to know which level of production could be obtained in reality. I believe that a first-class farmer with excellent equipment probably could produce 75% and a very poor farmer with traditional farm management measures 5 or 10% of the potential computed.

6. THE AUSTRALIAN STUDY

A recent study on the potential of Australia has been published by Gifford *et al.* (1975). The aim was to investigate the potential production of food and water in Australia, given the proven technology and present consumption trends, in order to find out how many people could live in Australia. They found that Australia could support 200 m people (present population 13.1 m) if labour-intensive subsistence farming is applied, which includes high risk, low security and poor existence. However, if Australia wants to keep the present standard of living, it has to maintain its food exports, produced by modern farm management. Then the population should be stabilized between 20 and 30 m people. It seems to me that the last figures are somewhat low because the assumptions on future crop yields are rather low and the area of potential cropland is much lower than in the global studies of the White House report (US Report, 1967) and of Buringh *et al.* (1975). I got the impression that the authors did not want to give too optimistic an idea about population possibilities in Australia; how-

ever, this may be wrong. On the other hand, the figures given above show clearly that the estimated number of people that could live on this planet highly depends on the standard of living which is supposed to be acceptable.

7. RECENT, MORE DETAILED STUDIES

The Canadian Department of Agriculture has published two booklets (Nowland, 1975 a + b) on the agricultural productivity of Ontario and Quebec and on the Atlantic Provinces. This author has calculated from soil maps and potential yields (those that can be expected under good management), that the potential for the increase of agriculture production is 116% in Ontario, 25% in Quebec and 150% (or 800% if forest clearance is practised) in the Atlantic Provinces. Data like these can also be found in many soil and land classification reports of various countries and of the FAO. This study shows that it is very useful to make such investigations, because there are important regional differences. Moreover Nowland (1975a) has drawn attention once more to the process whereby urbanization is taking over irreplaceable high-quality farmland. Between 1971 and 2001 large areas of the food-producing land may be lost. In Ontario this is 12% and in Quebec 26%. This is at an annual average rate of 0.4% in Ontario and 0.9% in Quebec. Such figures and possibly even higher ones could be produced for the increasing non-agricultural land use in various other countries.

Another study I want to refer to is by van Liere (1976), who investigated the Mekong drainage basin in Southeast Asia and who proves that the agricultural potential of that region is much greater than was expected. According to van Liere that region could become a new food basket for the world that is even equal to the present food basket of the USA and Canada. Until now it was always said that Southeast Asia is a very difficult part of the world because of a very rapid increase in population, having almost no potential to increase food production. This example shows once more that more investigations in all parts of the world have to be carried out. We really do not know the exact food production potential of our planet. The MOIRA study with a subdivision of the world in 222 regions is the most detailed global study made up to now; however, it is still a study on a high level of generalization that can be improved considerably. When Eckholm (1976) and some other authors try to convince us that the tropics will never be the food basket of the world, our only comment is: it is not true.

8. DISCUSSION

We have tried to indicate in a general way the different approaches in the various studies. Several authors have made calculations on production based on areas of suitable land and average yields or on 'potential yields', mainly yields obtained on experimental fields. Other computations are based on production expressed in calories and the average food requirement expressed in calories per person, in order to calculate the number of people who could live on our planet. Meadows (1972) has calculated how much land will be needed for each person in order to conclude how many people could live on earth. The MOIRA study shows that there is a real limit — it could be somewhat lower, most probably somewhat higher — but there is a limit in food production as a consequence of limits in photosynthesis.

The US study and the MOIRA study indicate almost the same limit as to the land that could be cultivated, taking into account the present state of available knowledge and experience. That does not mean that there are no problems to be solved before the potential yield could be reached. For example there are problems concerning plant diseases, plant breeding, farm management. On the other hand there are the problems of soil losses by erosion, soil salinization and the rapid increase of non-agricultural land use of actually cultivated land, etc.

The food production potential of the world is decreasing every day. I once calculated from various data that we are losing at least 10 ha of arable land each minute (five because of soil erosion, three because of soil salinization, one because of non-agricultural use and one because of soil degradation). This is corroborated by calculations made by some other authors.

The problem of whether it is better to increase the production of food crops on the existing arable land, which is quite possible and probably not too difficult, or to extend the area by reclaiming non-cultivated land, has not been sufficiently studied. The answer often will depend on the local situation but even more on the political and economic situation.

It is my feeling that in most countries it is better to increase the often low production on the present arable land first and to reserve the reclamation for future generations. It probably costs less, it will be more effective and gives much quicker results.

Besides, we also need food for the animals. This can be produced on the grazing land which potentially has a much higher production than is achieved nowadays. That is part of the land not included in the area of potential agricultural land. Moreover, part of the arable land at present is and in the future also will be used for production of animal food for which a system of modern farm management can be applied.

As can be seen from the American and MOIRA figures there is still enough land left for wild life, recreation, etc. At least in the MOIRA study, in all regions only 80 or 90% and in some regions only 50% of the land that really could be potentially arable is used in the calculations. This means that ecologists should not be afraid that higher food production will lead to destruction of nature and of the global ecosystem. There are even large portions of non-agricultural land in almost all regions, except the glacial and desert regions, that can be improved, reforested, etc. There is no need at the present time to cultivate all available land. However, it is true that there are real ecological dangers, in particular in densely populated regions. Air and soil pollution, soil destruction and soil erosion have to be stopped, and we know the techniques with which to do this. In my opinion the present generation does not have the right to reclaim all the non-cultivated potential agricultural land now. In this respect attention has to be drawn to the Russians (Brejnev, 1974) who are reclaiming very large areas in semi-arid regions and to the Americans (Eckholm, 1976) who just started to invade the Amazon basin with large-scale reclamation of land. These recent land reclamations are part of the world food war that has started some years ago, although most people do not realize it. It will be a long war and the poor people in the poor countries will be the victims. In this connection a new science is being developed — 'food intelligence' — in which earth satellite images and remote sensing are the most important tools.

The availability of fertilizers is another problem. It has already been studied by some specialists. I learned that this will not be a big problem in the future (Baade, 1960; Schuffelen, 1965) as long as the prices are not too high. Those who are not familiar with modern agriculture and crop production believe that high applications of fertilizers are needed to achieve the potential high yields. This, however, is not true because in modern farm management mostly other factors than fertilizers are limiting the crop production, e.g. plant diseases, soil deficiencies and the lack of minor elements. Another misunderstanding is that these high applications of chemical fertilizers are needed almost everywhere. In order to prove this, very often the high amounts used in the Netherlands are given as an example. In those cases one has forgotten to mention the specific climatical conditions in the Netherlands.

I did not yet mention the energy needed to reach the absolute maximum food production. In countries with well-developed agriculture with average yields of approximately 50% of the absolute maximum yield, agriculture needs about 7 to 10% of the total fossil energy consumption. If there were a shortage of energy, it seems to me we would have to spend some of the still available energy on food production. On the other hand, in many poor regions food production could be doubled with almost no extra input of fossil energy. If animal power is replaced by tractors, large areas now used to produce animal food will become available for human food production, because to feed one horse or one cow we need approximately the production of one hectare of productive land. Of the total number of farm families estimated at 350 m, only 10 m of them use a tractor.

From the foregoing it is learned that the potential to produce more food exists. Making a computation of the absolute maximum food production (Buringh, van Heemst and Staring, 1975; Linnemann (in press)) seems to be somewhat crazy, because such production cannot be obtained. However, at present we do not need a level of food production that is 30 times the present production; in the near future when the population is doubled, we will perhaps need three times the present food production. This food can be produced and often even without reclaiming new land. According to Koppejan (1976), the world population growth will decrease and after approximately

150 years the population will be at an almost constant level of 12,000 m people. They will need approximately five times the food we produce now. This is no problem from an agricultural point of view. Psomopoulos (1975) found that even 22,000 m people could live on our globe in an 'high environment'. The political leaders in the world have to decide if they want enough food for everybody and if so, they have to decide how to help to improve agriculture, in particular in poor countries in order to use their full potential. It is a matter of policy in which economic and social conditions have to be changed not only in the poor countries but even more in the rich countries as is shown in the economic part of the MOIRA study (De Hoogh, 1976). It is left to the readers and other authors in this volume to think about the political implications of the world food problem.

The future cannot be predicted; we can only do research on it in order to facilitate taking decisions that shall determine the future of our world.

9. SUMMARY

Until recently, little research was done on the food production potential of the world. Studies have been made by USA, FAO and Dutch specialists, as well as some specific country studies. The results of these studies have been discussed here. Taking into account the regional conditions of soils, climate and farm management, all studies show that enough food can be produced for a population that is 5 to 10 times and even more the present world population. In the Dutch MOIRA study, the authors even attempt to compute the absolute maximum food production as a basis for other studies. If politicians succeed in improving social and economic conditions, agriculturists can produce enough food.

REFERENCES

Baade, F., *Der Wetlauf zum Jahre 2000* (Oldenburg: 1960).

Baker, O. E., 'Land utilization in the United States: geographical aspects of the problem', *The Geogr. Rev.*, Vol. 13, No. 1 (1923), pp. 1–26.

Brejnev, L. I., 'Un grand exploit du parti et du peuple', Discours à Alma-Ata (Moscow: 1974).

Brown, L. R. and P. Eckholm, *By Bread Alone* (New York: 1974).

Buringh, P., H. D. J. van Heemst and G. J. Staring, 'Computation of the absolute maximum food production of the world' (Wageningen: Agricultural University, 1975).

Clark, J. and S. Cole, 'Model of world food supply, demand and nutrition', *Food Policy* (1976) pp. 130–142.

Eckholm, E. P., *Losing Ground* (New York: 1976).

FAO, *Provisional Indicative World Plan for Agricultural Development* (Rome: 1969).

FAO/UNESCO, *Soil Map of the World, 1:5,000,000* (Paris: 1971–76).

Garbutt, J., H. Linnemann, *et al., Mensen tellen* (Utrecht: Aula 553, 1976).

Gifford, R. M., J. D. Kalma, A. R. Aston and R. J. Millington, 'Biophysical constraints in Australian food production: implications for population policy', Symposium 45th ANIAAS Congress (Perth: 1975); *Search*, Vol. 6, No. 6, pp. 212–223.

Gruhl, H., *Ein Planet wird geplündert* (Frankfurt: 1975).

Heady, E. O., 'The agriculture of the US', *Scientific American*, Vol. 235, No. 3 (1976), pp. 106–127.

Heemst, H. D. J. van, 'De bovengrens van de voedsel-productie op aarde', *Landbk. Tijdschr.*, Vol. 88, No. 6a (1976), pp. 202–205.

Hoogh, J. de, 'Voedsel voor een verdubbelde wereldbe-volking, een studie over de wereldvoedselsituatie op lange termijn', Symposium 'Voedsel voor allen, plaats en rol van de EEG' (Utrecht: 1976), pp. 4–23.

Hoogh, J. de, M. A. Keyzer, H. Linnemann and H. D. J. van Heemst, 'Food for a growing population. Some of the main findings of a study on the long-term prospects of the world food situation' (Amsterdam: Economic and Social Institute, Free University, 1976).

Kellogg, Ch. E. and A. C. Orvedal, 'Potential arable soils of the world and critical measures for their use', *Adv. in Agron.*, Vol. 21 (1969), pp. 109–170.

Keulen, H. van, 'Simulation of water use and herbage growth in arid regions', (Wageningen: Pudoc, 1975).

Koppejan, A. W. G., ' "Linnemann and after": het perspectief van de wereldvoedselvoorziening en de rol van de EEG', Symposium 'Voedsel voor allen, plaats en rol in de EEG' (Utrecht: 1976), pp. 60–65.

Kovda, V. A., *Biosphere, Soils and Their Utilization* (Moscow: 1974).

Liere, W. J. van, *World Food Production in Southeast Asia* (1977, in press).

Linnemann, H. and M. A. Keyzer (eds.), *MOIRA – A Model of International Relations in Agriculture* (Amsterdam: 1977 (in press)).

Meadows, D. and D. *et al.*, The Limits to Growth (New York: 1972).

Mesarović, M. and E. Pestel, *De Mensheid op een Kruispunt* (Amsterdam–Brussels: 1974).

Moen, H. J. and K. J. Beek, 'Literature study on the potential irrigated acreage in the world', (Wageningen: ILR Inst., 1974).

Mückenhausen, E., *Die Produktionskapazität der Böden der Erde* (Rheinisch-Westfälische Akademie der Wissenschaften, Vorträge N234, 1973), pp. 7–74.

Nowland, J. L., *The Agricultural Productivity of the Soils of Ontario and Quebec* (Ottawa: 1975a).

Nowland, J. L., *The Agricultural Productivity of the Soils of the Atlantic Provinces* (Ottawa: 1975b).

Psomopoulos, P., 'Man – his impact and dependence on the environment', IFIAS rep. no. 11 (Stockholm: Nairobi Workshop, October 1975), pp. 42–45.

Sanchez, P. A. and S. W. Buol, 'Soils of the tropics and the world food crisis', *Science*, Vol. 188 (1975), pp. 598–603.

Schuffelen, A. C., *Kunstmest voor Voedsel* (Wageningen: Diësrede, Landbouwhogeschool, 1965).

Simonson, R. W. 'Present and potential usefulness of soil resources' (Wageningen: An. Rep., IIL Recl., 1967), pp. 7–25.

US Report, *The World Food Problem. A Report of the President's Science Advisory Committee*, Vol. II (Washington: The White House, 1967).

World Development, 1977, Vol. 5, Nos. 5–7, pp. 487–495. Pergamon Press. Printed in Great Britain.

Assuring Our Food Supply – Technology, Resources and Policy*

SYLVAN H. WITTWER

Michigan State University, East Lansing

Summary. – This paper treats the problems of how to enhance agricultural output per unit of land area per unit of time – how to increase the productivity of the individual farmer. The author emphasizes the importance of combining a biophysical approach with a socio-politico-economic approach. He discusses new technologies related to food production, resources needed for crop and livestock production and policies required to achieve these new 'frontiers' of production, combining techniques with incentives.

INTRODUCTION

An adequate food supply should be the concern of all. It requires more than biophysical production technology. There are a host of socio-politico-economic, organizational, and institutional constraints and food policy issues. One of the most important is price with expectation of profit. Many countries still follow a cheap food policy which discourages production.

Food production must be doubled in the next 25–30 years. If people are to be fed it will come from increased production of plant and animal resources. The production of foodgrains alone must be increased at the rate of 25 million metric tons per year to keep pace with population increases and rising demands.

That people today are malnourished or starving is a question of food policy and distribution, resources and economics, not agricultural production limitations. There is enough food now produced to feed the world's hungry. We are producing more food *per capita* than ever before.

The people of the world today have about 20% more food *per capita* than 20 years ago. New records in food production were established in many nations in 1976 including the USA, USSR and India. The problem remains one of delivery. It is putting – or producing – the food where the people are, and providing an income so they can buy it. Only poor people go hungry.

Plants provide directly, or indirectly, up to 95% of the world's food supply. Increased production of crops can come from a combination of three approaches: (1) bringing more land into production; (2) enhancement of yields per unit land area; and, (3) increasing the number of crops produced per year. With livestock, increased output relates to better feeding, genetic improvement and environment and disease control. This paper will emphasize the enhancement of output per unit of land area per unit of time, and for each increment of water, energy, fertilizer and pesticide used. The productivity of the individual farmer must be

---

* Journal Article Number *7962* of the Michigan Agricultural Experiment Station. This paper is an extension, updating, and further amplification of three previous documents by the author: 'Research recommendations for increasing food, feed and fiber production in the USA' (Washington, D.C.: National Science Foundation, 1974); 'Food production: technology and the resource base', *Science,* Vol. 188 (1975), pp. 579–584; 'Increased crop yields and livestock productivity', *World Food Prospects and Agricultural Potential* (N.Y.: The Hudson Institute, 1977). Other resource documents included those of the Board on Agriculture and Renewable Resources (BARR) of the National Research Council, National Academy of Sciences, 'Agricultural production efficiency' (1975), 'Enhancement of food production for the United States' (1975), and 'Climate and food' (1976); the Proceedings of the International Conference, 'Crop productivity–research imperatives', jointly sponsored by the Michigan Agricultural Experiment Station and the Charles F. Kettering Foundation (1976); and the Report of the Office of Technology Assessment (US Congress) Panel on 'Assessment of alternatives for supporting high priority basic research to enhance food production'.

increased. This can be achieved by the development of new technologies, by farmers learning how to use them, and providing incentives to put them to use.

There is a great potential for increasing crop yields per unit land area per unit time. Bangladesh is an example. It is often said that every inch of land is cultivated. While 85% of its work force is in the field, it still fails to grow enough food. Yet, rice yields are only 50% as great as the world average, 25% of the USA, and only 15% of what it achieves in its own research stations. There is no technical reason why rice yield could not be doubled in Bangladesh. The answer must be in failures of information delivery systems, food policy issues, management of resources and/or the lack of incentives for farmers to produce.

Production strategy of the past has been to grow two ears of corn or two blades of grass where one grew before. We have been remarkably successful — never before have we produced so much food on so few hectares. There are now, however, storm clouds on the horizon. Global yields of grain per unit land area have plateaued. Recent increases in production have been achieved only by cultivating more land.

Enhancement of crop and livestock productivity should still be our first priority. There are now, however, other important and not always complementary objectives. We must also seek technologies which result in stable production at high levels, which are scale neutral; with the least possible inputs of the non-renewable resources of land, water, energy, fertilizer, and chemical pesticides; with achievable minimum environmental impacts; and with accompanying improvements in nutritional quality.

There have been many recent assessments of research priorities for increasing plant and animal resources for human consumption. One is impressed by the number of studies, as well as the alternatives. An increase of investment in research relating to the biological processes that control or limit crop and livestock productivity is a common theme. There is the consistent undertone that we know far more than is being put to use, and the ever present challenge to make operational the knowledge we now have. Thus far, the biopnysical research approach has been pursued, primarily and with vigour, but not without recognition of the significance of socio-economic-political institutional and policy aspects of the food problem. The description of opportunities which follow for increasing plant and animal resources for mankind are no exception. One looks to the biological processes that control productivity.

But, first of all, what is food for man and where does it come from? Chief among the major food crops, in approximate order of importance, are the cereal grains — rice, wheat, maize, sorghum, millet, barley, oats and rye; the seed legumes — field beans, peanuts, chick peas, pigeon peas, soybeans, mung beans and broad beans; the root and tuber crops — potatoes, sweet potatoes, cassava; the sugar crops — sugarcane and sugar beets; the tropical crops — bananas and coconuts. A great variety of fruits and vegetables are secondary staple crops that seldom get into economic surveys. Processed and fresh, they add personal enrichment and pleasure to eating and essential dietary nutrients. Hundreds of millions of people depend primarily on what is produced in gardens or small holdings. The consumers are the producers. Several crops a year may be grown. Hay, forages, pasture crops, trees and shrubs provide feed units for herds and flocks. Wastes and by-product utilization figure strongly in the production of swine and poultry.

Cereal grains constitute the most important food group on earth. They provide 60% of the calories and 50% of the protein consumed by man. 20% of the protein comes from seed legumes. About 25% of man's protein requirements and 10% of the calories and significant amounts of calcium and phosphorus are provided by livestock and poultry. Fish constitute 5% of man's protein needs.

FRONTIERS IN FOOD PRODUCTION

Attention should be directed to development of technologies for increased efficiency in photosynthate accumulation and partitioning, greater efficiency of biological nitrogen fixation and use by plants, and the development of new techniques for genetic engineering. These should include an expansion of those for conventional plant breeding as well as *in vitro* techniques for asexual approaches and wide crosses.

Crop yields are dependent more than anything else on the net accumulation of photosynthates in usable organs of the plant, and the availability of adequate supplies of nitrogen. Advances in photosynthetic efficiency and nitrogen fixation, in turn, depend on the integration or recombination of new types of genetic material. Recombinant DNA research will become important and the required specialized containment facilities to do it. The ultimate perfection of tissue culture techniques will provide a rapid means of screening genetic materials for more efficient mechanisms for accumulating and partitioning photosynthates and in utilizing applied fertilizer and enhancing biological nitrogen fixation. New technologies for greater photosynthetic efficiency, biological nitrogen fixation, and unconventional approaches to plant breeding and greater efficiency in nutrient uptake by plant roots are non-polluting, without noise, literally add to the resources of the earth for all mankind, and are non-political. They are permanent and without limit.

Photosynthesis

The most extraordinary mechanism ever devised is the photosynthetic process. Green plants, as yet, are the primary harvesters of free solar energy and net producers of food and energy on a renewable basis. Agriculture is basically a solar energy processing machine. It is the only industry that utilizes today's incident solar radiation, and is man's largest current user of solar energy. Agriculture can achieve a uniquely distinctive role in the energy balance of the world. Harvesting the sun, however, requires the management of land, and often irrigation water, fertilizer and other proxies. The geometry of agriculture demands that crops be distributed over the land in a layer of a few inches thick for maximization of the capture of sunlight. Livestock must also be dispersed for most effective utilization of grazing, pasture, savanna, and prairie lands. The sun strikes everywhere. It is, therefore, the business of agriculture to collect and store solar energy as food, feed and fibre in plant and animal products and to do it with utmost efficiency. Man has specialized in and depends on the culture of sun-loving crops.

There are many researchable alternatives for enhancement of photosynthesis. They include identification and control of the mechanisms that regulate and could reduce the wasteful processes of both dark and light induced (photo) respiration; mechanisms responsible for redistribution of photosynthates which in turn regulate yield and maximize the 'Harvest Index'; resolution of the hormonal mechanisms that control flowering and leaf senescence; improvements in plant architecture and anatomy, cropping systems, planting designs and cultural practices for better light reception; and carbon dioxide enrichment of crop atmospheres.

Biological nitrogen fixation

This is the second most important and magnificent process on earth. It is the primary source of food protein. It is agriculturally important with legumes, some non-legumes, and has potential for many crops.

The first initiative for new technology in biological nitrogen fixation should be with legumes. They have a demonstrated efficient system with good chances for a quick payoff. Furthermore, legumes make important global contributions to yield improvement and continuing productive food systems in the tropics, sub-tropics, and for temperate zone agriculture. They provide seed pods for man, forages for livestock, and a means for soil improvement and ground cover for alleviation of soil erosion. All legumes have rhizobial associations in root nodules which provide a built-in nitrogen source. Nevertheless, legumes often obtain 75% or more of their nitrogen from that already in the soil. Only 25% is fixed in the nodules. Yet, this 25% rate is limiting for growth. Production of all legumes could be substantially increased if nitrogen fixation in the nodules could be improved. It has been dramatically demonstrated that photosynthates are a major limiting factor in nitrogen fixation. A major effort should be directed toward increasing the photosynthetic energy source in legumes. A second approach should be the development of super strains of rhizobia for each of the several species that infect the major food legumes. The alternative is to improve the host plant and its environment; explore the effects of variety, age, pH, temperature, and soil nutrient levels.

Blue-green algae in tropical soils and in rice paddies offer a special opportunity. A special blue-green algal relationship has been noted. It involves the minute aquatic fern, *Azolla*, and the algae, *Anabena*. The fern becomes 'infected' with algae. The amount of nitrogen fixed under this relationship may exceed 600 kilograms per hectare per year. Unlike legumes, nitrogen fixation is not limited by available energy since both the blue-green algae and the tiny fern have built-in energy sources. The science and art of *Azolla–Anabena* culture poses a fascinating opportunity for improvement of yields of rice without the addition of, or with a minimal amount of, nitrogen fertilizer.

Genetic improvement

Some of the most remarkable increases in food crop productivity have occurred here. The standard techniques of selection based on phenotypic expression, controlled hybridization, and more recently, selection for better nutritional qualities have given us super strains of rice, wheat, maize, sorghum, millet, some legumes, and many fruits and vegetables of excellent nutritional quality.

While standard plant breeding techniques will likely predominate in the forseeable future, there are other frontiers. One is a modification of conventional breeding technology developed by International Agricultural Research Centres. It consists of massive high volume crossing, broad use of existing genetic material, and wide regional evaluation of huge segregating populations by teams of agriculturists. Significant advances have also occurred in defining techniques for isolating protoplasts (plant cells without walls), their fusion and subsequent regeneration into new plants. These new cellular approaches to plant breeding could become a major avenue for new species building with greater yield, resistance to stresses, toxins, and improved nutritional quality. Results of studies on transformations and regeneration of parasexual hybrids from fixed protoplasts could revolutionize agriculture.

The collection, preservation and utilization of genetic materials of food crops is vital for alleviation of genetic, climatic and chemical vulnerability. Merely broadening the genetic base of major food crop varieties will not prevent disease epidemics or crop disasters. Germplasm is the key. The natural variation must be preserved that exists in cultivated and wild species. This is a major natural resource. The preservation of genetic materials of the principal food crops is now proceeding on a systematic and world-wide basis. The process is relatively simple for the cereal grains, the seed legumes, forages, and many vegetables. Those that are vegetatively propagated (potatoes, sweet potatoes, cassava, fruit trees), however, pose a special problem. There is now an effort to freeze meristems in liquid nitrogen for the preservation of genetic stocks of vegetatively propagated food crops. This will require high technology.

Genetic improvement in nutrient components

Cereals dominate in the diets of most people. Progress in raising levels of protein and critically deficient amino acids with cereal grains has been singular. Rice, wheat and barley selections have been identified with higher protein levels. There is no cheaper, better or quicker way to solve the protein needs of people in most agriculturally developing nations than to improve the cereals that they eat. Both the biological value and the level of the protein of maize have been enhanced using the opaque-2-recessive gene, and, more recently, in corn of normal background. Rice, wheat, and barley selections of higher protein levels have been identified. Triticale, the new synthetic species, with its improved nutritional contributions, great adaptability, and high yields is now receiving limited commercial acceptance. Recent evidence indicates that the protein quality of cereals is inversely related to their prolamine content. The following is indicative.

Prolamine content of cereals

5–10%	30–40%	50–60%
Rice	Wheat	Maize
Oats	Barley	Sorghum

Maize and sorghum are high in prolamine, and while photosynthetically efficient under hot-dry conditions (C_4 plants) are designated as 'coarse' grains; whereas rice and wheat, being less efficient in fixing solar energy and carbon dioxide (C_3 plants), are known as the 'nobel' grains. The combining of high productivity with superior protein quality, and 'nobel' grain characteristics remains as one of the great research challenges.

There are other opportunities. Some indigenous, highly productive, high protein and potentially important food crops could be utilized. Two examples are legumes with built-in nitrogen sources. One is the pods and seeds of the desert mesquite. The other is the winged bean of the tropics. All parts of the winged bean plant may be harvested for human food.

There is the strong suggestion that the world's food problem, from the standpoint of a balanced diet, is not one of protein deficiency, but caloric adequacy. If sufficient calories are provided through conventional cereals and seed legumes and the biological values of the proteins of these same crops are genetically upgraded, there would be no protein problem. Indeed it has been demonstrated that most of the clinically-observed 'protein malnutrition' is the secondary consequence of a caloric inadequacy that occurs with people whose diets contain sufficient protein but which they are unable to assimilate when caloric uptake is inadequate.

This observation should cast new interest for the potential of the high energy root crops –

sweet potatoes and cassava. These food crops predominate in much of the developing world. Their further promotion might well be predicated on the fact that calorie deficiencies are very common with hundreds of millions of people in South America, Southeast Asia and in Equatorial Africa. The intent with cassava should not be to develop a major food protein source but one of calories. Here the potential is tremendous. Yields of up to 50 metric tons per hectare have already been achieved in Brazil.

Roots, mycorrhizae, and nutrient uptake

Fertilizer manufacture is the most important industrial input into agricultural productivity. Yet only 50% of the nitrogen and less than 35% of the phosphorus and potassium applied as fertilizer in the USA are recovered by crops. The recovery of fertilizer nitrogen in the rice paddies of the tropics is only 25–35%. The balance is lost to the environment. Denitrification loses nitrogen to the atmosphere and encourages losses in the soil from leaching. Food production could be greatly improved if these enormous losses, particularly of nitrogen, in the warm soils of the tropics could be partially reduced. Much of the loss of nitrogen occurs from bacteria-induced nitrification and subsequent denitrification. Nitrification inhibitors, both natural and synthetic, applied with ammonia or urea are effective deterrents to leaching and atmospheric losses of nitrogen. Their use is just beginning on a global scale. Expenditures for fertilizer could be greatly reduced. Non-renewable resources would be preserved, and our food supply could be greatly improved. It has been estimated that biological denitrification alone depletes the soil of 120 million tons of nitrogen annually. This is almost 3 times the amount which is chemically fixed as fertilizer.

An important approach to better recovery of soil applied fertilizer and also to increased crop productivity on marginal soils is a further microbiological one. In sharp contrast to the action of nitrifying bacteria which greatly reduce fertilizer nitrogen utilization, other micro-organisms – the mycorrhizae – specifically the endomycorrhizae, may result in large increases in the uptake of phosphorus and other poorly mobile ions. Almost all food crops respond. Mycorrhizae are obligate parasites. They can be viewed as fungal extensions of root systems. They can help roots absorb nutrients, and they can stimulate growth and nitrogen fixation by legumes, especially on phosphorus

deficient soils. There are super strains of mycorrhizae and crops can be inoculated with them. Mycorrhizal fungi have been reported to significantly increase yields of both legumes and cereal grains. Research with mycorrhizae in particular, and in soil microbiology in general, has scarcely been initiated.

There is another grossly neglected researchable area in food production and delivery which involves technology, resources and policy. It relates to the effects of changing climatic and weather patterns on agricultural productivity and what can be done about them. Weather and climate are still the most determinate factors in food production. We should no longer ignore the potential, through research for precipitation enhancement and the alleviation of major droughts, for making our crops more climate proof. Year-to-year, or season-to-season, fluctuations in temperature, precipitation and sunlight are far greater than any long-term climate trends which have thus far been identified. There is much that can be done to alleviate weather stain. These include crop variety development, cultural practices, pest management, and judicious use of land and water resources.

Pest management

Crop losses from insects, diseases and weeds are enormous. They range from a high of 46% for rice to a low of 24% for wheat. The aggregate is 35% of potential production for all crops. It is astonishing that the greatest loss of all occurs with rice, the number one food crop on earth. Losses from pests are derived from that which is in large part already synthesized by the green plant. A mere 10 to 20% reduction in losses from pests would provide food for hundreds of millions of people. Effective pest control practices could eliminate 50% of the current losses in food.

Toxic chemicals, heretofore, have provided the main foundation for contemporary pest control practices. Here crop protection technology becomes obsolete at an alarming rate. More than a billion pounds of pesticides are used in the world each year.[1] Meanwhile, systems of integrated pest management are emerging and can be created for all crops. These are a combination of all pest control technologies and their integration into crop production. Included in such pest management strategies are natural enemies, resistant varieties, cultural practices, and chemicals. The concept is environmental management – to ally with components of nature, getting the greatest return in food production with the least expenditure of resources. The intent is to manage pests with the least cost to man and the environment. The result is to alleviate pesticide shortages, reduce costs, minimize environmental contamination and to increase and stabilize the food crop production. The technology is useful for all crops on all pests in every region of the earth.

Allelopathy for weed control is an emerging technology. It is defined as mutual harm, where chemicals produced and released by one plant species inhibit the growth of another. There will still emerge new ways to fight pests with less chemical and energy inputs.

Chemicals known as bioregulators can be expected to have exciting impacts on agricultural productivity. They often duplicate genetic effects. There is new hope and interest in improvement of yields of agronomic crops prompted by the use of chemical ripeners that enhance sugar yields by as much as 10% on sugarcane. Better test methods and low volume application will open new frontiers for useful application.

Land, water, energy, human labour

These are primary resources for crop and livestock production. They are interrelated and one can be partially interchanged or substituted for the others. The recent decrease in the output–input ratio for energy into crop production in the USA resulted in millions of hectares of land freed from corn production as a result of the adoption of new technology. Soybean hectarage expanded almost proportionately. It requires less fossil fuel energy inputs than corn because of a built-in nitrogen supply through biological nitrogen fixation; and less energy is needed for drying the harvested product.

Land, water and energy interrelationships are quickly apparent in irrigated areas, where an additional energy input is required for water management. Fossil energy power can be used to reduce the labour–manpower input and vice versa. Likewise, increasing the intensity of land management (through the use of water, fertilizer, pesticides) can reduce the amount of land needed, and the reverse is true. The land and water base can also be changed with time and technology.

Two major problems are now placing restrictions on the natural substitutability of energy, labour and land in agricultural production.

First, prime agricultural land is disappearing on a global scale because of irreversible use; and second, it is being seriously degraded by erosion.

Problems of soil erosion are global. For 40 years, the Soil Conservation Service of the US Department of Agriculture has promoted sound conservation practices, supported by technical and financial assistance, education, persuasion and appeals to good land stewardship. It hasn't been too effective. After 40 years, only 25% of our farm lands are under approved conservation practices. Meanwhile, enormous losses of topsoil from our best lands continue.[2]

More energy efficient land and water utilization and conservation strategies can be designed. New conservation technologies can be developed for increasing yields of small and large holdings. The introduction of resource conservation oriented science into farms of all sizes would be to exploit one of the greatest opportunities for the enhancement of global food production. In the USA a series of agricultural technologies has been developed with labour-saving equipment, for large-scale units, and with huge inputs of capital, management and resources. Much of the world may not want nor can it handle such technologies where energy, land and water are in short supply, where unemployment is rampant, and management is lacking. Food producing technologies should be sought after that are scale-neutral, labour-intensive and result in stable production at high levels and with a minimum of capital, management and resource inputs.

Reduced tillage is one. The plough, long a symbol of American agriculture, has caused irreparable losses from wind and water erosion. The use of appropriate chemicals for weed control has now established the reality of improved crop productivity without plowing the land. The plough is gradually being retired. Over 7 million acres in the USA were planted in 1976 without tillage, and on over 50 million acres tillage was reduced from the conventional level. Reduced tillage is the most significant technology man has yet developed for control of soil erosion, for maximization of cover on the land, and for the conservation of energy, labour, water, soil fertility and organic matter for the main food producing areas of the earth.[3] In addition, a higher proportion of land in hilly areas can be brought into production or planted to more profitable crops.

The number of kilograms of water needed to produce a kilogram of food is a most important variable. Practically no research has been done in this area. Large differences in transpiration losses exist among species varying from a scale of 100 for pineapple to 400–500 for cereals and seed legumes to over 1,000 for some fruits and vegetables. The water requirement of sugarcane per unit land area in Hawaii is 5 times that of pineapple. Why these differences? Research can give the answers.

Equally important are new water management technologies for food crop production. Efficiency of usage of irrigation water varies from 20–40% in the United States to 80–85% in Israel. Drip or trickle irrigation will reduce by 50% the water now used in conventional irrigation systems (flooding, sprinkling, furrow) for food crop production. There are many other concurrent advantages for high value crops. Soil erosion is reduced to a minimum. No land is wasted to build irrigation ditches. There is no leaching, run-off or drainage water pollution. Weed control and fertilizer can be optimized and crop and soil management and harvest operations can be conducted without interference. Even greater promise for efficient water use with less capital investment, resource inputs, and management are the prospects for high frequency irrigation.[4]

Food losses

It has been estimated that losses of energy and waste and effluent in food processing could be reduced by 35 and 80% respectively. Food losses between harvest and consumption could be reduced by 30 to 50%. All this could increase the available food by 10–15% without more land or increasing yields. Annual production of crop and animal wastes in the USA exceeds 800 million tons of dry matter. The US produces 1.2 billion pounds of seafood waste and 35 million tons of fruit and vegetable processing wastes. Globally, approximately 150 pounds of cellulose is produced daily for each of the earth's 4 billion inhabitants. This is equivalent to 1.7×10^{11} tons of dry biomass annually, of which only about 1% is currently used for fuel and about 1% for food and feed. The vegetation of the earth through its photosynthetic ability produces every year 12 times as much energy as all human beings consume. Economic incentives as well as inadequate technologies are not yet conducive to improved utilization of these vast resources in food, feed, fibre and energy production systems.

Forage production and range management

Forage and range production is not a direct food source for man, but indirectly provides a food supply for approximately 2.5 billion ruminant animals useful to man. It is technically and economically feasible to double this production on the range and pasture lands of temperate zones. Land and water resources for forage production in the tropics are enormous. There are three distinct areas that extend from the Tropics of Cancer to Capricorn remarkably adapted for forage production – the lowlands, the high elevations and the cerrada or savanna. Tremendous productivity is possible in the tropics with yields approaching 60 tons of dry matter per hectare per year. There are at least four frontiers of technology for global improvement of forage crops for livestock: higher yielding types, increased nutritive values, improved harvest techniques, and the merger of production and utilization systems.

Animal productivity

Livestock numbers of the earth are double the human population. Domestic animals produce meat, milk and eggs from nutrients derived from crops, forages, and by-products that have less value elsewhere. Food resources produced by animals fall into two categories: those derived from ruminants (dairy, beef cattle, water buffalo, sheep, goats, llama, alpaca) and the monogastric (swine, poultry, guinea pig, rabbits). Ruminants provide foods of the highest quality from range and grassland, forages, plant by-products, crop residues and browse. Swine and poultry are providers of food derived from consumption of many products not edible by man.

Livestock in agriculturally developing nations serve as important sources of food, dietary improvement, income, power, fuel and fertilizer, and are a living food reservoir. The latter exceeds the present world-wide commercial grain reserves (40 days compared to 27), and is not concentrated in a few surplus nations. An increase in livestock resources can come from improved production and utilization of feeds, disease control and genetic improvement. The opportunities for better feeding lie in forage and range production. Yield increases of 2% a year are reasonable and within reach. Utilization of by-products for feed could be tripled. The low reproductive efficiency of livestock now results in 50% of potential animals lost. Twinning in dairy and beef cattle can become a reality through hormone treatment for super ovulation, controlled breeding, recovery of fertilized eggs and non-surgical embryo transfer to recipient females of lesser breeding value.

A loss of $20 billion occurs annually from animal diseases in the US. It is much greater abroad. Reductions in loss from epidemic and infectious diseases up to 50% is a possible and realistic goal.

Farming systems

Technologies relating thereto are the most promising of all for enhancement of the supply, increase of dependability, and improvement of the nutritional quality of food. They at the same time are the most difficult to design and execute. Management of farming systems research is contrary to the traditional disciplinary approach. Special and expanded administrative skills are required. Future progress in increasing crop and livestock productivity from research must come from packages that articulate simultaneous efforts on several frontiers.

The number and array of sub-systems at the farm level are enormous. There are diverse systems for land, water, energy, fertilizer, mechanization, labour, waste, pests and climate. There are cropping systems, livestock systems and tillage practices which bridge all the above resource systems. There are many alternatives systems for managing beef cattle operations, swine units, dairy herds; and the production of corn, cassava, cotton, soybeans or sugar beets. Farming systems technologies must be broken down into local geographical and ecological areas, and to cite specific socio-economic, food policy, institutional and political conditions.

Food systems must extend beyond the farm gate. There are diverse processing, handling, storage, transportation, packaging and marketing systems. Domestic and international trade and port facilities are involved. There are regulatory inputs; taxation of inputs and products; availability of credit and subsidies; institutions to serve and create new technologies; a complex of public and private support; food policies, and an infrastructure to provide supplies and services — to supply food for people everywhere.

POLICY[5]

The success of any food production and delivery system resides not only in the application of science and new biophysical technology, but in economic, social and political incentives to produce, based on the promulgation of a free-enterprise system and a family farm base. Prices are the key signals for farmers to produce. Unless these signals indicate an expectation of profit, production will slow down, and often cease beyond that required for farmers' families.

Half the people of the world depend upon a subsistence type of agriculture, and 40% of the cultivated land of the world is in the hands of subsistence farmers. Government regulations and political constraints frequently establish price and control profits. There is little incentive to produce beyond that needed for immediate survival.

Storage capability of indigenous production in subsistence agricultural systems is grossly lacking, but if available would provide production goal incentives for farmers, family food security, opportunity to manage a part of the market system, and a means of improving seed stocks.

Small-scale, labour-intensive, capital and resource scarce farming is the one great and unexploited food production frontier. Intermediate technology is the prerequisite. It is built upon meeting simple equipment needs. The incomes of a billion people depend on farms of less than 5 hectares. The output per hectare on these mini-holdings can exceed by one-third that of large US farms. Increments of fertilizer or pesticides or other technologies or economic and social incentives in Southeast Asia, Latin America or Africa or even the USSR would have telling effects on food productivity.

South Korea has during the past year become 95% self-sufficient in the production of rice, its No. 1 food crop. Technology made its contribution through the introduction of 'Tongil', a new dwarf type of rice that is cold tolerant, early in maturity, and resistant to blast. Equally important was the profit incentive to the farmer encouraged by government policies and a strong market demand that resulted in a price increase of 121%.

Technologies that would enhance yield stability of food crops could be as important as an increase in yields for encouraging farmers to adopt new practices. An example is pest control. Without a sense of stability, farmers are not likely to make investments in agriculture that require more than one growing season to amortize. Enhancement and stability of production in aggregate with the possibility of profit can be regarded as positive incentives to produce.

CONCLUSIONS

Only scientists develop new technologies. Only farmers produce food. Motivation and incentives are important both for scientific discovery and food production. Food policy, political will, and institutions also play a key role. The time between a basic research discovery and its application averages 13 years. The time from introduction of a new technology until its adoption reaches the expected ceiling is 35 years. It now takes 6–10 years to train scientists to do research. Hence we must lengthen the stride and quicken the pace of agricultural development. New technologies must be tailored to each local condition. This can best be done by scientists who also know how to farm – a combination which is becoming rare, indeed.

Photosynthesis is the most important single process on this planet and has considerable unutilized potential in the production of an adequate food supply. Only green plants can convert sunlight to chemical energy which provides man with food, feed and fibre. However, scarcely 1% of the sunlight which falls on the plants is captured. Thus, research must be carried out to correct this deficiency and to fully exploit this great resource.

NOTES

1. 'Contemporary pest control practices and prospects', the Report of the Executive Committee Study on Problems of Pest Control, Environmental Studies Board of the National Research Council, National Academy of Sciences, Washington, D.C. (1975).

2. E. P. Eckholm, *Losing Ground, Environmental Stresses and World Food Prospects* (New York: W. W. Norton and Co., 1976), 223 pp. D. Pimental, E. C. Terhune, R. Dyson-Hudson, S. Rochereau, R. Samis, E. A. Smith, D. Denman, D. Reifschneider, and M. Shepard, 'Land degradation: effects on food and energy resources', *Science,* Vol. 194 (1976), pp. 149–155.

3. G. B. Triplett, Jr. and D. M. Van Doren, Jr., 'Agriculture without tillage', *Scientific American,* Vol. 236, No. 1 (1977), pp. 28–33.

4. S. L. Rawlins, 'High frequency and green revolution food production', Paper presented to the New York Academy of Sciences (Philadelphia: 1–3 December 1976).

5. Some thoughts expressed here were derived from a paper prepared by the author for the United States Information Agency, Washington, D.C., in January 1977, entitled, 'The challenge to science for food production'.

World Development, 1977, Vol. 5, Nos. 5–7, pp. 497–506. Pergamon Press. Printed in Great Britain.

Projections of World Demand for and Supply of Foodgrains: An Attempt at Methodological Evaluation

ROMESH DIWAN*

*Rensselaer Polytechnic Institute,
Troy, New York*

Summary. – This paper deals with some of the problems involved in making projections of world demand for and supply of foodgrains. The author evaluates and compares the projection methods used by the Food and Agriculture Organization, the US Department of Agriculture, and the Organization for Economic Co-operation and Development. The paper raises some questions about the usefulness and reliability of the various projections.

INTRODUCTION

Any economic policy requires some idea about probable direction and magnitudes of relevant economic quantities in the future. Projections of economic quantities, thus, are extremely important tools of economic policy. It is particularly so in the supply of and demand for food where large disequilibria can, literally, lead to famine, mass deaths and massive economic dislocation.[1] Yet, projections of food supply and demand are comparatively recent. Basically, these started in the 1950s; one of the earliest being made by Sinha.[2] In early 1960s international organizations entered this field. The United States Department of Agriculture (USDA) commissioned a number of studies for projections of agricultural commodities for various countries. These came out in the early 1960s.[3] The Food and Agricultural Organization (FAO) produced its first set of international projections in 1962[4] and another in 1966.[5] The Organization for Economic Co-operation and Development (OECD) published its own projections in 1968.[6] In the 1970s, these projections have been revised or updated. In 1971, FAO and USDA came out, separately, with a set of projections for 1980. Again in 1974, both FAO and USDA published, separately, projections for 1985.[7] Last year, OECD also joined in with its own projections

for 1985. In addition, during the last six years there have been many projections for individual countries. This paper, however, is concerned with international projections only. It is restricted to the projections that have come out from the three agencies – FAO, OECD and USDA – since 1970. Its purpose is to evaluate and compare the various projections.

FOODGRAIN PROJECTIONS FOR 1980 AND 1985

Tables 1 and 2 (*overleaf*) give projected values of demand and production of foodgrains for 1980 and 1985, respectively. The projections are for the world, developing countries, developed countries and centrally-planned countries. FAO and USDA provide projections for 1980. FAO, OECD and USDA have projections for 1985. However, OECD has published its projections by bits and pieces only[8] so that projections for aggregate areas in Tables 1 and 2 are not available. Accordingly, Table 2 does not contain projections from OECD. USDA, on the

---

* I have gained very much from discussions with, and comments on an earlier draft from Radha Sinha. An earlier version of this paper was presented to a seminar at Cambridge University. I am thankful to Ajit Singh for helpful comments.

Table 1. *Projection for cereals in 1980*
(in million metric tons)

Region	Base Year 1964–66		Projection Year 1980			
	FAO	USDA	FAO	USDA		
				Set I	Set II	Set III
Developing						
P	263.9	246.1	435.8	390.5	458.8	346.9
D	275.5	261.7	439.3	426.3	469.5	399.1
B	−11.6	−15.6	− 4.5	−35.8	−10.7	−52.2
Developed						
P	357.0	344.4	510.8	482.7	475.8	487.4
D	337.4	326.4	447.0	440.4	451.4	433.1
B	+19.6	+18.0	+63.8	+42.3	+24.4	+54.3
Centrally Planned						
P	329.4	313.7	480.8	440.8	440.4	441.0
D	343.5	327.2	479.4	442.4	442.7	442.3
B	−14.1	−13.5	+ 1.4	− 1.6	− 2.3	− 1.3
World						
P	950.4	904.2	1427.4	1314.0	1375.0	1275.3
D	956.5	915.3	1365.7	1309.2	1363.6	1274.8
B	− 6.1	−11.1	+ 61.7	+ 4.8	+ 11.4	+ .8

Source: FAO, *Agricultural Commodities Projections 1970–80,* p. 892. USDA, *World Demand Prospects for Grains in 1980,* pp. 78–79.
Notes: P = Production; D = Demand; B = Balance=(P-D). Developing, Developed and Centrally Planned refer to FAO's Class II, Class I and Class III respectively.

Table 2. *Projections for cereals in 1985*
(in million metric tons)

Region	Base Year 1969–71		Projection Year − 1985				
	FAO	USDA	FAO	USDA			
				Set I	Set II	Set III	Set IV
Developing							
P	585	443	853	632	648	626	721
D	590	466	929	691	726	678	743
B	− 5	−23	−76	−59	−78	−52	−22
Developed							
P	654	638	NA	918	972	877	925
D	617	596	796	857	892	823	900
B	37	42	NA	61	80	54	25
World							
P	1,239	1,082	NA	1,550	1,620	1,504	1,646
D	1,207	1,062	1,725	1,548	1,618	1,502	1,644
B	32	20		2	2	2	2

Source: USDA (1975), p. 35, Table 16. The details of these estimates and the differences between FAO and USDA projections are given in this source. Developing countries include Asian centrally-planned countries and developing market economies.

other hand, has 3 sets of projections for 1980 and 4 for 1985.

Looking at Table 1, for projections for 1980, one finds that FAO projects a huge surplus in the world while USDA projects a much smaller surplus — USDA III virtually nil. FAO projects a very large surplus for developed countries and a small deficit for developing countries. USDA, by comparison, projects a much smaller surplus and much larger deficit.

In Table 2, for 1985, USDA projects just about equilibrium for the world. UN (1974) does not provide projections for the developed countries, and, therefore, for the world. The major difference between the two projections is that FAO projects a surplus in centrally-planned Asian countries as against a deficit by USDA. Also FAO projects a very large deficit for the developing countries in general and more so in particular for the developing market economies. USDA projections, in this respect, are just the opposite.

If one were to formulate policy measures on the basis of these projections, policies implied by FAO projections are quite different from, even opposite to, those implied by USDA projections. For example, FAO projects a large surplus for 1980 so that one can argue for a policy to reduce production; USDA projections, on the other hand, would imply a policy to encourage production. A policy-maker can be, and is, genuinely confused. Whom should he/she believe?

Whenever one compares two projections, one naturally asks the question: which of these projections is 'better'? However natural or simplistic this question, the answer is not obvious; it may never be categorical. Comparisons are not easy. The projections are the end result of a large exercise involving purpose, methodology, data etc. Every projection, therefore, has to be analysed in depth. Thus, one has to answer the prior question of how good a particular projection is. The following sections are an attempt to provide information on this question.

GENERAL METHODOLOGY

Projections, basically, are conditional forecasts. A projection involves the determination of the value of a variable, Y, at a future date, $t + S$, given the value of some other related variables, $X_1, X_2 \ldots X_n$, and their values at that future date. Thus, it implies a relationship between Y and X_i ($i=1\ldots n$). Such a relationship may be expressed mathematically, and is known as a model. The simplest form of a model is a single equation.[9] It may be written as

$$Y = f(X_1 \ldots X_n)$$

where Y is the variable to be projected, f the form of the function and X_i ($i=1\ldots n$) the variables taken as 'given'.

Projection procedures involve the following steps. (i) Choice of X_i. This is determined by question at hand, availability of data and the received economic theory. (ii) Determination or specification of the form f; should it be a linear, log-linear, polynomial, etc? In all cases, it is defined by a number of parameters, A_i ($i=1\ldots n$). (iii) Estimation of A_i. This depends upon the nature of the model, size of the data set, computer facilities and estimation techniques available from statistical and econometric theory. (iv) Forecasts of X_i ($i=1\ldots n$) for the projection period, $t + S$. Forecasts for Y, then, follows mechanistically. It needs to be emphasized that all these four steps are highly interrelated and interdependent.[10]

Once the projections have been made, evaluation raises quite a few questions. The most important of these questions are related to the criteria for evaluation. There is very little literature on the evaluation of projections and still less on the relevant criteria.[11] In view of the lack of a standard, or generally acceptable, criteria set, we suggest below two sets of criteria based on (i) the various steps in making projections, and (ii) general considerations and commonsense.

Taking Set I first, the following six criteria can be laid out.

(Ia) Model: Is the model simple or sophisticated? Does it answer the basic questions, if any?

(Ib) Data: Are these available? Are these reliable?

(Ic) Estimation: Have the coefficients been estimated scientifically — by statistical or econometric techniques — or a priori? Are these coefficients plausible based on economic theory?

(Id) Forecasts of exogenous variables: Are these made by projectors themselves? Have these been borrowed? How 'reliable' are these?

(Ie) Prediction errors: Certain statistical estimation techniques ensure that the variance of prediction errors is minimal. Can prediction errors be estimated? How large are these?

(If) Performance: How do these projections compare with the past quantities, i.e. if the projections are made for the past periods, how would they compare with the actual quantities? How do they perform in the future?

In Set II we suggest three other criteria:

(IIa) Comprehensiveness: How comprehensive are these projections?

(IIb) Cost:[12] Is the cost of making projections high or low or minimum?

(IIc) Reputation of the projector: What sort of biases are liable to be introduced by the institution that is making projections?

It needs to be emphasized that it may not be possible to give a categorical answer to the question: is a projection good or bad? The criteria are multi-dimensional and much will depend upon the judgement of the evaluator.[13] In the following we examine various projections on the basis of the above criteria.

FAO METHODOLOGY AND PROJECTIONS

FAO methodology for projections has been described in detail in FAO (1971), Vol. II.[14] This volume contains projections for 1980. Projections for 1985 are upgraded and presented in UN (1974).[15] The projections are made for a large number of commodities including cereals. Cereals are divided into 3 sub-groups: wheat, rice and coarse grains.[16] The projections are made for 132 countries, divided into 22 sub-regions and 11 regions.[17]

By and large, the methodology consists of developing two single equation models; one each for production[18] and demand. The production model is the simplest. Conceptually, it is $\log Q_t = Q_o + A_t$ where Q refers to production and t to time. The production projections, thus, are straightforward extrapolations of the trend; more specifically, extrapolations of the exponential growth rates. For 1980, the production trends were based on the period 1955—1969/70. However,

> extrapolations were not in themselves the projections of production but rather a guide to the commodity specialist who . . . . modified the trends — or sometimes discarded them completely — according to their assessment of likely influences.[19]

The starting point for these projections is the period 1964—66 average. 1985 projections, on the other hand, are based on the trends for the period 1961—73, with the starting point as 1969—71 average.[20]

Demand projections were made by relating demand for food with income and population; in some cases time trend was also included. Conceptually, the relation is given by $D_t = A_1 Y_t + A_2 P_t + A_3 t$ where D, Y and P refer to demand, income and population, respectively, and t stands for time period. Coefficients A_1, A_2 and A_3 were estimated separately. They were *not* estimated jointly by a multivariate regression. A_1, the elasticity of income,[21] was estimated for each country on the basis of various studies: some on historical data for average national *per capita* consumption and income, others on data from family budget surveys, and still others on the basis of international comparisons.[22] A_2, the effect of population on food demand, was developed from food balance sheets for every country for the period 1964—66. From these balance sheets indices of increase in *per capita* demand were developed. A_3, the trend factor, was estimated, in some cases only, by conditional regression.

Initially, projections for 1970, 1975 and 1980 were made on the basis of the 1964—66 data base. 1970 actuals were then compared with 1970 projections. In the final form projections for 1975 and 1980 were corrected by the ratio: 1970 actual/1970 projected. The difference between 1980 and 1985 is basically the difference between 1980 and 1985 forecasts of income and population.[23]

EVALUATION OF FAO METHODOLOGY AND PROJECTIONS

To evaluate FAO methodology and projections, on the basis of the criteria suggested above, let us start with Set I. Looking at the model — criterion (Ia) — one finds that the model is a very simple one. In 1980 projections the particular question — or a set of questions — that the projections are supposed to help answer, is never posed. It seems it is a technical exercise to project quantities in the hope these will be useful. The question for 1985 projections, on the other hand, is well articulated; it is to assess the food situation. The choice of variables is rather limited — basically income and population. Obviously, there are other important variables: urbanization, distribution of income, prices, etc. to name a few. Mention is made of other factors; but they remain only at that level.

In view of the size of projections for 1980, the data needed — (Ib) — is very large indeed. One is doubtful if these data are (a) available and (b) reliable for a very large number of developing countries.[24] In view of these data inadequacies, one wonders if it is wise to present such detailed projections.[25] As regards estimation of coefficients — (Ic) — by and large, income elasticities have been estimated by Ordinary Least Squares. However, there are a number of estimates based only on 'judgement'; the distinction between the two, unfortunately, has not been made clear. In view of the 'messaging' of these estimates, they do conform to the logic of economic theory. The forecasts of income and population – (Id) – have been taken from the United Nations and not made in FAO. It does raise a conceptual question: are population and income growth independent of each other?[26] Since the estimates of the coefficients have been made by 'judgement' or *a priori* expectations, it is not possible to work out the prediction errors – (Ie) – in terms of statistical theory. FAO projections make no attempt to provide these errors. One can safely assume that these errors, if these can be estimated, are neither zero nor minimum.[27] So far as performance – (If) – is concerned, the exercise is not possible for 1980 or 1985 at this time. One wished FAO had presented year by year projections. In that case, some of the projections could have been compared with actual quantities. FAO also has not provided the result of the exercise of comparing the projections for the previous years, say 1965–70, with the actual quantities.[28] One wishes it had done so.

Coming to criteria Set II, FAO 1980 projections do seem rather comprehensive (IIa). As has been pointed out above (Ib) regarding data, the comprehensiveness may be more apparent than real. No data on costs – (IIb) – is ever given, hence there is no way to judge their 'efficiency'. Knowing international – for that matter national – organizations, one can safely assume that the costs are quite high. They are by no means minimal.[29] At this stage it is difficult to gauge the reputation – (IIc) – of FAO in terms of its capability to make projections. It can certainly acquire the best talent and data yet it is severely handicapped by political decision-making.[30] One would thus expect it to be biased towards comprehensiveness and against accuracy.

Overall, FAO projections seem to be simple-minded, technically deficient, and rather expensive. They contain immeasurable biases and errors. Having presented only one projection, without reference to possible errors due to a large number of reasons, they give a wrong impression of scientificity and accuracy. The only redeeming features are that 1985 projections are well directed to a meaningful purpose and 1980 projections are apparently comprehensive. In spite of all these deficiencies, they are still useful, since they provide some idea –

even if not the right one – about future quantities.

OECD METHODOLOGY AND PROJECTIONS AND THEIR EVALUATION

OECD provides, inter alia, projections for three grains[31] for the years 1975 and 1985 in OECD (1968). These projections are *only* for OECD and Oceania countries. The base period is the 3-year average centering on the 1962–63 agricultural year. Methodology is similar to that of FAO. Income elasticity is based on all 3 data sources:[32] household comparison surveys, time series of consumption *per capita*, and international comparisons. Consumption projections have been based on 'composite elasticities', reflecting the influence of all factors without distinguishing between them.[33] Production estimates have been made on the basis of separate estimates for land and yield. These are of the nature of growth rates rather than any functional relationships.

OECD (1976), on the other hand, provides some projections for 1985 for countries outside OECD and Oceania. These countries or areas are: Poor Developing Countries, Eastern Europe, USSR, Africa, and Latin America.[34] These projections are made, it seems, by different methodologies. There is no attempt to aggregate these projections for such aggregates as developed, developing countries etc. Actually, no attempt is made to describe or explain how these projections are made. This is not a study in, or even an attempt at, projections.[35]

In view of the above, it is very difficult to evaluate these projections. The comments made about the FAO projections for 1980 would apply to the projections for OECD and Oceania in OECD (1968), except that the data for OECD countries is liable to be more widely available.[36] On the other hand, their projections for other areas seem of a much more ad hoc nature.

USDA METHODOLOGY AND PROJECTIONS

The USDA methodology for projections is described in USDA (1971). It contains projections for 1980. Projections are made for 22 regions aggregated into four groups: developed, centrally planned, less developed and world. Projections are made for cereals divided into 3 grains: rice, wheat and coarse grains. The data base relates to 1964—66. Projections for 1985 are contained in USDA (1974) and are for cereals only and for regions: world, developed and developing (developing are further divided into market and centrally planned). The data base is for the period 1969—71 average.

'The major objective of this study is to estimate 1980 world demand prospects for grains, and to outline the implications of possible production and trade policies and programmes on the world grain economy'.[37] Accordingly an ambitious simultaneous equation model is formulated. Basically, this model is made up of supply, demand and price equations. There are four basic sets of price equations: (i) relationships between farm and wholesale prices, (ii) consumer and wholesale prices, (iii) import (or export) price and wholesale prices, and (iv) the assumption that wholesale prices in consuming and producing regions are the same. For every one of these six equations, there are 66 equations; one each for 22 regions and 3 commodities. There are 3 market clearing equations; one each for every commodity. In addition, there are $63(21 \times 3)$ equations relating import and export prices. In all, therefore, there are 462 unknowns, made up of 66 supply, 66 demand, and the remaining 330 (66×5) prices.[38]

There is absolutely no explanation about this model. What is its rationale? Why is it so large, and why has it taken this form? Regarding the estimation of coefficients, we are told,

Because the model was *synthesized,* the coefficients in the equations were developed from several sources to reflect the relationship among the variables. Data for 1964—66 were used to determine the value of the constants in the equation. In short, 1964—66 is the base for projecting to 1980.[39]

It is also suggested that:

the model has been synthesized to be consistent with economic theory and statistical findings to the extent possible. It is not a product of a direct statistical fit because of its size.[40]

The price elasticities of supply and demand are used in the projections; exactly how, it is not clear. Even though the model involves, endogeneously, 330 prices, none of these are projected. The projections are of supply, demand, exports and imports. The projections for supply are based on time trend and for demand on income and population.

For 1980, three sets of projections are made based on the assumption about developing countries. Thus Set I refers to medium, Set II to high and Set III to low.[41] Basically, Set I

refers to trend projections. Projections for 1985 are given under four alternatives,[42] depending upon assumptions about growth and imports.

EVALUATION OF USDA METHODOLOGY AND PROJECTIONS

The most serious problem this author has is the model (Ia). Nowhere is it explained why it is what it is. There is no rationale for the introduction of so many prices, and margins therein. This is neo-classicism gone berserk; particularly when the prices are not projected.[43] Its relevance to the stated purpose is not obvious. For trade, a model based on export—import quantities would have been far more realistic. Demand and supply equations, in the last analysis, are rather simple, even simplistic. One would have thought a team interested in such a large and sophisticated looking model would have taken into consideration such important factors as urbanization, income distribution, stocks, inputs in production, etc. Further, the model speaks as if there is a supply equation; in reality it is no better than a sheer production equation.

The quantity of data — (Ib) — needed for such a large model is enormous. One doubts if such large amounts of data are available. No doubt aggregation into regions would help. Still some of these data are hard to come by. The estimation — (Ic) — of so many coefficients would need a very large amount of data. Also, the basic parameters are highly under-identified. It is, therefore, no wonder the estimates were 'synthesized' — whatever synthesization means. One wishes they had given some explanation of this 'synthesization'. The forecasts — (Id) — were made of population and income only. These were taken from UN sources. There is no way one can estimate the prediction errors — (Ie). Similarly, in terms of performance — (If) — the comments made for FAO projections also apply here.

In terms of the second set of criteria, the projections are not that comprehensive — (IIa); far less comprehensive than the size of the model would suggest. Again like FAO, both costs — (IIb) — and reputation — (IIc) — of USDA in this respect are unknown.

Overall, the USDA model appears to be large and sophisticated. When analysed, it turns out to be quite simple and limited. It provides a wrong impression of being a large econometric model — it is technically pretentious and not comprehensive. Since it does not follow statistical procedures of estimation, its projections are not 'best' in the statistical sense.[44] It is also liable to be quite expensive. However, its usefulness lies in providing a range of projections; even if one is not sure whether the particular projection set is related to the assumptions.

FAO AND USDA METHODOLOGIES: A COMPARISON

We come back to our earliest question: which of these projections is 'better'?[45] As mentioned earlier, it is not easy to compare two projections from different institutions. These are like complex products produced by different corporations in an oligopolistic market, where competition, if any, takes the form of product differentiation.[46] One or a few elements in the product are genuinely different so that the whole product — which is after all a package — is not easily comparable. The major difference in the projections of the two organizations lies in their purposes. FAO projections look for a possible course in future of economic quantities and are more concerned with the issue of hunger and malnutrition; it becomes very important in 1985 projections. USDA, on the other hand, looks at the problem from the farmer's point of view and is interested in trade, prices and profits. In spite of these differences in purpose, both end up with projections of production and demand.

Table 3 below compares the methodologies used by FAO and USDA. It is self explanatory. The major difference is that USDA incorporates some, even if limited, information on prices through price-response coefficients and projects trade quantities as well. FAO projections, on the other hand, are based on a much larger body of data, follow — at least partly — statistical methods of estimation and are more comprehensive.

CONCLUSION

An evaluation of the methodology of projections by FAO and USDA has suggested that one is not sure if these projections have any particular meanings.[47] One fully realizes and appreciates the difficulties, pitfalls and frustrations in making projections. Projections are necessary. It will, therefore, be helpful, if institutions involved in making projections, like FAO and USDA, can make available to the reader — at least the interested reader — ancillary information so that the reader can evaluate these projections. Information on the following issues will be particularly useful.

1. Year-to-year projections.
2. 'Errors' when projections are made retrospectively for the past years.
3. Distinction between 'judgement' and 'scientific' estimates.
4. High and low estimates. These can be presented easily as percentages. For example,

$$X \overset{+}{-} \frac{a_1}{a_2}$$

where x is the trend projection; $x + a_1$ high and $x - a_2$ low; a_1 and a_2 are obviously percentages.
5. Projections or forecasts for: (a) disaster situations, (b) maximum possible production or potential.

The effect of this ancillary information will be to place projections in some perspective.

Table 3. *Comparison of FAO and USDA Methodologies*

Item	FAO	USDA
Model	Single equation	Simultaneous equation
Variables		
Exogenous-Demand	Income, population, trend	Income, population, trend
Exogenous-Supply	Trend	Trend
Endogenous –	Nil	Prices
Data	Historical and cross-section	Cross-section
Estimation	OLS and judgement	Synthesization: non-econometric techniques
Detail	132 countries, 22 sub-regions, 11 regions, 40 commodities	22 regions and 3 commodities
Projections	One set	3 sets

NOTES

1. In India, for example, such disequilibria have been quite frequent during the late 19th century; even in the early 20th century. These resulted in mass starvation and population migrations of whole regions.

2. Sinha (1961). It gives projections for India for 1975–76.

3. These studies were for the following countries individually; Australia, Austria, Denmark, France, Ghana, India, Mexico, Netherlands, Nigeria, Pakistan, Philippines, Saudi Arabia, South Africa, West Germany and West Indies. These studies were conducted generally by one of the Universities in the country. They were completed anywhere from 1962 to 1968.

4. FAO (1962). These are projections for 1970.

5. FAO (1966). These projections are for 1975 and 1985.

6. OECD (1968). These are projections for OECD countries only for 1975 and 1985.

7. There is no obvious relationship between the projections by FAO and USDA either for 1980 or for 1985. The fact that both of these institutions produced these projections in the same year is purely coincidental.

8. OECD (1968) gives projections for OECD countries only. OECD (1976) does give projections for USSR, Latin America and Poorest Developing Countries. It does not give projections for the world or large sections of the world as a whole.

9. A complex model is based on a system of simultaneous equations. It may be written as

$$BY + AX = V$$

where Y and X are matrices of variables Y_i and X_i, B and A are matrices of coefficients and V is a vector of either constant or variables. Y are the endogenous variables and X the exogenous variables. Given B, A; and V and forecasts for X, the projection for Y follows.

10. Few examples should make it clear. 1. Since X_i have to be forecast (Step iv), it effects their choice (Step i). 2. Since A_i have to be estimated, (Step iii), it effects the form of f (Step ii). It is this interrelationship that explains why so many functional forms are linear; or can be linearized. 3. If the model is made up of a simultaneous system (Step i), it will effect estimation of a_i (Step iii), since the technique of estimation will depend upon whether a_i are identified, under-identified, or over-identified.

11. No doubt some implicit criteria are always there in the very method and use of projections. What is being suggested here is that no standard, or generally acceptable, criteria have been presented in the literature.

12. This criterion is an important one — particularly these days — in view of the great desire for the organizations, and parts thereof, to be accountable. Also, budgets everywhere are under pressure and 'efficiency' — in terms of 'minimum cost' — has become all the more rational.

13. The fact that it involves judgement should not deter one from drawing a conclusion. Evaluation, after all, is also a matter of judgement. Judgements are made virtually, in every decision.

14. FAO (1971), *Agricultural Commodity Projections: 1970–80*. It is divided in two volumes: Vol. I contains the actual projections; Vol. II describes methodology and gives some projections.

15. United Nations World Food Conference (1974), *Assessment of the World Food Situation: Present and Future*. Even though this is listed as a UN publication, the work has been done basically by FAO Secretariat.

16. Coarse grains are further divided into 6 grains; namely, maize, barley, oats, millets and sorghums, rye and others.

17. These details are for 1980 projections. Projections for 1985 are available for very large aggregate areas only.

18. It must be noted that projections are for production and not for supply of foodgrains.

19. FAO (1971), Vol. II, p. LVI. Incidentally, the volume does not give any clue as to which coefficient is based on judgement and which on exponential growth rate.

20. For 1985, there is a change in methodology in view of the aggregation. Thus, extrapolations were made of the indices of total food and feed production for 64 countries. Estimates were added for the aggregate production of countries not covered individually. Mathematical projections were, in some cases, 'adjusted on a judgement basis'. UN (1974), p. 107.

21. Note that it is an elasticity and not a marginal coefficient.

22. Once again, it is not clear for which country coefficients were estimated and by what method.

23. 1985 forecasts make use of the more recent population forecasts of 1974 and the income forecasts take into consideration the information for the late 1960s and early 1970s.

24. Even for developed countries the data obtained by food surveys is neither sufficient nor reliable. To quote, 'It has been found that few household consumption surveys are available in a form suitable for the present study. In most of the countries covered, such surveys, if they exist, are too out-of-date or too

incomplete (often covering only an unrepresentative section of the population). Moreover, even in cases where the results of these surveys are given in *quantities* of product consumed and not just in terms of expenditure, the definition of the product often makes it difficult to apply the elasticity coefficient obtained to a product as it appears at the production stage (for instance an elasticity coefficient for 'bread' cannot simply be applied to 'wheat')'. OECD (1968), p. 70. Also see FAO *Production Year Books.* For the deficiencies and difficulties of food balance sheets see also Sinha (1975), Appendix 1, pp. 146–152. FAO (1971) also shows that they are quite aware of many of these, and other, problems.

25. One has a nagging suspicion that some of the 'judgement' estimates may be a cover for lack of adequate data. This suspicion arises particularly from the fact that 1985 projections are based on data for a much smaller number of countries even though these relate to later years – see footnote 20.

26. If income and population are not independent of each other, the projections may be upward-biased in poor countries and downward-biased in developed countries.

27. Since part of the projections have been made by statistical methods, these prediction errors can be estimates; see Johnston (1971). The effect of substituting judgement coefficients maybe to increase these errors. Also R^2 in many cases is low indeed. Furthermore, the functional form used is not the same. Thus there may be two tendencies: (i) aggregation, reducing errors at the aggregate level, and (ii) dissimilar methods, increasing errors at the aggregate level.

28. This sentence implies that FAO did do such an exercise. The assumption may not be true. On the other hand, there is no good reason why FAO cannot, and should not – even at this late date – do so.

29. There are a few Ph.D. theses that seem to have produced a reasonably large part of such projections. See Bjarnason (1967) and Blakeslee (1967).

30. This will be particularly pertinent in its capacity to cast doubt on a certain class of data. It may be forced to mix the good with the bad.

31. The three grains are: bread, rice and coarse. OECD defines total grains = bread grains + coarse grains. It excludes rice.

32. OECD (1968) is particularly concerned about the lack of data. See footnote 24.

33. 'To calculate the coefficients for these composite elasticities, the series of *per capita* consumption for each product, taken from the food balance sheets, has been related to the series of disposable *per capita* incomes'. OECD (1968), p. 71.

34. Projections for these areas are given on the

following pages, respectively: 104, 185, 187, 255 and 276, in OECD (1976).

35. In a larger vein, one wonders about the usefulness – to a reader – of this publication, particularly in view of the fact that resources are getting more scarce. At best, it is a statement of thinking by the OECD. One wishes – perhaps, in vain – that it had raised issues for discussion and provided information to the reader to compare other alternatives. But then, strange are the priorities and decisions of international agencies.

36. OECD may also argue that their concept of 'composite elasticity' is a shade better than 'income elasticity' used by FAO in so far as the former takes into consideration, even if indirectly, the evolution of prices.

37. USDA (1971), p. 1.

38. In the chapter on the model, the discussion is in general terms; n regions, m commodities. The numbers had to be worked out. They may be different by a few since in actual practice, such general theories never work fully. The basic model is as follows:

1. $QS_{ij} - \sum_{i=1}^{m} a_{ij} PS_{ij} = A_{ij}$

2. $QD_{ik} - \sum_{i=1}^{m} b_{ik} PD_{ik} = A_{ik}$

3. $\Sigma QS_{ij} - \Sigma QD_{ik} = O$

4. $PS_{ij} - C_{ij} PW_{ij} = MS_{ij}$

5. $PD_{ik} - d_{ik} PW_{ik} = MD_{ik}$

6. $PW_{ij} = PW_{ik}$

7. $PW_{ij} - e_{ij} PE_{ij} = ME_{ij}$ or $PW_{ik} - e_{ik} PI_{ik} = MI_{ik}$

8. $PI_{ik} - PE_{ij} = M_{ijk}.$

where $i = 1,...m; j = k = 1,...n; m = 3; n = 22; i$ stands for commodity; j for producing region; and k for consuming region.

Q = quantity; S = supplies; D = demand; P = price; W = wholesale; E = Export; I = import; M = margin: A refers to factors affecting supply and demand. In reality $A_{ij} = f_o + f_{ijt}$, and $A_{ij} = g_o + g_{ik}Y_k + g'_{ik}P_k$; where Y and P refer to income and population.

39. USDA (1971), p. 55 (emphasis added).

40. USDA (1971), pp. 54–55.

41. Set I assumes a 'continuation of present food and fibre policies in the less developed countries; allowing for moderate gains in productivity consistent with some improvement in available technology'. USDA

(1971), p. 50. There are two variants of Set II: IIA and IIB based on export and import assumptions.

42. Alternative I assumes a slow but accentuated growth in the 1970s and 1980s; II is a high world import demand situation; III is low demand and low growth; and, IV is low import demand by developing countries.

43. One has a strong suspicion that the analysts were over-impressed by largeness for largeness sake or perhaps trying to impress — whom one does not know — by the use of sophisticated 'technology'.

44. In statistical theory, 'best' is generally defined as 'minimum variance of errors' for a particular class of estimators or predictors. Thus predictions based on the method of least squares are 'best' within the class unbiased linear estimators.

45. See page 499 in this text.

46. Persons involved in the purchase of a computer, even a car, would appreciate the nature of problems that arise in such a comparison.

47. One feels like saying:
'Projections are like leaves, and where they most abound,
Much fruit of sense beneath is rarely found',
with due apologies to Alexander Pope. See Alexander Pope, 'An Essay on Criticism'. I have substituted 'projections' for Pope's 'words'.

REFERENCES

Bjarnason, H. F., *An Economic Analysis of 1980 International Trade in Feed Grains*, unpublished Ph.D. thesis (University of Wisconsin, 1967).

Blakeslee, Leroy, *An Analysis of Projected World Food Production and Demand in 1970, 1985 and 2,000*, Unpublished Ph.D. thesis (Iowa State University, 1967).

FAO, *Production Year Book* (Rome, annual).

FAO, *Agricultural Commodities: Projections for 1970* (Rome: 1962).

FAO, *Agricultural Commodities: Projections for 1975 and 1980* (Rome: 1966).

FAO, *Agricultural Commodities Projections: 1970–80*, 2 volumes (Rome: 1971).

Johnston, J., *Econometric Method* (New York: McGraw Hill, 1971).

OECD, *Agricultural Projections for 1975 and 1985* (Paris: 1968).

OECD, *Study of Trends in World Supply and Demand of Major Agricultural Commodities* (Paris: 1976).

Sinha, R. P., *Food in India* (Bombay: Oxford University Press, 1961).

Sinha, R. P., *Food and Poverty* (London: Croom Helm Ltd., 1976).

UN World Food Conference, *Assessment of the World Food Situation* (Rome: 1974).

United States Department of Agriculture, *World Demand Prospects for Grains to 1980* (Washington D.C.: 1971).

United States Department of Agriculture, *World Food Situation and Prospects to 1985* (Washington, D.C.: 1975).

World Development, 1977, Vol. 5, Nos. 5–7, pp. 507–518. Pergamon Press. Printed in Great Britain.

Climatic Variation and Implications for World Food Production

REID A. BRYSON

and

JOHN E. ROSS

Institute for Environmental Studies,
University of Wisconsin, Madison

Summary. – The authors of this paper show, based on some examples from climatic history, that climate can change rapidly and that these changes can have drastic effects on world food production, as well as on other aspects of economic and cultural life. The historical examples are the Arctic expansions of around 1900 B.C. and A.D. 1200. The authors also describe a presently occurring Arctic expansion and its world-wide effects on climate to date.

This changing situation poses certain questions for those countries which continue to have the capacity to increase their food production. The authors propose that a world food policy should be devised to pre-empt world food shortages and/or to deal with such situations when they occur.

INTRODUCTION

Slowly, but steadily, the collective eyes of the world are converging on the question of our ability to feed human beings, more than 4.2 thousand million of us at this time.

More pessimistic forecasters see population and food supplies on a collision course, perhaps as in a slow-motion film, but nevertheless an inevitable impact, already in its early stages.

More optimistic forecasters see some room to manoeuver. For example, Sterling Wortman, vice-president of the Rockefeller Foundation, writing in a special issue of *Scientific American* on 'Food and Agriculture', says, 'There are two components to the solution of the food problem: increased production of food, primarily in the developing countries, and widespread increases in family incomes, particularly among the poor' (Wortman, 1976).

More forecasters, and there are now many, see the problem as primarily a matter of technological adaptation, of economic priorities, or of social will, with a natural environment that is generally amenable to greatly increased production, if we can just get it together.

But there is a real possibility that one of the major environmental variables is missed or ignored in many of the current analyses. That variable is climate. If it has been missed, and if it is a limiting factor in even some of the coming years, then our forecasts on food production could have some excruciating errors.

The evidence of this decade suggests that we cannot take climate for granted, as a random variable or as essentially benign. The evidence looks as follows:

A decade-long drought in Sahelian Africa. Erratic monsoons in India. A drought in Western Europe, including Britain. Crop losses to weather anomalies in Russia. Drought and other climatological problems in that mighty fortress of agricultural technology, the United States.

In the early 1970s, droughts, storms, floods and frosts occurred in patterns and combinations that surprised us because they appeared to be beyond the range of normal climate. Concomitant poor crop seasons in many countries depleted world foodgrain reserves, at a time when technology appeared to be gaining on hunger.

Were these isolated, chance events in the course of climatic variation, or were they part of a developing pattern essentially different from the 'normal' period in the first half of the 20th century?

There is a growing awareness that the world pattern of climate has been changing. The overriding question is whether that change will continue. The rash of climatic problems certainly did not abate in 1976.

Meanwhile, there is a tendency among those concerned with food supplies to think in annual cycles; to conclude that this year 'we're going to have to tighten our belt a notch, or we can loosen our belt a notch'. But the climate patterns are not totally revealed from one year to the next and annual belt tightening is clearly an inadequate policy if we expect to increase food production from 3—5% each year.

GENERALIZATIONS OF CLIMATE CHANGE

Climate research has not yet produced a deterministic model of world climate that can predict the character of the coming decades or even what next year will be like. However, there are lessons that can be learned from climatic history. If we combine what we know of the history with knowledge of atmosphere—earth mechanics, we see patterns that can be used to assess the probable future course of the climate:

1. *Climate is not fixed.*

On a long-time scale it has varied from a condition of vast continental glaciers to non-glacial. The last 10,000 years have been non-glacial, probably inter-glacial. On the scale of centuries there have also been significant climatic changes associated with significant changes in living systems. For example, the 19th century was part of what has been called 'the little ice age'. It was significantly cooler then than in the first part of the 20th century.

2. *Climate tends to change rapidly rather than gradually.*

By that, we do not mean overnight, the way weather can change with the advance of a cold front or a warm front. Rather, the change from a glacial climate to a non-glacial climate may take less than a century, though full response of the environment, specifically biota, may take longer. Smaller, but still significant, changes may occur in a few decades, for example in the amounts, geographic distribution and seasonal timing of rainfall, i.e. droughts or cool and wet spells.

3. *Cultural changes usually accompany climatic changes.*

The climatic changes within the past ten millennia have changed the human possibilities of the environment enough to make important changes in cultures (Bryson *et al.*, 1974; Wendland and Bryson, 1974). It is important to note that these are not the global changes one would expect from major glaciation, rather they have occurred within the most recent inter-glacial period. It is also important to note that mankind survived and evolved during the last glaciation.

4. *Those of us alive in this century have an image of normal climate.*

However, our image is not normal in the longer perspective of recent centuries. It is, in fact, abnormal.

5. *When the high latitudes cool, the monsoons in tropical countries tend to fail.*

The high latitudes have been cooling the last three decades. We would expect to have seen increasingly erratic behavior in monsoons. We have.

6. *Cool periods of earth history are periods of greater-than-normal climatic instability.*

One might expect that if the earth or the hemisphere were cooling then everything would cool down, summer and winter, year-by-year. But that is not so. Rather, unexpected events occur. Extremes of various kinds occur. New records are set. There are some explicit reasons why this happens.

The atmosphere, and thus the climate, is driven by solar energy. The unequal heating of high latitudes and tropics, which arises from the sunlight falling on a spherical earth, produces a temperature differential that controls the circulation pattern of the atmosphere in an interaction with the distribution of land and sea. This in turn determines the distribution of rainfall.

Climatic records show that the variation of the contrast between tropical and high-latitude temperatures is primarily due to temperature changes at high latitudes. Thus, times of warming or cooling in the sub-Arctic are critical times to examine. Because there has been rapid sub-arctic cooling in recent decades, the following paragraphs will concentrate on some similar times in the past.

We are all familiar with the changes of climate which accompany high-latitude temperature changes, for these changes occur every year to produce the seasons. Thus, cooling of

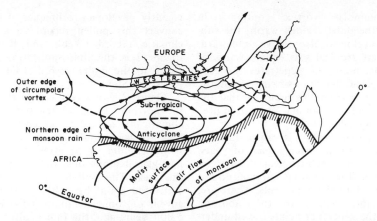

Figure 1. *The sub-tropical anticyclones,* clockwise eddies which produce the great sub-tropical deserts, are at the outer edge of the westerlies of the circumpolar vortex. The monsoon rains, between the anticyclones and the equator, follow the anticyclones north and south with the seasons. If the anticyclones do not move as far poleward in summer as usual, the monsoon rains are also less extensive and the desert reaches closer to the equator. The light arrows represent air flow in the mid-atmosphere and the heavy arrows represent the air flow near the ground.

the polar regions in winter produces polar caps of cold air that surge down to the sub-tropics. In the summer's warmth these cold-air caps retreat. But there can also be decades and centuries of cooler sub-arctic temperatures with periods of more extensive cool polar air, and with a more wintery character, than normal.

THE ARCTIC EXPANSION AROUND 1900 B.C.

North of the forest of Canada lie the treeless 'barren grounds' of the tundra. Extending into the tundra, beyond the area occupied by forest, lie bands of forest palaeosols. The forest formerly extended farther north (Sorenson, *et al.,* 1971). A layer of charcoal lies at the top of the soil profile where the fossil forest soil has been buried by wind-blown sand. Dating of this charcoal shows that the forest extended its maximum distance poleward in 1900 B.C. but its northern edge had retreated at least 200 km southwards by 1800 B.C.[1]

The climate was favourable to forest for at least a millenium. The northern border of the boreal forest is the southern edge of the cap of arctic air in summer (Bryson, 1966). Then, for some reason, the arctic air regime expanded and the forest border retreated southwards – not to return even part of the way for about 700 years.

Climate is a world-wide integrated system. Significant changes cannot take place in one part of the system without other changes occurring in other places. There are dynamic connections that interlink climatic changes in various parts of the globe.

At the outer edge of the polar cap of cold air is the region of maximum lateral contrast of that air with the warm air of lower latitudes. In the region between the outer edge and the North Pole there is a general poleward decrease of temperature, and this produces westerly winds in the upper air which flow about the Pole in a circumpolar vortex. Near the outer edge of the circumpolar vortex, over the region of maximum temperature contrast, lies the *jetstream,* and around the outer edge of this are the eddies known as the sub-tropical anticyclones (Figure 1). The sinking air in the anticyclones produces the sub-tropical deserts of the world. But the position and movement of the anticyclones strongly influences the location and duration of the monsoon rains.

---

[1] When B.C. dates are given here and following, they refer to calendar dates, whereas 'years ago' refer to radiocarbon dates. Calendar dates of 1900 B.C. are comparable with radiocarbon dates of about 3,500 years before the present.

The circumpolar vortex contracts in summer. As the polar regions warm, the subtropical anticyclones also move poleward. Where there are tropical seas equatorwards of the continents, moist air penetrates the continents to replace the dry, sinking air of the anticyclones. It is from this moist air that the monsoon rains fall – the annual 're-birth of life' in the monsoon lands.

The circumpolar vortex is larger and can become more dominant over a span of years. Then the associated sub-tropical deserts are closer to the Equator and monsoon rains do not penetrate as far into the continents. There are, of course, more details to the monsoon systems, but the general principle is well understood.

Most important, there is a connection between high-latitude cooling, the size of the circumpolar vortex, and the monsoons.

The fossil soils in the sub-Arctic show that there was an arctic cooling and expansion about 1900 B.C. Was there a related reduction of the northern hemisphere monsoons? The evidence shows that there was, and with drastic consequences.

In the millennium before 1900 B.C., an empire developed in what is now north-west India and Pakistan. Its greatest cities, Harappa and Mohenjo-Daro, were on the Indus River, but lesser cities and towns spread over nearly all of what is now the Rajputana Desert area. It was an agricultural empire, with huge granaries. It paralleled and traded with Sumer. After 1900 B.C. the cities were abandoned. Some towns were buried under sand dunes. Seven hundred years later, Aryan nomads arrived, building their settlements on other sites, or occasionally on the dunes over the old towns. The 'new town' of Osian, near Jodhpur, was built around 500 B.C. on dune sand which covers the walls of an 'old town' beneath. The dunes tell of the monsoon's failure, the failure of rains that watered the fields of the Indus civilization.

Earlier than that, during the last ice-age, when the polar regions were very cold and the circumpolar vortex was very large year-round, dunes had formed in Rajputana. There was *no* monsoon. When the ice-age climate ended 10,800 years ago (Figure 2) the monsoons began, the ground-water level rose, and freshwater lakes formed between some of the dunes. (Singh *et al.,* 1972). Into these lakes fell the pollen of the plants that grew in the area or that blew in from surrounding areas (Singh *et al.,* 1973). As the sediments accumulated in the lakes, the pollen was buried to provide a record of the vegetative history of the area. Using

recently developed techniques, it is possible to convert this pollen record to a quantitative climatic record (Webb and Bryson, 1972). Figure 2 is the first application of this technique to the pollen record from Lunkaransar, Rajasthan State.

Figure 2 shows very clearly that the area at the northern fringe of the Indian monsoon is climatically hazardous at best, with century-long average rainfall varying by a factor of two. A millennium or so after the advent of the post-glacial monsoons, there was agriculture in the area. The pollen record begins to show cultivated grains by 9,400 years ago. With the advent of somewhat more reliable rains about 5,000 years ago, the Indus culture spread over the area. As the rains decreased some 4,000 years ago, the freshwater lakes turned salt, then dried up as the ground-water level fell, and the Indus civilization disappeared. When the Arctic cooled, the monsoons failed, not only in India, but in the Sahel region of North Africa as well (Geyh and Jakel, 1974). This record reveals that the monsoons tended to fail over a period of seven centuries, and in 'modern times' climatologically speaking.

The pollen technique shows corollary time-scale evidence in North America, Figures 3a and 3b.

THE ARCTIC EXPANSION OF A.D. 1200

When the Arctic cools, the effect is also apparent in northern Canada, the far-north

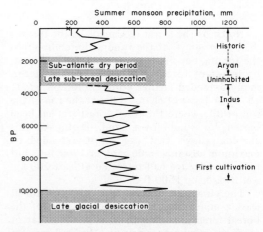

Figure 2. *Tentative reconstruction of the summer monsoon rainfall in Rajasthan over the past 10,800 years, based on fossil pollen accumulated in a lake. The lake contained fresh water until shortly before it dried up about 3,500 years ago.*

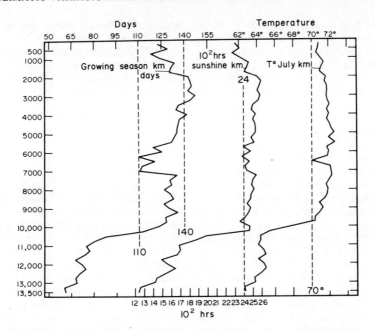

Figure 3a. *Reconstructed climate of the last 13,500 years at Kirchner Marsh, Dakota Co., in Southeastern Minnesota.* PGS stands for precipitation during the growing season. Notice the abrupt change of climate, starting 10,800 years ago as the Pleistocene 'ice age' ended.

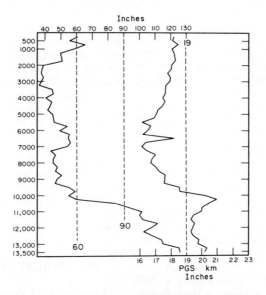

Figure 3b. *Reconstructed climate of the last 13,500 years at Kirchner Marsh, Dakota Co., in South-eastern Minnesota.* PGS stands for precipitation during the growing season. Notice the abrupt change of climate, starting 10,800 years ago as the Pleistocene 'ice age' ended.

Atlantic, and Scandinavia. Indeed it is in northeastern North America and Scandinavia that the great continental ice-sheets of the last great glaciation were located. Cooling of the far-north Atlantic expands the sea-ice cover.

As the average temperature in Iceland is closely related to the ice conditions, it is possible to construct a thousand-year history of Icelandic temperature (Figure 4). When the Vikings settled in Iceland and Greenland there was little sea-ice in the region and the climate was mild enough for some grain cultivation. During this warmer period, the forest in northern Canada had once again advanced northwards — but only half as far as it had done prior to 1900 B.C.

Then came the cooling and expansion of the Arctic. Around A.D. 1200, or just before, the sea-ice of the North Atlantic expanded, chilling Iceland, and the forest in central Canada retreated southwards. The main landmark in Greenland towards which the Vikings sailed had been called Black Mountain, but became known instead as White Mountain, as the snow and ice-cover increased (Pettersen, 1914).

Climatic theory tells us that the circumpolar vortex should have expanded, sweeping mild, showery Atlantic air into western Europe, and shifting the summer westerlies southwards, from southern Canada into the northern United States. Here the air would be dry and sunny as it descended the east face of the cordillera.

It is possible to construct a hypothetical rainfall map for such conditions, using modern climatic data (Figure 5). There is enough year-to-year variation in the climate for one to select those years which have the indicated features of the circulation, and average them to produce a climatic chart that represents the pattern of an era in which that circulation pattern prevailed (Bryson and Baerreis, 1968). This suggests reduced rainfall in the northern plains, corn-belt, west Texas, and much of the intermontane west of the United States, but increased rainfall in the Pacific north-west, the south-east, and much of the east coast region.

But Figure 5 is a hypothetical map, and an hypothesis must be tested. This can be done by the methods of palaeoecology and environmental archaeology for North America, and with historical evidence for Europe. There once was a culture known to archaeologists as Mill Creek near the boundary between the tall-grass prairie region that is now the US 'corn belt' and the short-grass prairie plains that are now the spring-wheat region. These people were representative of a complex of groups of corn farmers who had spread across the plains to the

base of the Rocky Mountains in the centuries preceding A.D. 1200.

The villages of the Mill Creek people had been established around A.D. 900. Pollen evidence shows that they lived in a region with tall-grass prairie on the uplands, and woods on the valley terraces and valley floors. They hunted the deer that browsed the woods and grew corn in the rich bottomlands. 97% of their meat came from the deer.

Then, with the expansion of the Arctic, the westerlies of summer shifted southwards to cross the Great Plains of the north-central United States. Instead of the moist south winds from the Gulf of Mexico, the dry westerlies prevailed and a long drought began. In perhaps 20 years the tall-grass prairies were replaced by short-grass. The few cottonwoods and willows along the stream banks were the only remnants of the forest that had once filled the valleys. The deer disappeared, and two-thirds of the meat eaten by the Mill Creek people came from bison, a grazing animal, though the people apparently had less of all kinds of food than formerly. Further west, the farming villages disappeared entirely. There were profound cultural changes. That drought lasted for two hundred years.

The integral behaviour of the atmosphere means that there must have been concomitant climatic changes in other regions. Europe, with its steady flow of showery maritime air, had widespread outbreaks of ergot blight of its grain, and large areas were essentially depopulated by the ravages of St. Anthony's Fire — chronic ergotism. The heavy clay soils of the English midlands were too wet to work, and were largely abandoned by the early part of the 14th century. The Black Plague was epidemic. World population declined.

As we saw in the earlier case, there should have been failures of the monsoon. There is some evidence that roughly a thousand years ago, when the sub-Arctic was warmer, the monsoon was better developed than in the cooler last 500 years. The cooler sub-Arctic was again associated with less rain in north-west India.

THE PRESENT ARCTIC EXPANSION

From A.D. 1600 until the present century, the sub-Arctic was very cool. The population of Iceland declined in a series of famines, the Arctic sea-ice expanded, and European winters were very cold (Bergthorsson, 1962).

Then, early in the present century the

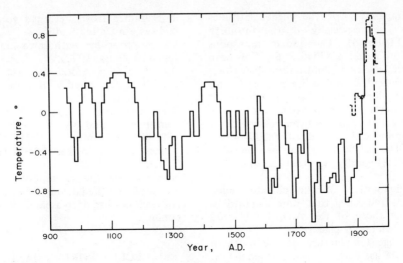

Figure 4. *Decadal mean annual temperature in Iceland over the past millenium, after Bergthorsson.*
The line (long dashes) indicates the rate of temperature decline in 1961–71 period, and the line (short dashes) shows the variation of mean temperature in the Northern Hemisphere plotted to the same relative scale.

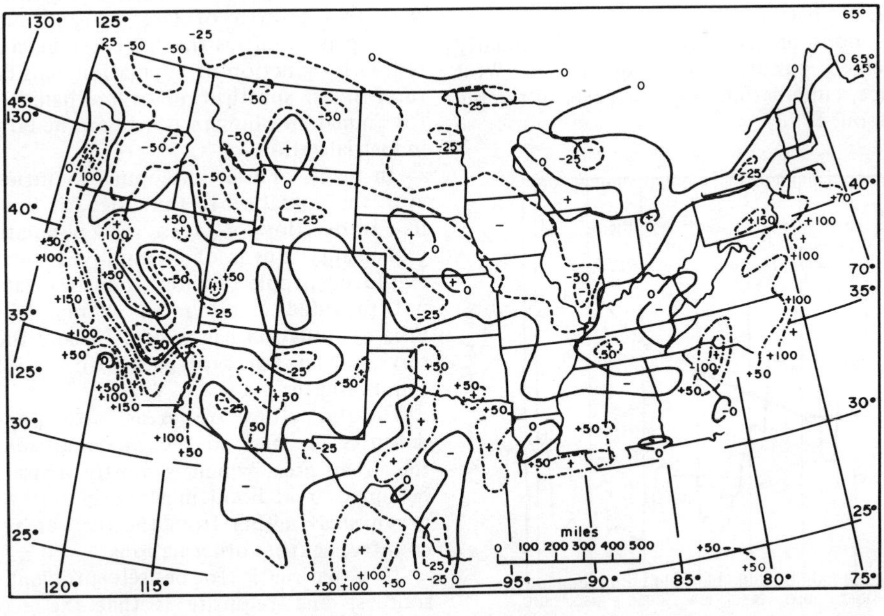

Figure 5. *July precipitation changes, in percent, to be expected with a southward shift of the westerlies, i.e., from weak westerlies over the 35–55 latitude band to stronger westerlies in that band.*

Based on 20 years of modern data.

average temperature of the higher latitudes started to rise, especially in the far-north Atlantic (Figure 4). The Indian monsoons became more reliable (Figure 6), European winters were less severe, and midsummer frosts in the north-central United States ceased. This very recent configuration is our image of normal. However, the *general* temperature level of the last 2,000 years has been below that of the mid-post-glacial period of 5,000–4,000 years ago. The last 50 years may be somewhat closer climatologically to that period circa 5000.

This amelioration of the climate ended about 1945, and since that time a return to climates like those of the A.D. 1600–1900 period has been taking place:

- The average temperature of the northern hemisphere has declined nearly as much as it previously rose.
- The average temperature of Iceland has declined to its former level.
- Since 1951 the surface temperature of the whole North Atlantic has declined about one-eighth of the difference between recent temperatures and full glacial temperature conditions, and the Gulf Stream has shifted southwards (Rodewald, 1973).
- The growing season in England has diminished by two weeks (H.H. Lamb, pers. comm.).
- The frequency of droughts in north-west India has begun to increase.
- The monsoon has gradually and irregularly retreated towards the Equator in West Africa, culminating in seven years of famine (Bryson, 1973).

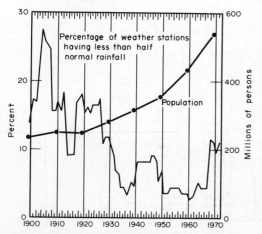

Figure 6. *Trends in the percentage of weather stations in northwestern India reporting less than half of normal annual rainfall in a given year.*
Overlapping ten-year averages.

- Midsummer frosts returned to the upper midwestern United States.
- The monsoon has withdrawn southwards in Japan (Asakura, 1972).
- The Canadian Arctic has had severe ice conditions compared with those of the past few decades.
- The snow- and ice-cover of the northern hemisphere suddenly increased by about 13% in the winter of 1971–72, and remained at the increased level (Kukla and Kukla, 1974).
- The size of the circumpolar vortex has increased and the latitude of the sub-tropical anticyclones has decreased (E.W. Wahl, pers. comm.).

RECENT WORLD CHANGES

During the last 30 years the world of mankind was also changing quite dramatically. In the poorer countries the world-wide spread of antibiotics and insecticides greatly reduced suffering from infectious diseases and malaria. The decline in death rates due to health care and increased food production produced an explosion of population that has about doubled the number of inhabitants and done even more in the monsoon countries.

One of the most dramatic changes has been the rapid growth of large urban centres. In developed countries this has often been associated with reduction of population density in the rural areas, substitution of mechanical power for animal and human power on the farms, and industrialization.

In many of the developing countries, however, the migration to the cities has been more like an overflow of excess rural population and vast shanty towns of unemployed and under-employed people develop. Industrialization has not provided employment as rapidly as the urban population has grown. Usually the social services have not kept pace with the influx of 'rural refugees'.

Clearly, cities are areas with population densities far beyond the carrying capacity of the urban area, which is mostly unusable and occupied area. Food must be imported to the urban areas, either from the rural areas of the country, or from other nations.

If a nation is to be self-sufficient in resources, one requisite is that the economic product of the cities be adequate to buy food for its inhabitants. Equally important is the fact that the farmers and herdsmen must be able to produce an excess of food above their own minimal requirements equal to the food requirements of the cities. The economic product of the urban population (and other non-productive segments such as armies and bureaucracies) must be approximately equal to the price of the agricultural excess so that the farmers can exchange the food for the product of the cities. No nations are now really self-sufficient. By choice or by need they are involved in foreign trade and balances of payments. In that case however, resources and value added to resources must, over time, be in balance. The food production excess must be sufficiently great that the income covers handling and processing the exported food, and/or there must be other resources for which there is a foreign demand, and/or a nation must be involved in technological processing.

If the rural population density is at the carrying capacity of the land, the existence of other exportable resources becomes a necessity if the urban population is to be fed.

The carrying capacity depends on the yield, directly, and also on the 'efficiency' with which the yield can be used. Many agricultural management schemes are designed to maximize efficiency by controlling the usable portion of the total photosynthetic yield, by elimination of non-usable species or by developing varieties of seed which produce a maximum edible fraction. Manipulation of the photosynthetic efficiency is a technique often used.

Clearly, if population density is at carrying capacity, given present technology, then any decrease of the yield must result in sub-minimal

food supply and starvation unless there is an inter-year carryover of stored food.

If the yield is less than the amount required for food, storage is negative indicating a reduction of reserve. Unfortunately, for the world as a whole, the integrated shortfall over the past few years has now approximately consumed the entire world reserve (Figure 7).

On the other hand, periods in which food production exceeds consumption make possible the creation of reserves — but also make possible an increase of the actual *per capita* food consumption. In regions where the population density is near the carrying capacity, increased yield, due perhaps to a long spell of good rainfall, not only increases the food consumption but the survival rate as well, especially of children. Thus the population rises towards the carrying capacity appropriate to the above normal yield associated with the good rains. This is also true of animal populations. The population is then above the carrying capacity when drought and low yields follow. Crisis ensues when reserves are depleted, unless additional food is obtained from reserves elsewhere.

In the case of deserts, including those lands on the northern areas of the monsoons, this variation of short-term carrying capacity is most important. In the absence of reserves, the population density must not exceed the minimum expected short-term carrying capacity. With reserves, the population density must not exceed that which can be sustained over the period of shortfall. Particu-

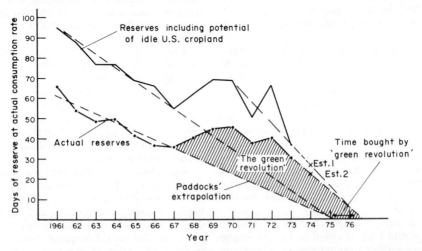

Figure 7. *World food-grain reserves, year by year, since 1961* show a rather steady decline with only a minor offset produced by the 'green revolution'. The graph shows that the world consumed more than it produced from 1961–67, then again after about 1970.

larly significant in this case is the non-linear effect of exceeding the carrying capacity, especially with animals. The production of plant biomass depends on leaf area, which is reduced by grazing. If the grazing (herbivory) exceeds the photosynthetic production rate (carrying capacity exceeded) then the production rate goes down *at an increasing rate*. When the remaining plant biomass is negligible or consists only of non-usable species, the region is *by definition* a desert.

Considering further this interrelation between grazing pressure and plant cover, this expansion of desert *if not reversible* is an increase of the unusable area. This is the equivalent of a long-term decrease of carrying capacity.

The annals of soil science and geomorphology are replete with examples of irreversible depletion of plant cover. Especially in semi-arid lands, dune mobility and erosion are non-linearly enhanced by reduction of plant cover.

It is clear, considering the above interrelationships that desertization and desertification cannot be regarded as either 'natural' or man-caused processes alone. The production of biomass depends on the climate *and* on human efforts, and the off-take of biomass depends on herbivory including human and domestic animal consumption. The balance between the production and off-take, which determines the rate of desertization, is thus related to the interplay of climate and human pressures on the plant ecosystem.

Changes in productivity of the land can proceed more rapidly than changes in population density, in the semi-arid lands where the standing biomass is small, but also in other areas of the world. Population densities much above that sustainable by the minimum expected productivity over the period covered by food reserves must inevitably result in famine, dependence on external food supplies, or migration. The viable human population density is a calculable value, *providing* the climate does not change. Recent and ancient evidence show that climate can change.

That rapid rate of population growth continues. As the world has become more crowded, the mobility of populations has decreased. It is no longer possible for a million Irish to emigrate in response to a famine. A mass movement of a nation of pastoralists to greener pastures would lead to bloodshed if the migration crossed national boundaries — and perhaps even if it did not.

For many years world reserves of foodgrains diminished after the post-World War II recovery

peak. There was a short-lived increase with the introduction of the higher-yielding rice and wheat of the 'green revolution' (Figure 7). Then the inexorable decrease resumed.

In 1972, a series of climatically induced crop reductions occurred. The Indian monsoon was weak, the west African monsoon failed, there was drought in Russia, and scores of other countries had climatic problems of food production. In 1973, things seemed a little better; 1974 appeared to be disappointing again as was 1975. The season just ended (1976) again appears slightly better. With reserves depleted, however, every year must be a success.

We know from the lessons of climatic history that significant climatic changes can occur rapidly, and that the changed climate can last for centuries. We know that great social disruption and the destruction of cultures can result. We know that the cooler periods of climatic history are periods of highly variable climate. (Look back at the A.D. 1600–1900 data of Figure 4 again!) We know that the high latitudes have been rapidly cooling, and that the people of the monsoon lands cannot reduce their food consumption much more and still survive. We know that world foodgrain reserves will prove inadequate if more years like the last few recur soon. And we know that the rapid expansion of high-technology agriculture would require large inputs of energy and capital, both of which are in short supply.

This changing situation, which we feel is fundamental, sets in motion a series of questions for industrial nations with current and/or potential food surpluses. A key issue is whether these countries try to stimulate vastly increased production (say a 300% increase in 30 years).

Food production breakthroughs in the US and other countries that now have industrialized agriculture have been built on the concept of 'limiting factors'. Technology is packaged to increase yields by controlling as many of the environmental variables as possible . . . . . fertilizer, water, tillage, competitors. Water is now 'the limiting factor' in increasing production even in these situations.

Agriculture becomes an energy-intensive mono-culture. To the extent that environmental variables cannot be controlled (corn blight, drought) technical agriculture is in sudden trouble. To apply this strategy in other parts of the world requires this same *total transfer* of technical structure. This was the miscalculation in the decline of the Green Revolution. It is a vulnerable strategy, given, for example, a climate shift.

Further, this strategy is quite pervasively dependent on oil. The relatively cheap food supply in industrial countries has been subsidized heavily by cheap oil and gas. Such systems have not begun to consider how to disengage from oil, either because of declining supplies or formidable prices. The easy way will be to modify coal to gasoline and synthetic natural gas. More difficult will be to mechanically process solar energy. There are probably some significant gains to be made in biological processing of solar energy.

A problem for the US is whether to import oil and export grain as a balance-of-payments issue, and American agriculture could end up paying more for the oil than it gets for the grain, unless energy conversion systems are revolutionized in American agriculture. A key question is whether the country can or will move back to a more labour-intensive agriculture.

There is now considerable debate on the question of arable lands, internationally and in the United States. There appear to be *some* undeveloped arable lands on the global scale, but the number of new acres per unit of time is declining. Capital investment for modern agriculture is as much as $2500 per acre. Assuming that an acre will support around 6 people with conventional systems, this means 15 million additional acres per year, and about $37.5 thousand million annual investment, not including operational costs. The ratio of 6 people per acre may be too high. Water is again a limiting factor.

There is considerable evidence of arable land degradation due to erosion, salination, and burning of organics (slash and burn, animal dung for cooking fuel). There is not conclusive evidence of the rate of degradation. It would appear however, that soil degradation is accelerating, in part due to climate change, but also to agricultural and urban development practices.

All of this adds up to a tightening situation in food supply, even assuming favorable climate.

What, then, does the future hold in terms of climate?

Climatic theory is not sufficiently developed to give a definitive prediction. Indeed, the scientific effort to develop this capability has yet to be made. However, we can still turn to the past for guidance.

SUMMARY

Studies of past climates show unequivocally what *can* happen to our atmospheric environment. From climatic history we can learn several very specific lessons.

The climate can change rapidly. Major climatic changes, such as the change from glacial to non-glacial conditions, can occur in a few centuries, even though the adjustment of biota and the wasting of continental ice-sheets may take longer. Smaller changes may take only decades.

Changed climatic states may persist for centuries or millennia. While the climatic excursion of this century appears to have lasted a half-a-century or so, the 'little ice-age' was at least three centuries long (roughly 1550–1850 A.D.), a North American drought period lasted two centuries, and there was a monsoon failure of seven centuries. These have all been recorded in the evidence of nature.

Climatic changes may occur in different senses in different parts of the world. This paper has outlined several cases where cooling in the sub-Arctic was associated with reduced rainfall or increased frequency of failure of the monsoon, and a case in which drought in North America was concomitant with wet weather in western Europe.

The climate we think of as normal is quite abnormal by the standards of the past few centuries, and the magnitude of the change since 1945 is significant by comparison with similar changes in the past.

Combining the nature of the recent climatic change with the present narrow margin of world foodgrain reserves, an urgent need to consider and react to the possibility of continued climatic variation is indicated.

We have doubled food production in the world in the last 40 years. We will undoubtedly try to double it again in the next 35 years. However, to do this will require allocation of oil to agriculture at the expense of other sectors, or a revolution in energy systems.

There will be, in this decade, some regional and national episodes of severe food shortages, and we will be heavily pressed to solve them in some cases because of a shortfall in production, and in other cases because of a failure in delivery and economic situations. If the weather conditions deteriorate further, then starvation will be upon us. The evidence is that climate conditions will impose perhaps a 5 to 10% 'tax' on food production between now and the end of the century.

For a series of reasons, humanitarian and economic, the food surplus countries will at least consider increasing their food production faster than the world population increase (5% a year). To do this will require energy allocation, a redefinition and implementation of land use policies, and some innovative pricing policies designed to buffer prices to farmers against short-term surpluses. The world community will continue to seek to develop a world food reserve and an innovative new programme in agricultural development.

In the prosperous countries there will be pressures by consumer groups to embargo some foreign shipments of food. This is exceedingly difficult to do, because of pressures from farmers in these countries to sell abroad and because of standing trade agreements. We may, however, have to regulate domestic prices or at least have enabling procedures.

There could well be some desperate nations in the next 10–15 years due to food shortfalls; some of them militarily weak, but perhaps some not. World food policy should be designed to defuse these situations.

REFERENCES

Asakura, Tadashi, *Unusual Weather and Environmental Pollution* (in Japanese) (Tokyo: Kyoritsu Shuppan, 1972), iv + 212 pp., illustr.

Bergthorsson, Pall, Paper presented at the *National Center for Atmospheric Research – Air Force Cambridge Research Laboratories Conference on the Climate of the 11th and 16th Centuries* (Aspen, Colorado: 16–24 June 1962), 23 pp.

Bryson, Reid A., 'Airmasses, streamlines and the Boreal forest', *Geogr. Bull.* (Canada), Vol. 8 (1966), pp. 228–269.

Bryson, Reid A., 'World food prospects and climatic change', Testimony before joint meeting of the US Senate Subcommittees on Foreign Agricultural Policy and Agricultural Production, Marketing and Stabilization of Prices (18 October 1973). Also, *Hearings, 93rd Congress, First Session* (17–18 October 1973), (Washington, D.C.: US Government Printing Office, 1974), (24–799), pp. 119–40.

Bryson, Reid A. & Baerreis, D. A., 'Climatic change and the Mill Creek culture of Iowa', Part 1, Ch. 1, 'Introduction and Project Summary', *Jour. Iowa Archeol. Soc.*, Vol. 15 (1968), pp. 1–34.

Bryson, Reid A., Lamb, H. H. and Donley, D. L., 'Drought and the decline of Mycenae', *Antiquity*, Vol. 48 (1974), pp. 46–50.

Geyh, Mebus A. and Jakel, D., 'Late-glacial and holocene climatic history of the Sahara desert derived from a statistical assay of ^{14}C dates', *Paleogeogr., Paleoclimatol., Paleoecol.*, Vol. 15 (1974), pp. 205–208.

Kukla, George J. and Kukla, H. J., 'Increased surface albedo in the northern hemisphere', *Science*, Vol. 183 (1974), p. 713.

Pettersen, O., 'Climatic variations in historic and prehistoric times' (Goteborg), *Sver. Hydrogr.-Biol. Skr.*, No. 5 (1914), 25 pp.

Rodewald, Martin, 'Der Trend des Meerestemperatur in Nordatlantik', *Beilage zur Berliner Wetterkarte des Instituts for Meteorologie der Freien Universitat Berlin* (1973), S029/73, 6 pp.

Singh, Gurdip, Chopra, S. K. and Singh, A. B., 'Pollen-rain from the vegetation of North-west India', *New Phytol.*, Vol. 72 (1973), pp. 191–206.

Singh, Gurdip, Joshi, R. D. and Singh, A. B. 'Stratigraphic and radiocarbon evidence for the age and development of three salt-lake deposits in Rajasthan, India', *Quaternary Res.*, Vol. 2 (1972), pp. 496–505.

Sorenson, Curtis J., Knox, J. C., Larsen J. A. and Bryson, R. A., 'Paleosols and the forest border in Keewatin', *Quaternary Res.*, Vol. 1 (1971), pp. 468–473.

Webb, Thompson, III and Bryson, R. A., 'The late- and post-glacial sequence of climatic events in Wisconsin and east-central Minnesota', quantitative estimates derived from fossil pollen spectra by multivariate statistical analysis, *Quaternary Res.*, Vol. 2 (1972), pp. 70–115.

Wendland, W. M. and Bryson, R. A., 'Dating climatic epsidoes of the holocene', *Quaternary Res.*, Vol 4 (1974), pp. 9–24.

Wortman, Sterling, 'Food and Agriculture', *Scientific American*, Vol. 235, No. 3 (Sept. 1976), p. 30.

World Development, 1977, Vol. 5, Nos. 5–7, pp. 519–523. Pergamon Press. Printed in Great Britain.

World Water Resources:
Perspectives and Problems

A. A. SOKOLOV

Director, State Hydrological
Institute, Leningrad

Summary. – On the basis of a careful study of all kinds of water and hydrological cycles on the Earth the author comes to the conclusion that mankind does not face any danger of water shortage even in the remote future. This optimistic conclusion is, however, valid on the assumption that an obligatory condition is fulfilled, i.e. the development and implementation of measures on the national and international level providing a rational use and protection of water resources of our planet against depletion and pollution.

The history of mankind shows that economic and cultural development results in a progressive demand for water use to satisfy the needs of population, industry, agriculture, fisheries and other branches of the national economy in all the countries. The increase of water consumption is particularly great during the 20th century. Between 1900 and 1975 water consumption for agriculture has increased 7 times (from 350 km^3/year to 2,100 km^3/year) and for industry more than 20 times (from 30 km^3/year to 630 km^3/year). A particularly rapid leap in water consumption all over the world was observed during the 1960s and is explained by technical progress started at that period.

The population growth, the development of power engineering and industry, the origination of different forms of production requiring water, and the extension of irrigated farming led to a catastrophically great water demand.

At present no branch of industry can be developed without water. The production of 1 t of petroleum requires 10 m^3 of water; 1 t of steel requires 20 m^3 of water; 1 t of paper requires 200 m^3 of water; 1 t of woollen stuff requires 600 m^3 of water, etc. Water demand is especially great due to the development of a chemical industry. The production of 1 t of acetate silk requires 2,660 m^3 of water; 1 t of lavsan – 4,200 m^3; 1 t of capron fibre – 5,600 m^3 of water. A modern heat power plant of 1 million Kw requires 1.2–1.6 km^3 of water per year, and atomic power plants constructed at present in many countries of the world require 1.5–2.0 times more water.

To satisfy the water demand of a modern city with 1 million people at least 0.5 million ·m^3 of water are required daily, and in future, with the improvement of living standards, up to 1 million m^3 of water.

The growing population should be supplied with food and clothes. To produce 1 kg of dry wheat grains at least 750 kg of water are essential. To irrigate 1 hectare of cotton, 5,000–6,000 m^3 of water are necessary and the irrigation of 1 hectare of rice requires 15,000–20,000 m^3 of water during a season.

Together with the growth of water consumption a progressive increase of waste discharges is observed, leading to pollution of natural water bodies, i.e. rivers, lakes, seas and ground water, which is dangerous for health.

The Rhine, Lake Erie and many other large rivers and lakes, to say nothing about small ones, have acquired a bad reputation due to their extreme rate of pollution. Inland seas and even the ocean are subject to a rapid pollution as well. Thor Heyerdahl, who crossed the Atlantic Ocean in Ra-I, wrote that he was staggered how quickly people managed to pollute the ocean. The famous traveller wrote that it was difficult to imagine how many sweepings were swimming in the open ocean from America to Africa.

The progressing quantitative and qualitative depletion of fresh water resources was the main reason for a sudden aggravation of the water problem which nowadays is becoming of a global nature. Together with developed countries, the developing countries pay much attention to this problem, since they do not want to repeat the mistakes of the previous historical experience, characterized by a chaotic, extremely thoughtless water resources development.

Nowadays water greatly affects the distribution and development of productive forces of the society. It is not a surprise, therefore, that the water problem during recent years has been the subject of discussion at summit talks, that it has become one of the key problems for many international organizations, such as UNESCO, WMO, IAHS, IOC, IAH, ICID, etc.

During 1965–74 a programme of international co-operation in hydrology – the International Hydrological Decade – unprecedented in its scale, was implemented by UNESCO to study world water balance and water resources, encompassing 108 member-states from all the continents.

During the implementation of the IHD programme, Soviet hydrologists made a detailed inventory of all kinds of water on the Earth.*

According to up-to-date data, total secular water resources on the Earth equal 1,386 million km^3 (Table 1). Its major portion is concentrated in the World Ocean; the volume of water there according to the latest data on the bottom relief is 1,338 million km^3, or 96.5%. Water storage in the Ocean is so great compared with the demand of mankind for water that if the water were suitable for wide use, mankind would face no water problem either at present or in the remote future. The use of sea water without freshening is possible within quite restricted limits; however, the

_____

* *World Water Balance and Water Resources of the Earth* (Leningrad: Gidrometeoizdat, 1974), 638 p.

Table 1. *World water resources*

Type of water	Area of distribution, km^2	Volume, km^3	Depth, m	Portion from world storage, %	
				from total water storage	from fresh water storage
World ocean	361,300,000	1,338,000,000	3,700	96.5	–
Ground water fresh water	134,800,000	23,400,000	174	1.7	–
including		10,530,000	78	0.76	30.1
Soil moisture	82,000,000	16,500	0.2	0.001	0.05
Glaciers and ice cover Including:	16,227,500	24,064,100	1,463	1.74	68.7
Antarctic	13,980,000	21,600,000	1,546	1.57	61.7
Greenland	1,802,400	2,340,000	1,298	0.17	6.68
Arctic	226,100	83,500	369	0.006	0.24
Mountain areas	224,000	40,600	181	0.003	0.12
Underground ice in permafrost zone	21,000,000	300,000	14	0.022	0.86
Lake water storage fresh water	2,085,700	176,400	85.7	0.013	–
including	1,236,400	91,000	73.6	0.007	0.26
salt water	822,300	85,400	103.8	0.006	–
Swamp water	2,682,600	11,470	4.28	0.0008	0.03
Water in stream channels	148,800,000	2,120	0.014	0.0002	0.006
Water in atmosphere	510,000,000	129	0.025	0.001	0.04
Biologic water	510,000,000	1,120	0.002	0.0001	0.003
Total water storage	510,000,000	1,385,984,610	2,718	100	–
Fresh water	148,000,000	35,029,210	235	2.53	100

freshening of sea water is too expensive to consider it as an essential reserve of water resources. They say that a Queen of England in the 16th century offered a great prize to a person who would propose an effective way of sea water freshening. But that premium was never paid to anybody. Storage of all kinds of fresh water resources, i.e. rivers, lakes, glaciers and ground water makes 35 million km³, or 2.53% of total water resources of the Earth. Moreover, the major portion of this amount is concentrated in glaciers and the snow pack of the Antarctic and Greenland; the water volume of these areas is evaluated as 24 million km³ or 70% of all fresh water resources of the Earth. These forms of water storage are hardly accessible for use though there are some proposals on the transportation of gigantic icebergs to arid coasts of America, Asia and probably Europe as well. If we neglect the possible use of sea water and glaciers of the Arctic and the Antarctic, then the real water resources available are presented by *streamflow*, which will be for a long time the basic source for the satisfaction of numerous water needs of human society.

The most important feature of streamflow among other kinds of natural resources is its annual recovery during water exchange between land and ocean, where water polluted on land is subject to physical and biological purification. Moreover, this remarkable capacity of river water for self-recovery and self-purification during the water cycle is one of the reasons for our thoughtless attitude towards rivers. Together with streamflow, ground water is sometimes considered as an independent type of fresh water resource. But during recent years hydrogeologists have made sure that the recovered ground water resources (which may be used without prejudice for secular storage) are contained in streamflow.

The recovered fresh water resources, according to up-to-date data, comprise 44,500 km³ of water per year (without the glacier runoff of the Antarctic). This corresponds to the amount of water annually discharged by all the rivers into the world ocean and inland endorheic basins.

It is supposed that the recovered water resources relative to secular water storage on the Earth are somewhat similar to the interest from constant capital and may be used without considerable prejudice for the environment. This is surely not so. Natural waters are unique, the use of streamflow from inland basins inevitably affects the regime and quality of water of inland seas, and will lead to the decrease of water levels, while (irretrievable) use of streamflow discharging into the world ocean will finally result in the disturbance of the existing distribution of water between land and ocean.

The quantities of recovered water resources are great but their distribution over the Earth is extremely uneven. Among other continents Europe is referred to as a continent with the minimum water supply *per capita*. About 20% of the population of the world lives in Europe, while European water resources constitute only 7% of world water resources. Comparatively poor water supply exists in vast areas of Central Asia. The worst water supply (per unit area) is found in Australia and Africa (Table 2).

Table 2. *Recovered water resources of the world*

Continent (with islands)	Runoff		Portion in total discharge, %	Water volume			
	mm	km³		area, thousand km²	Discharge l/s/km²	population, million persons (according to data of 1971)	runoff per capita, thousand m³/year
Europe	306	3,210	7	10,500	9.7	654	4.9
Asia	332	14,410	31	43,475	10.5	2,161	6.7
Africa	151	4,570	10	30,120	4.8	290	15.8
North America	339	8,200	17	24,200	10.7	327	25.1
South America	661	11,760	25	17,800	21.0	185	63.6
Australia (with Tasmania)	45.3	348	1	7,683	1.44	12.7	27.4
Oceania	1,610	2,040	4	1,267	51.1	7.1	287.0
Antarctic	165	2,310	5	13,980	5.2	No permanent population	—
Whole land area	314	46,800	100	149,000	10.0	3,637	12.9

Computations show that total water consumption by the year 2000 taking into account population growth and productive forces development may be as follows: Europe – 23%, Asia – 22.7%, Africa – 8.3%, North America – 15.8%, South America – 2.6%, and Australia – 2.5% from mean annual river runoff. As a whole for the continents it will constitute about 13% of the recovered water resources.

The above figures provide an optimistic conclusion for the future.

If we take into account an extremely non-uniform space and time distribution of streamflow and compare water consumption not with mean annual runoff but with a realistic runoff portion available for use (no more than 40%), the above figures should be increased at least 2 or 3 times. This means that in Europe and Asia, i.e. over the area where two-thirds of the world population live, water consumption by the year 2000 will exceed 50% of real water resources. But life will not cease after 2000. Therefore, if we want our descendants who will live in the 21st century not to accuse the 20th century of the depletion of water resources on our planet, we have to take urgent measures providing for rational water resources development and protection against pollution, streamflow in particular.

To this end it is essential to change quite resolutely our view of rivers and lakes as the last link of sewage systems. It is quite natural that the question is not about a simple change of some erroneous idea on the magic capacity of water courses and water bodies for self-purification, but about the necessity of large investments to build large structures for sewage treatment, and their cost will be a heavy burden for industry thus making industrial production more expensive.

Simultaneously it is necessary to re-orientate the system of water conservation measures into preventive inspection, which should be the basis to protect water resources against their qualitative depletion. To this end it is essential to reduce waste water discharges, even after treatment, into rivers and reservoirs in every possible way and eventually, to stop them altogether.

The ever increasing tension of water management balance in many regions of the world makes us conclude that the period of chaotic, unplanned water resources development should be left in the past.

Prevention of irretrievable water losses, control of water consumption, introduction of waterless technological processes into practice, prevention of water pollution, and water re-use are the most important measures towards which the attention of engineers and scientists engaged in hydrology and water management should be concentrated.

Nowadays we face an acute problem of a legislative control of public relations connected with the use and protection of water resources, with the elimination of sharp contradictions between water users and water consumers.

Such legislative measures determining a more reasonable order in water use (inventory, planning and control of water use, responsibility for breaking the law) have been taken recently in many countries. But the implementation of these laws is often difficult especially in capitalist society where private property in land and water exists. For example, in the USA, according to Ralph Nader's paper, 'Water desert', seven laws have been adopted during the last 15 years, a comprehensive programme of pollution control has been developed and three billion dollars have been spent, but the programme has come to grief.

The conditions for the water problem solution are more favourable in a socialist society with its planned national economy. The Supreme Soviet of the USSR adopted the 'Basis of water legislation of the USSR and Union Republics' in 1970. To realize this law an extensive State plan of water control measures, currently in progress, has been developed for the basins of the Caspian Sea, Black and Azov Seas, Baikal Lake, and for some other basins. Plans for inter-basin redistribution of water resources are being developed and implemented. A new system of water inventory and cadastre providing reliable data on the quantity and quality of surface and ground waters, their regime and use is being introduced.

The solution of the water problem requires an expansion of theoretical and experimental investigations for the study of the mechanism of hydrological events and processes, of all the elements of water balance, and consequently, of the energy and salt balances of basins and territories and their changes under the effect of man's activity.

These investigations will serve as a scientific basis to improve methods of hydrological computations and forecasts. They will provide the transition to compiling current water balances (for short time intervals) for basins of rivers, lakes, reservoirs, seas, and the control of water resources.

With the development of water management and hydrology it becomes more and more necessary to make a synthesis of a unique science on water highly differentiated during recent years, to combine efforts of hydrologists, hydrogeologists, oceanologists, meteorologists and other scientists concerned with the solution of the problem of rational use and protection of water.

The International Hydrological Programme (IHP) established by UNESCO and WMO in 1975 with the participation of scientists from all the continents is an important contribution to its solution.

World Development, 1977, Vol. 5, Nos. 5–7, pp. 525–536. Pergamon Press. Printed in Great Britain.

The World Fertilizer Situation

G. R. ALLEN

Institute of Agricultural Economics,
Oxford University

Summary. – Cyclical changes in world market conditions pose a potentially serious problem for LDCs sometime in the early 1980s notwithstanding their efforts for greater self-sufficiency in the manufacture of fertilizer. The author discusses the present and future capacity of the fertilizer industry and its effect on the world market and therefore on fertilizer availability to LDCs. Using the forecasts of the Commission on Fertilizers and others as a basis, the author considers the implications for world fertilizer use and thus, food production. In particular, various aspects of the macro-economic fertilizer price/demand relationship are presented. The cyclical outlook differs widely among various projections considered but the author's own projections lead to a relatively pessimistic conclusion, i.e. that shortages of capacity after 1980 may be exacerbated by an explosion of demand and that although LDC importers will be relatively less vulnerable to world market fluctuations, they may still be dependent to a critical degree on imported materials.

I

Probably the single most important policy issue relating to the world fertilizer industry is the vulnerability of the LDCs to shortages and high prices in international markets. Those countries in the mid-1970s consumed slightly less than one-quarter of all plant nutrients, and 29% of all nitrogen (the most critical nutrient for the time being in most Green Revolution situations), but produced only one-half of their own needs. In 1973 through early 1975 they found it increasingly difficult to purchase imports on the scale to which they had become accustomed, partly on account of price but partly because the governments of most export-ing DCs ensured that their own farmers had preferential access to the available supply – even if in the process export contracts to LDCs had to be broken. In 1974 it seemed highly likely that *per capita* food production in countries such as India would be severely reduced on account of inadequate fertilizer use.[1] It was exceptionally favourable growing conditions in non-Communist Asia in 1975/76, apparently the most beneficent in about a quarter of a century, plus the slump in world demand[2] which averted the crisis.

The dominating role of the DCs in the past development of the fertilizer industry is self-evident. Table 1 (*overleaf*) summarizes the situa-tion for the year ending June 1975. At that time North America, Western Europe and the Eastern European and Russian Bloc took respectively 24%, 22% and 27% of total world consumption. Communist China was the largest consumer among the LDCs at 7% of total nutrients, followed by India with about half the 8% of non-Communist Asia.

By 1981 the overall pattern will have shifted somewhat towards the LDCs — perhaps by two or three percentage points overall and slightly more for nitrogen.[3] By then the LDCs will be more self-sufficient and, depending on the growth of their fertilizer consumption, produc-ing in the aggregate 70–85% of their needs. Their search for self-sufficiency is being pur-sued, quite understandably given their recent experience, almost irrespective of the costs involved and of the large long-term benefits from developing international trade in fertili-zers, especially in nitrogen produced in the oil-rich states.[4]

There is a substantial body of literature on the macro-economics of fertilizer production and consumption in LDCs. This paper will not attempt to augment it. Instead it will address itself to the fact that cyclical changes in world market conditions pose a potentially serious problem for LDCs sometime in the early 1980s notwithstanding their efforts for greater self-sufficiency in the manufacture of fertilizer. One can take an optimistic view: the cobweb ten-dencies are probably less strong than in the last cycle and, if so, major LDCs should be less dependent on fertilizer imports, absolutely as well as proportionally, than they were in 1972—75. But significant chances remain of a less favourable combination of LDC demand and world market supplies.

II

In 1967—71 all three sections of the industry had experienced over-capacity, although less in nitrogen than in phosphates and potash. The effects have been most long-lasting for potash, principally as a result of the expansion in capacity following the technological advance in the early 1960s which made the Saskatchewan deposits mineable. Here excess capacity has become almost structural rather than purely cyclical. Technology was an important destabilizing factor in the case of nitrogen, with the development of the centrifugal compressor ammonia plants in the early 1960s. But, for all three nutrients there was a more general cobweb effect due to improving profitability in the mid-1960s reinforced by the optimism (for the

fertilizer industry) generated by the world food shortages of 1964—67. In the end phosphates have shown the strongest purely cyclical tendencies.

These patterns are revealed clearly in the absolute and relative price movements of the three nutrients in world markets and in the USA. Statistics on the use of world capacity are not sufficiently precise to reveal the relationship between price variations and demand/supply imbalances. Information on operating rates in the USA is reliable and at the same time provides a reasonable indication of the tendencies in international markets. It is shown in Table 1 together with information on capacity usage for North American potash producers.

Demand and supply are in balance and yielding normal profits when the industry shows an operating rate of 85—90% of effective capacity — although, of course, allowance must always be made for the level of stocks at the beginning of the fertilizer year. On this basis, Table 2 supports the fact that (1) phosphates experienced deeper and more prolonged cyclical over-supply than nitrogen; (2) with slightly different timings each of these sectors swung

Table 1. *Percentage distribution of consumption of manufactured plant nutrients in 1974/75*

By countries					
	Developed countries				
	North America %	Western Europe %	USSR and Eastern Europe %	Other %	Sub total %
Nitrogen	24	18	26	3	71
Phosphates	24	25	23	8	80
Potash	25	25	33	6	89
Total	24	22	27	5	78

By countries				*By category of nutrient: world consumption*
	Less developed countries			
	Non-communist Asia* %	Communist Asia† %	Other %	Sub total %	%
Nitrogen	10	11	8	29	48
Phosphates	7	5	8	20	29
Potash	4	1	6	11	23
Total	8	7	7	22	

Source: Calculated from the projected consumptions in Reidinger (1974).
*Excluding Taiwan
†Including Taiwan

back into a shortage situation in the early 1970s with exceptionally acute pressure on production in 1972–74; but, (3) by the beginning of 1976 serious over-supply had reappeared in phosphates and was possibly imminent in ammonia.[5]

World market prices rose rapidly after 1971. An approximate index of total world plant nutrient consumption valued at world market prices with 1967–69 = 100 had recovered to 114 in 1972 and then 'took off' to 520 in 1974 from which there has been a decline to 190 in 1976 and the prospect of around 200 in 1977. Table 3 (*overleaf*) shows the experience in more detail, together with the US GNP deflator, price series for cereals and other principal users of fertilizer – using crops (excluding grass in Europe and some plantation crops) and farm income data for the US.[6]

Table 3 supports the view that the main reason for the sharp rise in prices in 1973–early 1975 was the increased profitability of farming for most major users of fertilizers and that the important subsidiary influence was shortage of

capacity.[7] The rise in demand included an important element of panic buying, as well as more well-considered speculative activity, in 1973 and 1974; the one illustrated by world market purchases by various LDCs which they could not subsidize sufficiently for their farmers to afford and which have accumulated as excess stocks and the other by purchases for one year ahead by dealers and farmers in North America and Western Europe. (Oil prices and supplies had a minor effect on the overall world fertilizer situation in 1973–75. Their importance has been much exaggerated.)

The reversal of the foregoing demand factors in the spring of 1975 broke the cycle and were reinforced mainly by large-scale postponement of phosphate applications in developed countries[8] and by the expansion of phosphate capacity.

III

Additions to world effective capacity can be

Table 2. *Indicators of capacity use and fertilizer prices 1965–76*

| Year ending June 30 | Use as an approximate per cent of effective capacity | | | Average price paid per short ton of material by US farmers at April 15 ($ per short ton) | | |
	Ammonia USA	Wet Phosphoric acid USA	Potash North America	Anhydrous ammonia	Triple super-phosphate	Potash
	%	%	%	$	$	$
1965	95	91	91	123	81	60
1966	97	86	93	119	81	60
1967	92	77	88	113	84	58
1968	85	75	85	91	78	49
1969	83	72	81	76	74	48
1970	81	76	75	75	75	51
1971	82	84	77	79	77	58
1972	85	91	80	80	78	59
1973	90	94	82	88	88	62
1974	94	89	77	183	150	81
1975	84	84	76	265	214	102
1976	88	80	75	191	158	96

Source: G. R. Allen from various published and unpublished material.
Notes: Ammonia is the basic intermediate from which nitrogen fertilizers are produced and, at least in the United States, is used extensively as a fertilizer material without any further processing. Similarly wet phosphoric acid is the building block for the so-called high analysis phosphate fertilizers which represent virtually all of US phosphate production and are coming increasingly to dominate output elsewhere.

In order to get a clearer picture of the cyclical tendencies in prices it is necessary to consider the following points: (1) technical advances in production and distribution had reduced the long-run supply price of ammonia to around $95–$100 per short ton by 1967, or a reduction of $10–$15 per short ton in the space of 4 or 5 years; (2) the cost of sulphur, an essential ingredient in phosphate fertilizers, rose by the equivalent of around $6 per short ton of triple super-phosphate in 1967–69 compared with 1965 and much of 1966; (3) the long-run supply price of potash probably fell by around $5 per short ton from 1963–64 to 1967.

projected with reasonable confidence through the year ending May 1981 for nitrogen and phosphates. As regards the market economies, the new plants which will be brought into operation by mid-1979 in developed countries and by mid-1980 in less developed countries are to all intents and purposes already announced. Given the current low levels of profitability on new investments and in some cases difficulties over nitrogen feedstock it is unlikely that much

Table 3. *Fertilizer prices and selected indicators of changes in the demand for plant nutrients*

	Representative fertilizer prices in world markets				
Calendar Year	Urea (f.o.b. in bags European ports) $/m.t	Triple super-phosphate (f.o.b. in bulk US ports) $/m.t	Potassium chloride (f.o.b. in bulk Vancouver) $/m.t	Approximate weighted average for all fertilizers per ton of nutrient	
				Actual $/m.t	Index 1967–1969 = 100
1966	89	47	28	128	127
1967	79	47	26	117	116
1968	66	38	24	98	97
1969	56	39	22	88	87
1970	48	43	32	87	86
1971	46	43	33	86	85
1972	59	68	34	115	114
1973	95	100	43	173	171
1974	316	304	61	525	520
1975	198	200*	81	343	340
1976	115*	90*	53*	192	190
1977(F)	120	100	55	202	200

USA			World average export values							
GNP deflator	Total farm income									Mutton and Lamb
Index 1967–1969 = 100	Gross $ bill.	Net $ bill.	Maize $/m.t	Wheat $/m.t	Sugar $/m.t	Rice $/m.t	Wool $/m.t	Cotton $/m.t		$/m.t
91	50.5	14.0	58	63	103		1199	603		503
96	49.9	11.6	56	68	100	157	1170	597		493
100	51.7	12.0	52	64	101	173	989	631		464
105	56.3	13.9	55	65	107	158	1055	617		483
110	58.6	13.8	60	62	118	129	964	630		551
115	60.6	12.8	63	65	128	121	802	695		556
119	70.1	17.3	63	69	148	134	922	772		587
126	95.5	29.9	91	106	186	225	2057	876		873
139	100.2	27.8	122*	138*	345*	457	1900*	1299*		1211
151	98.2	22.7	110*	151*	444*	288	1800*	1221*		N.A.
159	102.0*	24.0*	100*	125*	300*	200*	1900*	1700*		N.A.
168	–	–	–	–	–	–	–	–		–

Sources: Fertilizer prices 1966–75: *UN Yearbook of Financial Statistics.*
US farm income 1966–75: USDA, *Statistical Yearbook* and *Agricultural Outlook* (December 1976).
World average export values 1966–73: FAO, *State of Food and Agriculture.*
* Estimated by G. R. Allen based on various sources and subject to revision.
Notes: (1) The estimates of export values may be slightly inconsistent with the FAO series for 1966–73.
(2) Urea (46% N), triple superphosphate (48% $P_2 O_5$) and potash (60% K_2 O) prices have been converted to a nutrient ton basis and weighted in the proportions 45, 30 and 25.

additional capacity, as yet unannounced, will be working by mid-1981 or even 1982. Incremental expansion in potash, especially in Canada, could be undertaken more rapidly, but is constrained by poor market prospects. For all three plant nutrients the Five-Year Plans of the communist countries take us to 1980. Their targetted capacity can be adjusted (downwards) on the basis of past experience.

There are, of course, a large number of assumptions which must be made in getting from announced date of start-up of *nominal* capacity to actual date of commencing operation and the *effective* capacity thereafter achieved. Possibly one of the greatest areas of doubt concerns the large expansion in China. However, there is broad agreement among analysts on these matters[9] which are a subordinate source of uncertainty in projecting capacity into 1981 or 1982. The more serious unknown for the next four or five years is the as yet unannounced closure of high cost plants. For example, Douglas (1976) shows that the US and European phosphate industries could be back in balance between demand and supply during 1979 if allowance is made for probable shut-downs, but not until 1980 or 1981 if they are ignored. Stangel (1975, pp. 91–93) indicates the possible closure of Japanese nitrogen capacity as its export markets to China begin to decline.

In brief, the present analysis uses the forecasts of the Commission on Fertilizers (FAO, UNIDO, World Bank and others) for probable capacity through June 1981, but recognizes that a five percentage points range on either side should be allowed, reflecting the net effect of yet unannounced closures or new plants and of discrepancies between assumed and actual time lags in plant start-up and in operating efficiency. The Commission's projections are shown later in Table 6.

Much greater uncertainty surrounds projections of consumption. We begin by outlining two important characteristics.

(1) Only a small proportion of the phosphates applied in one season become immediately available to a crop, the rest being fixed into the soil and released more slowly over a number of years. After a period of rapid increase in phosphate applications per acre, as in 1962–72 in most countries, the soil has a large nutrient reserve on which farmers can draw without serious effect on yields while economising in fresh applications. This happened in 1975 and 1976, particularly in Western Europe and North America. There is some disagreement over the extent to which it will remain a constraining influence on the

demand for phosphate fertilizers over the next two or three years.

(2) About half of total world manufactured plant nutrients are used on grains. Approximate estimates of the share on grains have been provided for individual countries by Reidinger (1974): USA, 53%; West Germany, 51%; Japan, 36%; France, 34%; China, 85%; India, 64%.[10] In some developed countries feedgrains take more fertilizer than cereals for human consumption. At the extreme about 45% of total fertilizer used in the USA is on maize, sorghum and barley. Feedgrain crops probably use 25–33% of the total plant nutrients applied in non-Communist developed countries.

If the underlying world-wide trends of fertilizer costs and of demand for agricultural output could be projected as extensions of the experience of 1952–72, there would not be much difficulty in projecting consumption. The writer would argue, as in 1974, that the use of plant nutrients would increase at a somewhat faster rate during the 1970s than in the previous two decades – emphasizing the overall tendency to diminishing returns to fertilizer use and an (assumed) offsetting willingness of governments to provide the necessary financial incentives, one way or another, to ensure a total food supply sufficient to raise *per capita* nutritional standards slightly.[11]

This approach is obviously no longer reasonable given the rather poor prospects for the global demand for agricultural products due to slow world economic growth. Change in real fertilizer costs following the OPEC price increases might be another substantial influence; yet, apart from one important contribution by Timmer towards deriving the needed macroeconomic fertilizer demand curve,[12] the necessary empirical basis for assessing the energy effect is virtually undeveloped. All of the forecasts of world consumption known to the writer are derived as extrapolations of past trends with some subjective assessment for the influence of energy costs and the like. The consensus strongly supports the view of the Commission on Fertilizers in June 1976 that world consumption will be around 120 million metric tons of plant nutrient in the year ending June 1981.[13] Yet, it still seems that the Commission's projection reflects an overreaction to the factors which have checked consumption in recent years – lack of supplies and high prices in 1973–75 and the above-normal reliance of the soil's phosphate reserve already noted – and to the expected influences of energy costs and other demand factors.

Fertilizers are now costly in terms of their

use of oil, natural gas and naphtha (derived from oil). Assuming that these inputs were priced on a strict opportunity cost basis and discounting for inflation, the effect of the OPEC situation would be an increase of around 20% in the real average cost of fertilizers to North American farmers by 1980 compared with the late 1960s and slightly less in most other developed market economies where before 1973 energy was comparatively more expensive. One is tempted to see a sharp curtailment in fertilizer use. The micro-economic long-run price elasticity of demand for fertilizers, i.e. the responsiveness, assuming all other relevant prices remain unchanged, is likely to be well over unity. but it is a misleading concept and mentioned here only because virtually all of the quantitative analysis of fertilizer demand employs it!

The first critical issue is akin to that of the incidence of an indirect tax: how far can the increased cost of fertilizers be passed on to the consumer and with what ultimate effect on the demand for farm products and on the derived consumption of plant nutrient? Timmer's macro-economic relationship must be used. The more inelastic the demand for agricultural output at the farm-gate, the more a given increase in fertilizer prices due to higher energy and feedstock costs will be passed on to the consumer and thereby offset the initial fall in fertilizer consumption.

For example, the National Economic Development Office (1974) suggests that a 21.1% increase in fertilizer costs (together with other energy-related cost increases) would raise the expense of agricultural production in the United Kingdom by 5.2% and that the consequent overall effect on the volume of food consumption would not be significant. The NEDO result is a reasonable indicator for most of the developed market economies. But the overall conclusion conceals a greater price elasticity of demand for feedgrains,[14] which take 25–33% of all plant nutrient consumed in these countries or some 11–15% of world disappearance. Add to this the effect of the comparatively high price elasticity of demand for all grains in LDCs and the brake of higher fertilizer costs on the expansion of use in the subsistence or largely subsistence sectors of Third World agriculture, and the possibility emerges of an important macro-economic check from energy and feedstock costs to world fertilizer use.

But there is another complexity. In one way or another most governments seem likely to negate, offset, or mitigate substantially the consequences of higher energy costs on fertilizer demand. In some cases feedstock for nitrogen is likely to be regulated well below the long-run opportunity cost: for example, probably for three or four years in the USA and much longer in the UK or, with the present development of the Bombay High oil deposits, India. In the Eastern Bloc and China it is probable that fertilizer plants will receive whatever energy and feedstock is necessary to realize fertilizer production targets, and there is no sign that these targets have been scaled down as a result of the post-OPEC situation.

Increased fertilizer subsidies are possible in the non-Communist LDCs. In 1974 some 43 had fertilizer subsidy programmes. Prior to the 1973 price increases the level of subsidy was commonly 25 to 50% of the farm-gate price.[15] But the scope for further expansion is severely limited. A more important mitigating influence from the side of demand is likely to be the consumer subsidies on food in the Eastern Bloc.

The final qualification in assessing the macro-economic fertilizer price/demand relationship applies principally to Western Europe. Here fertilizer on pastures and temporary grass is about equal to the total amount used on cereals but is generally much more profitable at the margin. It is the management problems of intensive grass production, rather than the price relationships between fertilizers and livestock products, which determine the rate of expansion in plant nutrient use on pasture, both pre- and post-OPEC.

It will be obvious that a much more rigorous treatment of the macro relationship is required than is set out above and that if a long period of adjustment well beyond the early 1980s were considered larger and wider reactions would be likely. But in the next four or five years the radical changes in the general energy situation will have but a very small effect on total fertilizer use. A best guess is that the net effect by June 1981 will be to have lowered world consumption by three percentage points below what it would have been otherwise, or by less than half of one years growth. The consequences of the rather slow pace of world economic expansion will be more serious.

Real GNP in the OECD countries increased by around 5.0% annually in 1959–71. Thereafter annual average increases have been 3.0% for 1971–76 and, according to the writer's reading of the macro-forecasters, will achieve 4.0–4.5% for 1976–81. The adverse effects of these recent and prospective changes on the demand for food are not likely to be compensated by other developments. The rate of growth of food aid is unlikely to increase, nor will there be income redistribution on a sufficient scale, either within or between nations.[16]

The recent changes in the trend of world grain consumption shown in Table 4 indicate in part the price effects of short harvests. By mid-1976 this constraint was no longer important and the projected outcome for 1976/77 reflects almost entirely the consequence of lagging demand for food. *Per capita* grain consumption in 1976/77 seems likely to show no more than a 0.3% annual average increase from the beginning of the decade, as against the annual 1.3% of the 1960s, and to be below the peak of 1973/4. In terms of the implication for fertilizer use the decline in feedgrain for livestock is particularly important.

World demand for food (and other agricultural products) almost certainly will expand more rapidly in the years immediately ahead than in the recent past but the net effect will be to leave the rate of increase in the decade to 1981 below that of the previous ten years. The changes in trend will be due almost entirely to the somewhat slower overall economic growth. Any increase in the real cost of food (due to energy prices or other effects) is likely to be a very small secondary influence.

These conclusions can be set in terms of the FAO Index of World Agricultural Production as a lead to using it as a basis for a projection of fertilizer consumption. As against its yearly average increases of 2.8% in 1961–71 and 2.2% in 1971–75, the prospective increases in demand should support an increase of 2.3–2.6% annually without shifting the market balance adversely for agriculture. This projection is the basis of the estimate of fertilizer consumption for the year ending June 1981, derived from extrapolation of mathematically fitted relationships between the Index and the logarithms of world fertilizer use for the period 1952–75, as set out in Figure 1. A semi-log extrapolation is,

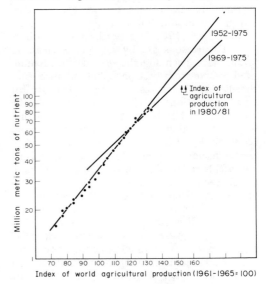

Figure 1.

Table 4. *Per capita world grain consumption*

	Animal feed	Direct human use	Total
	kg.	kg.	kg.
1960/61–1962/63	72.0	206.3	278.3
1969/70–1971/72	92.7	219.2	311.9
1973/74	94.5	229.0	323.5
1974/75	82.6	228.1	310.7
1975/76	82.9	222.5	305.4
1976/77 (forecast)	82.5	235.0	317.5
Annual average percentage increase:	%	%	%
1960/61–1962/63 to 1969/70–1971/72	2.8	0.7	1.3
1969/70–1971/72 to 1976/77	−1.9	1.2	0.3

Source: USDA, *World Agricultural Situation* (December 1976), p. 17.

of course, extremely sensitive to *slight* changes in the historical interpretation and to the projected values for the index of production. But on both counts due caution has been taken. First, the production, which it is expected projected demand will support, does not seem excessive. But, of far more importance, the relationship between production and fertilizer consumption chosen to make the extrapolation seems cautious, namely that for 1969–75 instead of that for 1952–75.

There may have been a sharp break in the agricultural production/plant nutrient use relationship since 1969 in a fertilizer saving direction. The reasons are by no means clear. In favour have been (1) the use of the accumulated reserve from past phosphate applications, already mentioned, as a partial substitute for fresh applications in 1974 and 1975, and the possibility that in future farmers will find that they can continue to use this nutrient more economically than in the past; (2) the much greater response to fertilizers obtained by using high-yield varieties in Asia in place of traditional seeds; (3) somewhat greater use of organic fertilizers in Western Europe; and (4) possibly a contribution from the land brought back into cultivation in the USA in the 1970s where *for a year or two* accumulated soil fertility might have more than compensated for the soil's longer-term poorish productivity. But on the other side is the tendency to diminishing returns to fertilizer use in many developed countries, as illustrated by American experience shown in Figure 2, and the possibility that the fertilizer saving aspect of the Green Revolution will be much weaker in the future than in the recent past.[17]

The impact of climatic influences is by no means clear. It might seem that 1971–75 has experienced generally unfavourable climatic conditions, the implication being that the global weather and, therefore, the production response to fertilizer use have been below 'normal'. But against that contention must be set the substantial body of opinion contending that the 1960s witnessed unusually favourable weather, especially in the North American grain areas, which permitted a given output from a 'below normal' fertilizer use.

One is tempted to use the longer-term relationship for 1952–75 except for the need to guard against possible errors of the semi-log extrapolation. However, its projection of around 157 million metric tons of plant nutrient consumption in 1980/81 must be kept in mind until we have, say, two more years data to provide a better test. In the meantime the

more cautious 1969–75 trend is used, giving some 130 million metric tons in 1980/81. This is 10.6 million metric tons more than the Commission on Fertilizers.

Projected plant nutrient consumption,
year ending June 1981
(million metric tons of nutrient)

	Nitrogen	Phosphates	Potash	Total
Fertilizer Commission	59.4	31.8	28.6	119.7
G. R. Allen	65.2	34.1	31.0	130.3

These alternative sets of projections are compared with the historical experience in Table 5 where the period 1950–74 has been broken down into four groups intended to highlight the main changes in the pace of increased consumption since 1950 and to point to the risks of giving too much weight to the short period of slow growth in 1974–76 when making a longer-term projection. In the periods 1950–55 and 1962–67 there were cyclical upswings in capacity and supply, and given the necessary price changes, in consumption. But in 1955–62 and 1967–74 consumption growth was constrained, in the first case probably more by weakish demand than by supply but in the second by lack of new capacity. We are now in

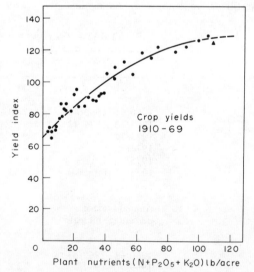

Figure 2. *The signs of diminishing returns to increased use of fertilizers in the USA.*
Source: National Academy of Science, *Agricultural Production Efficiency* (Washington D.C., 1975), using USDA statistics. See Allen (1976) for an evaluation of this and related evidence.

a phase of relatively rapid expansion of supplies and of consumption, subject to the constraining influence on demand of slow economic growth and whatever are the effects of increased energy costs.

IV

Table 6 (*overleaf*) highlights the widely differing positions on the cyclical outlook which this paper has examined. The analysis of the Commission on Fertilizers points to excess capacity continuing through the 1980/81 season, and possibly further for nitrogen and potash. Admittedly the Commission has made no allowance for closures of high-cost plants in the intervening period of oversupply but on the other hand its projections, if they are correct in all other respects, suggest a substantial build-up of stocks in the next four years. By contrast, the writer's projections of consumption for 1980/81, together with his implied estimates for earlier years, in combination with the Commission on Fertilizer's projection of supply capability point to a balance of demand and supply by 1979/80 at the latest, and possibly sooner for nitrogen. In addition, there is the prospect of continuing shortages for two or three more years, because (1) the industry is likely to be cautious in committing itself to new capacity in the next two years, even if demand expands in line with the writer's projections, and (2) the next phase of nitrogen expansion outside Communist countries will take place largely in the Middle East and other oil-rich areas where the effective time lag between initial planning and bringing new plants on

stream will be typically four years and possibly five.

There are sufficient signs for us to be greatly concerned that the early 1980s will see a return to severe shortages of capacity. Whether their consequences will be exacerbated again by an explosion of demand must remain an open question. In such circumstances Third World importers would be relatively less vulnerable to the vagaries of the world markets than they were in the 1970s by virtue of their own current expansions in fertilizer production. But, if the more pessimistic diagnosis is correct, they will still be dependent to a highly critical degree on imported materials.

Against this background one notes that, despite all the expressions of anxiety at the World Food Conference of 1974, there are no signs of international action on measures to minimize the cyclical tendencies in prices and supplies, or to ensure better provision for LDC importers than existed in 1973–75. The Commission on Fertilizers may be too influential! Admittedly, it is hard to see what might be done. In the event of serious shortages re--emerging governments of the principal exporting countries (North America, Western Europe and Eastern Europe and the USSR) are once again likely to give over-riding preference to domestic users, and it is an open question how far the expanding shipments from oil-rich states would be directed to LDCs which in the circumstances would probably not provide the most profitable markets.

Buffer stock proposals were aired by the FAO at the time of the World Food Conference but have come to nothing, perhaps partly because of the loss of the sense of urgency but

Table 5. *Annual average percentage increase in world fertilizer consumption,*
actual and projected

Year ending June	Nitrogen	Phosphates	Potash	Total
	%	%	%	%
1950–55	12.8	5.0	9.4	8.6
1955–62	7.9	4.3	4.8	5.9
1962–67	13.4	8.9	8.3	10.5
1967–74	8.6	5.9	7.0	7.4
1974–81				
Fertilizer				
Commission	6.3	4.0	4.6	5.2
G. R. Allen	7.7	5.1	5.8	6.5

Source: Calculated from FAO statistics of world fertilizer consumption.

Note: A graphical presentation of the basic data would show that the differences in growth rates between periods reflect the short-term changes in trends and are not the accident of inappropriately chosen dates.

Table 6. *Supply capability and consumption, 1974–81*
(million metric tons)

Year ending 30 June	Estimates and projections of Fertilizer Commission								Projections of supply capability by the Fertilizer Commission and of consumption by G. R. Allen
	1974	1975	1976	1977	1978	1979	1980	1981	1981
Nitrogen									
Supply capability	38.80	40.52	42.41	46.13	49.69	54.12	58.85	62.10	62.10
Consumption	38.76	38.87	42.18	45.34	48.57	51.92	55.60	59.38	65.20
Supply capability less consumption	0.04	1.65	0.23	0.79	1.12	2.22	3.25	2.72	-3.10
Phosphates									
Supply capability	24.10	24.60	27.21	28.93	30.23	31.25	32.37	33.18	33.18
Consumption	24.14	22.89	23.83	25.56	27.20	28.89	30.35	31.75	34.10
Supply capability less consumption	-0.04	1.71	3.38	3.37	3.03	2.36	2.02	1.43	-0.92
Potash									
Supply capability	21.10	21.71	28.06	28.74	29.27	29.61	30.75	31.37	31.37
Consumption	20.86	19.93	20.99	22.72	23.99	25.55	27.07	28.56	31.00
Supply capability less consumption	0.24	1.78	7.07	6.02	5.28	4.06	3.67	2.81	0.37
Total Nutrients									
Supply capability	84.00	86.83	97.68	103.80	109.19	114.98	121.97	126.65	126.65
Consumption	83.76	81.69	87.00	93.62	99.76	106.36	113.02	119.69	130.30
Supply capability less consumption	0.24	5.14	10.68	10.18	9.43	8.62	8.95	6.96	-3.65

Source: *Report to the Commission on Fertilizers, 8–11 June 1976*, AGS:F/76/2 (May 1976) except for supply capabilities in 1974 which have been estimated by G. R. Allen.

Note: Supply capability assumes that (1) plants are running at the levels of production required if demand and supply are in balance, and (2) no capacity in use in 1976 is shut down, temporarily or permanently, within the review period.

also because it is difficult to see how adequate finance could be provided to make this approach more than a minor policy instrument. The relevant demand and supply elasticities are too high and, at least for nitrogen products, wastage costs would be large; and the probable speculative profits from 'playing the fertilizer cycle' would not be a sufficient counter-attraction to governments. But the need for some inter-governmental cooperation in stockpiling must remain on the agenda — especially if serious excess capacity develops in nitrogen around mid-1978 as envisaged by the Commission on Fertilizers. In such circumstances the purchase and stockpiling of even one million tons of nitrogen over a two or three-year period would be well justified in cost/benefit terms.

One over-riding need is for prompt action to offset, or at least mitigate, the insufficiency of new investment which seems likely in 1978—80. Governments should be preparing now for an appropriate programme of counter-cyclical investment incentives in case the Commission on Fertilizers is seriously underestimating future demand.

And finally, the greatest single contribution towards more stability in the world fertilizer industry would be to operate on the side of demand; i.e. to implement measures for reducing fluctuations in international agricultural commodity prices, above all by a world grain reserve.

REFERENCES

Allen, G. R., 'Confusion in fertilizers and the world food situation', *European Chemical News, Chemscope Supplement* (18 October 1974).

Allen, G. R., 'Agricultural policies in the shadow of Malthus', *Lloyds Bank Review* (July 1975).

Allen, G. R., 'Some aspects of planning world food supplies', *Journal of Agricultural Economics*, Vol. 28, No. 1 (January 1976).

Commission on Fertilizers, *Report to the Commission on Fertilizers, 8–11 June 1976*, FAO, AGS:F/76/2 (May 1976).

Dalrymple, D. G., *Evaluating Fertilizer Subsidies in Developing Countries*, AID Discussion Paper No. 30, Bureau for Program and Policy Coordination, Agency for International Development (1975).

Reidinger, R. B., *The World Fertilizer Situation 1975, 1976 and 1980. Supplement to the World Agricultural Situation*, Economic Research Service, United States Department of Agriculture (September 1974).

Reidinger, R. B., *World Fertilizer Review and Prospects to 1980/81*, Foreign Agricultural Economic Report No. 115, Economic Research Service, United States Department of Agriculture (February 1976).

Shields, J. T., 'Estimating fertilizer demand', *Food Policy*, Vol. 1, No. 4 (August 1976).

Stangel, P. J., 'Impact of the energy crisis and other factors on the fertilizer industry of Asia', in *Impact of Fertilizer Shortage: Focus on Asia* (Tokyo: Asian Productivity Organization, 1975).

Timmer, C. P., 'Interaction of energy and food prices in less developed countries', *American Journal of Agricultural Economics* (May 1975).

Timmer, C. P., 'Fertilizer and food policy in LDCs', *Food Policy*, Vol. 1, No. 2 (February 1976).

NOTES

1. See Allen (1974).

2. See Table 4.

3. e.g. assessments of the relative contributions of price and non-price influences on demand.

4. Allen (1975) states: 'While one can always point to exceptions — often where there is partnership between indigenous and expatriate management — a critical set of unfavourable plant economics can usually be found in developing countries. Plants take five years to build, where two or three would be required elsewhere; their start-up problems are greater and more prolonged; they ultimately settle down at outputs of 60—75% of theoretical capability, as against 80—90% in North America or in Western or Eastern Europe; the technical infrastructure required to support the industry is more expensive.

Fertilizer manufacturing, especially the all-critical nitrogen, is one of the most capital intensive of industries and, except where an extremely favourable raw material situation exists (as with Middle East natural gas), cannot reconcile such poor performance factors with timely and cheap plant nutrient. While I have not made any precise calculation, inefficiencies to the extent indicated, taking one year with another, are likely to increase the cost of plant nutrient to the peasant farmer in, say, the market economies of Asia by 60—80% over that of imported material. Various cost/benefit studies are said to refute this conclusion or, at least, to invalidate its implications, when allowance is made for the foreign-exchange cost of imported materials and the opportunities to manufacture fertilizer plant components domestically. I believe that further investigation would show that such studies make insufficient allowances for differences in likely operating efficiency and times required to bring new plants on stream; do not allow adequately for the fact that domestic resources used to "save imports" by manufacturing plant components have an "opportunity cost" in terms of alternative activities which also save foreign exchange; do not set the 'shadow price' for capital high enough and assume (at least in some recent evaluations) that ocean freight rates on fertilizer materials will remain at the unrealistically high levels suggested by the circumstances of 1972–74.

5. Perhaps the reader will not object to the linguistic convenience of short-cutting the fundamental economic proposition that demand always equals supply!

6. Grain takes around 50% of world fertilizer use and developed countries account for about three-quarters of total disappearance.

7. It is recognized that agricultural prices in domestic markets in many countries did not rise in line with those in world markets, but increases were generally sufficient to support the argument above.

8. See below.

9. For further information see Reidinger (1976) and Commission on Fertilizers (1976).

10. The UK is probably around one-third.

11. Allen (1974) states: 'If a serious world recession is avoided and if the developed countries have the political will to maintain or increase their aid to the underdeveloped parts of the world, two broad conclusions will follow:
(1) The rate at which fertilizer converts into food is declining. But market forces and, where necessary, government action will ensure that the necessary amount of fertilizer is used to produce the food required in the long run. This reasoning provides the fundamental basis for my rejection of the more conservative fertilizer projections which have been made in the last year or so. They imply long-run food shortages, mostly in the under-developed countries, on a scale which, one hopes, the world will not tolerate . . . . .
(2) Demand and supply will balance, with consumption and production growing at 2.5–2.6% annually between 1972 and 1980. Improved real prices to farmers will be (a) the principal means whereby necessary fertilizer application rates are achieved, (b) a necessary incentive in sustaining the forward momentum of production in the face of any slow down in the development of new agricultural technology.
On the basis of these two conclusions a 9.2% annual growth rate for world fertilizer use through 1980 is considered reasonable as the high projection.

A more pessimistic note is now necessary. First, the anti-inflationary policies likely to be implemented in the USA and elsewhere and the difficulties of handling the international liquidity problems resulting from increased oil prices mean that a free world economic recession is virtually certain, and possibly severe and prolonged.

Second, it is doubtful whether the rich countries have the political will to do more than maintain their present real level of aid to under-developed countries, let alone to raise it . . . . The low projection of fertilizer consumption, growing at 8.1% annually . . . . . is intended to reflect the more pessimistic expectations'.

12. Timmer (1975 or 1976) allows not only for the reduced plant nutrient consumption initially attributable to higher fertilizer prices but also for the partially compensating effects as the resulting reduction in output causes improved agricultural product prices.

13. See Shields (1976) for some further information. There are a number of other estimates which have been prepared since Shield's article and which have been borne in mind above.

14. Used to obtain products with own price elasticities of demand two or three times as large as for food as a whole.

15. See Dalrymple (1975), pp. 9–10.

16. Witness the dragging of DC feet over the New International Economic Order.

17. There is some evidence that the fertilizer/yield response curve is shifted upwards by the HYVs without greatly changing its shape. See Allen (1976), p. 108.

World Development, 1977, Vol. 5, Nos. 5–7, pp. 537–547. Pergamon Press. Printed in Great Britain.

World Grain Markets:
A Functional Analysis

WALTER C. LABYS

Department of Resource and Mineral Economics
West Virginia University, Morgantown

Summary. – The understanding of world grain markets is necessary for analysing problems of world food and agriculture as well as for developing policies to solve those problems. Although several commodity models already exist for explaining the behaviour of those markets which could be commented upon, the purpose of this paper is to examine those mechanisms or relationships deemed most important to understanding overall grain market performance. Following an introduction to the general characteristics of grain markets, consideration is given to a number of critical areas of market behaviour: supply, demand, inventories and prices, futures exchanges, and importance for trade and development.

THE GRAIN MARKETS

World grain markets have been taken here to consist of wheat, rice and the coarse grains: barley, maize, oats, rye and sorghums. In terms of relative importance, world trade in 1973 reached the following levels: wheat and wheat flour – 63.1 million tons; maize – 44.6 million tons; sorghum – 10.5 million tons; barley – 8.0 million tons; rye – 1.3 million tons; and oats – 1.4 million tons.

With the exception of rice, production of grains takes place mostly in the developed regions of the world. In fact, only a few countries account for most of the grain output and exports. As shown in Table 1, the United States, Canada and Australia account for 75% of wheat exports, 68% of barley exports and 58% of oats exports. The United States and Canada supply 51% of total rye exports, while the United States itself produces 69% of the maize exports, 58% of sorghum exports and 25% of rice exports.

When examining production in the developing regions, only for Burma, Cambodia, Thailand and Argentina do grain exports represent more than 20% of total export earnings. Grain production has increased notably in these countries over the last decade, mainly because of the adoption of new, high-yielding seed varieties for rice and wheat; however, the export earnings from grain production have not been highly favourable for these countries. As

shown in Table 2, prices in 1972 were roughly the same as in 1961 for most grains. The impact of the energy crisis in 1973 and of the accompanying world inflation has been to raise these prices, but since 1975 they have turned down. The relative instability of these prices is also an important factor in considering them for purposes of investment and for export diversification. Rice and barley are indicated to be the most unstable with the other grains not far behind, excepting sorghums.

A more complete description of grain markets can be obtained by examining the demand side, as shown in Table 3. Major markets for wheat have been Japan and the EEC among the developed countries and India, Pakistan, Brazil and the United Arab Republic among the developing ones. More than 85% of the wheat and 80% of the coarse grains supplied go to the developed countries. For rice, import demand has been concentrated in Asia. Rice production is not as geographically concentrated as for the other grains, and a number of regions supply these import needs. Actually, less than 5% of the world's rice production enters international trade.

Also included in that table are projections for expected changes in world demand patterns by 1980. The 'A' projection assumes a continuation of present policies and productivity increases, while the 'B' projection suggests higher productivity increases in the developing countries. Wheat import demand is shown to

Table 1. *International grain sources*
(Percentage of Export Contribution)
(1970−74)

Wheat	Rice[a]	Rye	Barley
US − 42%	US − 25%	EEC (9) − 30%	Canada − 40%
Canada − 21%	China − 20%	US − 29%	EEC (9) − 30%
Australia − 12%	Thailand − 16%	Canada − 22%	US − 16%
EEC (9) − 10%	Burma − 5%	Argentina − 5%	Australia − 12%
Others − 15%	Egypt − 4%	Others − 14%	Others − 2%
	Japan − 4%		
	Others − 24%		

Maize	Sorghums[c]	Oats
US − 69%	US − 58%	US − 30%
Argentina − 13%	Argentina − 25%	Australia − 20%
South Africa[b] − 5%	Thailand − 2%	Sweden − 20%
Thailand − 5%	South Africa[b] − 2%	Argentina − 12%
Brazil − 1%	Others − 12%	Canada − 8%
Others − 7%		EEC (9) − 6%
		Others − 4%

Source: FAO, 'Review of the grains situation and outlook', CCR:GR 75/4,
(Rome: FAO, 1975).

[a]   1972−74
[b]   Republic of South Africa
[c]   Includes millet

Table 2. *International grain prices**
(1961−75)

	Wheat	Rye	Barley	Oats	Maize	Sorghum	Rice
1961	2.28	125.0	135.0	71.4	1.11	2.01	136.5
1962	2.48	119.0	112.1	69.4	1.11	1.95	152.8
1963	2.42	131.0	108.7	69.6	1.24	1.97	143.3
1964	2.06	119.0	118.0	73.2	1.23	2.08	137.7
1965	1.83	116.0	130.0	66.4	1.28	1.98	136.3
1966	1.97	119.0	132.0	72.5	1.34	2.11	163.2
1967	1.92	115.0	124.0	70.2	1.27	1.96	205.8
1968	1.79	117.0	115.0	64.1	1.11	1.97	201.6
1969	1.80	113.0	108.0	63.2	1.21	2.07	186.9
1970	1.91	113.0	121.0	70.9	1.35	2.32	144.0
1971	1.77	100.0	116.0	67.5	1.39	2.05	129.0
1972	1.86	111.0	144.0	84.5	1.30	3.24	147.1
1973	3.33	182.0	200.0	108.0	2.19	5.38	350.0
1974	5.24	299.0	340.0	166.0	3.22	6.99	542.0
1975	4.60	278.0	360.0	167.0	2.92	6.50	420.0
Mean	2.48	143.8	157.6	85.6	1.55	2.97	213.1
Standard Deviation	1.08	61.6	81.4	34.6	0.67	0.49	124.0
Instability Ratio (%)	43	43	52	40	43	16	58

Source: *Survey of Current Business* 1962−76 (US Department of Commerce,
Washington, D.C.); *Commodity Price Bulletin* (UNCTAD, Geneva, various
issues).
* Price sources used: Wheat − US No. 2 Hard Red Winter, Kansas City, $/bu;
Rice − Broken milled, f.o.b. Bangkok, $/mt; Maize − US No. 3 Yellow,
Chicago, $/bu; Oats − US No. 2 White Minneapolis, ¢/bu; Rye − US No. 2
Minneapolis, ¢/bu; Barley − No. 3 Straight Minneapolis, ¢/bu; and Sorghum −
No. 2 Kansas City, $/CWT.

Table 3. *World trade in wheat, rice, and coarse grains,
average for 1964–66 and projections to 1980*

Region	Wheat			Coarse Grains			Rice		
	1964–66	1980A[a]	1980B[b]	1964–66	1980A[a]	1980B[b]	1964–66	1980A[a]	1980B[b]
	million metric tons						1,000 metric tons		
United States	21.2	19.3	14.8	21.8	30.0	21.0	1,527	1,063	147
Canada	13.8	11.9	8.7	0.7	1.1	0.4	-45	-64	-66
Central America & Mexico	-1.0	-2.3	-2.1	0.7	-2.2	-0.7	-367	-503	-394
E. South America	-3.0	-4.9	-5.0	0.2	1.0	3.0	382	158	379
W. South America	-1.2	-3.4	-3.5	-0.1	-1.2	-1.2	-71	-22	100
Argentina	5.1	5.2	6.2	5.2	7.0	8.4	29	43	81
N. Africa	-3.6	-8.9	-9.6	0.1	1.2	-0.4	341	538	662
E. Africa	-0.3	-0.7	-0.7	-0.1	1.2	3.3	-177	-454	-437
W. Africa	-0.6	-1.5	-1.6	0.1	-2.8	-2.2	-428	-791	-637
South Africa, Rep. of	-0.4	-0.4	-0.5	0.5	3.9	3.4	-73	-132	-137
W. Asia	-1.9	-5.0	-4.3	-0.5	-2.8	-2.6	-354	-575	-464
S. Asia	-9.3	-2.4	7.1	-1.3	-2.8	-2.4	-1,137	-770	-117
S. E. Asia	-0.2	-0.4	-0.4	1.3	1.6	2.9	2,419	2,480	2,791
E. Asia & Pacific Islands	-2.1	-4.2	-4.4	-0.3	-3.7	-1.3	-1,728	-1,627	-1,046
Australia & New Zealand	6.3	7.8	6.8	0.7	2.8	2.7	71	158	140
Eastern Europe	-5.7	-1.8	-1.8	-0.4	1.1	1.0	-290	-354	-367
USSR	-2.4	4.6	4.6	0.3	0.7	0.6	-247	-266	-287
Communist Asia	-5.7	-6.1	-6.1	0.1	-0.3	-0.4	903	768	574
Japan	-3.6	-6.5	-6.5	-6.0	-16.7	-17.2	-750	-170	-365
EEC	1.3	3.9	2.4	-11.9	-10.0	-9.3	-199	-302	-336
United Kingdom	-4.3	-4.5	-4.6	-3.5	-1.7	-2.9	-109	-134	-140
Other Western Europe	-1.3	0.5	0.6	-5.6	-5.1	-6.2	-29	-40	-82

Source: A. Š. Rojko, F. S. Urban, and J. J. Naive, *World Demand Prospects for Grain in 1980 with Emphasis in Trade by the Less Developed Countries*, Foreign Agricultural Economics Report No. 75, US Department of Agriculture (Washington, D.C.: 1971).

[a] Assumes a continuation of present food and fibre policies, allowing for moderate gains in productivity in the less developed countries.
[b] Assumes that agricultural productivity and economic growth in the less developed countries would be higher than projected under 1980A.

slow down in the developed countries; at the same time increased self-sufficiency occurs in Asia. However, these figures do not take into account the recent impact of increases in energy prices and of decreases in fertilizer availabilities. Coarse grain demand is expected to grow in the developed as well as in the developing countries.

A less well-known aspect of the grain market is the related operation of futures exchanges, as they are termed in the United Kingdom, and futures markets in the United States. Grains futures trading in the United States takes place on the following exchanges: Wheat: Chicago Board of Trade, Kansas City Board of Trade, Mid-American Commercial Exchange, and the Minneapolis Grain Exchange; Corn: Chicago Board of Trade, Kansas City Board of Trade, Mid-American Commercial Exchange, and the Minneapolis Board of Trade; Oats: Chicago Board of Trade, Mid-American Commercial Exchange, and the Minneapolis Grain Exchange; Rye: Chicago Board of Trade, Mid-American Grain Exchange and the Minneapolis Grain Exchange; and Sorghums: Kansas City Board of Trade. The principal grain futures exchange in the United Kingdom which deals with both wheat and barley is the London Corn Trade Association.

Futures trading in grain as well as other commodities has grown continuously since the early 1960s. Table 4 provides a comparison of futures trading in grains with actual amounts of the grains produced in the United States as well as amounts entering world trade from all sources in 1973. The measure of futures trading used is the volume of turnover which indicates the number of futures contracts bought or sold. For wheat and maize the volume of turnover is

substantial, reaching levels of 296.6 and 520.1 million tons respectively. In considering inter-relationships between futures price and spot price behaviour, it is important to examine levels of futures trading relative to actual amounts of the commodity supplied on the spot markets. About 5 times as much the volume of futures trading as exports occurred for wheat. The proportion traded on futures exchanges for barley and sorghums is much smaller.

UNDERSTANDING MARKET RELATIONSHIPS

The interest in understanding the functional mechanisms inherent to grain market behaviour stems from the difficulties encountered in applying traditional modelling approaches. Rather than provide a complete description of the supply—demand behaviour of these markets, the attempt is to examine those variables and mechanisms crucial for analysing the impact of market decisions and policies.

Market framework

The overall market framework within which the various functional mechanisms will be explained is given in Fig. 1. Those factors explaining supply behaviour within a typical producing and exporting country are divided according to yield and acreage determination. Similarly, factors relevant to demand behaviour within a typical consuming country also are featured. The intersection between supply and demand is shown at the world trade level,

Table 4. *Trading on grain futures markets, 1973*
(000 metric tons)

	Futures Turnover[a] US and UK	Production US	World Trade[b]
Wheat[c,d]	296,639	46,400	63,100[c]
Maize	529,141	143,400	44,600
Oats	48,768	9,700	1,434
Barley	1,391	9,200	8,000
Sorghum	0.1	23,600	10,500

Source: Association of Commodity Exchange Firms, Inc., New York; and private sources.

[a] Volume of futures contracts traded
[b] Exports
[c] Wheat including wheat flour
[d] US turnover = 295,160; London turnover = 1,479.

where tariffs, quotas, freight rates and related factors affect world grain distribution. Where a country does not produce substantial amounts of grains, then supply determination can be neglected and only import dependence considered. Also given are related market institutions such as futures markets and grain reserves and buffer stocks.

Supply

The factors shown to be important in explaining grain supply can be divided according to whether they influence yields or acreages. Yields are influenced by cultural practices in each country. Government policies influencing farmer behaviour are important as are questions dealing with the prices of inputs such as subsidies and loans for fertilizers. Yields in a year are smaller or larger depending on a variety of biological, agronomic or meteorological conditions. For example, yields can be influenced by methods used to control insects and crop diseases, the strains or quality of seeds, the nature of fertilization and irrigation, and climatic conditions. Relationships explaining the effects of weather conditions on yields are just beginning to be understood. Interest in them has recently increased because of declines in world inventory levels as well as information provided by satellite weather forecasting.

Acreages planted in grains are also influenced by cultural conditions such as patterns of land ownership and factor endowments. The decisions as to whether to expand or contract acreages depends on the expected price of one grain compared to expected prices of other grains or of other competitive crops. The expected prices of livestock come into play, in

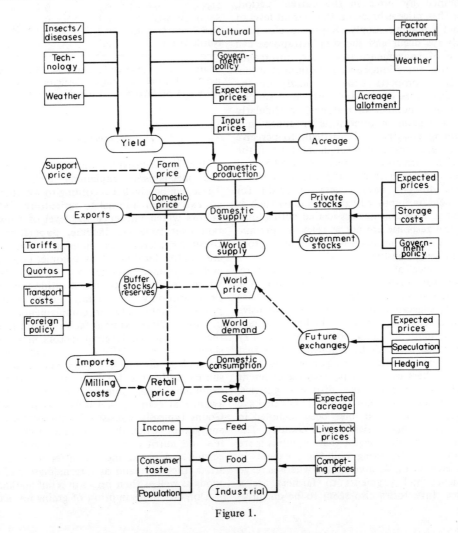

Figure 1.

so far as the grains are used for feed purposes. Inventories are also important; there is a feedback from the relative inventory condition on world markets to acreage expansion.

The economic mechanism used to explain grain production relates to the dynamics of short- and long-run price responses of farmers. Short-run price response is important for explaining crops of an annual nature such as grains. Output from these crops depends on influences arising since the previous harvest. The mechanism by which farmers regulate their planting according to their perception of present prices and their expectations of future ones has been based traditionally on the 'cobweb'. Here supply cycles are hypothesized to occur in two-year patterns. The supply process begins in one period but is realized only in the next. The linkage of response over time is recursive, with supply in the next period determined by price in the current period, where that price is based on the current level of demand equalling supply. Supply cycles need not always occur and the supply response can be one of convergence towards or divergence away from some long-run equilibrium position. This latter property depends mostly on the price elasticities of demand relative to supply.

But in a number of instances, particularly where the grain of interest is produced in a developing country, it is difficult to perceive such a lagged response mechanism. Such is the case where farmers are near subsistence levels of income and the grain is a staple food or where farmers do not have access to credit for investment in improved variable inputs such as fertilizers. Relationships associated with a long-run price response are not as relevant, pertaining more to the production of perennial crops or of fuel and non-fuel minerals.

Some idea of the magnitude of price responses for grain can be gleaned from the elasticities reported in Table 5. A lower price elasticity suggests that farmers are unresponsive to price changes, while a higher elasticity suggests more of a response. Inter-country comparisons are complicated by the fact that prices in one country may have changed more than in others or that it possesses a different agricultural structure and different policies. Also data are often not comparable nor have weather and other variables been included in estimating the elasticities in each country. The reported elasticities suggest that supply is more responsive in exporting countries, except in those such as the United States where acreage allotments and payments to farmers are a practice. Inventories also seem to be an influ-

encing factor regarding farmer response in the United States and Canada as well. Because of the predominance of central planning in the USSR, the supply elasticities are somewhat lower. For the elasticities selected for the three developing regions and Argentina, the values in some cases are comparable to the developed countries listed. This can be accounted for by those regions containing producing countries which are also substantial exporters.

Table 5. *Selected grain supply-price elasticities*

	Wheat	Coarse grain	Rice
Argentina	0.3	0.3	0.4
Australia	0.4	0.3	0.3
Canada	0.1	0.4	0.3
EEC	0.3	0.25	0.3
United Kingdom	0.4	0.3	0.2
United States	0.2	0.3	0.2
USSR	0.2	0.2	0.3
Southeast Asia	0.1	0.3	0.3
East South America	0.2	0.3	0.4
North Africa	0.3	0.1	0.3

Source: W. C. Labys and J. Hunkeler, 'Survey of commodity demand and supply elasticities', Res. Memo. No. 48, UNCTAD/RD/70 (Geneva: 1974).

Demand

Fig. 1 also provides hints as to the variables and mechanisms explaining grain demand. These can be divided according to whether they are external or internal to agriculture. External factors which influence the level of consumption over time are income, population, and consumer preferences. Internal factors which are jointly determined by income, population, and consumer preferences. Internal factors which are jointly determined within the agricultural economy are mainly prices, including prices of substitute or complementary commodities. While external factors relate more to the long run and internal factors more to the short run, both affect the composition of demand at all stages of economic growth and, subsequently, the total demand for grains. In examining total demand, one must also be aware that grain market differentiation is high. Grains typically consist of a number of classes and grades which differ in milling characteristics and nutritive value. Costs of milling, processing and marketing the different grains also affect their demand as intermediate and final goods as well as their prices in retail markets.

Domestic consumption of grains normally is

divided into food for human consumption, feed for animals, and industrial uses and seeds. Food consumption consists of unprocessed and processed grains such as flour and flour products, pearl-barley, oatmeal, unprocessed and processed grains such as flour and flour products, pearl-barley, oatmeal, cornmeal, rice and breakfast foods. Industrial consumption in addition to alcohol includes starch, oil and molasses. Seed consumption depends on expected planting acreage, while feed consumption varies with livestock prices and the prices of feed substitutes.

An important mechanism in assessing changes in grain demand is the relation of the grain/meat ratio to the relative stage of economic development of a country. At early stages of development, grains such as rice or wheat are considered diet staples and are consumed as food. As development increases and incomes rise, the diet improves mostly with a higher consumption of livestock products. As shown in Table 6, larger amounts of grain consumed are now fed to livestock. Shifts also occur in the choice of grains for food consumption, mostly in favour of wheat.

The economic mechanisms of interest in explaining grain demand are the related price and income elasticities. Price elasticities of demand vary between grains and markets. They tend to be lower where substitution between grains and other commodities is less likely. Measurements of price elasticities as well as cross-price elasticities between grains over time have proved difficult. Even more so since substitution tends to be of an economic as well as of a technical and quality or taste nature. Income elasticities also have been difficult to measure. The degree to which a grain responds to changes in income depends on the income elasticity of the particular end product to which the grain is related. Those products with

Table 6. *Critical ranges in the development sequence of a world grain–livestock economy*

Trend in human consumption per capita		Grain allocation to livestock	Grain–meat ratio	Income range per capita
Grain	Meat			
Rising fast, nearly proportional to income	None	None	0	Under $60
Rising	Under 10 kg rising more than prop. to income	Under 1% of domestic disappearance	very low – below 1.0	$50–$100
About level	10 to 20 kg rising prop. to income	1 to 12% of domestic disappearance	low – but doubles to about 2.0	$100–$200
Falling	Moderate to high – rising at 60 to 80% of income rise	Rising from 12 to 75% of domestic disappearance – about prop. to rise in meat cons. pc.	Moderate to high – doubles again to over 4.0	$200–$300
Critical level 1	Minimum income elasticity of meat consumption 0.55			$350
Critical level 2		Minimum income elasticity of feed grain share – 0.55		$500

Source: D. Regier and O. H. Goolsby, *Growth in World Demand for Feed Grains Related to Meat and Livestock Products and Human Consumption of Grain,* Foreign Agricultural Report No. 63, US Department of Agriculture (Washington, D.C.: 1970).

a relatively low income elasticity tend to experience fewer demand fluctuations than those with a higher elasticity.

Some estimates of price and income elasticities are given in Table 7. For both the developed and developing countries among the major grain-producing regions, the food demand for grains such as rice and wheat is relatively inelastic, implying only a small response to prices by consumers. However, in the developed countries feed demand such as that for the coarse grains tends to be more elastic, reflecting the price elasticity of livestock products. The reported income elasticities do not conform as strongly to prior beliefs. They do not appear to be higher in the developing as compared to the developed regions, as would be expected, nor do the income elasticities appear to be much higher for the coarse grains, which would indicate a growth in the demand for meat.

Inventories and prices

It is important to consider inventories and prices together in deriving any relationships which would link them to overall market behaviour. Given the above magnitudes of the price elasticities of supply and demand, it is apparent that market adjustments work themselves out more in terms of relative inventory and price movements. Farmer response on the supply side also is based to a considerable extent on inventory levels as well as prices.

There have been historic differences in the levels of inventories held among the various grains. The major wheat-producing regions have produced well over their consumption levels. Inventories stimulated by domestic support policies have been sufficient to offset domestic as well as international shortages. This has not been the situation in the major rice producing regions which also have been the major consuming regions. Substantial quantities of surplus rice have never existed for purposes of stocking or export.

Where grain stocks have appeared or presently exist, what mechanisms can be employed to help explain their fluctuations? Where producers hold inventories for speculative purposes and prices are rising, this does not necessarily lead to sales out of those inventories; in fact it can lead to further inventory accumulation in anticipation of further price increases. Where consumers hold these inventories for further processing, inventory levels normally vary with expected price changes and levels of consump-

tion. But here precautionary and speculative motives as well as transactions motives come into play. Until the costs of storage become too high, inventories provide these processors with a convenience yield as well as a stockout yield.

Although it would be useful to examine price elasticities of inventory response similar to supply and demand, these elasticities are even more difficult to measure. Inventories are held by governments, manufacturers, processors, elevator operators, merchandisers, importers, exporters and traders — all of whom hold inventories for different purposes. Since records on these inventories, for the most part, are held in propriety, there are few descriptive data. There is also the question of the network of prices linked to inventory adjustments. For the grain markets the following different forms of prices exist: spot prices, forward or contract prices, futures prices, import prices, export prices, farmer prices, retail prices, and support prices. There may also be others.

But this does not preclude the evaluation of some aspects of inventory price response. Approximations of the volume of inventories needed for stabilizing international grain prices have been made within the context of the UNCTAD integrated programme. Estimated volume requirements for a grains buffer stock (wheat, coarse grains and rice) are given in the range of 18 to 36 million tons. For a food reserve stock, the FAO suggests a volume of 45 to 50 million tons.

Futures exchanges

The role played by futures exchanges in international grain markets also needs to be clarified. Futures exchanges or markets consist of hedgers and speculators. A hedger is one who holds a position in the futures market opposite to that he holds in the spot market. Hedgers in grain markets normally can be identified as producers, merchandisers or processors. Speculators, on the other hand, cannot be identified as such. They simply hold a net short position for gain and not incidental to operating a business.

Futures exchanges arise in grain markets because of the uncertainties of buying and storing grains along the traditional pipeline of movement: from off-farm sales to country elevators, sub-terminal markets, terminal markets, processors and to end-users. Starting with off-farm sales, the farmer or an agri-business firm can utilize futures markets by hedging a grain crop before it is sown or harvested. They normally would sell grain futures contracts to protect a crop against a price fall. The country elevator operator would place his hedge in an opposite position. A long hedge would be placed by buying futures contracts to protect against a price increase, where commodities have been sold before they are actually produced.

By far the greatest proportion of hedging is undertaken by the larger elevator operators and the grain merchandisers. These merchandisers who operate in wheat, corn, oats, rye, barley, sorghums and rice provide grains for domestic and export markets. They typically maintain large stocks of these grains and conduct their commercial operations under a policy of being fully cover hedged at all times. Hedging becomes a 'risk management' objective in this context. When the merchandiser makes a sale, he covers himself with a long hedge. Similarly when a purchase is made, he obtains cover using a short hedge.

Millers and processors are responsible for the remainder of total grain market hedging. Their principal goal is to ensure an inventory position at the right price and quality which will facilitate production of all end products. Hedging is used not only to provide future grain availabilities but also to mitigate against adverse grain price fluctuations.

This explanation of the functioning of futures exchanges has not dwelled upon some of their deficiencies such as the price fluctuations stimulated by excess speculation or the cornering of positions. Indeed other studies have shown the need to reconsider the efficiency of the exchanges during times of major economic upheaval, when price fluctuations become amplified. But both aspects of futures market behaviour have to be taken into account.

Table 7. *Selected grain demand price and income elasticities*

	Wheat	Coarse grain	Rice
ARGENTINA:			
Price	−0.3	−0.4	−0.3
Income	−0.3	0.0	0.3
AUSTRALIA:			
Price	−0.1	−0.1	−0.3
Income	−0.2	0.0	0.2
EEC (6):			
Price	−0.3	−0.5	−0.3
Income	0.0	0.6	0.2
UNITED KINGDOM			
Price	−0.2	−0.7	−0.4
Income	−0.2	0.6	0.2
UNITED STATES			
Price	−0.2	−0.4	−0.2
Income	−0.3	0.4	0.2
USSR			
Price	−0.2	−0.3	−0.4
Income	0.0	0.5	0.3
SOUTHEAST ASIA			
Price	−0.04	−0.1	−0.5
Income	0.3	0.0	0.5
EAST SOUTH AMERICA			
Price	−0.2	−0.3	−0.3
Income	0.2	0.2	0.2
NORTH AFRICA			
Price	−0.2	−0.3	−0.5
Income	0.3	0.5	0.6

Source: W. C. Labys and J. Hunkeler, 'Survey of commodity demand and supply elasticities', Res. Memo. No. 48, UNCTAD/RD/70 (Geneva: 1974).

Importance for trade and development

World grain trade and development is influenced by effects of space and resources as well as by domestic and foreign policies. Space effects refer to the costs of transferring grain from one region to another. Such costs represent an aggregation of several activities: (1) handling by the grain elevators, loading for transfer to the port, inland transportation, unloading at the port; (2) loading on an ocean-going vessel, ocean transportation, unloading at the port; and (3) unloading for transfer to the consumption centre, inland transportation, unloading and further handling. A major factor in arranging for ocean shipments is the determination of shipment rates. These rates vary substantially from month to month and year to year. Rates are negotiated on an individual basis for each cargo by dealers or millers of the importing countries and the shipping companies. Rate variations depend on the size of the ship, the volume of the shipment, the distance involved, the nature of the return cargo, and the time of the year. Uncertainty in these factors together with a rate structure which favours long hauls to short hauls makes shipping an important factor in understanding grain trade patterns.

Resource availabilities are important in determining which regions of the world will provide greater or lesser quantities of grain. The total stock of land available for grain production is limited; further land to be brought into use in the developing countries would be difficult. Those countries with abundant energy are likely to have a greater capability for maintaining or increasing grain production, since high energy prices will prevent marginal lands from being brought into use. Finally, fertilizers are a critical input to grain production. Where gaps in fertilizer availability exist or are foreseen, grain production will be affected.

With few exceptions, most of the grain output is protected by foreign and domestic policies. Grain exports from the developed countries are restricted by trade barriers which include fixed import duties, *ad valorem* import duties, variable import levies, fixed import quotas, and percentage import quotas. Grain production in the developed countries is protected by a combination of the above barriers and domestic price supports, acreage allotments and subsidies. The estimates of the elasticities of supply in Table 5 reflect that this high degree of protection has resulted in substantial expansion of grain output. If free trade in grains would be instigated, the low price elasticities of demand in Table 7 suggest that grain food consumption would rise only slightly, with the consumption of grain for livestock feed increasing substantially. Grains which have been provided historically as a form of aid reflect output that cannot be sold at existing price support levels, and thus represent a problem to the region that has generated the excess output.

CONCLUSIONS

This paper attempts to provide a better understanding of the variables and relationships important for analysing international grain markets. There are many questions concerning policies of the grain trade and related international development which remain to be answered. What would be the impact of an international grain buffer stock or grain reserve programme on grain prices, production and consumption? What would be the effect on grain import demand if concessional terms of trade are made available? Even if developing countries increase production of grains to stimulate foreign exchange earnings, what will be the impact of increasing self-sufficiency in grain by those countries capable of generating an exportable surplus? And how would the pricing of wheat competitively as a feedgrain affect those developing countries which have the potential of becoming exporters? But because such questions are too complex to be resolved in a paper such as this, it is hoped that the insights provided will lead to better approaches to answering them.

REFERENCES

Arthur, H. B., *Commodity Futures as a Business Management Tool* (Boston: Harvard University Graduate School for Business Administration, 1971).

Borgstrom, G., *World Food Resources* (New York: Intext Publishers, 1973).

FAO, 'Review of the grain situation and outlook', Committee of Commodity Problems, Intergovernmental Group of Grains, CCP: GR 75/4 (Rome: FAO, 1975).

Granger, C. W. J., *Trading in Commodities* (Cambridge: Woodhead and Faulkner, 1974).

Kost, W. E., 'Trade flows in the grain—livestock economy of the EEC', in W. C. Labys (ed.), *Quantitative Models of Commodity Markets* (Cambridge: Ballinger Publishing Co., 1975).

Labys, W. C., *Dynamic Commodity Models: Specification, Estimation and Simulation* (Lexington: D.C. Heath and Co., 1973).

Labys, W. C., (ed.), *Quantitative Models of Commodity Markets* (Cambridge: Ballinger Publishing Co., 1975).

Labys, W. C. (ed.), *Quantitative Models of Com-* demand and supply elasticities', Res. Memo. No. 48, UNCTAD/RD/70 (Geneva: 1974).

Labys, W. C. and H. Thomas, 'Speculation, hedging and commodity price behaviour: an international comparison', *Applied Economics*, Vol. 7 (1975), pp. 287–301.

Regier, D. and O. H. Goolsby, *Growth in World Demand for Feed Grains Related to Meat and Livestock Product and Human Consumption of Grain*, Foreign Agricultural Report No. 63, US Department of Agriculture (Washington, D.C.: 1970).

Rojko, A. S., F. S. Urban and J. J. Naive, *World Demand Prospects for Grain in 1980 with Emphasis on Trade by the Less Developed Countries*, Foreign Agricultural Economics Report No. 75, US Department of Agriculture (Washington D.C.: 1971).

Schmitz, A. and D. L. Bawden, *The World Wheat Economy: An Empirical Analysis*, Giannini Foundation Monograph No. 32, California Agricultural Experiment Station (Berkeley: 1973).

Tolley, G. S. and P. A. Zadrozny (eds.), *Trade, Agriculture and Development* (Cambridge: Ballinger Publishing Co., 1975).

UNCTAD, 'An integrated programme of commodities: the role of commodity stocks', Committee of Commodities, UNCTAD TD/B/C. 1/166/Supp. 1/Add. 1 (Geneva: 1974).

World Development, 1977, Vol. 5, Nos. 5–7, pp. 549–558. Pergamon Press. Printed in Great Britain.

The World Grain Economy
and the Food Problem

ROBBIN S. JOHNSON

Cargill, Incorporated
Minneapolis, Minnesota

Summary. – This paper examines world food prospects in terms of shifting market forces, arguing essentially that freer trade in agricultural and industrial commodities would make a powerful contribution to enhanced food security. The author acknowledges the importance of other factors affecting the world grain economy but focuses on four: production, consumption, exports and carryover stocks. To combat the situation arising from the impediments to adjustment caused by inflexible farm and trade policies, the author proposes several food security options: increased grain production in developing countries to keep up with population growth; increased earning power in developing countries to offset detrimental effects of temporary grain price rises; increased adjustment of consumption in industrial nations to match fluctuating supplies so that the full burden does not fall on the poorer countries; and, food aid and grain reserves.

INTRODUCTION

Mounting concern about world food prospects led, in November 1974, to the first World Food Conference. Though called to consider new approaches with medium-term time horizons, the Conference was compelled by urgent food needs in a number of countries to concentrate on problems posed by current shortfalls in grain output. Food aid and grain reserves attracted special interest.

Since then, world grain output has expanded, and grain stock levels should rebound significantly this year from recent lows. Not surprisingly, this turnabout has stalled several of the initiatives launched two years ago. Yet, both the timing and the understanding of agricultural development problems justify action more than ever before.[1] Moreover, easing of grain supplies has permitted attention to shift back toward structural questions. In response, some new ideas have been offered for planning how to cope with periodic fluctuations in regional or world grain output.[2]

This paper attempts to examine world food prospects in terms of shifting market forces. The world food situation has other dimensions which should not be ignored. Among them are the special nutritional needs of children and nursing mothers, the hunger and malnutrition which continues even when aggregate food supplies are adequate, and general dietary deficiencies.

All dimensions of the food problem are important. Individual well-being, political stability and basic human rights are all at stake. This paper does not intend to ignore them. But, it focuses on the forces of supply and demand at work in the world grain economy in order to shed light on one pervasive facet of the food problem: the ability to produce, distribute and pay for food is central to any concerted effort to relieve hunger. Examining the constraints which limit this capability will not cover all dimensions of a very complex problem, but it may highlight ways to harness market forces in service to human needs.

THE WORLD GRAIN ECONOMY

The world grain economy is diverse but increasingly integrated. Food developments in any individual region today often have global significance. Their effects are no longer localized. They are knitted together by the persistent pressures of supply and demand.

For purposes of this analysis, the world grain economy will be broken down into four component parts – production, consumption, exports and carryover stocks. Each plays an important part in explaining the experiences of the last few years.

1. *Production*

World grain production has generally been increasing (see Table 1). Output has risen from 881 million metric tons at the beginning of this decade to 1,040 million metric tons this year. To some extent, however, this comparison overstates the capacity for growth demonstrated in this period. Several countries — most notably the US and Canada — were withholding land from production at the beginning of the decade in an effort to reduce what were then regarded as burdensome surpluses. This land has been returned to production in more recent years, giving total output a one-time boost.

A more realistic picture of the trend in world food output can be drawn from the 20-year period between 1954 and 1973. During that period world food production increased at an annual rate of 2.8%. Food output grew at 2.7% per year in developed countries and 3% per year in developing nations.

Most analyses project total world food production to grow at about the same rate for the balance of this decade. The rate of growth in food output is expected to accelerate in developed nations. Unless policies change, however, the rate of growth will decline in the developing countries.

Though growth has been strong, it has not been consistent. Variations in annual grain production have been especially pronounced over the past eight years. Heightened concern about world food security stems in large part from this increased variation combined with the emerging disparity in annual growth rates between developed and developing countries.

2. *Consumption*

The trend in world grain consumption has been more uniform. World grain consumption rose steadily between 1969–70 and 1973–74. It fell by nearly 45 million tons in 1974–75 before resuming its steady upward climb. Significantly, 80% of that temporary reduction in grain consumption occurred in the United States, as wheat and feed grains were diverted from domestic livestock feeding into exports.

Grain consumption is increasing for two reasons. A 2% annual increase in population adds about 80 million new people each year. Second, as *per capita* incomes rise, demand for meat, milk, poultry and eggs increases. The net result is higher grain use *per capita*.

This latter trend has been criticized on the ground that it diverts grain from humans to animals. Such criticism ignores the relationship that exists between production and consumption. Demand for grain to produce animal products provides an incentive to expand grain output. This interaction between demand and supply, in fact, has led to a decline in real grain prices in the face of rising consumption.

Table 1. *World: total grain (excluding rice)*
supply–distribution market years
1969–70 through 1976–77
(million metric tons)

	Carryover stocks *	Production	Total exports †	Consumption total
1969–70	192.5	881.4	102.7	898.2
1970–71	175.7	885.7	109.7	924.8
1971–72	136.6	970.5	113.5	951.2
1972–73	155.9	947.1	141.2	986.4
1973–74	117.1	1,032.3	151.5	1,029.9
1974–75	119.5	976.1	137.3	985.1
1975–76 Prel.	119.6	979.9	161.5	983.9
1976–77 Proj.	106.6	1,041.6	149.0	1,017.0
1977–78 Proj.	131.2			

* Represents aggregate of local marketing years and does not represent world stock levels at a fixed point in time.
Numbers underestimate actual stocks as data is not available for all countries.

† Data based on aggregate of local marketing years and therefore differ from July–June data.

The resulting increase in total grain supply also has reduced the potential threat to food supplies from a periodic poor crop. When market forces are allowed to reflect tightening conditions of supply through higher prices — as they were in the US in 1974—75 — grain is diverted from marginal animal feeding. In effect, livestock feeding serves as a secondary reserve of grain.

This process provides the world grain economy with some .powerful tools for adjusting consumption downward to match tighter supplies without jeopardizing essential food needs. Of course, this does not solve the problems of those who cannot pay for the supplies freed up. But, the point to be stressed here is that solutions to those problems should take account of the broad market forces that act to adjust production and consumption to changing supply and demand relationships.

3. *Exports*

Total exports — the third important component of the world grain market — is basically a residual factor. On the one hand, it represents the surplus supply above local demand for grain at prevailing prices in exporting nations. It is an additional supply of grain available to meet world needs elsewhere. On the other hand, it is the residual demand for grain in importing countries above what is met by local production. Total grain exports represent only about 12 to 15% of either world production or consumption.

This residual character of grain exports means that they are typically more variable than either production or consumption. How well exports work to cover shortages elsewhere depends largely on the trade policies pursued by grain-surplus or grain-deficit nations. As we shall see shortly, those policies frequently impede international grain flows, at times subjecting the export sector of the world grain market to intense pressures.

4. *Carryover stocks*

Carryover stocks are also a residual factor. At a minimum they equal the quantity of grain that must be in the marketing pipeline to keep grain moving steadily into consumption from one harvest to the next. Such stocks cannot fall to zero without disrupting the entire grain economy and forcing people to go without food. How low these stocks can go without

physically interrupting the steady flow of food is not clear. Many felt that minimum pipeline levels were being approached when world grain stocks fell to about 100 million tons two years ago.

Even when supplies are not physically interrupted, uncertainty about their adequacy can be extremely disruptive. For example, concern about dwindling US stocks of wheat intensified during the winter of 1973—74. Fear of a wheat export embargo, triggered by the US soybean embargo the preceding summer, aggravated the situation. Between 23 November 1973 and 24 February 1974 wheat prices rose $1.55 per bushel — from $4.80 to $6.35.

When it became clear that the US would not impose export controls to protect its wheat supplies prices reversed, falling $2 per bushel between 24 February and 19 May 1974. During this six-month period from November 1973 to May 1974, the US Department of Agriculture revised its export estimate upward by only 50 million bushels or about 5%. Clearly, volatile wheat prices during the winter of 1973—74 resulted from concerns about governmental policy, not from changing views of total available supplies.

By contrast, high carryover levels become a price-depressing surplus. World carryover stocks in 1969—70 of 192.5 million tons represented nearly one-quarter of total annual consumption. With no foreseeable need for stocks of this quantity, the world experienced very low prices and deliberate efforts to restrict output.

The level of residual — or carryover — stocks, then, poses a critical policy dilemma for the world grain economy. Stocks that are too small result in high, volatile prices disruptive to grain consumers. Stocks that are too large remove the incentive to expand grain output. At the extreme, they can discourage investment in production resources needed to supply the steady growth of world consumption.

The level of stocks has another, political effect. Stocks that are too small prompt consumer demand for grain reserves. Stocks that are too large build farmer resistance to grain reserves.

IMPEDIMENTS TO ADJUSTMENT IN THE WORLD GRAIN ECONOMY

It would appear from this analysis that the case for reserves rests mainly on production uncertainties. Unfortunately, the case for reserves is not that straightforward. As D. Gale Johnson points out, year-to-year fluctuations in world grain production are relatively small and would not, if there were free trade in grains, make the holding of grain reserves in excess of working stocks an economic investment more than one year out of five.[3]

In other words, a short grain crop in one area of the world could be covered by relatively more plentiful supplies from other areas, if grain could move freely among nations.

Unfortunately, grain flows are not unimpeded. Many nations – like the European Community (EC), the Soviet Union and Japan – maintain agricultural and trading systems that insulate their domestic grain economies from world developments. As a result, their patterns of grain use do not change significantly in response to external events.

For example, the European Community stabilizes its grain economy through its Common Agricultural Policy. In most years grain prices within the Community are higher than those prevailing in world markets. The EC protects domestic grain production by adjusting its variable import levies to guarantee a margin of preference for internal production. This discourages grain consumption in the EC, encourages unnecessary grain output and shifts the burdens of surplus onto farmers in major exporting nations. The net effect is to add to rather than reduce the periodic surpluses which arise in world grain supplies.

When world grain supplies tightened in 1973, the Community reversed this policy and converted its variable grain levies into variable export taxes. The effect was to hold grain supplies within the Community, artificially encouraging domestic grain use at the same time that grain supplies were extremely tight in the rest of the world. EC grain production plus net imports between 1972–73 and 1974–75 remained remarkably stable, fluctuating about 2 million tons or less than 2%. By contrast, US domestic wheat use varied 13% and coarse grains consumption 22%.

The European Community is not alone. The Soviet Union, for example, maintains fixed grain prices to consumers and to livestock farmers. Prior to 1970, however, the Soviet Union also absorbed the consequences of this artificial arrangement. In years of large Soviet harvests the additional grain was consumed rather than stored. When its crops were poor, the Soviets cut back consumption by wholesale slaughter of livestock.

Apparently, Soviet policy changed about 1970, and the country embarked on a concerted effort to increase production of meat, milk, eggs and poultry to meet the rising expectations of its people. Thus, when it experienced a poor crop in 1972, it entered world markets and purchased more grain than necessary to cover the actual shortfall. Good harvests – like its 1973 crop – apparently failed to result in a significant stock build-up. Instead, its grain and livestock pricing policies encouraged immediate internal consumption in spite of relative shortages and high prices elsewhere in the world.

The costs of such governmental interventions were largely concealed in the 1960s by the willingness of the US and Canada to carry excessive grain stocks and to release them at relatively low prices. US and Canadian grain stocks in 1961 of 137 million metric tons equalled nearly four-fifths of total world stocks. Release of stocks owned by the US Commodity Credit Corporation was authorized whenever grain prices reached or exceeded 115% of the loan level (plus carrying charges) at which they were acquired. As a result, annual grain price fluctuations in the US never exceeded 20% in the 1960s, and this set the tone for world grain markets as well.

In summary, increased concern for world food security has been triggered by a series of relatively poor harvests and declining world carryover stocks. The problems presented by disappointing harvests would not have been as severe as they were, however, had nations responded differently. Protective policies in a number of industrial nations prevented the relatively modest adjustments in consumption levels that would have accommodated the crop shortfalls. This underlines a new – and significant – cost of the failure to liberalize world trade in grains.

The government-financed stocks in the US and Canada which had long cushioned consumers were reduced or eliminated to cover the past few years' needs. Both countries are understandably reluctant to accumulate burdensome stocks again. Changing Soviet policies aggravated the situation, exposing world markets to the stresses of fluctuating Soviet harvests at a time when world production also became at least temporarily more volatile.

In other words, inflexible farm and trade policies lie at the heart of world food problems. They concentrate the brunt of needed adjustments in grain use on artificially restricted international markets and on the few countries whose domestic prices do reflect international conditions. Weather may return to a more normal pattern but, unless some new initiatives are launched, the policies which have compounded problems will remain unaltered.

FOOD SECURITY OPTIONS

1. *Increased grain production in developing countries*

Developing countries have been able to expand grain output more rapidly than population growth, and projections of the Food and Agriculture Organization (FAO) suggest that this can continue. Even so, FAO projected total grain demand in these nations to grow more rapidly than local output. Unless policies change, developing countries as a whole could be confronted by 1985 with the staggering need to import 85 million tons of grain annually. It is doubtful that imports at this level could be managed either physically or financially.

Increases in *per capita* food consumption will depend in part upon future rates of population growth. While population is growing at about 1.0% annually in developed countries, it is expanding at a rate above 2.5% in developing market economies (see Fig. 1). Continued population growth at this rate limits the degree of improvement that can be achieved in *per capita* food consumption. Long-term progress toward solving food problems, therefore, hinges on the ability of developing nations to curb excessively high rates of population growth.

Fig. 1. *Annual population growth rate – selected areas.*

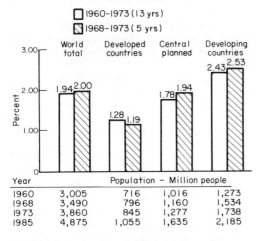

Year

Year	World total	Developed countries	Central planned	Developing countries
1960	3,005	716	1,016	1,273
1968	3,490	796	1,160	1,534
1973	3,860	845	1,277	1,738
1985	4,875	1,055	1,635	2,185

Centrally Planned – USSR, East Europe and China (PRC). Reason for large annual growth rate is attributed to China:

Annual growth rate – percent

	China	USSR	East Europe
1960–73	2.1	1.19	0.73
1968–73	2.4	0.96	0.69

Indigenous grain production in developing countries also must be expanded. There is ample room for progress. In some cases, additional land can be brought under cultivation. 'Perhaps twice as much land is available for food production as is presently being used. While bringing this land into production would involve some costs, these costs are not prohibitive'.[4] In fact, while the land area under cultivation in developed countries changed little between 1960 and 1971, it has increased 1.1% annually in the developing world. In parts of Africa and Latin America, cultivated acreage has increased from 2.0 to 3.7% annually.

Though there is no overall shortage of agricultural land, ' . . . there are serious regional problems resulting from a combination of population pressure on land and difficulties of increasing agricultural production with the technologies used in these regions'.[5] In these areas – including such heavily populated countries as India, Bangladesh and Egypt – the focus will have to be on more intensive, land-conserving methods of production.

Progress on this front through increased yields is quite feasible. For example, while corn yields in the US equal about 5.8 tons per hectare, 112 countries have corn yields below 3 tons and 81 below 1.5 tons per hectare.[6] The sharp rise in grain yields in North America and Western Europe is largely a post-World War II phenomenon, though the technologies on which those gains were built were first available in the 1930s. Moreover, though the initial yield gains from hybrids were large, improved varieties and continuing dissemination of better cultivation practices through farm extension services have sustained strong advances in yields each subsequent decade.

Application of high-yielding grain technologies to the farm systems of developing countries only began in a concerted manner in the 1960s. The work of the International Maize and Wheat Improvement Centre in Mexico (CIMMYT) and of the International Rice Research Institute in the Philippines brought on the 'Green Revolution' of that decade. Since these initial successes, the land area devoted to high-yielding grain and rice varieties in Asia has grown significantly, but there are vast areas there and in the rest of the developing world where they have not yet spread.

As seeds and production techniques are adapted to local conditions, important yield gains can be achieved on a sustained basis. This will require more research expenditures, greater concentration of research efforts on developing varieties adapted to local conditions and major investments in providing the extension services and farm credit mechanisms crucial to securing practical applications. And, of course, the full package of inputs — water, fertilizers and pesticides as well as high-yielding seeds — must be available to farmers from the beginning, or adoption will be frustrated.

New production inputs will not solve problems alone. They must be supported by incentives to produce and market. The techniques of the 'Green Revolution' involve a high proportion of purchased inputs and substantial cash outlays prior to planting. Farmers adopting them are more vulnerable to financial disaster because of poor crops or low prices than is the case with traditional cultivating practices.

> Controls placed on prices below the equilibrium level discourage producers from planning future expansion and may drive marginal producers out of business. Price controls also discourage farmers from using more productive inputs such as improved seeds, fertilizers, irrigation, insecticides and pesticides that are needed to increase production.[7]

Provision of these incentives may involve steps that only the developing countries themselves can take. For example, a recent USDA survey of 50 developing countries revealed that 46 of them had policies which discouraged expansion in domestic agricultural production.

> Disincentives revealed by the survey include: (1) controlling the selling price of the producers; (2) controlling the retail price to the consumer; (3) non-competitive buying (procurement policy); (4) export controls; (5) export taxes; (6) importing for sale at subsidized prices; (7) exchange rate controls; (8) restrictions on credit, land tenure and farm size; (9) restrictions on domestic movement of agricultural products, as from one district to another.[8]

No doubt, the cheap food policies that result in production disincentives often reflect serious development problems. Allowing grain prices to rise as an incentive to production seriously harms low-income groups who spend most of their income on food. It also offends urban groups which are important sources of support for many governments. And, where landholdings are concentrated in relatively few hands, higher grain prices can further distort existing inequalities. These problems are real, but resolving them at the expense of incentives to expand indigenous grain production is likely to be ultimately self-defeating.

Plans to improve the production and distribution of foodstuffs in developing countries also must reflect the differing farming conditions of each area. For example, in Africa concentration on destroying 'river blindness' — a disease carried by the black fly — would open up some of the most productive land in West Africa currently held out of production. Similar efforts to control the tsetse fly would substantially boost livestock development. The Near East must concentrate on developing water resources and expanding production of legumes. Countries in that region also need improved grasses adapted to increasing the carrying capacity of their range land. In South Asia and the Far East development strategies must centre on improving water resources, increasing the intensity of land utilization and expanding the supply of basic agricultural inputs such as fertilizers and pesticides.

The developed nations can do much to help make available needed inputs, technical assistance and capital. But, the transfer of resources to help these countries develop their rural economies and agricultural productivity must recognize that increasing food supplies is not enough. Food problems in developing countries also reflect serious problems of distribution. This is an important point that deserves special emphasis.

Expanding aggregate food supplies cannot be divorced from the need to attack the social and economic causes of chronic, grinding poverty. Increased output must result in expanded employment opportunities. Ability to produce must be matched by ability to purchase the additional supply of food. Productivity gains that exacerbate income inequalities will do little to relieve hunger and may produce social unrest, threatening the ability to sustain growth.

Consequently, the capital-intensive, labour-extensive technologies of the West will be inappropriate for most developing countries. Under-employment of people and resources characterizes the agricultural sectors of virtually all developing countries. New technologies, therefore, must be adapted to the surplus labour conditions characteristic of the heavily populated developing world. Unless expanded output is achieved by increasing the capacity and productivity of traditional agriculture, large segments of rural populations will be by-passed.

In other words, increasing food production must be part of an indigenous policy of agricultural and rural economic development. Placing a priority on distribution as well as on the rate of growth will require some very difficult decisions by governments with limited resources, overwhelming needs and political structures skewed toward cities and urban dwellers. Developed nations can help support change, but the major initiatives must come from within the developing countries themselves.

2. *Increased earning power in developing countries*

Expanding food production in developing countries is one step toward greater food security. Raising *per capita* incomes in those nations is another. The purchasing power created by higher incomes can make it easier to provide incentives for expanding local output. It also softens some of the harshest effects of temporary grain price increases.

Fig. 2 indicates the strong correlation existing between higher income levels and higher rates of grain consumption. Persistently low *per capita* incomes translate directly into hunger, malnutrition or even starvation in periods of temporary crop shortfalls. Substantial progress toward heightened food security will only come with accelerated development of developing nations' economies.

Much of this investment should flow into the rural areas of developing countries – agriculture, roads, water control, processing and light industry. The rural areas still contain most of the people. They are burdened with underemployment. They lack capital. And, if they do not develop, they will continue to pour people into increasingly unmanageable urban slums. Stronger rural areas can anchor an economy that will support higher incomes and improved standards of living across the board.

What is true for individuals is also true for nations. More foreign exchange earnings through expanded exports helps generate the money with which to pay for needed production inputs or food imports. Here the industrial nations can make a clear, positive contribution. By opening their markets to the raw material, tropical product and light manufacture exports of developing countries, industrial nations can help build both employment opportunities and foreign exchange earnings for them.

The current trade negotiations under the General Agreement on Tariffs and Trade (GATT) offer an opportunity to take some significant steps in this direction. Tropical product exports will receive special attention. Tariff preferences for developing countries have already been implemented by many countries but could be harmonized and enlarged. And, the negative impact of escalating tariffs as the degree of value-added from processing or manufacturing rises is receiving new attention. Exports can be a powerful force in pulling along industrialization in countries with limited local markets. Where developing countries have a comparative advantage, trading rules should encourage them to exploit it.

3. *Increased adjustment in industrial nations*

A third step toward greater food security would be to break down barriers that insulate many industrial countries from the need to adjust consumption to match fluctuating supplies. Experiences over the past few years underline the disparities which can arise. For example, while real wheat prices in the US increased 150% between 1969 and 1974, the real price of wheat in France and Japan remained stable or actually declined. Consumers in these latter countries enjoyed stable prices at a time when other nations – including many developing countries – were forced to adjust to scarcity.

Such disparities arise because of efforts to support and protect high-cost domestic produc-

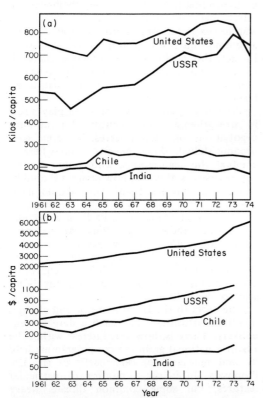

Fig. 2. Per capita *consumption of major grains for selected countries.*

tion. No doubt, European agriculture faces difficult economic, social and political problems of adjustment. But, when those adjustment burdens are shifted by variable levies and variable export taxes onto others, they impose unjustifiable costs.

The current GATT trade negotiations offer an opportunity to reduce those costs. The Community need not reshape its Common Agricultural Policy, but it could make concessions in the use it makes of border measures to sustain that policy. Greater tolerance within the EC — and in other industrial countries — for changes in grain prices and consumption levels would ease the burdens others bear in adjusting to periodic production fluctuations.

Bringing greater stability to Soviet grain importing patterns could also help. In fact, over the last 15 years variations in Soviet net trade have accounted for more than half the fluctuation in world exports. For wheat the Soviet share has been nearly 80%.

There are some hopeful signs of progress on this front. The recently concluded 5-year grain agreement between the US and the Soviet Union requires the Soviet Union to import at least 6 million tons of grain annually from the US and to consult before raising purchases in any one marketing year above 8 million tons. Moreover, there are indications that the Soviets are building additional grain storage capacity, although whether it will be used to accumulate reserve stocks is not known. Finally, while Soviet internal prices remain rigidly fixed, its strained foreign exchange position is likely to make it more sensitive to grain import costs, especially when unit prices are high.

4. Food aid and grain reserves

Even with good progress toward a more open grain economy, pockets of protection will remain. Efforts to isolate economies from the world market will limit the ability to correct regional imbalances through trade flows. For this reason food aid and conscious grain reserves have important roles to play in increasing world food security.

Administering both food aid and reserves will be challenging. Food aid must meet the requirements of needy countries and people without encouraging unnecessary dependence. It must also avoid discouraging growth in food output within the recipient countries themselves. Finally, it must become more than a means of disposing of unwanted surpluses. Use of food aid as surplus disposal has tied food aid

flows historically to supply availability in donor nations. Unfortunately, reduced supply availability often can coincide — as it did in 1974 — with increased emergency food aid needs.

This suggests several guidelines for food aid programmes. First, they should not attempt to cover all food aid requirements at no cost to the recipient, since experience has shown that unlimited availability of cheap food supplies under aid programmes can perpetuate agricultural underdevelopment in recipient countries.

Second, they probably should not cover the entire shortfall between production and consumption. Sharing the adjustment burden with recipient countries may encourage them to make some decisions on their priorities — e.g., whether to reduce internal consumption, carry stocks to avoid reduced consumption or use foreign exchange to purchase imports to cover reduced supplies. This both reduces the cost to donor countries of providing food aid and encourages agricultural development in recipient countries.

Finally, food aid should not be an obligation of food-surplus-producing countries alone. Developing countries can help each other out by expanding trade flows among themselves to offset regional shortages. Wealthy nations — whether exporters or importers of grain — share a common interest in providing food assistance. In fact, this might be more widely accepted if food assistance took the form of transfers of money to buy needed grain rather than transfers of grain itself.

Conscious grain reserves also can play a role in strengthening food security. International negotiations on food reserves, however, have become stalled. Disagreements about where to conduct the negotiations, who should control any reserves established, how reserves should be acquired and released and who should have access to them have all held up progress.

The United States finds itself in a peculiar position in these negotiations. As its grain production and carryover stocks increase, other nations appear to be losing interest. It seems that many believe the US will be forced, for its own reasons, once again to carry the lion's share of world food stocks.

The costs to the US of that role and changes in public attitudes make such a development unlikely. There is, however, interest within the US in a national grain reserve programme held by and managed for the benefit of the US. Proposals differ on a number of particular features, but some common threads weave through a number of them.

First, greatest interest centres on a grain

reserve to cover commercial as well as concessional requirements. Such a reserve would not attempt to stabilize prices within the narrow range which characterized the 1960s. Rather, the purpose of such a reserve would be to provide reasonable assurance of supplies in periods of real need. In other words, such a reserve would function as a shock absorber rather than as a perennial grain inventory.

Second, grain reserves substitute for the adjustments which governmental interference with market forces prevents. They are being held, however, to protect against events – like poor weather – which are inevitable but whose timing and duration cannot be foreseen. Private parties will hold grain stocks when they can foresee reasonable opportunities for profit. The value of reserves to society, however, comes from their availability when the unexpected arises. Conscious reserves, then, are held to meet the unanticipated, the unforeseen. This requires governmental rather than private financing.

Government ownership brings with it certain risks. Farmers especially are concerned that government-owned reserves could be used to depress prices for political reasons. To protect against this, stocks must be carefully and effectively insulated from the market. There must be a firm agreement on the conditions under which grain will be acquired for the reserve and released from it.

Similar concerns explain support for placing limits on the total quantity of grain that government could hold in a reserve. To avoid bearing down unfairly on grain prices or raising reserve costs too high, this quantity should be relatively modest. For the US it might be no more than 20 million tons of grain. Perhaps a third of this amount would be in wheat, half in feed grains and one-sixth in soybeans.

Finally, market forces should be permitted to accommodate normal supply or demand fluctuations without recourse to the reserve. This means that release prices from the reserve should be well above acquisition levels. In the US such a band could be created by preventing release from reserve stocks at prices less than twice their acquisition level.

This approach to reserves has a number of advantages consistent with increasing world food security. It would permit modest consumption adjustments while ensuring supply availability in times of extreme need. It would also avoid undercutting incentives to farmers to increase production – the only lasting solution to shortage.

Reserve stocks effectively insulated by a wide price band also reduce the probability that the US would again have to rely on export controls. This, in turn, should reduce uneconomic pursuit of grain self-sufficiency by countries concerned about access to supplies. The result would be a more efficient distribution of the world's scarce agricultural resources.

Limits on stock levels and a wide band between acquisition and release prices should encourage other nations to build reserve stocks. Importing nations especially will either have to assume more of the burden of carrying stocks or be more willing to adjust their consumption to changing supply conditions.

CONCLUSION

This last point returns to a fundamental thesis of this paper. Food security is not a goal that should be pursued mainly through food aid and reserve policies. Those measures are expensive, essentially interim steps necessitated by resource imbalances and protective farm and trade policies. Freer trade in agricultural and industrial commodities would make a powerful contribution to enhanced food security.

Opening markets in developed nations to processed and industrial exports of developing countries would help build jobs, economic vitality and financial strength. This would mean more income and more foreign exchange to spend on food imports, farm inputs and agricultural development. The industrial nations would be improving the ability of developing countries to pay by extending to them the means to earn.

Freer farm trade would also broaden the consumption base on which adjustments to production variations could take place. This is important in holding down the costs of food aid and reserves. It also would help minimize imbalances that create the need for special assistance

Several grain importing developed nations have been extremely reluctant to move in this direction because of complex internal social, political and economic forces. Their decision to subsidize their domestic farm production, however, is made easier by concerns over supply availability. Trade-inhibiting measures simply follow as a means of supporting that policy.

This is where trade liberalization and grain reserves can be especially helpful when considered together. Freer trade in grains would provide supply assurance at less cost. By freeing up market forces yet assuring supplies when needed, a reserves programme could serve as a bridge between current protective policies and a more open, genuinely stable world market in the future.

NOTES

1. See for example the article by Sterling Wortman entitled 'Food and agriculture' in *Scientific American,* Vol. 235, No. 3 (September 1976), pp. 31–39.

2. One of the best was offered by D. Gale Johnson in 'Increased stability of grain supplies in developing countries: optimal carryovers and insurance', Univ. of Chicago, Office of Agricultural Economics Research, Paper No. 76:14 (26 April 1976); also in *World Development,* Vol. 4, No. 12 (December 1976), pp. 977–987.

3. Johnson, op. cit., p. 6.

4. *The World Food Situation and Prospects to 1985,*

Economic Research Service, USDA Foreign Agricultural Economic Report No. 98 (Washington, D.C.: December 1974), p. vii.

5. *World Food Situation,* p. 59.

6. Wortman, p. 37.

7. 'Disincentives to agricultural production in developing countries: a policy survey', by Abdullah A. Saleh in *Foreign Agricultural Supplement* (March 1975), p. 1.

8. Saleh, op. cit., p. 1.

World Development, 1977, Vol. 5, Nos. 5–7, pp. 559–571. Pergamon Press. Printed in Great Britain.

Agribusiness and the Elimination of Latin America's Rural Proletariat

ERNEST FEDER

Instituto de Investigaciones Economicas,
UNAM, Mexico D.F.

Summary. – This paper studies the impact of agribusiness on Latin American agriculture in general and the rural proletariat in particular. It deals with the structural changes accompanying modernization – the domination of agriculture by industry. In describing the process of ownership and production concentration and monopolization, it relates how the rural proletariat has become dispossessed of its land, of its opportunities for employment and of its livelihood, and how the natural resources and agricultural potential of Latin America are endangered.

The paper is critical of the involvement of foreign business, governments and aid agencies in reinforcing this political and economic process. The author takes a pessimistic view of the possibilities of reversing or halting this process unless the rural proletariat somehow takes political action to change the system.

I

To fully appreciate the impact of *Agribusiness,* which I will define below, on Latin American agriculture and on the rural proletariat, the peasants and the landless, one must visualize the profound transformation of the agricultural sectors of the industrial capitalist countries during the last three decades, above all the US, foremost protagonist of Agribusiness. After World War II, modernization proceeded at great speed. With some exceptions, all productive processes were mechanized within the space of a few years. Good fertilizer, pesticides, animal feeds and high-level management, improvements in animal health and quality of livestock products contributed to rapidly rising productivity of land, capital and beasts. Large areas were provided with irrigation to minimize weather risks. Total output rose. What is more: the potential for still larger production and exports increased. Where operations are not yet mechanized, strenuous efforts are made to replace man by machines. Broad-scale research promises ever greater productivity of land and labour. These processes have resulted in powerful agricultural sectors functioning practically without people, structurally incapable of providing new employment opportunities or absorbing any portion of unemployment during periods of economic crises.

Modernization brought about other significant structural changes. Mechanization, which demands heavy investments and large operating-capital needs became major factors in bringing about concentration of land-ownership and production. This meant the speedy displacement of small ('inefficient') producers. The structural changes at the farm level were moreover accelerated by changes in the industrial sector. Agriculture-related industries and services became fewer in number and larger in size. Their monopoly power *vis-à-vis* the producers increased, both in buying produce and selling inputs. But they also penetrated the productive processes themselves. Giant or medium-sized 'food corporations' are now engaged in farming on a large scale directly through ownership and operation of land; or they control output and distribution through the *production contract system*. Giant manufacturers supply producers with all kinds of inputs, but put them constantly under heavy pressure to replace 'outmoded' models by new ones. Agriculture has thus become excellent business for industry, so much so that even corporations previously engaged exclusively in non-agricultural activities are now either producing or peddling food and fibre products or supplying inputs,[1] creating thereby a still more powerful relationship of dependency of producers on industries and services. The interdependence between agriculture and industry, which now goes under the name of Agri-business, is thus not an alliance, or 'coordination', between two sectors of equal bargaining power, as the apostles of Agribusiness will have us believe, but the domination of the former by the latter.

An illustration of ownership and production concentration and monopolization of agriculture-related industries and services is the fruit and vegetable sector of the US. According to statistics proudly presented by Ray Goldberg of the Harvard Business School, the foremost advocate of Agribusiness, between 1959 and 1969, in five important vegetable producing states the number of farmers reporting vegetables harvested for sale decreased 'dramatically' by 48% and the number of farmers with land in orchards in two states decreased by 32%, while harvested acreage for vegetables decreased slightly (6%) and increased for orchard production (19%). Yields were rising steadily. On the other hand, US vegetable and melon production increased by about 18% and orchard produce by 31%. Between 1954 and 1970, the number of canning plants decreased by 39%, and between 1963 and 1970 freezing plants declined by 12%.[2] However after 1970, these trends were accentuated sharply, a process which Goldberg did not include in his statistics.

The rapid disappearance of small producers has so far not caused major social and political upheavals because of the existence of alternative employment opportunities; the profound changes have proceeded smoothly. But undoubtedly the status of many farmers who remain in agriculture is deteriorating. Wherever the production contract system was introduced, the 'agricultural entrepreneur' is turning into some sort of high-level sharecropper or employee whose productive activities — what, where, when and how to plant and harvest — are decided for him by the contracting corporation.[3] As the production contract system is bound to spread with the growth of the monopoly power of the giant food firms, the status of farmers is bound to decline further.

It is crucial that Agribusiness and its apostles, such as the Harvard Business School economists, are firm believers in the 'efficiency' of giant enterprises and their ability to bring increased welfare to agricultural producers and the rural economy throughout the world. They transfer the fetish of bigness in farming and elsewhere to the underdeveloped countries and seek to impose on them the model of modern capitalist agriculture of the industrial countries.[4]

II

Since the mid-1960s, the activities of giant Agribusiness concerns have spilled over from the industrial countries, particularly the US, to Latin America and other continents. In Latin America, all important and an increasing number of 'modernized', 'dynamic' agricultural sectors and related industries and services are controlled today by US capital and technology. The subjugation of these agricultural sectors and their rural populations is the result of a long-run global strategy whose various components and consequences I shall attempt to outline briefly in the following paragraphs. This raises immediately three fundamental questions: (a) what caused the sudden interest of giant industrial capital to invest in the poorly-performing agriculture of Latin America? (b) what do we understand by Agribusiness? and (c) what mechanisms are applied to bring foreign agriculture under the control of the industrial countries?

The first question is the most complex. It has a political and an economic dimension. After the Cuban revolution and agrarian reform, which eliminated the landed oligarchies and Cuba's economic and political dependence upon the US practically with one stroke, and since Cuba's socialist agriculture predictably showed impressive results in terms of organization, output, diversification and improved status of its rural workers, the US and Latin American governments and their landed oligarchies were struck with terror at the thought that the Cuban example might spread to other countries and wipe out the existing power structure also with one stroke — and without compensation. What is more they also feared this would upset the relations between the US and the hemisphere. Such an event was within the realm of possibility: not only because without exception Latin American agriculture is characterized by rigid agrarian structures (like pre-revolutionary Cuba), an increasingly unequal distribution of wealth, income and power, spreading unemployment and rising poverty — all responsible for an increasingly poor agricultural performance — but also because the Cuban revolution electrified the peasantry and the landless causing a wave of organized peasant movements to sweep through the hemisphere.

The response was swift and twofold. Through the Alliance for Progress, Latin American governments were promised financial assistance to increase their agricultural output through so-called land reforms. With one exception, each country set up land reform legislation and institutes to qualify for US dollar aid. The aid arrived, but the reforms were never carried out, except at best on a pilot-project basis or through colonization projects baptized 'agrarian reform' to pacify the peasants. Simultaneously, through its military apparatus and alliances, the US set in motion a hemisphere-wide campaign to end, *manu militari,* both peasant movements and organizations. By the mid-1960s, the peasants' political pressures in favour of incisive agrarian reforms had ceased to exist, except in Chile which had to wait until the 1973 fascist putsch to settle the peasant question there once and for all.

Once launched by sheer necessity on the road to 'do something' about the hemisphere's failing agriculture, the US and Latin American power elites soon discovered that neither pilot-project-type land reforms nor bloody peasant repressions could solve the production problem. It was urgent to respond to the challenge in a more constructive manner. The answer was the modernization of Latin America's latifundio-sector. By strengthening the landed elite economically, politically and militarily, and by coaxing traditionally inefficient land monopolists – who operate only a tiny portion of their huge holdings intensively and use the remainder in extensive enterprises or not at all – into adopting modern capitalist farming methods, the proletariat could be neutralized for a long time to come; and one of the arguments in favour of reforms, namely that (to use the innocuous vocabulary of the reformists) the land owned by the landed elite did 'not fulfil its social function', would fall by the wayside.

This new strategy was inspired by the 'Mexican model': the Green Revolution, whose birthplace is Mexico, or more precisely by the miracle – (wheat, maize and sorghum) seeds – producing offices and laboratories of the philanthropic Ford and Rockefeller Foundations and CIMMYT, supported by enormous subsidies from Mexican governments following the Cardenas regime, willing to curtail the achievements of Mexico's agrarian reform. Mexico's Green Revolution, which with US assistance soon became Mexico's principal source of exports, was the most efficient counter-reform programme ever devised by helping to establish a powerful capitalist neo-latifundio sector, by occupying the best farming areas, by producing the bulk of the country's exports, an important portion of domestic foods and animal feeds, and by systematically displacing the peasants from the land they had acquired through the reform.[5]

Actually modernization of Mexican and subsequently of Latin American agriculture proceeded in two phases. The strengthening of the latifundio sector proved to be a time- and money-consuming effort, given that large landowners had to be cajoled by extraordinary means into modifying their antiquated farming systems : iron-clad markets, guaranteed prices and other truly enormous subsidies. Subsequently modernization was achieved directly by intervention of foreign, mainly US, capital and technology, with the already mentioned result that important sectors and agriculture-related industries and services were owned and operated by overseas investors. This has significant political implications for land monopolists, peasants and governments. Erich Jacoby pointed out recently that

> In their capacity as agents for the application of advanced technology [the rural elites] have turned into a commercial elite which is quite different from the rural elite of their fathers who used to act as patrons to their peasant clients. . . . . .however the actual participation of the new elite is of marginal importance only for the smooth functioning of the transnational mechanism. It may even be claimed that the once powerful elite has been *politically expropriated* and that its former economic functions have been transferred to transnational corporations. . .[6] (My emphasis)

The implications for the rural proletariat are much more serious : the old class struggle between the peasants or the landless and the local elite has increasingly broader international connotations. Rural labour is not facing just a powerful national class enemy anymore, but transnational investors and corporations whose political and economic power is infinitely greater than that of the former since they are backed by the economic, political and military machines of the industrial nations which they actually represent. The integrated international operations of transnational agribusiness affect all countries in a like manner, so that it becomes increasingly unrealistic to speak, as many still do, of national agricultural or agrarian problems. The fact is that these problems are now hemisphere-wide, as international agribusiness and its allies *impose* upon the proletariat a hemisphere-wide response to the challenge of their activities. Since peasant organizations are notoriously weak on the national level, it is not difficult to realize the enormous task they now face on the wider level, and it is doubtful whether they are up to it in the foreseeable future without substantial outside assistance.[7] And the major task the rural proletariat faces is to prevent the liquidation of the peasants and the elimination of the rural proletariat even in a physical sense.

The rural population cannot even count any more on the modest and marginal support with which Latin American governments furnished them from time to time. The influence of agribusiness and their allies has become so pervasive that it excludes the possibility of adopting even the mildest plans and programmes for redistribution of wealth and income. National agricultural programmes and institutions are now shaped so as to support exclusively international agribusiness ventures overseas.

The counter-reform element of the modernization strategy might well have remained less effective, if modernization had not been stimulated simultaneously by economic factors which contributed to the rapid expansion of agribusiness overseas operations. Since the mid-1960s, investment opportunities and profit repatriations from non-agricultural overseas ventures declined and industrial capital was forced to seek new investment outlets. It found them in foreign agricultures. Contrary to widely-held opinion, agricultural ventures turned out to be very remunerative, once they were made broad enough to include the combined control over productive processes, processing, distribution and input sales. Transnational corporations earn and repatriate larger profits than they could earn 'at home' — even super-profits[8] — because of low and super-low production, processing or distribution costs, because inputs are sold under uniquely favourable conditions and because of the high mobility of capital and technology, always in search of super-low costs. Super-profitable overseas ventures of US corporations now include — a new historical development — staple foods, animal feeds, fruit and vegetables, livestock and meat including the sale of high-quality breeding animals, artificial insemination, cotton and other fibres, seeds of all kinds including grasses for pasture, timber and related items, and the traditional tropical and sub-tropical products. There is hardly an agricultural enterprise for moderate climate, sub-tropical or tropical conditions which is not on the list. *Thus we are witnessing a unique process of the transfer of the agricultures of the industrial countries to Latin America where an entirely new form of enclave economy is being created which exceeds in scope, importance and impact the old plantation-enclave-economies beyond comparison.*[9] As a matter of fact, agribusiness and its apostles consider their overseas ventures simply as part of the US marketing system, as the accompanying graph — 'US fruit and vegetable market system, 1971' — which is summarized

from one of Ray Goldberg's graphs, illustrates.[10]

Fig. 1. *Global integration of agriculture: An agribusiness view of the 'US fruit and vegetable market system, 1971'.*
(Summarized graph)

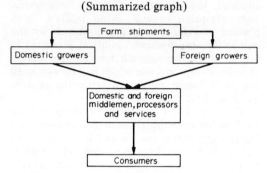

Source: Goldberg, op. cit. pp. 44, 110.

III

Now anyone seriously looking for an answer to what agribusiness in Latin America is all about would be hard put to find it in the verbose literature devoted to the subject by the Harvard Business School or the pronouncements of leaders of giant food corporations who are prone to express themselves freely on the subject. Fortunately the answer is relatively simple. Agribusiness in underdeveloped countries is a conglomerate of diverse, interdependent agencies and operations to assist large and medium-sized corporations (or in a few cases, individual investors) engaged in agriculture or agriculture-related industries and services on a hemisphere-wide scale for the practically exclusive benefit of the latter. It is like a giant set of wheels — agribusiness firms properly speaking — assisted by an effective lubricating system to keep the wheels turning faster — the agencies which keep world-wide agribusiness capitalist-style in constant expansion. We can distinguish three types of firms :

- multinational corporations engaged directly either in the production or distribution of agricultural products, or in both at the same time;
- corporations engaged in the production (or local assembly) and distribution of agricultural inputs;[11]
- corporations or firms engaged in supplying services.

The latter category is normally overlooked. But these firms play an important multifunctional role in that they operate on their own behalf and on behalf and in support of the other two categories of concerns. Among them are : export and import, consultant, law, public relations and advertising firms, as well as technical and management advisors at the farm, processing or distribution levels. Many of these activities are in support of profit repatriations and therefore assist in draining underdeveloped countries of their agricultural resources.

These firms could not operate at the level and with the financial means with which they now function if it was not for a number of institutions which serve to organize and improve the infra- and super-structure for their world-wide activities. Among them are :

- private (super) agencies formed by agribusiness firms which coordinate the activities of transnational corporations, elaborate plans and projects for new overseas investments and seek new financial (private or public) support from other sources;
- private banks operating on a world-wide basis, supporting agricultural ventures overseas;
- bilateral and international technical assistance or lending institutions, such as USAID, the US Export—Import Bank, the World Bank, the Inter-American Development Bank, the United Nations (UNDP, UNIDO for example) and FAO (FAO/Industry Cooperative Programme);
- other agencies or organizations which support on a world-wide basis overseas agribusiness ventures directly or indirectly, such as the large 'philanthropic' foundations (Rockefeller, Ford, Volkswagen, etc.), international research stations (CIMMYT, IRRI, etc.), and religious organizations;
- national government or private organizations collaborating in one way or another with any of the above categories;
- and last but not least, the institutions, such as the Harvard Business School and 90 universities in the US and other countries, which have 'established agribusiness programmes or courses'[12] and supply giant corporations with new ideas and beautify their public image.

A prominent, characteristic case is the World Bank because of its powerful financial resources and widespread, well-heeled loan projects. Bank loans for agriculture — not to mention loans for agricultural industries and infrastructural improvements in the countryside, such as electrification, roads or irrigation works or financial support for CIMMYT and other research projects always directed exclusively towards crops cultivated by large commercial farm producers — are *all* of financial interest and profit for agribusiness firms properly speaking, and in fact, the transnational corporations *expect* additional business from World Bank

loans and are unhappy if this does not occur.[13] With such an array of financial and technical support from powerful agencies, all focusing on 'saving' underdeveloped agriculture from certain disaster by expanding capitalist ventures there — and thereby precipitating the very disaster they wish to avoid — it is little wonder that agribusiness has evolved as rapidly as it did during the span of only a few years.

IV

In the normal process of expanding their business transactions overseas, transnational 'food corporations' and input peddlers obtain and maintain control over modernized agricultural sectors in Latin America in four ways : transfers of fixed and operating capital to establish production, processing and service facilities and to keep them in operation; transfers of technology at the various levels; the marshalling of local financial, personnel and institutional involvement to support the foreign ventures; and political pressures. A few comments may dispel some agribusiness-induced misconceptions about how agribusiness functions in the poor countries. I focus on the operations of firms engaged in production or distribution of agricultural products, rather than on input peddlers, but the activities are closely interrelated. The larger the firm, the greater the chance that it will be engaged in all activities — production, processing, distribution of food or fibre, plus manufacture (or assembly) and sale or distribution of inputs — simultaneously. In a complete reversal of a policy announced some years ago[14] industrial capital now invests fixed and operating capital in farm land and its operation. It is impossible to determine the scope of these investments (purchases, leases or concessions) because of the common use of 'strawmen' to hide real ownership. Methods of controlling land vary from country to country partly in accordance with local legislation. In Brazil, according to a confidential parliamentary enquiry, purchases of land by US investors, between 1964 and 1970, amounted to 32–35 million ha and are now surely much larger, without counting enormous concessions granted to non-agricultural enterprises.[15] In Mexico, rentals are more common. The process of land acquisition by foreign investors is a fact in all countries from Surinam to Brazil, and now Chile, and it has an upward trend.[16] Land and farming operations are controlled also by the production contract system and more indirectly through foreign (e.g. World Bank) loans via the lenders' right to supervise the execution of the loan projects. In addition, existing or new agricultural industries are purchased or built by foreign capitalists.[17] Control over the necessary related services follows. The processes of capital transfers are paralleled by technology transfers.[18] Since the objective of all these transfers is to obtain control over entire commodity systems, capital and technology transfers tend to go hand in hand. Hence the probability is extremely high that, once the productive processes with respect to a specific commodity are dominated by foreign capital and technology, its processing or handling is also dominated in the same way, either by the same firm(s) or through loose or formal cooperation of several corporations and vice-versa. To illustrate, in Mexico some 45 agricultural industries showed varying degrees of participation by transnational corporations in 1970 (see Table 1).[19] A realistic hypothesis is therefore that, where there is participation of such corporations in a given industry, its direct or indirect participation in farm-level production is also bound to occur, and that the higher the degree of participation at the industrial level, the higher its participation at the farm level.

That foreign capital is able to marshall local resources to support its business ventures has been well documented by the vast literature on dependency. It should be noted however that this general rule may have its exceptions whenever the use of local resources threatens to weaken the hold of foreign investors over the commodity system.[20] The marshalling of local personnel and the use of local institutions in support of overseas agribusiness ventures is a 'horse of a different colour' because, without exception, these ventures draw upon an out-of-proportion number of qualified personnel or government agencies to keep the venture well-oiled and to assure the repatriation of profits. Since qualified personnel in the poor countries is scarce and government agencies under-staffed, the consequence is an unavoidable neglect of other agricultural sectors, mainly the peasant sector, and the proliferation of corruption. The very presence of transnational concerns makes the effective execution of programmes other than those in support of agribusiness a practical impossibility. To enforce the adoption of measures to marshall local support for their operations, agribusiness concerns employ subtle or brutal methods, which go all the way from bribery to the artificial creation of new or the fostering of old social and political conflicts,[21] without even bothering to seek the cooperation of their own governments, although political pressures can include the threat of military or para-military intervention. *This is not any more the type of staging of the small-Banana-Republic-type where a powerful plantation owner bamboozles a weak executive. It is a war-game with heavy artillery, with (figuratively speaking) atomic warheads, which becomes the fiercer, the more industrialized and 'developed' the poor country has become.* The margin of independent action on plans, policies and programmes by local governments decreases in geometric proportions with the rising penetration of foreign capital and technology into their dependent capitalist economies — the only alternative permitted by the capitalist system whereby an underdeveloped economy is allowed to climb on the road to 'progress'.

V

Whether part of a hemisphere-wide conspiracy or simply the 'natural' outgrowth of an expansionist system running wild, moderniza-

Table 1. *Degree of participation of transnational corporations in 45 Mexican food industries 1970*

Percent of production attributable to transnational corporations	Number of industries
Less than 10%	2
10–49%	28
50–90%	12
Over 90%	3

Source: CIDE, unpublished
Note: Except for curing tobacco, the manufacture of cigarettes and of condensed, evaporated or powdered milk, the number of transnationals as percent of all establishments was relatively low in each industry.

tion via the functioning and growth of transnational agribusiness must result in the gradual but rapid elimination of Latin America's rural proletariat. Although this sounds exorbitant, I have reached this conclusion after careful examination of the issues involved, and on the basis of the fundamental fact that the new process of capitalist expansion in agriculture requires in the longer run for its success neither the land of the peasants nor the labour of most of the landless.[22] Its elimination comes about directly, both through the activities of agribusiness firms and allied strategies originating with the industrial countries; and indirectly through the impact of the former on the future availability of natural resources and Latin America's potential for maintaining production.

Let me begin with the peasants – smallholders, owners, tenants, sharecroppers or occupiers of small plots. Even before the activities of agribusiness spilled over from the US to Latin America, their status had become increasingly precarious. Unable to obtain access to land and other resources, they proliferated on just about the same total farming area; average size and quality of their plots declined – hence both a numerical increase of the poor and a lowering of their already inadequate income. Now, their very existence on the plots is threatened in various ways, principally through the agribusiness-induced expansion of large-scale, modernized, commercial agriculture and the two-pronged action of the two types of agribusiness concerns mentioned earlier.

The eviction of smallholders operates like a pair of scissors. On one side, through modernization, particularly mechanization, capital replaces labour. (As we saw earlier, modernization in industrial countries had to result in production and ownership concentration and 'dramatic' labour displacement.) There is an abundant and confusing literature on the employment effect of modernization in underdeveloped countries which usually ignores what took place in the industrial countries and which tries to demonstrate for selected cases that innovations can create new employment opportunities and are therefore socially desirable. This may be so. But these studies never draw up a balance sheet of the aggregate effects of all innovations in agriculture as a whole.[23] In my view, in the aggregate, the elimination of jobs must exceed the creation of new employment in a 'modernizing' capitalist agriculture under conditions of underdevelopment, otherwise rural unemployment and underemployment would be decreasing at least in relative terms.[24] But obviously this is not so in any Latin

American country, either absolutely or relatively. As far as smallholders are concerned, modernization requires reorganization of labour management in the sense that on large holdings traditional labour use patterns (small tenants, sharecroppers, etc.) are replaced by the direct exploitation by the commercial producers accompanied by the eviction of the plotholders from the land.[25] Furthermore the expansion of commercial agriculture threatens directly the survival of smallholders whenever commodities are involved which are traditionally produced by the latter since they cannot compete, production-wise or in the agribusiness-dominated market place, with the former. We have seen earlier that agribusiness ventures are likely to exist in most any commodity system, hence the adverse impact on smallholders is bound to be increasingly severe. This is the panorama when studied from the input side.

The other blade of the scissors is operated by the big corporations engaged in commodity production, processing or distribution. They solve their supply problem by engaging directly in producing on owned or rented land – an 'extreme form of vertical integration' – by purchasing from independent producers or through the production contract system. In all three, the firms prefer and foster large-scale farming operations. They bring the fetish of bigness to Latin America because bigness is what they created and cherish at home. Hence agribusiness has a built-in anti-peasant bias which is compounded by the anti-peasant institutions rampant in Latin America. However, in the production contract system, now widely used and bound to cover ever more commodity systems, the situation is complex. Agribusiness likes the system for economic and political reasons. Economically, it makes the contracted growers dependent upon the buyer as he furnishes them with needed inputs and 'assistance'; he makes additional profits and secures additional profit repatriations from input sales; and the system makes his supply operations flexible in that he is for all practical purposes free to accept or reject the growers' (particularly the small growers') output without any cost to him, in accordance with market conditions. Politically agribusiness can and does argue that it is a 'less extreme form of vertical integration', politically more acceptable since the system 'preserves the autonomy of the growers'. Obviously this is untrue: the system provides the buyer with about the same amount of control over growers and output as the 'extreme form'. But the argument works. In underdeveloped countries, transnational food corporations *nolens volens* are forced to contract small growers because for every large landowner there are thousands of smallholders. But the system can be used effectively to drive smallholders out of business and off their plots through relentless mechanisms on which I need not elaborate here.[26] In practically all cases where production contracting has functioned for some time in a commodity system, production and ownership concentration has been achieved at the expense of the peasants.

VI

The fatal consequences of modernization for the rural proletariat in the dependent capitalist countries of Latin America — greater unemployment, poverty and potentials for unmanageable conflicts — did not escape its promoters. What has been their reaction? Beyond military repression, they are taking what appear to be by many criteria near-desperate economic and political measures.

The first is the recent effort to expand capitalism in the smallholder sector through a broad system of 'credit for the poor'. The ramifications of this highly synchronized programme are astounding : there is hardly a development agency or agribusiness concern which is not now involved in it on a small or a large scale. By far the most important is the 1973 World Bank scheme to 'assist' 700 million poor on smallholdings (only) throughout the Third World, which is likely to involve the largest amount of funds. Its alleged objective is to pump credit and thereby 'modern' inputs into the smallholdings, excepting however most of the sophisticated inputs available to large landowners. Of course, its aim is not to abolish smallholdings, a bottomless source of supply of cheap labour for large rural employers. It is meant to rescue the peasants from what the Bank calls 'absolute poverty'. Such a rescue operation is bound to have at best a temporary and marginal effect, unless the fundamental cause of rural poverty, the lop-sided agrarian structure, is solved through the abolition of the landed elite and the organization of an equitable land tenure system, as in Cuba. In practice, its consequences may very well be to set loan beneficiaries against the remainder of the peasants, as limited credit funds have to be doled out over years in piecemeal fashion, and it is practically certain that the available funds can only reach a fraction of the 700 million poor, even if the World Bank does not lose patience in the execution of this formidable task. In order to survive in the World Bank- and agribusiness-fostered capitalist ex-peasant economy, the lucky loan recipients will be obliged to start a small capitalist-style process of monopolization of their own, at the expense of the more unlucky fellow peasants not yet included in the scheme, who will be starved out of their plots and become still more absolutely poor. Even worse is the likelihood that since the landed monopolists continue to be strengthened by the entire agribusiness apparatus operating in the Third World, the chances of survival even of the loan beneficiaries are slim indeed and their improved land, into which credits have been sunk, will become attractive real estate for the land-grabbing elite. Thus the Bank scheme to wipe out 'absolute poverty' must end up in a proliferation of absolutely poor with which even ten more World Banks could not cope.

Control of population growth is an equally serious threat to the physical survival of the rural proletariat. It is inspired by the proposition that a reduction in the number of mouths to feed will do away with poverty. It is not the absurdity of this doctrine which concerns us here,[27] but the effects of its implementation. There are two types of mechanisms now planned or employed to reduce the number of people in Latin American agriculture. The first type is through open or clandestine measures to prevent births. It involves the dissemination of contraceptives and the education for their use. In rural Latin America, this encounters severe obstacles because of the aggressive opposition of the Catholic Church and because of its relatively high costs. It may also involve the sterilization of men or women. Sterilization can be voluntary, but is rarely practised; or, it can be done on an involuntary basis or surreptitiously. Reports about the latter, particularly on women, from various parts of the hemisphere, including areas inhabited by poor indigenous communities, are now so frequent that they cannot be dismissed as anti-imperialist propaganda. Although in all likelihood such involuntary sterilizations are still carried out through small pilot projects, there exists the probability that they could be used on a much broader scale as a desperate means to reduce class conflicts which threaten the control by industrial countries and their transnational concerns over agriculture and economies. That such broad-scale programmes can be undertaken by undemocratic regimes has been demonstrated by India. In the unhygienic conditions under which sterilization of men or women takes place, the victims may not be the not-to-be-born children, but the people on whom it is practised. There are indications that loans from international lending agencies are now being tied to the condition that the recipient governments undertake effective birth control measures, which could, under the proper conditions, involve large-scale involuntary sterilization.

The second type is population control by starvation through systematic economic strangulation. This is now being tried out effectively in Chile. Lest the reader think that this is the product of the author's exalted imagination, let us remind him that pronouncements to that effect by prominent personalities from industrial countries are reported periodically in the press in recent years.[28] In this context, it is surely no coincidence that the World Bank's poverty scheme, which was outlined above, includes only a rescue operation for the smallholders who can buy inputs produced by the transnational agribusiness corporations or sell them their output, since they have a plot of land to contribute to capitalist accumulation. The landless are omitted from the scheme although they are as numerous as the absolutely poor smallholders, and are therefore left to their own devices, as far as the World Bank is concerned (not to mention their own governments): death sentence by remote control.

VII

My final remarks concern agribusiness-induced uses of natural resources and their longer-run effects on Latin America's ability to feed itself and export the surplus, and how this affects the rural labour force. I start with the realistic assumption that in the Latin American hemisphere there are today, broadly speaking, ample land, water and forest resources, good soils and climatic conditions, including virgin areas not yet incorporated in agriculture, adequate to feed a population much larger than the existing one, with the exception that according to available evidence, forest resources are smaller than official statistics show. The historical expansion of agriculture with the traditional agrarian structure, which decisively fashioned the pattern of resource uses, has beeen characterized by enormous wastes through the systematic 'mining' of the soils, which obliged the latifundio owners to constantly shift their production to new unspoiled areas. Latin America's has always been a 'migrating' agriculture. This process continues today. Statistically it is shown by the fact that

increases in output are due principally to an increase of the farming area rather than of per hectare yields. With such a resource-use pattern, aggregate output would have to decline whenever new virgin areas become unavailable, unless producers were willing and able to shift to scientific, intensive land-use practices.

With the advent of international agribusiness, one can discern contradictory patterns, all of which, however, threaten seriously over the longer-run (which may be no more than 2–3 generations) the preservation of agricultural resources. These patterns relate to agribusiness-style exploitation in relatively intensive cultivation, to the expansion of the livestock industry, and to the systematic destruction of forests, i.e. the gradual elimination of virgin areas – the latter two being incidentally closely interrelated.

The wasteful use of cultivable land which has gone on for generations now is bound to be compounded sharply by the new processes of modernization. This appears to be a paradox, but can be explained easily by the special conditions which giant foreign agribusiness firms encounter in Latin American agriculture and which they exploit to the hilt. The purpose of modernized commodity systems dominated by foreign capital and technology is to produce and market commodities at minimum costs and to maximize the repatriation of profits. This can be achieved at the farm level by firms engaged in production, either directly or through the production contract system, by using irrigated or rain-fed soils of good quality, i.e. with high initial yields, and taking advantage of and attempting by all means to maintain low and super-low production costs such as low land values, rental payments, wages, costs of construction, or services. This is elementary economics. It is not surprising therefore that the modernized, 'dynamic' foreign-dominated sectors occupy today the best farming areas available. Similar observations can be made for processing and distribution. Now there is no doubt that foreign investors, with experience in production and handling of agricultural commodities in industrial and underdeveloped agricultures all over the world, have at their fingertips a complete knowledge of the best and most up-to-date farming and handling methods. They are in a position to transfer their entire bag of technological know-how to the poor countries. However, under the conditions prevailing in the latter, this just does not occur, although agribusiness and its apostles arrogantly try to convince everybody that it does. The transfers of know-how are bound to be partial and selective,[29] even involving technologies of inferior quality either because this means lower costs, or because the transfers involve surplus or obsolete technologies not used or prohibited in the industrial countries, or because technologies are transferred which are well-adapted to the conditions of industrial agricultures or industries but ill-suited to the conditions of the poor countries, or because in the final analysis the commodities may be produced for the industrial markets and have to suit the industrial countries' consumer preferences or, last but not least, because partial, selective technology transfers maintain or increase the dependency of the underdeveloped agricultures on the transnational corporations, as it permits the permanent control over all such transfers by the foreign 'innovators' (as agribusiness apostles like to call them) which they would never give up voluntarily.[30] If as a consequence of these practices, land and water resources are wasted, yields decline and soils are infected or eroded. This is of no particular concern to the foreign innovators because under conditions of plentiful supply of good land, there is no need for them to preserve the capital (resource) base of their productive operations, which they are obliged to do in the industrial countries. If the quality of the soils declines or water becomes scarce, the solution lies in shifting the operation to a new area and the process will start all over again. This now occurs on a large scale throughout Latin America. The reader will therefore note at once that modern agribusiness operations employ precisely the same pattern of resource use as the traditional landed elite, except on a considerably higher level of sophistication. While the mode of operation of the old landed elite threatened to destroy the best agricultural resources over a long period of time lasting generations, capitalist exploitation in foreign-dominated commodity systems is likely to destroy them foreseeably in a matter of a few decades. The traditional latifundio sector relied on expansion for survival, but so does capitalist exploitation in the poor countries, except at lightening speed.[31]

A similar pattern can be observed in extensive enterprises such as livestock (cattle). Here the selective transfer of technologies is still more obvious. Basically, foreign-controlled livestock enterprises use the same extensive management practices as traditional Latin ranchers, including for example the time-tested separation of livestock and cropping. Modernization is likely to affect only certain specific phases of the operations, such as better disease prevention, methods to decrease mortality rates and improvements in transportation. The basic patterns are likely to remain unchanged except for the moderate improvements mentioned, since extensive livestock operations require little capital investment, low operating costs and little labour, and land is still plentiful. But there is a more important aspect: namely that a large proportion of all foreign capital transferred to Latin American agriculture has been and continues to be invested in livestock enterprises. As a matter of fact, the US, one of the largest livestock and meat producing and importing countries, now appears to be engaged in a programme of very large scope to expand relentlessly Latin America's livestock and meat industry and bring it under its control — a process which now has gone on for about 10 years, but has shown an upward trend in recent years. The implications for Latin America's resources are far-reaching. In any Latin American country with a livestock industry — and this includes most of them — the overwhelming proportion of the land in farms is occupied by pastures destined for cattle; and in countries where agriculture has expanded, the added area is preferentially devoted to cattle raising. Not all land in pastures is fit for cropping, but a very high proportion is. As the livestock industry grows under foreign ownership and control, it can be predicted that an increasing share of land suitable for cultivation will be inaccessible for cropping, putting the burden of increased production of food and fibre on the remainder of the land, i.e. mostly on the land which is already used for field crops. This contradictory process of capitalist expansion of modernized farming and of the livestock industry, both competing for agricultural resources, and which might or might not be an indication that competing foreign capitalists are involved, has a built-in threat for the former. It may actually imply that the limits of expansion for cropping might be reached in the foreseeable future. But far from being an incentive for the foreign investors to transfer more capital and technology into a highly scientific land use and management mode of operation, exactly similar to that employed in the industrial agriculture, it is on the contrary likely to force them into gradual withdrawal, because the very motivations for producing in Latin America — namely low and super-low production costs and maximum profit repatriations — would cease to exist. This would leave Latin America 'holding the bag', as the popular saying goes.

The exploitation of forest resources pursues two objectives: extraction of lumber and opening up new areas for livestock. In the process of lumber extraction, the vicissitudes and wastes of capitalist exploitation under conditions of underdevelopment appear to reach their apex. This accounts in large part for a pace of deforestation which is bound to have the most serious consequences, not only on the future of the lumber industry which with rational forest management could provide employment and income for the peasants, but in terms of future climatic conditions, as it is likely to provoke droughts and floods of catastrophic proportions. In the face of the capitalist-style extinction of forests, it is unrealistic to think of reforestation and no one now appears to be seriously interested in it. In the second objective of forest exploitation, we are again dealing with a time-tested phenomenon prevailing in Latin America, but which under agribusiness stimulus is turned from a mere phenomenon into a process with practically devastating consequences, compounding the effects of irrational lumbering. For generations, the expansion of the agricultural frontier was largely achieved through the labour of settlers in search of a livelihood in virgin areas. They cleared the land which was subsequently taken over by cattle ranches and moved on to clear more land with the same result. With the advent of foreign capital and technology, however, the clearing of forested areas in preparation for grazing can be and is being undertaken with great speed, with and without settlers. In many areas of the hemisphere, e.g. Colombia, Brazil or Mexico, this has the additional consequence that many indigenous communities are evicted, if not actually exterminated.

I reach the somber conclusion that the process of capitalist expansion by transnational agribusiness firms and their take-over of Latin American agriculture is conducive to the rapid displacement of peasants from the land, without their having the slightest possibility of finding employment elsewhere, given the already existing excess supply of labour in each and every country. It saps the very basis of livelihood of the entire rural proletariat by destroying Latin America's farmland and forests or by making them inaccessible for sustenance and employment. Although it is to be expected that agricultural output and exports can be maintained and even somewhat increased over the next few years, Latin America's capacity to produce food and fibre over the longer run is being gradually and rapidly undermined. The result will be increased dependency on the industrial nations, particularly the US for food for domestic consumption. This is not of particular concern to the foreign capitalists and innovators, since they are in a position to re-transfer their capital and know-how back to the industrial nations whose resources are now being saved-up for future use by the present-day transfer of their agricultures to the Third World.

Only a global view of the different agricultural strategies of the capitalist industrial countries, instrumented at home and overseas by giant agribusiness firms and their allies — some of which I do not hesitate to qualify as near-desperate measures to save the capitalist system by any, even the most destructive means — is capable of furnishing insights into the colossal plundering of Latin America's agricultural resources, in which the industrial nations, combining their economic and military power and modern, even if only selectively employed, technology, are now engaged. The only hope remaining is that with the growing awareness that this internationalized process is destroying relentlessly the means of survival of the rural proletariat, the latter will soon become convinced of the need for a hemisphere-wide response, over and above the heads of their dictatorial and repressive governments, and will seek the establishment of an equitable, constructive, independent and rational resource-use system which will operate first of all for the benefit of Latin America's rural and urban proletariat. And that can hardly be the capitalist system under foreign domination.

NOTES

1. See for example Agribusiness Accountability Project, *A Summary Report on Major US Corporations Involved in Agribusiness* (Washington, D.C.: July 1973). The corporations include firms such as Sears Roebuck, Aetna Life and Casualty, Bank of America, Boeing, Kodak, ITT, etc., all engaged either in land-holdings, production, processing or distribution of foods or inputs. The same phenomenon exists in other industrial countries. For example Volkswagen owns immense areas of land in Brazil, for livestock operations.

2. Ray A. Goldberg, *Agribusiness Management for Developing Countries – Latin America* (1974), pp. 32–56. The title of this book is misleading because it deals with the potentials for expanding fruit and vegetable production in *Central America* for export to the US, not Latin America. In this context it is difficult to obtain an idea of the nature and objectives of Agribusiness without a careful reading of the Harvard Business School literature. It is devoted to US and other investors and describes the advantages which can be derived from investing in Latin American agriculture. The careful reader will soon discover, however, how disastrous agribusiness operations turn out to be for local producers, handlers and processors, without even having to read between the lines. Cf. my 'Agribusiness in underdeveloped agricultures: Harvard Business School myths and reality', *Economic and Political Weekly* (Bombay: 17 July 1976); and 'Agribusiness: in sheep's clothing', *Ceres* (FAO), (July–August 1976).

3. This is of course strenuously denied by agribusiness itself by insisting that the production contract system 'preserves the autonomy of the growers'. But this is false. See for example a typical contract in Goldberg, op. cit., p. 334, where the corporation expressly declares that the contracted grower is not an employee of the firm. This may be true in law, but not in fact.

4. Cf. for example Lester Brown, *Seeds of Change* (1969).

5. For the disastrous consequences of the Green Revolution in Mexico, see Cynthia Alcantara, *The Social and Economic Implications of Large-Scale Introduction of New Varieties of Foodgrains in Mexico* (Geneva: UNRISD, 1975). Production-wise, the Green Revolution was also a failure as Keith Griffin proved convincingly in *The Political Economy of Agrarian Change* (1974).

6. 'Structural changes in Third World agricultures as a result of neo-capitalist developments', *The Developing Economies* (Tokyo: Sept. 1974).

7. In his recent *The Latin American Peasant* (1975), Andrew Pearse begins by defining the contemporary – and I would add, the tragic – problem for the peasants of Latin America as follows:

How can the rural majorities in the post-colonial countries find a way of *coming to terms* with the acquisitive expansion of the industrial urban nucleus, which is rapidly undermining their land-bound security, but is niggardly in offering them advantageous places in the new society'. (My emphasis), p. ix.

If one examines Latin American agriculture, as Pearse does, as one great class struggle, it is obvious that this has had its historical ups and downs although in the long run the peasants seem to have been consistently on the losing side. After the Cuban revolution, it appeared as if the peasants might come out 'on top'. But the point I am trying to drive home is that the opportunities for the peasants to 'come to terms' with their old and new class enemies are now rapidly vanishing – or perhaps have already vanished.

8. See Barnet and Miller, *Global Reach* (1975), p. 17.

9. It will not escape the reader that this process is highly contradictory if one recalls the previously mentioned increased potential of the industrial agricultures to expand production. To what extent the overseas investments and ventures of transnational food corporations are contrary to the interests of the industrial nations' farmers is a subject which has not yet been adequately evaluated.

10. Goldberg, op. cit., pp. 44, 110.

11. For our purpose here it is immaterial whether firms in these two groups are wholly-owned subsidiaries, mixed-capital concerns or whether they operate under a licensing agreement.

12. Goldberg, op. cit., p. 5.

13. For details see my forthcoming, 'Capitalism's last ditch effort to save underdeveloped agricultures', *Journal of Contemporary Asia* (Special Issue, 1977), where I attempt to substantiate the claims made in the text on the basis of information furnished by the World Bank.

14. For example, United Brand of banana-fame allegedly divested itself of its holdings. But political opposition to this firm or others was not due to the amount of land they controlled, as they pretend, but to their crude methods of exploiting human and physical resources and the unrestricted repatriation of their profits. At present, local opposition has vanished due to the considerably greater political and economic influence locally and the omnipresence of giant food corporations.

15. Concessions for exploiting petroleum or minerals afford investors control over land and people.

16. Current devaluations cheapen the acquisition of assets.

17. Preference is for acquiring established plants. See for example F. Fajnzylber and T. Martinez, *Las Empresas Transnacionales* (Mexico: 1976).

18. For details see my *The New Penetration of the Agricultures of the Underdeveloped Countries by the Industrial Nations and Their Multinational Concerns,* Institute of Latin American Studies, University of Glasgow, Occasional Papers No. 19 (1975).

19. See unpublished report by the Centro de Investigacion y Dociencia (CIDE), *Agroindustria en Mexico* (1976). After 1970, the transnationals' participation in Mexico increased sharply.

20. An example is Mexico's fruit and vegetable export sector. US investors and middlemen furnish most of its fixed and all of the operating capital. This is likely to occur in countries with a certain level of private capital accumulation which might permit local capital to compete effectively with foreign investors.

21. See my *Strawberry Imperialism, An Enquiry into the Mechanisms of Dependency in Mexican Agriculture,* (The Hague: Institute of Social Studies, Research Report, 1976). In Spanish *Imperialismo Fresa* (Mexico: Editorial Campesina, 1976). In German, *Erdbeer Imperialismus* (Suhrkamp, 1977).

22. The well-known sociologist Rodolfo Stavenhagen has put forward the argument that a capitalist agriculture *requires* the existence and consistent regeneration of a peasant sector as a source of cheap exploitable manpower and in order to exact a surplus from their productive labour. Up to the present, this theory has a great deal of plausibility, as periodic 'land reforms', colonization schemes and the expansion of the farming area into virgin lands via poor settlers seem to prove. But the modernization of agriculture through agribusiness implies precisely the ability to produce more (with the qualifications made below) with cheap land and other resources, not including labour, which makes the regeneration of a peasant sector and even the availability of cheap landless labour a superfluity.

23. Such a balance sheet would have to account for employment creation and elimination in all the various sub-sectors (e.g. elimination of jobs through mechanization, new jobs through diversification or expansion of farming, etc.) in relation to the available and expanding labour force.

24. Another way of looking at the employment problem is that output per worker increases. Several observers (e.g. Erich Jacoby) regard this in itself as an ominous development. In his final report on the worldwide 'Social and economic implications of large-scale introduction of new varieties of foodgrains' (Geneva: UNRISD, 1976) (unpublished so far), Andrew Pearse appears to reach a conclusion similar to mine with regard to the overall employment balance although it is presented in the cautious language befitting a UN agency.

25. They may or may not be re-employed as wage workers, mostly depending on the degree of mechanization. Of course employment must also be evaluated in terms of the changing status of the workers.

26. They include discriminatory practices in the distribution of inputs, preferential treatment of large growers in pricing and grading, and less subtle methods.

27. I am of course not against the control of population growth.

28. See for example 'The new let 'em starve theory', *The Observer* (20 April 1975).

29. For example, marketing know-how is never transferred.

30. For an interesting example see my *Strawberry Imperialism,* op. cit.

31. Obviously this type of argumentation is the opposite of that of the Club of Rome.

World Development, 1977, Vol. 5, Nos. 5–7, pp. 573–583. Pergamon Press. Printed in Great Britain.

The Changing Structure of US Agriculture: Implications for World Trade

W. B. SUNDQUIST

University of Minnesota

Summary. – The reciprocal cause and effect relationship between the structure of US agriculture and world trade is the central theme of this paper. The author highlights those dimensions of the structure which could have a significant impact on trade: farm numbers and size, ownership and control of farmland, changes in the value of production assets, proprietors' equity in farm assets, ownership of farm debt, sources of operating funds, changes in farm employment, changes in production technology, coordination of production and marketing, changes in the structure of commodity markets. The concluding section briefly assesses which of these factors have a major effect on trade.

INTRODUCTION

Past changes in the structure of US agriculture have had significant impacts on world trade. Future changes will have their impacts as well. It is to this line of causality that this article is addressed. We would be remiss, however, not to recognize that both (1) the demand for agricultural products in world markets and (2) the institutional arrangements under which trade occurs, e.g., tariffs, export subsidies, food aid programmes, regulations concerning quality and form of products, and the financing of trade (to mention only a few) also have their impacts on the structure of US agriculture. Thus, in the relationships between structure and trade, causality is a two-way street.

We, in the US, when we think of trade, tend to think rather exclusively in terms of our exports of agricultural commodities. There are, however, a number of agricultural commodities produced domestically, e.g., sugar and wool, for which US producers do not produce adequately to supply total domestic market requirements. There are other commodities such as coffee, tea and bananas for which the domestic US market requirements are provided for almost exclusively via imports. Finally, there are several livestock and livestock product groups for which most of the domestic market needs are currently supplied by US producers,

but for which trade (both imports and/or exports) might be modified significantly under certain structural conditions for the domestic production sector. Since our focus in this article is on the structure of the US agricultural sector, our interest is primarily in those commodities for which US farmers supply at least a significant portion of the domestic market.

Table 1 (*overleaf*) indicates what the large-volume US agricultural export commodities have been in recent years. This list is not complete in that it omits some livestock products and a number of other minor export commodities. Clearly, feedgrains, wheat and flour, and soybeans and soybean products dominate the commodity set of US agricultural exports. These are all commodities which are produced in large volume for domestic markets as well.

It appears useful to define briefly those dimensions of agriculture to which the term structure applies. The list presented here is not intended to be an exhaustive one but rather one which highlights those dimensions of structure which could have a significant impact on trade. These include the size, number and type of firms in both the production and marketing sub-sectors of the agricultural industry; the source of ownership, control and management of these firms; the source, type and volume of financing for their operations; the mix of capital inputs such as land, durable plant and equipment, and the variable inputs such as fertilizer which they utilize; their utilization of labour and management; the degree of technological sophistication with which they operate; and their legal form of organization.

Several of these dimensions of structure normally exhibit a high degree of multicollinearity. Thus, the form of legal organization, for example, may generate its major influence through other dimensions of structure such as size, source and type of financing, management and degree of technological sophistication. Legal organization is also interrelated with commodity type since, for example, larger-than-family-scale corporate firms in production agriculture are concentrated more in the production of those commodities which service the less volatile and more lucrative domestic markets than in those produced for export markets. This is not the case, however, on the export marketing side where the large financial, managerial and organizational inputs required for servicing export markets both effectively exclude the small marketing firm, on the one hand, and provide opportunities for profits for the larger, more sophisticated corporate firm, on the other hand.

Finally, by way of introduction, as US agriculture has developed in the last four or five decades, and particularly in the post-World War II period, it has become increasingly dependent on purchased inputs from off the farm. In the process, a large and many-faceted farm input industry has become an important contributor to the agricultural production process. One

could spend a good deal of time and effort describing this purchased farm input sector. But its changing structure has been well described elsewhere. With the exception of petrochemicals, purchased farm inputs do not appear to have great potential for affecting future agricultural trade. Even in the case of the petrochemical industry, it is not so much structural change in the industry as the potential for reduced supplies and higher costs which could be critical in the future. Thus, I have chosen to give minimal attention in this article to changes in the structure of the purchased farm inputs sector.

THE CHANGING STRUCTURE OF THE AGRICULTURAL SECTOR

Major changes have occurred in the US agricultural sector since the 1930s when the six million or more farms used massive labour inputs and massive amounts of home-produced power (horses and mules) which were fuelled largely by home-produced feed supplies. Most farm tasks had, however, been mechanized by the 1950s; tractors and other power sources had largely replaced horses and mules by that time. Thus, it is the changes which have occurred in more recent years, together with expected future changes which are probably most relevant to the topic at hand. The documentation of historical changes in the structure of US agriculture in this article goes back only to 1960.

Table 1. *US agricultural exports:*
volume of selected commodities fiscal years 1974, 1975 and 1976
(million metric tons)

Commodity	1974 July–June	1975 July–June	1976 July–June	Average 1974–76
Wheat and flour	31.05	28.01	31.46	30.17
Feedgrains	43.74	34.33	46.37	41.48
Rice	1.58	2.23	1.54	1.78
Soybeans	14.05	11.01	15.41	13.49
Vegetable oils	1.05	1.07	0.82	0.98
Oilcake and meal	4.98	4.26	4.63	4.62
Cotton, including linters	1.33	0.88	0.75	0.99
Tobacco	0.31	0.29	0.27	0.29
Fresh fruit	1.10	1.30	1.33	1.24
Animal fats	1.14	1.16	0.89	1.06
Total*	100.31	84.53	103.48	96.11

Source: *World Agricultural Situation,* Economic Research Service, US Department of Agriculture (October 1976).
*Decimal figures may not check due to rounding error.

As US agriculture has taken on more and more of the characteristics of a 'value added' rather than those of a natural resource-based industry, a larger and larger volume of productive inputs flow through the farm firm on a regular production-cycle basis. For some crops this cycle is an annual one but the production period varies widely particularly for some livestock and poultry products. We are constrained by most available data to perform our assessment of production assets in agriculture in terms of an 'annual' accounting schedule. At the same time we know that in some types of farming the intra-year turnover rate for inputs and products has become an important determinant of business volume and profit rates. Ownership and control of some durable inputs to the production process, particularly land, are still described by the more conventional, though often analytically inadequate terminology of land tenure and legal organization.

Farm numbers and size

Table 2 shows recent changes in numbers and size of farms. These changes summarize to about a 30% decline in farm numbers and a 31% increase in farm size since 1960. This type of change will probably continue into the future but at a slightly diminished rate. These data tend to mask, however, the rapidity with which change has occurred in the commercial farming sector because of the relatively large number of small, non-commercial farms which changed very little during the post-1960 period. Along with an increase in size, commercial farms have become more specialized, more market-oriented, and more price-responsive. Most commercial farm operators as of 1976 were probably, for economic survival reasons, pretty well locked into production at or near the capacity level of their fixed factors, particularly land. But, many can and do shift between crops depending on the relative prices and profitability of alternative crops. And, they can and do vary the intensity with which they use variable inputs, such as fertilizer, depending on their profitability in use. Going back to structure, we need to be reminded that farm size, in terms of acres of land, provides us with a measure of change not in output but in an input, albeit an important one.

A commonly used output measure of farm size is that of business volume. Table 3 shows the number of farms within various sizes and sales classes. This table illustrates that farm numbers with sales of $100,000 or more increased in number by about 380% from 1960 to 1975 while those with sales under $20,000

Table 2. *US farms:*
number and average size, 1960–76

Year	Farms (thousands)	Average Size (acres)
1960	3,963	297
1965	3,356	340
1970	2,954	373
1975	2,808	387
1976	2,786	389

Source: *1976 Handbook of Agricultural Charts*, Agricultural Handbook No. 504, US Department of Agriculture.

Table 3. *US farm numbers by size of sales class, 1960–75*

Year	Number of farms (in thousands) with sales			
	$100,000 and over	$40,000– 99,999	$20,000– 39,999	Under $20,000
1960	23	90	227	3,623
1965	36	125	280	3,043
1970	55	178	343	2,378
1975	110	339	565	1,794

Source: *1976 Handbook of Agricultural Charts*, Agricultural Handbook No. 504, US Department of Agriculture.

dropped by more than one-half. A portion of these changes in sales volume are clearly the result of increases in production per farm. A portion are also due, however, to the price effects associated with the higher commodity prices in 1975 as compared to earlier years.

One could cite a number of other changes in the size and number of farms but perhaps the most important implication is already embodied in Table 3. This implication is that a rapidly increasing proportion of production now comes from a sub-set of commercial farms which are large business firms and which have a rapidly increasing exposure to the prices and other conditions of the input and commodity marketplaces and which are dependent on external sources for servicing their capital and credit needs. In addition, an ever smaller proportion of total farm production is used to serve the captive (on-the-same-farm) markets for feeding livestock and for feeding horses and mules kept as draught animals. An exception is the case of many small- to medium-size dairy farms which still produce most or all of their needed feed supplies. An increasing proportion of other livestock are, however, located on farms other than those producing most of the feed supplies which they utilize. Thus, the vagaries of the organized marketplace increasingly affect the well-being of most commercial farmers.

Ownership and control of farmland

Table 4 shows the current ownership of farmland in the US. These numbers indicate that most of the farmland (about 87.5%) is owned by individuals, partnerships and estates. A relatively small percentage (about 7.1%) is owned by corporations of which a significant portion are family-scale corporations. Thus, about 60% of the land is owned by the individuals or firms which operate the land. This is a high percentage historically, and suggests that land control and operation are not excessively separated. Excessive separation would be exemplified by excessive insecurity of tenure for operators and/or excessive investment by non-operators for speculative, as contrasted to productive, purposes. Neither condition appears to be the case currently. In addition, most current purchases of farmland are by farmers who are expanding the size of their operating unit for economic reasons.

Though not identified in Table 4, a tenure category which has increased significantly in recent years is that of part-owners. Part-owners are farm operators who own some land but who rent in an additional acreage in order both to spread fixed machinery costs and to increase the income generated by their farming operation. The phenomenon of increased part-

Table 4. *Ownership of US farmland*

	Acres (millions)	Percent of total
Land owned by operator:		
Individuals	403	43.90
Partnerships	90	9.80
Corporations	49	5.34
Sub-total	542	59.04
Ownership of land rented out by owner:		
Farm operators	40	4.36
Individuals, estates and partnerships	270	29.41
Corporations	16	1.74
State, federal and Indian lands	50	5.45
Sub-total	376	40.96
Total all farmland	918	100.00

Source: *The Food and Fiber System – How It Works,* US Department of Agriculture, Economic Research Service, Agriculture Information Bulletin 383 (March 1975).

ownership is explained largely by the increased price of land to potential farm operator purchasers on the one hand, and by the desire of retired farmers and other investors to share in future land value increases through retained ownership, on the other hand. Overall, recent changes in the structure of land ownership and control do not appear to have major implications for world trade. Increases in the incidence of part-ownership and decreases in the incidence of full-renter categories of tenancy probably do, however, increase the propensity for production of cash crops as compared to livestock and livestock products. Increased corporate ownership of farmland in the US does not appear to be a major factor affecting trade since (1) its incidence is low in the aggregate and (2) such ownership appears to centre principally on land for development purposes or for use mainly in the production of speciality crops to service profitable domestic markets.

Changes in value of production assets

Table 5 illustrates the rapid increases which have occurred in the value of farm production assets since 1960. Magnitudes are shown for total asset values, values per farm and values per farm worker. The major increases in the value of production assets result mainly from much higher values for farm real estate and from a much more expensive complement of machinery and equipment. The increase in value of production assets per worker results both from the large increase in aggregate asset values and from the interrelated decline in the total number of farm workers. The significance of this capital—labour shift will be elaborated further in a later section. Within the several categories of production assets, real estate increased its percentage share of the total from about 73% in 1960 to 78% in 1976. Livestock's share dropped from 9.7% in 1960 to 6.0% in 1976 while the share of machinery and motor vehicles held about steady over the same period. Shares of other miscellaneous categories of production assets declined slightly. Livestock assets are the most volatile category of production assets and undergo rather wide swings in value (both up and down) from year to year. Thus their lower share of total asset value in 1976 may not be significant. In sum, though the value of production assets (the capital base of agriculture) increased dramatically from 1960 to 1976, there were no major inter-category shifts of importance. What we observed happening during this period were the three-fold developments to (1) bid up the price of a scarce economic good: farmland; (2) substitute, on a mass scale, capital and new technology for labour in farming; and (3) absorb the general inflationary pressures which were present in the general economy.

Proprietors' equity in farm assets

Despite major increases in the value of production assets between 1960 and 1976, US farmers in the aggregate maintained a strong debt-to-asset balance. Farm proprietors' equity in farm real estate assets, for example, totaled about 90.8% in 1960 and declined only slightly to about 88% by 1976. Similarly, proprietors' equity in farm non-real estate assets stood at 82.7% in 1960 and declined to about 75.6% in 1976. These are very high equity ratios relative to those in other industries and suggest that farmers are not excessively in debt in an absolute sense. Neither is the agricultural

Table 5. *Value of US farm production assets: total, per farm and per farm worker, 1960–75*

Year	Total value of production assets (billion dollars)	Value per farm (dollars)	Value per farm worker (dollars)
1960	157.2	42,585	21,416
1965	188.4	59,885	30,832
1970	249.0	89,447	54,229
1975	430.0	163,885	97,601
1976	490.2	188,360	112,114
% 1976 is of 1960	311.8	442.3	523.5

Source: *Balance Sheet of the Farming Sector 1976*, Economic Research Service, US Department of Agriculture.

industry excessively in debt to other economic sectors. So we conclude that the aggregate debt-to-asset ratios of farm proprietors for both broad categories of real estate and non-real estate production assets remained at healthy levels in 1976. But, since many proprietors owned their assets debt-free, the equity position of some other farmers could be at vulnerable levels. This could be the case especially for those operators who increased the size of their units rapidly or who made major and costly shifts to new technology. Such vulnerability might be crucial should farm real estate prices or commodity prices fall back significantly from their current levels. Such vulnerability is not unique to the current time period, however. In fact it is almost the case, by definition, in a competitive economic sector in which some firms enter and others exit.

Ownership of farm debt

It is often postulated that those who own the debt of farmers also exercise substantial influence on their destiny. Table 6 shows the distribution of farm real estate debt in 1960 and again in 1976. The major proportional shift in lending appears to be in the form of increased lending by the Federal Land Bank over time and a decrease in lending by life insurance companies which generally were able to find more profitable and less risky loans elsewhere. On the non-real estate debt side, commercial banks, farmer-owned cooperatives and governmental lending agencies increased their proportional holdings of farm debt between 1960 and 1976. Individuals and others have declined in relative importance in non-real estate lending. One can probably safely conclude that changes in the structure of farm debt in the US between 1960 and 1976 had little if any significance either for control

of the farming sector or for the future competitive position of US farm commodities in agricultural trade. In fact, some of the external speculative investment capital present in cattle feeding and beef cow herds in the late 1960s and early 1970s had shifted mainly to non-farm areas by the mid-1970s.

Sources of operating funds

Measured in terms of the 'annual net flow' of new funds into farming, internally generated funds (about $13 billion in 1975) continue to be the single most important net fund source though external borrowing (about $9 billion in 1975) has increased proportionately over time and may soon bypass internal funds in importance. Funding provided by integrators via contractual arrangements with producers is difficult to measure as are other input contributions to the production process made by integrating firms. It appears to be the case, however, that contributions by integrators to the flow of funds have taken on importance only in the production of a few speciality crops, poultry and some other livestock subsectors.

Overall, there seems to be very little evidence that changes in the capital structure of agriculture have or will induce major impacts on agricultural trade. This situation could change, however, as succeeding generations of farm operators undertake to re-finance the extremely high value production assets of the agricultural sector. Clearly, the major increases in capital requirements have resulted from two sources: (1) inflation in land prices and (2) increased use of purchased farm inputs. The latter expenditures totalled $66 billion in 1973[1] and are still climbing. Though declines in product prices could generate a decline in farm real estate values, such a loss would likely be

Table 6. *US real estate farm debt outstanding 1960−76*

	Federal land bank	Farmers home administration	Life insurance companies	Commercial banks	Individuals and others	Total
1960						
(million dollars)	2335	676	2820	1523	4828	12,182
Percent of total	19.17	5.55	23.15	12.50	39.63	100.00
1976						
(million dollars)	15,950	3369	6533	6296	18,728	50,876
Percent of total	31.35	6.62	12.84	12.38	36.81	100.00

Source: *Balance Sheet of the Farming Sector 1976*, Economic Research Service, US Department of Agriculture.

absorbed internally within the domestic agricultural sector and would not affect trade in any major way. Further increases in the cost of purchased farm inputs, on the other hand, could adversely affect the competitive position of US farm commodities in world trade. The latter, of course, is partially dependent on what happens to input prices in other producing countries.

Changes in farm employment

Table 7 depicts the rapid decline in US farm employment which has occurred in recent years. Total worker numbers in 1975 were only 62% of 1960 numbers. Much of the recent adjustment in labour use has been by way of increased mechanization and specialization on commercial farms coupled with the dropping of numerous small, and usually inefficient livestock enterprises on farms where they had survived the 1940s and 1950s. Labour efficiency during the critical production periods is now at extremely high levels on those farms specializing in the production of feed and foodgrains, cotton and oil crops. These also are the major current US farm export commodities (see Table 1). Producers of these crops are dependent on export markets for a sizeable portion of their output (output from 100 million acres was

exported in 1975).[2] These farmers will be extremely reluctant to shift back to livestock enterprises and forage production. In fact, it is due partly to the increased labour costs relative to other inputs that many farmers have shifted to production of cash crops and have substituted capital (in the form of machinery, fertilizer, pesticides, etc.) for labour. Once the shift has been made to these labour-efficient crops and to new labour-efficient production technology, the change is largely irreversible. Once having left the farm, those workers formerly engaged in farm work will not be easily attracted back into this vocation. Moreover, there is little evidence that agriculture can successfully attract new workers from the non-farm sectors even when unemployment rates are high in these sectors. In sum, many producers are now locked into the production of a set of commodities which are highly labour-efficient and for which current and expected future production levels require large export markets.

Changes in production technology

Table 8 describes well in summary, if not in detail, the two key changes which have occurred in agricultural production technology since 1960. These are the rapid decline in labour use

Table 7. *US farm employment, 1960–76*

Year	Total workers (thousands)	Family workers (thousands)	Hired workers (thousands)
1960	7,067	5,172	1,885
1965	5,610	4,128	1,482
1970	4,523	3,348	1,175
1975	4,357	3,033	1,324

Source: *1976 Handbook of Agricultural Charts*, Agricultural Handbook No. 504, US Department of Agriculture.

Table 8. *Use of selected farm inputs in the US*
(1960=100)

Year	Labour	Farm real estate	Mechanical power and machinery	Agricultural chemicals	All other inputs	Total inputs
1960	100	100	100	100	100	100
1965	75	99	97	154	109	98
1970	62	97	102	221	120	102
1975	56	93	107	253	111	100
1976	56	94	106	272	113	102

Source: *1976 Handbook of Agricultural Charts*, Agricultural Handbook No. 504, US Department of Agriculture.

and the rapid increase in the use of agricultural chemicals. The latter category of inputs includes mainly fertilizer, fuel products and chemical pesticides. Use of these chemicals is particularly high in the labour-efficient crops, e.g., fertilizers on feedgrains, pesticides on cotton and corn, petroleum in field crop production generally, etc. It is quite conceivable that alternative energy sources (e.g. solar energy) or other new technology can reduce materially the petroleum (and natural gas) energy inputs for such tasks as grain drying. But it appears unlikely that effective substitutes will soon be found for (1) petroleum products to fuel labour-efficient power units in the field, (2) fertilizers to maintain production volume (both per acre and in total), or (3) chemical pesticides which permit use of highly labour-efficient technology to produce cash crops for export markets. Some key implications of this dependence on the petrochemical industry for trade will be presented in the final section of this article. Computers, environmentally controlled technology and increasingly sophisticated managerial inputs in farming do not appear to have significant trade-related implications.

Coordination of production and marketing

Corporations and producer cooperatives have, in recent years, become active contributors to structural change through their efforts to coordinate the production and marketing of some agricultural products. Table 9 represents a rather crude set of estimates for the incidence of such coordination in 1970. Though difficult to document, it is clear that the incidence of coordination in vegetable crops and turkeys spread rapidly during the decade of the 1960s. The same was true for several other speciality enterprises, both crops and livestock. Among the chief export crops, however, only in the case of cotton was there any significant amount of production under contracts or vertical integration by 1970. And, even for cotton such coordination was not very important. Grains, soybeans and cotton are all commodities which are produced by many farmers, are easily bought and sold by standard grades in public markets and do not rapidly deteriorate in quality as they move through the marketing, storage and transportation processes. Thus, there is little incentive to coordinate their production and marketing processes. There is little evidence to suggest that structural changes in the coordination of production and marketing will have any significant effect on export trade in these commodities.

Changes in the structure of commodity markets

The farm commodity market sector can be divided into two components. One operates mainly to move farm products into processing

Table 9. *Methods of coordinating production of selected agricultural commodities, and 1970 estimates of percent of production*

Commodity	Corporate		Producer cooperatives
	Vertical integration	Contracts	
Sugar cane	60.0	23.0	17
Fluid grade milk	3.0	15.0	80
Broilers	7.0	85.0	5
Processing vegetables	10.0	69.0	7
Oil bearing crops	0.5	1.0	—
Foodgrains	0.5	2.0	—
Feedgrains	0.5	0.1	—
Hay and forages	—	0.3	—
Cotton	1.0	11.0	—

Source: *Contract Production and Vertical Integration in Farming 1960 and 1970*, ERS-479, Economic Research Service, US Department of Agriculture (April 1972), and *The Food and Fiber System — How It Works*, Agriculture Information Bulletin 383, Economic Research Service, US Department of Agriculture (March 1975).

and manufacturing to service domestic markets. Some processed products do, of course, also move into foreign trade. The other component of the farm commodity market sector operates mainly to move farm commodities into export markets. Though the domestic market is fairly evenly divided between livestock and crop commodities, grains and soybeans account for nearly 80% of the agricultural export market. Active futures markets as well as cash markets exist for the major grain, soybean and cotton commodities. Also, a large number of private and cooperative firms provide open markets to which delivery can be made by producers or other intermediaries, both private and cooperative.

With respect to those commodities moving to export outlets, the commodity marketing sector serves mainly as an intermediary to move commodities (mostly unprocessed) between producers and exporting firms. Thus, though there have been significant structural changes in the domestic marketing and processing sector since 1960, these changes have not affected major export commodities in any significant degree.

The US grain export industry is one in which rapid growth has occurred since 1960, and even since 1972. The capacity of this industry has expanded several fold in recent years in order to handle the much larger volume of commodities moving into export markets. A recent report[3] dealing with the structure of this industry indicates that five major grain export firms account for 85% of US grain exports. In recent years this includes an estimated 93% of the wheat exports, 90% of the foodgrain exports and 86% of the soybean exports. These multinational firms have world-wide computerized market intelligence systems and operate complex commodity procurement systems in the US to serve their overseas customers. They also operate and coordinate complex management systems to effectively merchandize, transport and finance the commodities which they export.

Despite the highly oligopolistic structure which exists in the grain export industry, there are strong incentives for these firms to maximize the volumes of US produced wheat, feedgrains and soybeans which they move into export markets. There seems to be little interest by or incentive for these firms to integrate backwards into the farm production stage of the commodities which they export since they have no commodity acquisition needs or competitive advantage to do so. Thus, the grain export industry appears to operate mainly to maximize profits from a predetermined supply of commodities by moving these commodities into their most profitable market outlets. With increased interest from farm cooperatives and other firms to enter the grain export industry, there seems to be little reason to expect that the grain export industry will not operate aggressively and reasonably efficiently in the future. It has substantial incentives to expedite future trade in those commodities which have broad based overseas markets and to which large-volume exports can be made.

CONCLUSIONS

Several kinds of major conclusions seem to stand out as one assesses implications of the changing structure of US agriculture for trade.

First, production and marketing of most agricultural products, including the major ones in trade, are broad-based and reasonably competitive. Exceptions in the production sector are mainly for some speciality crops and for some livestock products which are not important in trade. Exceptions in the marketing sector (though not studied intensively in this article) are mainly in the processing, manufacturing and distribution of products servicing domestic markets. Although the grain export industry has an oligopolistic structure, it is probably relatively efficient and aggressive with strong incentives to operate on a large-volume basis. Thus, structure of the agricultural industry as measured by 'degree of concentration' does not appear likely to generate major impacts on the US agricultural export trade.

Second, the agricultural production sector, particularly those farms engaged in the production of most large-volume export crops (feed and foodgrains, oil crops and cotton) has become highly labour-efficient. This structural change is the result of high per unit labour costs, expanded off-farm employment opportunities and the availability of labour-efficient production technology. Clearly these factors are interrelated and have resulted in shifts to use of labour-efficient technology and to the production of labour-efficient crops. Moreover, incentives exist for even further shifts in these directions.

Third, the use of petrochemical inputs (fertilizer, fuel and pesticides) has become intensive in the several labour-efficient, high-volume export crops. Also, the energy embodiments in chemical fertilizers and pesticides are high. Major increases in energy prices or substantive constraints on the use of petrochemical inputs generally could generate very substantial increases in the cost structure with resulting shifts (upward and to the left) in the supply schedules for grains, soybeans and cotton.[4] The impact of higher energy prices would be particularly great if, for example, energy prices to the US farmers increased not only on an absolute basis but also relative to those for competitive producers in other countries. Thus, more than for any other structural change in agriculture the move to heavy dependency on the petrochemical industry to undergird the production of major export commodities stands out. The possibilities of higher prices for energy and inputs with high energy embodiments and of shortages of petrochemical inputs and/or substantive constraints on the use of these inputs (for economic or environmental reasons) point up the supply vulnerability of these several major export commodities.

Finally, past structural shifts in the capital structure of farming, as measured both by the value of production assets and by the ownership and control of these assets, do not appear to have major implications for trade. Moreover, major declines in the price of these assets, particularly farmland, should they occur, would mainly provide a lower cost structure from which to produce for export markets. The capital loss impacts, though they could be of major consequence to the owners of the assets, particularly landowners, would be absorbed internally within the domestic agricultural industry.

NOTES

1. US Department of Agriculture, *The Food and Fiber System — How It Works*, Economic Research Service, Agriculture Information Bulletin 383 (March 1975), p. 15.

2. US Department of Agriculture,*1976 Handbook of Agricultural Charts*, Agricultural Handbook No. 504 (October 1976), p. 47.

3. Stanley P. Thurston, Michael J. Phillips, James E. Haskell and David Volkin, *Improving the Export Capability of Grain Cooperatives*, US Department of Agriculture, Farmer Cooperative Service Research Report 34 (June 1976), p. 17.

4. Several studies have shown that modest increases in the prices for fertilizer, pesticides and fuel would not cause major inter-commodity production shifts or shifts to alternative production technologies. Thus, very substantial price increases would be needed to reduce the aggregate supply of food and feedgrains and soybeans in the absence of intervention in input or product markets.

REFERENCES

Brake, John R. (ed.), *Emerging and Projected Trends Likely to Influence the Structure of Midwest Agriculture, 1970–85*, College of Law, Agricultural Law Center, The University of Iowa (Iowa City: June 1970).

Brandao, Antonio and G. Edward Schun, 'The changing structure of US trade: implications for agriculture', *Purdue Farm Management Report*, Agricultural Economics Department, Purdue University, October 1976.

Commoner, Barry, *The Poverty of Power* (Alfred A. Knopf Publishers, 1976).

Evans, Carson D., Philip T. Allen, Richard W. Simunek, Larry Walker and James B. Hottel, *Balance Sheet of the Farming Sector, 1976*, US Department of Agriculture, Economic Research Service, Agriculture Information Bulletin No. 403 (September 1976).

Frey, H. Thomas and Robert C. Otte, *Cropland for Today and Tomorrow*, US Department of Agriculture, Economic Research Service, Agricultural Economic Report No. 291 (July 1975).

Krause, Kenneth R., *Large Cotton, Feed Grain and Wheat Farms: Number and Importance*, US Department of Agriculture, Economic Research Service (November 1973).

Moore, C. V. and J. H. Snyder, *A Statistical Profile of California Corporate Farms*, Giannini Foundation of Agricultural Economics, No. 70–3, University of California (December 1970).

Rosine, John and Peter Helmberger, *Economic Changes in the US Farm Sector, 1948–72*, College of Agricultural and Life Sciences, Research Division, R. 2755, University of Wisconsin—Madison (February 1976).

Thurston, Stanley K., Michael J. Phillips, James E. Haskell and David Volkin, *Improving the Export Capability of Grain Cooperatives*, US Department of Agriculture, Farmer Cooperative Service Research Report 34 (June 1976).

US Department of Agriculture, *Costs of Producing Selected Crops in the United States — 1974*, Economic Research Service, Prepared for the Committee on Agriculture and Forestry, United States

Senate (Washington D.C.: US Government Printing Office, 1976).

US Department of Agriculture, *The Food and Fiber System – How It Works*, Economic Research Service, Agriculture Information Bulletin 383 (March 1975).

US Department of Agriculture, *1976 Handbook of Agricultural Charts*, Agricultural Handbook No. 504 (October 1976).

US Department of Agriculture, *Market Structure of the Food Industries*, Economic Research Service, Marketing Research Report No. 971 (September 1972).

US Department of Agriculture, *The US Food and Fiber Sector: Energy Use and Outlook*, Economic Research Service, Prepared for the Committee on Agriculture and Forestry, United States Senate (20 September 1974).

US Department of Agriculture, *World Agricultural Situation,* Economic Research Service, WAS-11 (October 1976).

World Development, 1977, Vol. 5, Nos. 5–7, pp. 585–593. Pergamon Press. Printed in Great Britain.

Marketing Alternatives for Agriculture in Developed Countries

V. JAMES RHODES*

University of Missouri, Columbia

Summary. – Alternatives, some new and some in use in parts of US agriculture, are examined for their possible application. Electronic markets for spot commodities and perhaps for future delivery contracts offer improvements for open markets. Exclusive agency bargaining may be the model for farmers with neither open markets nor vertically-integrated cooperatives. Those farmers who seek control of much of the market channel need to consider tighter forms of cooperation and forward integration. Governmental assistance would be needed in implementing several of the above as well as in provision of Marketing Orders or Boards, mandatory price reporting, and the ensuring of more competition in agribusiness.

In developed nations the marketing system has metamorphosed over time from a rather routine, even docile, intermediary role between producer and consumer into a giant entity of not only considerable economic power but also a structure and operating practices which are sharply at variance with the make-up of the markets for farm products. Shaffer has called marketing the 'system of markets and related institutions which organize the economic activity of the food and fibre system'.[1] As marketing institutions have become crucial to the organization of the food and fibre system including farming itself, there is a new urgency in exploring alternatives.

In the United States, extension economists have led the research and academic scholars in addressing marketing options. A set of papers, *Marketing Alternatives for Agriculture,*[2] written for educational efforts with farmers, has much of interest to professionals.

The ten alternatives suggested in the above publication fall under three broad classifications: improved price discovery, group action, and broad regulatory reform. There was no attempt to deal with all problems nor to include all practicable alternatives. Most of the alternatives are of relevance to only parts of agriculture; in a few cases they happen to be mutually exclusive. The series is more analogous to entrees in a cafeteria than to a medical prescription. Several involve changes in the political rules of the game. In all characterizations, a risk was run between raising false hopes

on the one hand and being too cautious on the other. Time will tell whether the authors were effective political economists.

While these alternatives are explicitly producer-oriented, the public interest is not forgotten. There are no suggestions that would match the ordinary advertising agency in its willingness to exploit consumer weakness for private advantage. Few, if any, of the authors would subscribe to the old view that it is the task of marketing merely to sell whatever farmers choose to produce. At the same time, they recognize the struggle for power within the marketing channel. Alternatives are proposed which may help to insulate farmers from agribusiness power or help them build their own power base. One can advise farmers to be market-oriented without advising them to become the bottom tier members of a new feudalism. Most of us are more comfortable with Boulding's exchange system than with his threat system.[3] But questions of power and equity can hardly be ignored in agricultural marketing. Paarlberg[4] and Breimyer[5] have emphasized that the horizontal and vertical integration of agribusiness raise important questions about pricing practices and operating procedures. There is general professional acceptance that governmental monitoring is essential to workable competition and the protection of equity. Of course, agreement about the need to

---

* The author appreciates the helpful comments of his colleague, Harold F. Breimyer.

balance or curtail private power may easily slide into disagreement about the justifiable balance.

I. IMPROVEMENTS IN PRICE DISCOVERY IN OPEN MARKETS

Price at the first change of ownership beyond the farm gate is determined in a variety of ways: individual negotiation, organized markets, price setting by either buyers or sellers, group negotiation, or governmental price setting. Traditional markets link price making with transfer of title and physical delivery. These functions are variously disassociated in alternate systems. Attention is directed for now to the first two methods as those by which price may be discovered in open markets. In a large part of US agriculture, price is determined by spot negotiations of individual sellers and buyers, or their representatives, at the time of delivery. These negotiations are naturally influenced by information as to the 'going price' immediately preceding negotiations. Those prices reported from such public (organized) markets as auctions and terminals are frequently the most readily available and they may be regarded as the most reliable indicators of the 'going price'. An increasing proportion of negotiated transactions use such public market prices as a price determinant, via some 'formula'. While price discovery in public markets has the smaller volume, it tends to be disproportionately important because of its use as a source of information and as a determinant in formula pricing.

Electronic commodity markets[6]

The centralized, public market offers substantial advantages over individual negotiation in terms of pricing efficiency, easy access of all buyers and sellers, and equitable, impersonal treatment of all buyers and sellers. However, the costs of physically assembling commodities and buyers and sellers in the same place are substantial. When production was in many, tiny production units and the processors were clustered around a few central markets, as once was true in US Midwestern slaughter livestock, the costs of physical assembly were not assessed to the pricing function, and the markets flourished. Central markets, once very important in livestock, eggs, poultry, fresh fruits and vegetables, have been increasingly bypassed in the past half-century.

Electronic markets offer the pricing, access and equity advantages of the traditional central market without the costs of physical assembly. The electronic aspects may vary from the simple to the complex but all require a modern area-wide telephone or teletype communication system linking potential buyers and sellers.

Successful operation depends upon several conditions:

(1) widely understood descriptive terms for the commodity, possibly including official grades, which permit trading without inspection;

(2) interest of both buyers and sellers in such a competitive market or legislation requiring its use, as was obtained for hogs in some Canadian Provinces; moreover, there must be a potential for competitive bidding;

(3) sufficient volume to spread the sometimes sizable overhead costs of the system; and

(4) the market rules which insure performance of contract.

The feasible electronic mechanisms depend upon the available volume and the desired frequency of trading. The manual trading house and telephone auctions are low-overhead operations requiring no technology other than access to telephones. Growing use of the former in the egg industry has led to plans for computerization.

Telephone auctions operate exactly like the ordinary English or American auction except that the auctioneer and a set of bidders are linked by a conference telephone call. These 'Teleauctions' have been used in limited geographic areas by farmers selling feeder livestock to other farmers and their use is slowly expanding to other regions and other commodities.

Teletype auctions, used in Canada for slaughter hogs, are an obvious alternative for a large volume commodity with buyers large enough to afford the teletypes. Producers list their prospective sales with a central selling agency which 'Dutch auctions' them via a leased teletype network.

A computerized trading house, imitating the matching of a manual trading house, would be adaptable to handling accurately a huge number of transactions at high speed, while providing instant market news, and full accounting services. Brief experience has been obtained with the marketing of cotton by a Texas cooperative.

These markets have potential efficiencies which suggest that their adoption represents a positive sum game for society, although outmoded agencies would be harmed.

Beginning an electronic market requires considerable capital to promote the system and develop the volume necessary to low unit costs. Cooperatives and industry groups, not private entrepreneurs, have been the initiators in the US. The far greater success of the Canadian system of marketing slaughter hogs suggests the possibility that farmers should seek government subsidies or mandated use to initiate an electronic market for large volume commodities.

Forward deliverable contracts markets[7]

In an accompanying paper, the authors define types of contracts and examine motivations for their use. Processors have generally initiated contracts when they anticipated benefits from the control of quantity, quality and the timing of product delivery. Farmers have used contracts to set prices at other than delivery times, to obtain or maintain market access, and to reduce their price risks. These reasons likely are not comprehensive, nor do they explain adequately the differences in uses of the three main types of contracts.

Starting with the assumption that contracting is beneficial or perhaps inevitable, the authors propose a public, organized exchange for the trading of contracts. There is an obvious resemblance to futures markets since standardized contracts for future delivery would be traded. The contrast is that the rules of the FDCM would be designed to encourage delivery rather than discourage it. The market mechanism could be a trading pit such as the Chicago Board of Trade, or more likely an electronic market.

Both market specification and production management contracts could be traded. Farmers and agribusinesses could make contracts within the market rather than seeking each other out in the field. The advantages of a centralized, public market over private negotiation would apply in contracts as in spot or cash markets. Likewise, the necessary conditions for an electronic market − widely understood descriptive terms, etc. − would apply.

Since the FDCM is a new concept, it is difficult to anticipate all of the operational problems. How is confidence in the validity of contracts to be maintained if literally tens of thousands of farmers are involved? Livestock farmers have been very sporadic in their use of market specification contracts; they are reluctant to fix price in advance except when they have a much more bearish view of the market than is reflected in the relevant futures prices. Large fluctuations in volume including long periods of virtually no trading pose special problems in financing such a market. Can a spot market, an FDCM, and a futures market coexist for the same commodity? Can contracts for cannery crops be standardized and sold widely when canneries utilize very specific contracts with farmers in specific localities to meet their coordination needs?

Educational efforts and start-up time are likely to be longer than for a more easily understood electronic spot market. Governmental assistance may be essential.

The FDCM is a new idea. Many questions remain. The costs and benefits are not clear. Yet the promise of improving a major weakness of contracts by public trading is enough to warrant further pursuit.

Mandatory public reporting of market transactions[8]

An efficiently operating market exchange economy depends upon individuals and firms obtaining a wealth of timely information about market and production opportunities. In recognition, US agriculture has a Market News Service and a Statistical Reporting Service to gather and disseminate information on market prices and quantities and on crop and livestock production and production intentions. The official agencies have depended almost entirely upon voluntary cooperation by farmers and agribusiness.

There is growing concern as to the adequacy of the voluntary system. Some farmers refuse to report production information and intentions. Some agribusinesses and farmers refuse to report their privately negotiated transactions. Evidence has been found of selective reporting. The decline of public markets and the increases in both vertical integration and contractual marketing have reduced sharply the flows of price information.

Little information is available with which to evaluate the cost and benefits of a mandatory reporting system. It is difficult to anticipate all the legal implications and operational problems of such a legislated change in market rules. Both private and public costs are likely to be increased. Consumers are likely to benefit from better working of the market-place. Those agribusinesses which have benefited from controlling information are likely to lose by its disclosure.

The authors go beyond their proposal for market news and suggest a need for much more information essential to planning and investment by both farmers and agribusiness. For example, line of business reporting is essential to prevent conglomerates from obscuring potential returns on investment in various industries.

The implementation of these rules changes would not be easy and may not be possible unless and until the needs can no longer be ignored. There is an extremely strong American tradition of individual privacy which has been stretched to treat giant, publicly-franchised corporations as if they were individual persons. Moreover, many citizens do not find the economic analysis persuasive. Even farmers find it easy to believe that any information is of more benefit to 'them' than to 'me'.

The point was made earlier that these alternatives are not presented as a system. Quite obviously, if electronic cash markets and the FDCM were widely adopted, the greatly enhanced flow of market information would obviate the need for mandatory reporting of market news. There is much to be said for a systematic approach by national policy-makers, but it was not deemed critical for the objectives of this effort in extension education.

II. GROUP ACTION

The next set of papers involves a medley of group action. Some would require authorization through new legislation. These institutional arrangements are aimed at providing or maintaining market access and, likely, greater price stability. They generally look not to better public market price discovery but rather to greater producer power.

Most agricultural economists are concerned about the impact upon the public interest of the marshalling of power by an interest group. The traditional argument for greater farmer power is Galbraith's countervailance. Even if that argument should be accepted fully, there is still room for debate as to a proper balance. The alternatives suggested below range along a power spectrum. These papers will draw a very mixed response among farmers.

Vertical integration through ownership[9]

The emphasis is upon forward integration by farmers as a group through cooperatives, although individual forward integration is also mentioned. The necessary requirements for effective cooperative action of capable management, adequate capital, and efficient operation are discussed.

An unusual presentation of cooperatives argues that (1) there must be firm, long-term commitments of adequate capital and all of a member's marketings; (2) members must accept some sort of pool or average price for the marketing period; (3) the cooperative as a strongly market-oriented firm may specify varieties to produce and even the extent of output; and (4) the cooperative must integrate forward as far as profitable. Thus farmers are urged to consider a vertically integrated cooperative which is not just another market outlet, but rather their unique marketing effort.

There are advantages which may adequately offset the obvious disadvantages to farmers. Returns to farmers in the long term should be greater because of more efficient marketing, better market orientation of both production and marketing efforts, and market power. Fluctuations of market income stemming from price variations through the season would be eliminated. Moreover, there is an enhanced security of market access.

Impacts upon society depend upon the situation. The entry of such a cooperative into an oligopolistic industry may enhance competition and might not raise consumer prices. On the other hand, it is possible to project a cooperative with market power which uses it to extract gains from consumers.

Implementation obviously requires the commitment of many producers and able leadership. In some commodity areas, the entry barriers are fairly high. Moreover, the authors note that a permissive political environment cannot be taken for granted.

Joint ventures between cooperative and agribusiness marketing firms[10]

Joint ventures are treated as a specific enterprise jointly owned and controlled by a cooperative and a private business. Strictly contractual agreements, on the one hand, and mergers, on the other, are not included, nor are joint ventures between two cooperatives or between two private businesses.

Joint ventures are not part of the usual experience of either farmers or agricultural economists.

One example, however, is joint ownership of United Vintners, wine makers. An 82% share was owned by Heublein, a medium-size conglomerate, and 18% was owned by Allied Grape Growers, a California cooperative. The joint venture has apparently not been a satisfactory one as it is currently in litigation.

A more positive instance, albeit more complex, is Agway-Curtice-Burns-Pro-Fac. In 1960, Agway, a large Northeastern cooperative, acquired a 58% interest in Curtice-Burns, a smaller canner. Pro-Fac was then formed as a cooperative of growers of cannery crops.

Nearly 90% of Curtice-Burns' volume is provided by Pro-Fac members, who receive their payment as a pooled residual of net proceeds from the cannery sales, after Curtice-Burns' costs are paid.

The Pro-Fac growers have secure market access. Their net returns have likely improved. The processor's corporate management has incentives of stock options which would not be available if it were a cooperative.

A joint venture may be viewed as a particular form of vertical integration. As such, it likely shares most of the advantages and disadvantages discussed in the previous paper.

There are obviously additional considerations. By combining forces with a private firm, a cooperative may obtain better access to processing, marketing and merchandising facilities and management. The joint venture may provide successful product and/or merchandising innovations which yield price premiums to the cooperative members. To the extent that cooperatives and private businesses operate in different frameworks as far as regulations, taxation, sources of credit, etc., there are some opportunities for a joint venture to obtain the best of both worlds.

As the Heublein example suggests, the joint venture may have some disadvantages as compared to simple, forward integration. Control is shared and a very considerable interdependency of the two firms may develop through the linkage of the joint venture. If either or both parties find the relationship to be disadvantageous, the problems of dissolution may become serious.

It is impossible to project a certain set of consequences for a joint venture. So much depends on how it works out. The joint venture may be large enough to have good or bad impacts upon competitive structure. Consumers may benefit from greater efficiencies in the firms servicing them or may pay the price of greater market power facing them.

Exclusive agency bargaining.[11]

This is a proposal that a producer association be authorized to act as an exclusive bargaining agent for *all* producers within a defined bargaining unit. The proposal meets the free rider problem which typically plagues bargaining associations by including all eligible producers, whether they join the association or not. It also involves a governmental definition of a bargaining unit, such as all Florida citrus producers, for example, and the recognition of a cooperative or association as an exclusive bargaining agent.

The nearest US example is fruit and vegetable bargaining in Michigan as authorized by a 1973 Act. Though designed there for the industry level, formalized bargaining as a principle bears some resemblance to the practice in certain European countries of a general farm organization being recognized as the exclusive bargaining agent for all of agriculture in price negotiations with the government.

Enabling legislation would be needed. It is suggested that a Bargaining Board be established in the USDA to implement the enabling legislation.

The authors keep their discussion of operational possibilities fairly general to fit numerous situations. They are specific, however, on certain key provisions in which they are apparently striving for a balance that yields 'just the right amount' of market power. A bargaining unit could include only one commodity; producer entry into the bargaining unit would be free but marketing quotas would be permitted; neither buying nor selling would be permitted to bypass the bargained terms; the producer bargaining agency must be operated democractically with due regard for the rights of members and non-members alike; bargained prices could be reduced by a national commission if judged to represent undue price enhancement.

No tidy little package can encompass the possible consequences of bargaining, because so much depends upon the situation. The possible benefits to farmers include assured market outlets at acceptable terms of trade with equal treatment of all. Possible costs as compared to a free market include reduced farmer independence, substantial organization costs, inevitable conflicts of interest among producers, and likely litigation over authorities and procedures. Some farmers may consider vertical integration through cooperatives to be superior to this complex and doubtlessly controversial bargaining approach.

Buyers could experience some benefits from a highly organized production and marketing system, including early information about industry-wide supplies. However, buyers would lose some freedom of action, and might have to pay higher prices.

Consumer price effects depend upon whether any efficiencies produced are more than offset by greater farmer bargaining power. In sum, consumers are hardly likely to support this bargaining power for farmers but they might tolerate it if they think the balance of power protects their interests.

The difficulties of implementing are great. Many farmers and their organizations must become convinced before the necessary lobbying and educational efforts can be done. Strong opposition from agribusiness interests can be taken for granted. While the present political and economic climate of US agriculture is not conducive to implementation, it may be a good time for farmers to get acquainted with this concept of strong bargaining.

Marketing Orders[12]

Federal Marketing Orders, administered by the Secretary of Agriculture, permit producer groups certain limited market power to deal with some specific problems. When Orders are approved by a required majority (usually two-thirds) of farmers, certain rules are prescribed for all handlers of the commodity within the geographic area covered. These rules solve the free-rider problem within the group, although minor competing areas are often not covered by an Order.

Marketing Orders continue to have two principal applications in the US. They are used for many fresh fruits and vegetables and a few speciality crops to accommodate natural production variability (quantity and quality) to market demand. Various devices are used to control the qualities shipped, to space time of shipment, and even to control total volume marketed in a season. Restrained use of such devices can provide a more uniform product, smooth out the seasonal flow, and generally contribute to orderly marketing and more stable pricing. Unrestrained use can push up prices, and likely gross receipts, in the short run, but the ensuing production response sharply limits any long term gains.

Federal milk Marketing Orders have been used as a mechanism for price discovery. The market is stratified into milk for fluid use and for processing. The latter market has been the elastic buffer which reconciled a reasonably stable year-round inelastic demand for fluid with a variable supply. Stratification has the additional objective of increasing gross revenue. Prices in the primary market for fluid use are negotiated within the Order mechanism with

due regard for supply and demand forces. Easy entry into milk production prevents the mechanism from becoming a cartel even if the administration were to allow such an attempt.

The development of a few very large milk cooperatives in the 1960s and their powerful participation in the milk negotiation process, as well as into political lobbying in some instances, provided a basis for some public concern as to balance of power. The rapidly rising food prices of the early 1970s ignited consumer accusations and governmental investigations.

Against this background, the authors catalogue a set of possible extensions of Orders. The list includes extension to additional commodities and areas, and administration of electronic markets, mandatory reporting, or commodity research and information programmes.

The point is that marketing orders are a very flexible device which can be tailored to do many different things. It is incumbent upon producers of any given commodity to analyse whether it can be a means to an end.

Marketing Boards[13]

Marketing boards, long established in several nations, are still an unknown in the US. This paper describes several versions and suggests an application to grain exporting.

A producer marketing board is described as a producer-oriented organization with legal powers of compulsion over producers, and perhaps over handlers, of an agricultural commodity. Such boards may be established under general enabling legislation or by specific enactment. Generally there is an explicit goal of representing producers' interests, subject to certain constraints of the public interest.

In the wake of dissatisfaction in the US in the 1970s with the performance of the private grain exporters, questions have arisen as to the possibly better performance of public control of grain exporting. While declining to answer that question, the authors suggest that public control might be exercised through a marketing board.

The board would have a monopoly of US grain exports. It could be assigned other functions such as administration of price supports or reserve stocks. It would hire existing firms to perform the physical functions of export. It would not engage in domestic grain trading. It would obtain supplies for export by purchases in the open market or by requiring proportionate deliveries by all producers. Producers would receive their due share of the pooled export receipts.

The discussion becomes much less specific when the crucial questions of control, accountability and social balance are faced. Is the board elected or appointed? What are the criteria and mechanisms for reconciling producer and consumer interests, for upholding producers incomes and earnings of foreign exchange while restraining food prices?

Some consequences are apparent while other important ones are not. The unpalatable consequence to producers of possibly mandatory deliveries is apparent. Unfortunately, the important question of comparative returns to farmers depends on too many unknowns. Consumer interests would have an obvious focal point for expressing their interests, but the board's response is unpredictable. The private grain exporters would be hurt through loss of their sales function.

Implementation in the form of enabling legislation would require far greater understanding of the issues among the citizenry, and a much more precise development of mechanisms. Still, this paper is a small step in the education process.

III. BROAD REGULATORY REFORM AND INDUSTRIAL RESTRUCTURING

Because of their orientation to producer initiatives, most alternatives have been close to farm level. They are concerned with farm commodity pricing and marketing, not the proportion of promotional costs in grocery manufacturing nor the impact on costs of dual distribution of processor and retailer brands. The next two papers are different; they range across the whole economy and particularly the entire agribusiness economy. A third paper provides a summary.

Fine tuning the present system[14]

The thesis is that much can be done by better administration of the existing laws. Fine tuning is a medley of facilitating and regulatory strategies to serve the public interest better. Adjustment to the changing times may sometimes mean more regulation and sometimes less.

The authors classify their regulatory improvements in terms of three perceived major problems of farmers: (1) to reduce effects of monopoly in agriculture; (2) to improve the producers' market position; (3) to improve

market information and pricing. Their concerns quite obviously overlap those of earlier papers.

Among their suggestions for reducing market power in agriculture is a proposal to establish an agency in the USDA to monitor input, farm and food prices for evidence of undue price enhancement and price rigidities. Farm cooperatives would receive particular scrutiny as would retail margins.

The authors argue that new, vigorous initiative by producers is needed to improve their market position. The cooperative movement needs to be revitalized, but producer initiatives to do for themselves should also include individual vertical integration, producer corporations, and other legal forms.

There are several suggestions for improving market information and pricing. The more novel include regular reporting of farm input prices, reporting of the terms of all types of agricultural contract prices, and the development of a standard contract for each commodity. Reacting to the famous 1972 Russian grain sale, they make several recommendations about practices designed to ensure that grain exporters do not profit unduly from farmers because of advance knowledge.

The consequences of fine tuning are to improve market access and enhance competition. The position of producers might be somewhat enhanced relative to agribusiness. The general public would pay for a greater degree of regulation but would benefit from more competitive markets. Whether the latter is as visible as the former to the taxpayer is an important question.

Implementation would require pressure on both the Congress and the Executive Branch to get things moving and to provide the needed funding.

Industrial restructuring: a policy for industrial competition[15]

This paper presents the most sweeping and likely controversial proposal of all. It reflects a willingness, which has generally been greater in the US than in other nations, to take some steps to preserve a competitive economy.

It is argued that divestiture of highly concentrated and important industries is now the only practicable way to continue our anti-trust, pro-competitive policies. Traditional anti-trust procedures on a case-by-case basis are too few, too expensive, too time-consuming, and too often ineffective against the giant firms. The countervailing power policy alternative is rejected as leading to many abuses of competition by unequal power blocs.

Divestiture is not as radical in the US tradition as it might first appear. Standard Oil of New Jersey was split into 33 pieces in 1911 and the American Tobacco Company into 16. Economists such as George Stigler and Carl Kaysen have argued its case.

The authors' approach of divestiture is along the lines of former Senator Hart's proposal: The Industrial Reorganization Act. The Act would: (1) provide a Congressional mandate for restructuring key industries; (2) define the possession of monopoly by specific standards including market share, pricing conduct, and profit levels; (3) establish a regulatory framework and new agencies with power to reorganize key monopolized industries so as to enhance competition.

The more probable candidates for divestiture in agri-marketing would include breakfast cereals, tobacco and grain exporters. Other possibilities with important inputs into agriculture might include steel, automobiles, cement, tires and oil-refining. Labour unions and farmer cooperatives would not be exempt from the monopoly test.

Consequences would include favourable social and political effects. They would also include considerable economic savings to consumers. The more basic consequence, however, is the contribution to preserving a competitive market economy.

Implementation faces the tough job of obtaining legislation against the opposition of very strong interests. Farmers' support will be needed if it is ever accomplished. Whether farmers will support measures involving this degree of economic abstraction is yet to be seen. Measures to build their own market power could easily be more attractive.

The options in perspective[16]

The varying themes are pulled together by several comparisons. The alternatives are rated as to the levels of producer initiative and governmental involvement required to implement them. The electronic exchange is rated as not very demanding on those scores. On the other hand, industrial restructuring would require a high political initiative by producers and a high level of governmental involvement. Ownership integration rates low on governmental involvement and producer political initiative but high on financial and market initiative by producers.

Caution is urged in the assessment of consequences. Seldom can all consequences be foreseen. Seldom is a group of farmers or agribusiness in such similar circumstances that all are affected equally or even in the same direction. Gains and losses have a way of being exhausted fairly quickly by market adjustments in the more competitive parts of the economy.

Even so, an assessment of consequences to major groups is important to a realistic examination by producers of their marketing alternatives. For some alternatives, the distribution of consequences suggests the potential of consumer support; for some, consumer acquiescence; and for some, consumer opposition. The same sort of assessment applies to agribusiness. The assessment of consequences reminds producers that they live in an economically, politically and socially interdependent society.

NOTES

1. James Shaffer, *A Working Paper Concerning Publicly Supported Economic Research in Agricultural Marketing,* US Department of Agriculture, Economic Research Service (1968), p.1.

2. Olan D. Forker and V. James Rhodes (eds.), *Marketing Alternatives for Agriculture: Is There a Better Way?* Cornell University, National Public Policy Education Committee Publication No.7 (November 1976). Also see related papers: Harold Breimyer (ed.), *Bargaining in Agriculture,* North Central Regional Extension Publication 30, University of Missouri, Ext. C911 (1971); and Harold Guither (ed.), *Who Will Control US Agriculture?,* North Central Regional Extension Publication 32, University of Illinois Special Publication 27 (1972).

3. Kenneth Boulding, 'Towards a pure theory of threat systems', *American Economic Review,* Vol.53 (1963), pp.424–434.

4. Donald Paarlberg, 'Statement ... before the Department Operations Subcommittee', Committee on Agriculture, House of Representatives (1 November 1971).

5. Harold Breimyer, *Economics of the Product Markets of Agriculture* (Ames, Iowa: Iowa State University Press, 1976).

6. See paper by Dennis Henderson, Lee Schrader and Michael Turner in Forker and Rhodes, op.cit.

7. See paper by Thomas Sporleder and David Holder in Forker and Rhodes, op.cit.

8. See paper by Kirby Moulton and Daniel Padberg in Forker and Rhodes, op.cit.

9. See paper by William E. Black and James E. Haskell in Forker and Rhodes, op.cit.

10. See paper by Lester Myers, Michael Phillips and Ray Goldberg in Forker and Rhodes, op.cit.

11. See paper by James Shaffer and Randall Torgerson in Forker and Rhodes, op.cit.

12. See paper by Walter Armbruster, Truman Graf and Alden Manchester in Forker and Rhodes, op.cit.

13. See paper by Martin Abel and Michele Veeman in Forker and Rhodes, op.cit.

14. See paper by Ronald Knutson, Dale Dahl and Jack Armstrong in Forker and Rhodes, op.cit.

15. See paper by Leon Garoyan and H.M. Harris, Jr. in Forker and Rhodes, op.cit.

16. See paper by Ronald Knutson and Olan Forker in Forker and Rhodes, op.cit.

World Development, 1977, Vol. 5, Nos. 5–7, pp. 595–601. Pergamon Press. Printed in Great Britain.

The UNCTAD Integrated Programme
for Commodities and the
World Food Problem

ALAN R. LAMOND*

UNCTAD Secretariat

Summary. – This paper outlines the kind of international arrangements which would be needed to fulfil the objectives of the UNCTAD Integrated Programme for Commodities with respect to basic foodstuffs, especially cereals. The treatment of the various issues demonstrates the importance of extensive international cooperation in order to attain a solution to the world food problem. At present, cereals are excluded from the Integrated Programme and the paper suggests that the International Wheat Council take appropriate action in the spirit of the Prgramme's objectives. The paper also treats the question of the role of stocks in market stabilization and the possible solutions to the problems of improving access to markets and achieving reliability of supply of food commodities. The author emphasizes that these economic measures would reinforce the positive effects of technical and financial assistance for food production in LDCs.

Although the world food problem may be seen as essentially a technical problem of ensuring that the expansion of production of basic foodstuffs in developing countries matches the growth of population, and that reserve stocks are maintained at levels adequate to provide security against temporary shortfalls in production, the problem is also to an important extent an economic one, which requires for its solution a high degree of international cooperation. In fact, the technical problem of expanding food production in developing countries cannot be separated from the economic problem facing many of these countries of determining how close to self-sufficiency, or how far beyond it, they should be aiming in their food production policy.

While, given the necessary external assistance and/or investment, there is undoubtedly scope for a considerable expansion of production of basic foodstuffs in many developing countries, a rational allocation of resources would require the expansion to stop short of self-sufficiency in some cases and to go beyond it in others. Although some countries — Brazil and Sudan are examples — appear to have the potential to become exporters of cereals on a substantial scale, other countries would continue to face the economic choice between growing food on their limited cultivable land or growing other crops and importing food.

In either of these cases, rational decision-making would clearly be greatly assisted by stabilization of the prices of cereals and other foodstuffs on the world market and also by stabilization of world prices of alternative crops. In addition, developing countries which are, actually or potentially, competitive exporters of basic foodstuffs would need assurance that the size of the competitive export market which is to be stabilized is not going to be artificially restricted by protection. If it were so restricted, such countries might find that price stability could be maintained only if they, together with other competitive exporters, limited their output in order to accommodate an increasing volume of protected production.[1]

Developing countries which will continue to rely to some extent on cereal imports will also need an additional assurance that, in the event of an unexpected and severe global shortage which undermines an international stabilization

* The author is a staff member of the UNCTAD secretariat. The views expressed in this paper, however, are those of the author and do not necessarily reflect those of the UNCTAD secretariat.

arrangement for basic cereals, an allocation of vital grains would be made to them at or near the ceiling price under the stabilization arrangement, and that scarce supplies would not simply be rationed by price, as happened in 1973 and 1974 at heavy cost in foreign exchange to many food-importing developing countries.[2]

THE RELEVANCE OF THE 'INTEGRATED PROGRAMME

The implicit acceptance of these arguments by the World Food Conference in 1974 was demonstrated in its unanimous adoption of a resolution on 'International trade stabilization and agricultural adjustment' (Resolution XIX), which called for both liberalization of world trade in food products and stabilization of world markets,

> ... particularly for foodstuffs and specially through international arrangements aimed, *inter alia,* at increasing food production, particularly in developing countries, alleviating food shortages, ensuring food security, and promoting prices which are remunerative to producers and fair to consumers, and which give particular attention to the interests of developing countries as importers and exporters.

In addition, recognizing the relevance to these objectives of the initial proposals for an integrated programme for commodities which had already been put before UNCTAD, in response to the call for preparation of such a programme contained in the UN General Assembly's Programme of Action on the Establishment of a New International Economic Order, the Conference urged UNCTAD in the same resolution,

> ... to intensify its efforts in considering new approaches to international commodity problems and policies and in elaborating further the proposals for an overall integrated programme for commodities, with particular reference to foodstuffs. ...

Since then the proposals for an integrated programme have undergone considerable elaboration. In its final form, as adopted by UNCTAD at its fourth session in Nairobi in May 1976, the Integrated Programme now consists of two main elements. The first is a series of negotiations to arrive at agreements to stabilize and strengthen markets for a wide range of commodities of export interest to developing countries. The second is the negotiation of a Common Fund for financing buffer stocks and other measures to be applied within the framework of the individually negotiated commodity agreements.

In contrast to the previous piecemeal approach to the commodity problem, the Integrated Programme aims to attack it in a comprehensive fashion. The negotiations on individual commodities will differ from those held in the past in that they are all to be completed within a given time-limit (the end of 1978) and within a framework of agreed common objectives and principles. Moreover, an *ad hoc* Intergovernmental Committee has been established within UNCTAD to coordinate the negotiations under the Programme and to deal with major policy issues that may arise, including the commodity coverage of the Programme.

The agreed objectives of the Programme include several which correspond to the policy prescriptions contained in the World Food Conference resolution cited above. The relevant objectives are:

> . . . to achieve stable conditions in commodity trade, including avoidance of excessive price fluctuations, at levels which would:
> (a) be remunerative and just to producers and equitable to consumers;
> (b) take account of world inflation and changes in the world economic and monetary situations;
> (c) promote equilibrium between supply and demand within expanding world commodity trade;
>   to seek to improve market access and reliability of supply for primary products and the processed products thereof, bearing in mind the needs and interests of developing countries;
>   to diversify production in developing countries, including food production. . . .

The Programme also contains a number of agreed measures.

> ... to be applied singly or in combination, including action in the context of international commodity arrangements between producers and consumers, in the light of the characteristics and problems of each commodity and the special needs of developing countries.

These measures include several which are highly relevant to the achievement of the objectives of price stabilization and trade liberalization for basic foodstuffs, namely:

> setting up of international commodity stocking arrangements;
> harmonization of stocking policies and the setting up of coordinated national stocks;
> establishment of pricing arrangements, in particular negotiated price ranges, which would be periodically reviewed and appropriately revised, taking into account, *inter alia,* movements in prices of imported manufactured goods, exchange rates, production costs and world inflation, and levels of production and consumption;

internationally agreed supply management measures, including export quotas and production policies and, where appropriate, multilateral long-term supply and purchase commitments;

improvement of procedures for information and consultation on market conditions;

improvement of market access for the primary and processed products of developing countries through multilateral trade measures in the multilateral trade negotiations, improvement of schemes of generalized preferences and their extension beyond the period originally envisaged, and trade promotion measures.

From the outset it was envisaged in the proposals for an integrated programme for commodities that foodgrains would be among the commodities to be covered by the programme. Developing countries, however, have tended to regard the Integrated Programme as being concerned essentially with commodities of interest to them as exporters rather than as importers, and have not pressed for cereals to be covered by the Programme. As adopted at Nairobi, therefore, the Conference resolution on the Integrated Programme mentions sugar, vegetable oilseeds and oils and meat, but not wheat, coarse grains or rice, in the list of products covered by the Programme.[3] The resolution makes clear, however, that the list is an open-ended one and that other products could be included by decision of the intergovernmental coordinating committee referred to above.

ACTION ON CEREALS

If cereals continue to be excluded from the Integrated Programme, it is to be hoped that the body which has primary responsibility for promoting international stabilization action on these commodities, i.e. the International Wheat Council, will act in the spirit of the Programme and take full account of the agreed objectives and measures contained in it, as well as the recommendations cited earlier contained in Resolution XIX of the World Food Conference. The International Wheat Council has in fact been studying for some time possible economic provisions for inclusion in a new international agreement on cereals to replace the existing Wheat Trade Convention (which has no economic provisions) of the International Wheat Agreement 1971, due to expire, after three extensions by protocol, on 30 June 1978.

However, the governments concerned have not yet agreed on the basic elements of such an agreement. Although most Council members apparently favour the inclusion of price provisions in a new agreement, at least one important exporting country seems to be willing to support such provisions only if they are of a highly flexible nature. It has not yet been decided, moreover, whether price stability should be sought through multilateral purchase and supply commitments of the type included in earlier Wheat Agreements, or through stock operations, or through some combination of these two methods. As regards stocking, the establishment of an internationally-held buffer stock seems to have been ruled out and discussions are proceeding on the assumption that any stocking operations under a new agreement would consist of the coordinated accumulation and release of nationally held and controlled stocks. At present, moreover, such coordinated stocking is envisaged only for wheat, although the possibility of extending the scheme to other cereals has not apparently been excluded. The nature of any food aid provisions which might be included in a new wheat agreement has also still to be decided.

There would seem to be some danger, therefore, that the current discussions in the International Wheat Council will give rise to a relatively loose new agreement which would not be an effective enough instrument for achieving the objectives of the Integrated Programme in relation to cereals. It could be argued, for example, that an agreement which incorporated a 'flexible' price range, without effective mechanisms for defending both the floor and the ceiling, could not achieve the objectives of reliability of supply or of price stabilization at levels which would 'be remunerative and just to producers and equitable to consumers' and which would 'promote equilibrium between supply and demand within expanding world commodity trade'.

In this regard it may be noted that while the minimum annual food aid target of 10 million tons of grains recommended by the World Food Conference has still to be met, and while no international reserve or stabilization stock has yet been established, wheat prices have fallen sharply since the middle of last year and in the first five months of 1977 were about 50% lower, in real terms,[4] than they were, on average, in 1974. The fall in the real price of rice since 1974 has been even sharper. In the absence of arrangements for establishing effective price 'floors' for these two cereals, there is a danger that such price falls will give the wrong signals to farmers and induce a cutting back of production which would quickly create another situation of world shortage.

What would seem to be required in any new

international arrangement for cereals, as an integral part of the attack on the world food problem, is the setting of price ranges with effective 'floors' which, after taking account of trends in production costs and world inflation, would be high enough to encourage and maintain production of wheat and rice at levels adequate to cover not only the prospective commercial demand for these cereals, but also that part of world food needs which, because of poverty, is not expressed in the form of market demand. This implies, naturally, that arrangements for expanded food aid should be an integral part of a new cereals agreement, but this would be in conformity with practice established under both the 1967 and 1971 international agreements on grains.

Once world production, of which developing countries would be expected to contribute an increasing share under the stimulus of the various measures taken in response to the recommendations of the World Food Conference,[5] had attained an agreed target level, world prices might start to come under pressure. Even then, however, a downward adjustment of the floor price under the arrangement should not be envisaged until world stocks, including a special reserve for emergencies as recommended by the World Food Conference, had reached a level adequate to provide security against major unpredictable downward fluctuations in production and thus the possibility of defending a ceiling price, over the short to medium term, in the interests of grain-importing countries, particularly developing ones.

THE ROLE OF STOCKS IN MARKET STABILIZATION

This immediately leads to the question of how such stocks would be held and managed. The defence of a price range for wheat (or any other cereal) on the world market through the international coordination of nationally-owned and held stocks, as envisaged by the International Wheat Council, would require a sustained and complex effort in international cooperation. Agreement would have to be reached among all the governments participating in the scheme on a set of rules for the holding and management of national stocks, including the stock-releasing and stock-accumulating obligations of each government when the world price reached (or approached) the upper and lower limits, respectively, of the range.

Arrangements designed to stabilize the world market through coordinated national action of this kind would have the greatest chance of success if governments permitted free trade in grains and thus allowed prices in their domestic markets to be aligned with world prices, at least as long as these prices remained within the agreed price range. If these conditions were not fulfilled, coordination of stock-holding for the purpose of stabilizing the world price would be more complicated and difficult.

For example, if some governments, having fixed minimum prices for their own producers higher than the agreed international minimum, defended these prices by means of import restrictions when the world price fell below the domestic minimum, such action would tend to destabilize the world price. There would be a similar destabilizing effect on the world price if any governments, in order to keep down prices within their domestic markets, imposed restrictions on the export of grains before the world price had reached the upper limit of the agreed price range.

If governments pursued such policies, their stock-holding and stock-management obligations for the purpose of stabilizing the world price would have to be defined in terms of obligations to purchase or sell given quantities on the world market, at the world minimum and maximum prices respectively, regardless of the situation in their domestic markets. There would be an obvious risk of conflict between such obligations and national interest, especially in periods of shortage, and such conflicts could put the arrangements under considerable strain.

For the above reasons, therefore, the use of an international buffer stock, the principal stabilization technique envisaged under the Integrated Programme for Commodities as an instrument of stabilization for the world grains market, would seem to deserve much more serious consideration than it appears to have so far received. Within the limits of the resources at its disposal, such a stock would be able to influence the prices of cereals on the world market directly, and hence more quickly, and its operation would not be dependent on the continuous concordance of the policies of different governments. Such a stock, therefore, could be envisaged either as the principal means of stabilizing the world market or as an instrument complementary to a system of internationally coordinated national stocks.

The global capital and storage costs of a stabilization system based entirely on an international stock would, in principle, be the same as those of a system based on perfectly co-ordinated national stocks, although they might be differently distributed. These costs, in comparison with the costs of stabilization stocks for other commodities, would no doubt be relatively high but they would be far outweighed by the benefits of greater stability in world cereal prices. For developed countries the principal benefit would be elimination of one of the sources of the inflationary 'shocks' imparted to their economies by sharp upward fluctuations in world prices of essential commodities, shocks which lead to losses in income because of the restrictive fiscal and monetary policies which usually have to be imposed to counter the inflationary pressures resulting from them.[6] For developing countries the benefits would include not only an attenuation of the risk of severe 'shocks' to the payments balances of importers resulting from sharp increases in cereal prices, but also the favourable effect which greater predictability of world cereal prices would have in facilitating rational agricultural planning.

Because it would be more effective and reliable as a price stabilizing mechanism, an international stocking system would be a surer way of realizing these benefits than a system of coordinated national stocks. It would be surer, moreover, than a system of multilateral trade commitments, which is also under consideration in the International Wheat Council, since such a system could not be expected to cover more than a limited portion of international trade in cereals.[7] A contractual system could, however, usefully complement an international stocking scheme, since it would reduce the size of the market to be stabilized by an international stock and hence the size of stock required. As suggested below, moreover, full attainment of the objectives of improved access to markets for exporters and reliability of supply for importers might require the inclusion in international agreements on basic foodstuffs of certain special commitments by governments.

In comparison with a system of coordinated national stocks, furthermore, an international cereals stock would provide a greater degree of world food security, since the stock would not be under the control of any one government. It could also be used to improve arrangements for food aid; if all the grain required for food aid was purchased and distributed by the buffer stock authority, this would have the following advantages:

(a) it would ensure a steadier and more reliable flow of food aid;

(b) it would minimize the real cost of this aid, since supplies would be purchased from internationally competitive producers, both developed and developing;

(c) it would permit an equitable sharing of the burden of food aid;[8]

(d) it would permit economies to be made in the administration of such aid.

ACCESS TO MARKETS

The Integrated Programme objective of improved access to markets will also need to be given attention in any new international agreement on cereals and, *a fortiori*, in any new international arrangements for sugar, oilseeds and meat, since virtually no progress has been made in the GATT multilateral trade negotiations in liberalizing trade in basic foodstuffs. While an international buffer stock would provide, within the limits of its resources, a sure outlet for export supplies of any commodity at the minimum price to be defended by the stock, it would not, as mentioned earlier, protect competitive exporters against erosion of their market by protection. Any increase in the yields of food crops produced under such protection, or in the margins of protection themselves, will tend to raise the volume of protected production. This, in turn, would exert a downward pressure on the price at which a stocking scheme could provide an assured outlet for competitive export supplies which increase at the same rate as world demand.

Wheat, coarse grains, rice, sugar and oilseeds are among the food commodities which are produced to a substantial extent under protection or subsidy in developed countries. Some degree of protection or support is provided for each of these in the United States, the EEC and Japan, although the actual rates of protection or support vary considerably. Ratios of production to consumption have been tending to rise with respect to each of these commodity categories in the EEC, with respect to coarse grains, rice and oilseeds in the United States and with respect to rice and sugar in Japan.

An example of the adverse effects of protectionist policies, for consumers as well as competitive producers, is provided by the case of sugar. In the 1960s, as production of beet sugar increased throughout the world under high and rising rates of protection and subsidy, the price of sugar in the residual free market declined, with fluctuations, until it reached a level, in the years 1966–68, which was below the cost of production in even the most efficient producing countries. The disincentives to investment in sugar production provided by this experience subsequently resulted in an unprecedented world shortage, which caused the world price to rise in 1974 to a level nine times higher, in real terms, than the average for 1966—68.

One way in which this problem could be overcome would be through the imposition of quantitative limits by governments on the amounts of each commodity with respect to which producers would be subsidized by protective measures. In this way governments could guarantee a minimum share in their domestic markets to external suppliers as long as protection was maintained.

An alternative possibility, however, which would allow governments practising protection much greater freedom of manoeuvre as regards their domestic agricultural support policies, would be for all such governments participating in a stocking scheme to guarantee in each year or season the import of a minimum quantity of the commodity concerned from participating exporting countries at not less than the floor price under the international stocking arrangements. Thus when the external market price reached the floor, any participating country which was then applying protective measures could be called upon by the stock authority to supplement its imports, by purchases at the floor price, until they reached the commitment amount.[9]

Such a system of import commitments, which could be operated preferentially in favour of developing exporting countries, would safeguard exporting countries participating in an international stocking system against any further erosion of their market as a result of protection. It would not in itself necessarily *reduce* protection. The hope would be, however, that if the system worked successfully and gave protecting countries confidence that it would provide stability of prices and security of supplies, these countries could be induced to reduce progressively their rates of protection.[10]

RELIABILITY OF SUPPLY

Just as a buffer stock with limited financial resources could not provide a guaranteed outlet for unlimited export supplies at a 'floor' price, it also could not guarantee unlimited availability of supplies to importers at a 'ceiling' price. Even a very large stock might not be able to defend a ceiling price in face of an unforeseen shortage of exceptional dimensions. In that case, as mentioned earlier, available supplies of the commodity concerned would thereafter be rationed by price, a situation in which poorer importing countries would be gravely disadvantaged. Richer importing countries also, however, might wish to avoid an international 'scramble' for scarce supplies.

The governments participating in a buffer stock arrangement for an essential food commodity might therefore agree that, in the event of the exhaustion of the buffer stock, exporting member countries would share out their available supplies among importing members in pre-agreed proportions until the supply situation returned to normal.[11] Sales under such a rationing system might be made at the ceiling price of the buffer stock or at some agreed higher price, and such arrangements might be operated preferentially in favour of developing importing countries. If exporting countries participating in a buffer stock scheme were unwilling to accept such a rationing arrangement they might reasonably be asked to agree, at least, to refrain from imposing artificial restrictions on production or exports in the event of the exhaustion of the buffer stock.

CONCLUSION

This paper has attempted to outline the kind of international arrangements which are needed to fulfil the objectives of the UNCTAD Integrated Programme for Commodities with respect to basic foodstuffs, particularly cereals. The relative importance or urgency of the measures described naturally varies from product to product, but all of them need to be seriously considered for each basic food commodity if the logic of the Programme as a comprehensive and multi-dimensional attack on commodity problems is to be respected. The effective implementation of these measures with respect to cereals and other basic food commodities, either inside or outside the negotiating framework of the Integrated Programme, would powerfully reinforce the various measures of technical and financial assistance for food production in developing countries being undertaken in response to the recommendations of the World Food Conference and would constitute a major step towards a lasting solution to the problem of world hunger and malnutrition.

NOTES

1. This is exactly how the rules of the sugar stabilization 'game' worked before the prolonged world shortage which appeared in 1972 made them unnecessary. The market which had until then been stabilized under the International Sugar Agreement was simply the market for residual world needs not covered by protected production, and competitive exporters were able to stabilize this residual market only by 'carving it up' by agreement among themselves on a system of export quotas.

2. The unit value of developing countries' imports of cereals rose by 50% in 1973 and by a further 62% in 1974. Since the volume of these imports also rose, their total cost to developing countries went up from $3 billion in 1972 to $6 billion in 1973 and $10.5 billion in 1974.

3. The full list of commodities mentioned in Conference Resolution 93(IV) is as follows: bananas, bauxite, cocoa, coffee, copper, cotton and cotton yarns, hard fibres and products, iron ore, jute and products, manganese, meat, phosphates, rubber, sugar, tea, tropical timber, tin, vegetable oilseeds and oils.

4. After taking account of the rise in prices of manufactured goods in world trade over the same period.

5. Care would have to be taken in this regard that the expanded food aid envisaged was administered in such a way that it did not constitute a disincentive to food production in recipient countries.

6. In this connexion, see the paper by Nicholas Kaldor, 'Inflation and recession in the world economy', published in *The Economic Journal* (December 1976).

7. The extent to which the world market for cereals could be stabilized by such a system would depend on the proportion of world trade which could be covered by matching commitments by importers and exporters

to purchase and sell at prices within the agreed price range. Whichever side (exporting or importing) was least willing to enter into such commitments would determine what that proportion could be.

8. In this connexion there are two possibilities. One is that the costs of the food purchased and distributed as aid would be combined with the costs of the buffer stock operation, and thus the countries participating in the financing of the buffer stock would share the costs of food aid and the costs of the buffer stock operation in the same proportions. The other possibility is that the buffer stock manager would keep separate accounts of food aid and buffer transactions, which would enable the costs of food aid to be shared in agreed proportions among any number of countries, including countries which might not be participating in the financing of the buffer stock.

9. In order to fulfil its import commitments, a government could adjust its tariffs, levies or quotas, as the case may be, until total imports for the period reached the guaranteed amount, thus ensuring that the additional quantities were imported through commercial channels. This might temporarily lower the internal price. If the government wished to prevent this, it could make price support purchases from domestic producers. Alternatively, it could itself make the necessary purchases from exporters at the minimum price and put the amounts concerned into stock. Naturally, countries which accepted an import commitment would need to accept a related commitment not to subsidize exports to the commercial world market.

10. In this connexion it may be noted that the need for stability of prices and security of supplies is often cited as a reason for and justification of protection.

11. The return to normality would be accomplished when any importing country could obtain as much of the commodity as it desired at the buffer stock's ceiling selling price.

World Development, 1977, Vol. 5, Nos. 5–7, pp. 603–611. Pergamon Press. Printed in Great Britain.

Grain Reserves and Government Agricultural Policies

TIM JOSLING

University of Reading

Summary. – This paper introduces some particular aspects of the role of grain reserve policies in world food security. The emphasis is on the interaction between government domestic agricultural policies and the management of reserves. The first part of the paper discusses the optimal stocks policy for a single country (or a group of countries with integrated policies and intra-group free trade), the degree to which such an optimal stocks policy is itself affected by the activities of other countries, and the necessity or otherwise for some part of global reserves to be held and distributed independently of the policies of individual countries. The second part reviews some of the implications of domestic farm policies for stock levels, and the final part proposes some possible solutions to world food security problems which integrate changes in farm policies, conscious reserve management and mechanisms for resource transfers to poor countries when disturbances occur on world cereal markets.

The 'grain reserve' question has become a popular topic for commentators on the world food and agriculture situation. The debate stems largely from the widespread concern of the run-down in grain stock levels in the past few years, and the feeling that conscious stock policies are necessary to prevent a repetition of the alarming rise in cereal prices of 1973. The idea that nutritional objectives in developing countries and inflationary considerations in developed countries can only be met if the world food system rids itself of its dependence on the bounty of each successive harvest has a strong intuitive appeal. I shall not attempt to review all the various aspects of the role of grain reserve policies in world food security. Rather, I wish to introduce some particular parts of the problem that have not received their due attention, and to place these observations in the wider context of the grain reserve issue. My particular emphasis will be on the interaction between government domestic agricultural policies and the management of reserves.[1] This interaction is important both because sensible discussion of desired stock policies must take account of government farm and food policies, and because many of those policies themselves are intimately linked with those aspects of market performance which grain reserves are supposed to influence.

The first section of the paper attempts to clarify some of the issues involved in the

formulation of a stocks policy. These seem to fall under three headings: the optimal stocks policy for a single country (or group of countries with integrated policies and intra-group free trade); the degree to which such an optimal stock policy is itself affected by the activities of other countries; and the neccessity or otherwise for some part of global reserves to be held and distributed independently of the policies of individual countries. These issues raise different questions, and require in turn the consideration of alternative policy actions. The second section reviews some of the implications of domestic farm policies for stock levels, and a concluding section introduces some possible solutions to the problems of world food security which integrate changes in farm policies, conscious reserve management, and mechanisms for transfer of resources to the needy at times of serious disturbances on world cereal markets.

GRAIN RESERVE ISSUES

(a) National stocks policies

The first of the three issues raised above relates to the question of whether, from the point of view of an individual country, the management of reserve stocks of a commodity such as grain should form an integral part of its food and agricultural policy.[2] Intuition would suggest that good market management would involve the husbanding of supplies in 'good' years to supplement availability of the product when yields are poor. Such intuition has the support of economic analysis under certain circumstances. If one makes the standard assumption of the diminishing marginal valuation to consumers, either as direct purchasers of grain or as indirect users through their purchase of grain-based products, then clearly a holding-over of some product from abundant to lean years will add to the value over time of the aggregated level of production. If an economy is self-contained, choosing not to trade with the rest of the world, then so long as that extra valuation exceeds the cost of storage (properly calculated to include not only physical storage costs but also the return foregone on capital 'tied-up' in grain) the policy will yield a net return. The 'matching' of food availability with food demand over time is a form of arbitrage which should yield positive benefits.

As to who, within the economy, receives such benefits is itself a matter of public policy: economic analysis cannot give a definitive answer. In fact, the operation of a reserve system which stabilizes consumer prices may, paradoxically, act against consumers interest *per se*.[3] Their ability to switch consumption patterns in favour of grain when prices are low and away from it when prices are high is impaired. There may be pressing reasons to restrict this 'freedom' in the case of food grains, since in high price periods, the poorest group of consumers may suffer disproportionately from the operation of the price system. Where grains are fed to livestock, it is less easy to see why quantities so used should not be allowed to reflect availability and hence enhance the efficiency of the livestock industry. Producers, similarly, may not appreciate such price stability policies even though technically they should gain. A buffer stock scheme might place upon their income levels the full impact of production variations — rather than such variations being offset by opposite changes in price levels. Gains may accrue, of course, to the buffer stock agency, if it buys cheap and sells on a rising market, but a self-liquidating fund will not even have a financial profit to show.

This leads to a real problem to be overcome by advocates of buffer stocks even in the simplest of all cases where domestic price fluctuations arise from variable domestic production and where the agency operating a price-stability scheme does not aim for a profit. The country as a whole gains, but these gains

may not be appreciated by either buyers or sellers of the product. In political terms, release from stocks will be popular when prices would otherwise rise, but support for such a programme will wane in times of abundance. Producers will complain of the price depressing effect of stock release, but support accumulation as providing a necessary floor to the market.[4] Price stability as such is likely to be politically popular if only for the fact that consumers will be restless when prices rise and producers upset when they fall: a buffer stock scheme appears to be a way of buying relative peace. But the absorption of the fluctuations in production by variations in the level of stocks will in turn lead to cries of 'surplus' when stocks mount and 'shortage' when they are reduced. The idea that instability can be hidden is an illusion: a stocks scheme translates price instability into variations in the level of stocks. It is not immediately obvious in all cases which variety of instability is the less acceptable.

So far, the market we have been considering has been self-sufficient in grain. The choice for countries which either can or do trade in grains is somewhat more complex. An optimal stocks policy in a trading environment will have to be formulated with the conditions on the world market in mind. Assume first that the main cause of potential instability is domestic production fluctuations, and that the country in question is not a major force on the world market. Domestic consumers can be immune from the effect of production variability merely by allowing import or export volumes to change. Again the principle holds that instability can be shifted but not hidden: in this case it re-emerges in the balance of trade. Foreign exchange reserves become in effect the grain stock policy. They are cheaper to hold and will bear a rate of interest. Appreciation of their value might be quite as likely as speculative capital gains on commodity holdings. Those who advocate stocks to even out domestic production fluctuations in an open economy have to show that these confer benefits over and above the holding of sufficient reserves of foreign exchange.

A slightly different choice faces countries which suffer not from domestic production variability but from 'imported' instability through world price changes. In this case we can again invoke the rule about transferring the incidence of variability. A fixed domestic price is easily maintained by means of variable trade controls, import levies and subsidies or their exporter equivalents which adjust to offset world price changes. The variability in this case is translated into fluctuations in receipts and expenditure on such trade measures, together with the corresponding element in the foreign exchange account. Again, an advocate of stocks would have to show that such a policy was superior to variable trade measures.

(b) Interrelations among national stocks policies

So far each country has been assumed to decide on a stocks policy without regard to those of others, either because it does not trade or because its trade represents only a small part of the world market. For many countries this situation might be realistic. However, the policies of the major trading nations are linked in a variety of ways not least with respect to their holding of stocks. At one level, major importers will have an interest in the adequacy of stocks held by exporters to maintain supplies when production temporarily declines. If they are convinced by the 'reliability' of their suppliers, then the only motive for holding reserves of their own would be to anticipate and hence make a capital gain on price increases. Once again the trading system acts to allocate supplies within a season to enhance their value in the same way that arbitrage over time in a closed economy through a stocks policy will increase the total value of that country's production. In this case, a major importer may feel itself vulnerable to adverse price movements when its own requirements increase due, say, to a drop in home production. Some reserve stocks would seem to enable it to restrict its purchases to more 'normal' levels. But as with any stock scheme, an evaluation of its economic benefits must take into account the accumulation as well as the dispersal of reserves. What it gains from lower prices when it reduces stocks must be set against the firmer price encountered as it builds them up. Again, economic theory cannot provide a definitive answer. There will however be a tendency for the 'grain from trade' to be greater if import demand is allowed to reflect differing domestic output levels than if stocks are used to offset such fluctuations. And the implications for domestic price levels can, as before, be countered by variable trade restrictions, though these will tend to prove expensive. If the major importer is concerned by world price instability generated by production fluctuations beyond its borders, trade policies offer a more attractive alternative to stockholding as a device for domestic price stability – at the cost of destabilizing its import bill.

An important exporter, by analogy with the producer in a closed economy, stands potentially to gain from reserve management to stabilize prices. The value over time of exports is enhanced, and the importer is denied the benefits that come from buying more in low-price periods and less when prices are high. The production instability, if domestically generated, will be translated into variability in foreign exchange earnings, and possibly income fluctuations for the producers. The scheme may not be domestically popular even if the country as a whole can be shown to gain. The trading system again, as in the case of the importer, promotes price stability, but in turn puts more burden on management of stock levels and on changes in the balance of trade. The policy decision of the government must rest with the relative value that it puts on the stability of each of these variables and upon the costs of achieving such stability.

If the exporter 'suffers' from fluctuating demand for its product, due perhaps to output variations in other countries, it is again faced with the choice of holding reserves or using trade controls. Domestic price stability can be bought at the cost of fluctuating exchequer and foreign exchange accounts, but with the strong implication that failing to take advantage of demand variations by changing trade volumes will result in lower 'gains' from trade. Here the similarity between exporters and importers becomes apparent. The importer may benefit from variations in export supply, and the exporter may benefit from fluctuations in import demand: they may choose to forego these gains by using trade policies or by holding stocks in order to cushion the impact on the domestic market. If instability is *internally* generated, the attitude of countries may change. Importers will tend to rank their policy reactions in the following way: allow variations in import volume; manage a stocks policy; or maintain domestic prices through trade controls. The exporter will tend to put stocks policies *first*, then variable export volumes, with trade policies as a third best solution.[5]

The link between countries' policies is therefore a complex of their own economic self-interest, the domestic political pressures which may conflict with these, and the attitude of other governments to similar problems of their own. In very general terms, one would expect stocks policies to be favoured in exporting countries wishing to allocate their own surplus production over time as well as between importers to their best advantage. To the extent that they do so, importers will be happy not to hold stocks, and will tend to use trade policies to preserve domestic price objectives. Where instability in world markets comes from variations in import demand, those importers may consider holding stocks as their trade policies become less attractive; the exporters in this case will tend to favour freer trade and have less incentive to hold stocks themselves. Moreover, they will have little reason to encourage other countries to develop an active stocks policy, and will find their own price-stabilizing trade policies becoming expensive.

(c) International stocks

The argument for stocks in the world as a whole mirrors that for the 'closed' economy case discussed above. In such an economy, the government must decide:

(i) whether the gains to the economy from market stability outweigh the costs of the storage required;

(ii) whether the resulting distribution of the gains is socially desirable, and, if not, whether a redistribution of these gains is feasible;

(iii) whether private storage decisions approximate to the optimal management of stocks, and, if not, whether government storage policies can supplement such private decisions, or regulate them, to attain an optimal policy; and

(iv) whether other types of policies can achieve the same objectives at a lower cost.

The task for an advocate of international stockholding is basically similar.[6] It seems fair to assume that the world as a whole does gain from the carryover of grain from one season to the next. Stocks do exist, and no one has suggested that a zero stock level would improve the performance of the trading system. Someone, somewhere, is profiting from the holding of stocks, and this implies that the value over time of the world's grain harvests is enhanced by such arbitrage. The question of the distribution of such gains is much more problematic. If it is true that producers gain, then it has to be asked whether such benefits are indeed desired by those who see grain stocks as helping developing countries. To be sure, much of the world's grain is grown in those countries, and does not move into international trade. But a stocks policy managed internationally is by definition going to have more effect on those whose links are strongest with the world market. The remote and largely self-sufficient village in a developing country will be much less influenced than the commercial wheat sector in a developed market economy.

This objection could be overcome if consumption patterns were noticeably improved in low-income countries. The main problem arises from the fact that social gains from stability do not show up in terms of standard measures of consumer welfare. In order for consumption levels and standards to be increased, there has either to be a conscious programme of income transfer to poor families out of the economic benefits from stability, or an implicit transfer by such means as differential pricing to allow the poor to purchase food at stable prices whilst the more affluent are allowed the luxury of altering consumption patterns in times of high prices. Nutritional and economic criteria appear to conflict: economic measures will indicate that a person or household free to spend income on available goods will choose the combination of purchases which yield him the most satisfaction. Nutritional criteria tend to indicate that the person concerned must devote his income to food consumption until a particular level is reached. It could indeed be questioned whether the calculation of consumer 'welfare' is appropriate in situations where the commodity in question is a staple food, rather than a luxury. A nutritionist might consider the whole question of consumer welfare as developed by economists to be an irrelevance. Consumption targets and 'adequate' diets take over from consumer choice. The economist can do little more than to indicate the problem and allow others to decide — and of course to point out that even a nutrition-related consumption objective has economic consequences and that it often requires measures of economic policy to implement.

A single government can ask whether the private trade is pursuing an appropriate stocks policy: the analogy at the global level is to enquire whether individual countries are together managing the total level of stocks (whether in governmental or private hands) in the most responsible way. This represents perhaps the strongest rationale for international stockholding for those who argue that governments and private companies are unlikely to absorb the risks involved in global stock management. Individual agencies have their own objectives and even when the level of altruism is high, the conflict of objectives leaves the world as a whole in a precarious position. This argument again defies simple economic analysis. It is probably true that private firms will tend to avoid risks which governments might for social reasons wish to assume.[7] Perhaps there are risks to the world's food supply which individual countries themselves are unwilling to assume. The richer nations might be willing to pay a form of insurance premium to prevent the impact of poor harvests on consumption levels in low-income countries. But the issue is not that simple. First of all, there is no world authority that can operate outside the constraints of major governments. The UN system, for example, is an extension of the foreign policy of governments and not a source of policy-making in its own right. Food stocks could well be administered by an international agency and be held in its name. But it would be unduly simplistic to assume that such an agency could operate without the consent of the governments that set it up and without the cooperation of those governments in implementing its policies. Some political 'laundering' of stocks to obscure their origin might be possible, as is the case with multilateral food aid. But it is not easy to see how an independent policy could be operated which conflicted with the aims of major grain trading countries.

Recognition of this has led to a tendency to fall back on inter-governmental cooperation in stock management as a more realistic target. If such agreement did have the effect of influencing national stock policies then the objective of an international stock might be achieved. But if the national stocks themselves are a function of domestic policies then clearly such an agreement cannot be devised without explicit recognition of this link. This in turn seems to hold the most hope for an improvement in the performance of the world food system. A coordinated set of policy changes, together perhaps with some conscious redistributional measures, may be needed before the way is clear to formulate an international stocks policy.

AGRICULTURAL TRADE POLICIES

The events of 1972–74 in the world grain market have taught many lessons.[8] One is the nature of the threat caused to the stability of that market by predatory purchases by centrally-planned economies that can combine the techniques of big business with the discipline of state trading. The lesson of these events lies in the exposure of the essential weakness of a trading system set up to facilitate the autonomous development of domestic agricultural policies. In hindsight one could imagine that world food security would have been enhanced

over that period if less of the world's grain stocks had been spirited from the commercial market almost overnight. But whatever one thinks about the manner in which the grain deal was conducted, the fault lies with the structure of the grain market in the years up to 1972. The structure was itself a function of government farm policies in the developed countries.

The key to understanding such policies lies in the fact that they start with domestic price objectives which relate to internal political pressures, views of farm costs, and concerns about inflation.[9] The result is that the rest of the world is faced with an excess supply of grain from exporters or a residual demand by importers largely isolated from the total world grain market situation. This causes a fundamental problem in the formation of prices in the world market. The price at which trade takes place becomes, as often as not, a function of these domestic decisions, the willingness to subsidize exports in surplus periods, and to restrict exports·in shortage years, the willingness of other countries with more flexible trade policies to enter the market to remove surpluses, and the extent to which governments and private firms choose to hold reserves. Rather than a smoothly functioning 'competitive' world market, one has a strange market structure composed of the complex of these policy decisions.[10] Whereas the grain markets up to 1972 had exhibited these characteristics, the world remained relatively unconcerned. Exporting countries strove valiantly to preserve and expand commercial sales by advocating trade barrier reduction in importing countries; their failure to achieve such liberalization led to higher subsidy costs, output restrictions, large concessional programmes, and accumulating reserves. Importing countries found that with weak world prices and adequate reserves, their own trade policies were very effective at protecting domestic interests. Developing country importers also found readily available grain to keep down food costs in urban areas, but may have neglected their own agricultural development on the assumption that such foreign supplies were likely to grow to keep pace with population increase.

The picture changed in 1972 in a way which is by now quite familiar. The purchase of the 'overhang' of stocks particularly in the US, Canada, and Europe by the USSR came at a time when world production dipped for the first time for many years. World prices rose *above* domestic support prices in the scramble for supplies, and hit the payments balance of importing countries just at the time when the price of oil and other raw materials jumped dramatically. Developing countries found food aid dwindling as well as commercial prices rising, and the serious threat to consumption levels provoked international concern about the future of the world's food supplies. The turnabout in the grain market was in fact the inevitable consequence of the market structure which had been built up over the previous decade. The role of stocks in the market needs to be related to this market structure if it is to be considered as an instrument of policy.

The decision to hold stocks, as with any other asset, depends on the price at which such stocks can be bought, the expectation of the price at which they will be sold, and the cost of holding such stocks between years. As the current price declines, more stocks will normally be held off the market. If export availability from a particular harvest is determined independently of import demand for use in that year then stocks perform the additional and vital function of reconciling these two trade volumes. Without stocks, the price itself is liable to be highly volatile if importers and exporters obstinately defend their domestic price targets. Stocks enter as a means of determining the market price. But the solution only works in the short run. A persistent surplus of export availability over import demand will steadily increase stocks, adding to their cost and driving the price down. In such a buyers' market, stocks become an embarrassment to the exporter who will tend to bear the burden. In contrast to our earlier discussion of a favourable attitude towards stocks as maintaining reliable export supplies, under these conditions the build-up of stocks is viewed as the inevitable and costly consequence of importer protectionism. The removal of such stocks arising from inconsistent domestic policies, by transferring them from the commercial market to the strategic reserves of the Soviet Union seemed to offer a chance to 'start again' with a firmer world market position which might even allow changes in domestic policies. If world harvests in 1972 had been normal, it is possible that we would now be facing a stable and more liberal grain market. But this was not to be: a fall in exports, a rise in import demand, and a drop in commercially available stocks conspired to raise the price way above the levels that would have been suggested by the relatively small output drop itself. Only the fall in the quantity of grain used for livestock feed saved the world's poor from an even more serious fate.

This puts the question of stocks in a somewhat parlous state. They have performed the function of allowing major trading nations to pursue independent farm and food policies. That function proved too much of a strain as the willingness to hold stocks diminished. Reserve levels proved inadequate at a time when they were most needed. The call for their replenishment came from those who had been most badly hit by the price rises. But can such stocks if they were to be rebuilt disentangle themselves from their former role? In other words, can the farm policies of advanced countries be adapted in such a way that a sensible stocks policy is adopted without having to bear the strain of reconciling disparate national agricultural objectives? Unless major changes are made in attitudes towards domestic policies it is hard to be optimistic for a rational grain reserve system.

SOME POSSIBLE SOLUTIONS

It is an occupational conceit of economists to try to answer the question that they have posed. Clearly the feasibility and institutional detail of solutions to problems rests with those who have responsibility. But a commentator can at least outline the type of policy initiatives which would seem to meet at least in part the problems that he perceives. Some such policy initiatives have indeed been evident in recent months. At the level of the individual country, the question of reserve stocks of foodgrain has entered into the general discussion of food procurement policies. Many developing countries have added storage capacity and improved distribution systems to enable them to counter production and price variability.[11] International agencies have encouraged such developments, and only time will tell whether the costs of such policies to those countries proves tolerable in relation to the benefits. The more general recognition of the impact on development of fluctuating import costs arising from grain price changes has led to a re-examination of the question of balance-of-payments facilities for low-income countries. So long as the renewed emphasis on agricultural development in these countries does not add to instability in their domestic output levels, this too will improve the security of their food supplies. Some impetus to the attainment of greater self-sufficiency has come from perhaps exaggerated fears of political hegemony arising from the reliance on food imports. So long as developing countries do not fall into the trap of stimulating high-cost domestic food production which then takes a large slice of their scarce financial resources to maintain, the rediscovery of the potential of the small farmer is a welcome development.

The major grain traders, meanwhile, have been meeting to discuss a new International Wheat Agreement, linked in a way not yet apparent with negotiations both in GATT and UNCTAD.[12] The FAO-inspired 'Undertaking on World Food Security' continues to concentrate the attention of governments on the formulation of reserve policies and to provide a valuable channel for information on stock levels.[13] The World Food Council in turn generates ideas on stock policies which both distinguish the various objectives of such stocks and attempt to coordinate the attitudes of governments and international agencies on such objectives.[14] Meanwhile, the improvement in the world supply situation for the main food-grains has provided an opportunity for such schemes to be contemplated without the emotional atmosphere that clouded the issues at the World Food Conference.

Despite these developments, which themselves have reduced the risk of another 'food crisis', the major issues are still not being faced. Three elements would appear to be essential to an improvement in the structure of the grain market. First, the major developed countries have to come to accept an obligation, in their own self-interest, to absorb more of the fluctuation in grain production than they have in the past. This primarily means that domestic price targets must be made responsive to world conditions, both in the short run, to absorb surpluses and alleviate shortages, and in the long run, to allow domestic markets to reflect the international valuation of grains relative to other products. This is the element of trade liberalization which should figure largely in the discussions within the GATT. Secondly, these countries must themselves develop a common approach to stocks which allows them to avoid recourse to trade disruptive measures at times of market disturbance. Whether such a coordinated stocks-management scheme is tied to price levels or to quantitative expectations of market conditions is largely immaterial: a proper stock scheme links the two.[15] The benefit to developing countries comes largely as a result of a more certain alternative to domestic output expansion but does not in itself reduce the value of wise investment in indigenous agriculture. The developed countries benefit from a more predictable basis on which to reformulate their own domestic farm and food supply policies. Trade measures which look attractive

from a single country viewpoint together give rise to market structure problems: stocks policies which seem expensive to the individual country become a viable alternative if the burdens are shared.[16] The gains from such cooperation spread far beyond the grain trade, extending to better commercial relationships in other fields and a healing of old diplomatic wounds.

The third element which might be superimposed on these developments is to institute a financial transfer system to link support for desirable nutritional and agricultural programmes in developing countries with constructive policy changes in the developed world. The closest approach to such a scheme so far is the proposal, occasionally aired, to return to developing countries the tariff revenue resulting from the imposition of such tariffs on their sales to developed markets. In the food sector, the policy might operate in the following way. If a developed country feels obliged to impose an export tax on grain, or a grain-based product, then the revenue from such a tax should be transferred to a fund which would in turn support nutritional programmes in the developing world. There would as a consequence be a disincentive to use such taxes on exports. Similar transfers might be made when consumer subsidies were employed in developed countries, a proportion of the expenditure on such subsidies being payable to the international fund. Other sources might be government revenues from import levies on grain-using livestock products. The attraction of such a scheme is that it does not infringe the sovereignty of the developed country to adopt such policies but merely imposes on them the full cost of so doing which at present tends to fall on the poorer consumer in developing countries. Whether political support for such a scheme would exist in rich countries is a matter for debate, but it does seem to avoid the difficulty of the 'one less hamburger' approach by linking altruistic intentions with observable results.

CONCLUSION

I have attempted in the paper to draw out some of the links between domestic agricultural policies and the question of national and international stocks. At the national level these links are apparent in the degree to which reserve management is one aspect of domestic policy. A national stocks policy takes its place in the list of options open to a country to regulate its agricultural markets. The attraction of such a policy rests crucially on the attitudes and actions of other governments struggling with similar problems. Security of world supplies therefore depends as much on the cumulative result of this complex of national policy decisions as on any overall decision on global stock levels *per se*. Until the links are clarified, conceptual proposals on a global stocks policy are unsatisfying and empirical work is likely to be misleading. It does not, for instance, make sense to ask the question 'what is a desirable level of foodgrain reserves for the world economy?'. Not only is it the management rules for such a stock that are important rather than the level, but the rules themselves will depend on the structure of the market, in turn determined by national trading policies. My contention is that an improvement of the market structure is essential both to complement a global stocks policy and also to reduce the burden on such a policy of attempting to reconcile conflicting national price policies. Or, to sum up the argument: unstable world production from year to year must be absorbed somewhere in the system either by consumption level changes or by stock changes. If consumption changes are intolerable to low-income consumers and are avoided by trade policies in high-income countries then stock levels *will* have to fluctuate. The trading system should, but does not at the moment, allocate production within a season and over time in a reasonably equitable way. Therefore changes in the trading system, and in rich country policies, will have to be implemented before stocks can fulfil their main function. Domestic price stability objectives in rich countries may be the casualty, but the beneficiaries will be those who cannot afford at the moment to bear the cost of supply variability.

NOTES

1. This aspect has also been emphasized by Johnson (1,3).

2. This is the question approached by Johnson (2).

3. The gains to the economy as a whole depend only on a 'downward-sloping' demand curve: the loss in consumer welfare is evident if such a demand schedule is linear, but could be reversed if demand became very inelastic in high price periods. See Sarris and Taylor (10) for a fuller discussion of this point.

4. The government can provide finance to 'sweeten the pill'. Broadly speaking, a buffer stock scheme which makes a loss is one which benefits producers; by contrast, one which makes a profit over a period of time reduces the 'burden' on consumers. The country as a whole, however, will benefit most from a self-financing scheme.

5. This does not rule out, of course, the possibility that policies which do in fact stabilize production *per se* might be implemented. My assumption is that in spite of such policies, fluctuations do remain.

6. The argument for international stocks has been made by a number of authors, for example Sinha (11).

7. See Sarris (9).

8. For a detailed analysis of these events see Johnson (3).

9. See Johnson (4) and Josling (5) for a discussion of the development of these policies.

10. An analytical attempt to draw the structural implications of such a market is to be found in Josling (7).

11. The most dramatic example is India which currently seems to have about 18 million tons of foodgrains in store.

12. For an account of current GATT negotiations on agriculture, and the links with other bodies, see Josling (6).

13. The undertaking itself is critically assessed by Sinha (11).

14. See WFC (12).

15. At present the discussions in the IWC seem to have got tied up in this question of triggers. The point is discussed in Josling (6).

16. For an elaboration of this point see Josling (8).

REFERENCES

1. Johnson, D. Gale., 'World agriculture, commodity policy and price variability', *A.J.A.E.* (December 1975).
2. Johnson, D. Gale., 'Increased stability of grain supplies in developing countries', *World Development* (December 1976).
3. Johnson, D. Gale., *World Food Problems and Prospects* (Washington: American Enterprise Institute for Public Policy Research, 1975).
4. Johnson, D. Gale., *World Agriculture in Disarray* (London: Macmillan, 1973).
5. Josling, T. E., 'Agricultural policies in developed countries: a review', *J.A.E.* (September 1974).
6. Josling, T. E., 'Agriculture and the multilateral trade negotiations' (London: Trade policy Research Centre), unpublished.
7. Josling, T. E., 'Government price policies and the structure of international agricultural trade', *J.A.E.* (forthcoming).
8. Josling, T. E., 'Towards our international system of grain reserves', in W. Henrichsmeyer *et al., Trade Negotiations and the World Food Problem* (London: Trade Policy Research Centre, 1974).
9. Sarris, A. H., *The Economics of International Grain Reserve Systems* (unpublished Ph. D. dissertation, MIT, 1976).
10. Sarris, A. H. and L. Taylor, 'Cereal stocks, food aid, and food security for the poor', *World Development* (December 1976).
11. Sinha, R., 'World food security', *J.A.E.* (January 1976).
12. World Food Council, *International System of Food Security*, WFC/22 (Rome: 1976).

World Development, 1977, Vol. 5, Nos. 5–7, pp. 613–621. Pergamon Press. Printed in Great Britain.

Food Security: Storage vs Exchange

R. S. WECKSTEIN

Brandeis University

Summary. – The author of this paper argues that the establishment of a new international grain reserve system will not provide the desired food security and it will be a very large and costly enterprise. Rather, he suggests that the world needs to integrate its national foodgrain markets so that when shortages occur, sharing of available food will be induced by market-price adjustments. He discusses why markets do not work properly now, including such factors as sale of US grain surpluses, farm-income- support policies, internal market disturbances, etc. He then treats various aspects of a reserve system in terms of its main objectives – stabilizing prices and insurance against catastrophe – and the potential conflicts/trade-offs between them. The author argues finally that better security would be found through 'broader markets' and puts forth a different proposal for food-financing on this basis.

As a sequel to the harvest disasters of 1972–73 that led to famine in parts of the world and to food-price inflation throughout the world, a number of proposals have been put forward urging the establishment of an international food (grain) reserve.[1] A new reserve is said to be desirable to replace the United States Government stocks which were exhausted in the early stages of the recent period of shortages. Before that final depletion the grain reserves of the United States and a few other countries were used more or less successfully to fill a world deficit and stem the tide of rising prices. This history is part of the basis for the common support for a new reserve, and if the United States does not plan to re-establish a reserve, then, the argument goes, an internationally coordinated policy is required.

Although this view is plausible it is, I believe, mistaken. To replace the finally dissipated US reserve with a new one will not provide the security we seek, yet it will be a large and costly enterprise. More important, the conventional interpretation of the recent history of food supplies and prices gives more credit to the US grain stock than is warranted. Much of the benefit gained in the last 30 years by consumers of American surpluses should be attributed to the associated agricultural export credit system, not to the stockpile of grain. The recent supply and price disaster took place when there still was a large US grain reserve on hand. It was fully deployed, sold into the world market, and still world grain prices rose tremendously. The operational management of that government stockpile was in fact often detrimental to the development of the world food economy. The security we seek can be found in other policies at lower cost. More than a reserve stock, the world needs to integrate its national foodgrain markets so that when shortages strike, widespread sharing of available food is effectively induced by market price adjustments. To the degree that there is such effective market integration stockpiles are unnecessary.

Accumulating stockpiles of foodgrains, and managing them to stabilize food prices, on the other hand, is a disincentive to the development of market institutions that cannot only stabilize ordinary price fluctuations but can provide protection against crop disaster.

WHY MARKETS DO NOT WORK NOW

It is all too evident that a serious crop failure now has very undesirable effects. If a country with such a problem is also poor, its population growth curve will be interrupted by starvation, even if only temporarily. And if the harvest failure is widespread enough, the unexpected bulge in the demand for food in the markets of the rest of the world creates a trauma of food-price inflation. It is understandable that the world concludes after such experiences that it needs a buffer stock to meet humanitarian needs and to stabilize prices. Moreover, during the period when the United States maintained a large official stock of surplus grain, the world had little of either of these problems, so it seems quite natural, now that the United States has finally succeeded in drawing down its unwanted surpluses, to seek to replace the American reserve with some official world reserve.

Part of the reason, however, for the failure of the grain markets to work acceptably during the past couple of years is related to those very same protective US grain surpluses. For, so long as the US Government held reserves which it was prepared to sell or give away, a lid was held on the world prices of grains; it was not profitable for others to invest in large stocks of grain, either private firms or other governments. Consequently one of the institutions of effective markets, speculative holdings, was simply missing, and when prices began to rise after the American surplus was sold out in 1972 there was no further backlog the rising price could dislodge.

United States grain policies in the past contributed to the concentration of grain production. A two-price policy was enforced whereby American consumers paid a price for food that assured high farm incomes in the United States. But that price was sustained by government purchase of the surplus that would have lowered the US price had it been offered in the domestic market. The surplus was then sold abroad at a lower average price, or offered on concessional terms. The sale of these US surpluses tended to pre-empt some of the market in the rest of the world that would otherwise have been supplied by an expansion of local farm capacity or by the other export countries. By holding down the average price of world grain, the United States slowed the development of farm capacity required to meet world demand, even allowing for the shrinkage of demand that may be attributed to higher prices. The bulk of world grain exports now come from only three countries: Canada and Australia, besides the United States. Other exporters would probably have been larger contributors had the United States not generated such large surpluses.

On the other hand, many food-import countries adopted farm-income-support policies by limiting their imports, perhaps being required to go farther in this direction than would otherwise have been necessary by cheapness of American export grain. But farm income protection in many countries, especially the great European national markets, would undoubtedly have been the policy of governments even if there had been a different US farm policy and prices had been somewhat higher, because the technological revolution in agriculture proceeded too fast for painless absorption of Europe's redundant farm labour and because farmers in democratic countries are an important political group. In any case, large fragments of world agriculture and the world food market have been tied off from the rest of the world with the result that what is now referred to as the 'world market' is either a small residual, operating as a free competitive market, or it is simply an imprecise way of speaking of many separated national markets which are aggregated only in the statistical records kept by the United Nations.

The actual world market, as opposed to the statistical one, can be described as a 'thin' market which means that its lack of breadth induces volatile behaviour. The price of grain changes greatly in response to moderate changes in quantities bought and sold. Under these circumstances it is almost as much a disaster for a country to suffer a bumper crop as a crop failure. The advent of a bumper crop forces a government to choose painfully between allowing the domestic grain price to plummet at the expense of farm income or to store the surplus to the detriment of the government's own budget.[2] What it cannot do satisfactorily is to sell grain in the open world market. To do so in any significant quantity would depress the price against the country with a bumper crop.

Alternatively, to supplement domestic production by imports would increase the price against a country with a poor crop. Over many years the expected value of physically balanced sales and purchases is thus algebraically negative. The magnitude may well be so large as to encourage each country to build its own reserve whenever it can even though the cost of such a reserve is very high. Thin markets and national reserves go together. If external purchases and sales are costly and sometimes actually infeasible, the accumulation of a national reserve permits self-sufficiency. But the possession of a significant reserve encourages a policy of autarky. For if domestic farm prices are supported by official stock accumulations at a level above external prices, imports must be restricted, or if domestic prices are being held below external prices by sales from stock, induced exports must be prevented. Thus the common policy of many governments of stabilizing internal markets by means of buffer stocks is responsible for the widespread grain-trade barriers. Much of the residual grain trade is that which arises as a result of governments' need to add to their own stabilization stocks.

For the affluent and developed part of the world stabilization stocks are a more or less open window to the rest of the world with the effect that the countries' food economies show the signs of integration. That is, price and quantity movements and also support-policy prices in the major world grain-exporting countries are fairly well matched by similar movements in EEC countries, for example.[3]

The policies of less developed countries however are influenced strongly by balance-of-payments constraints as well as farm- and consumer-price objectives and their food economies are as a result less well integrated into the world food economy.

Worse probably for the welfare of people of the developing world is the disintegration of grain markets within their own national boundaries. The severity of the losses is apparently sensitive to political disturbances that interfere with these internal markets. But even under quiet political and social circumstances the marketing margins required to store grain and to move it from surplus to deficit regions are strikingly large and shifting.[4]

Many of the great historical famines were local, many people starving while others not far away suffered no unusual shortages. This was recently the case in Ethiopia and was characteristically the nature of famines in the past in India. In these classic cases of acute physical maldistribution, poor and disorganized transportation facilities were often at fault. But transport failure is not the only source of trouble. The extremes of geographical and temporal price discrepancies in Indonesia in the 1960s were the result of restrictions placed on Chinese traders and the inadequacy of the Government's substituted agency, Bulog, to take over the rice trade. Years of severe hardship passed before the structure of rice prices returned more or less to normal.

Sometimes the causes of maldistribution of food remain obscure. In the case of the great famine in Bengal in 1942–43 there are at least two views and possibly a third to explain the death of as many as three million people by starvation and subsequent disease. The standard view is that there was a physical shortage. One version of this view is that the shortage was made acute in the coastal areas by flooding following a major cyclone.[5] But the region could not be supplied from outside because the Government had destroyed the boats in a policy of denying them to the Japanese in the event of an invasion. A second view is that if there was any shortage it was never enough to account for the great number of deaths.[6] The trouble was not shortage but market disruptions which were sparked perhaps by military demand and hoarding laid on top of general inflation which deprived a large group of the purchasing power to continue to buy their subsistence. Those whose labour was no longer necessary to produce the goods in demand as real incomes fell, or whose earnings were too small to buy subsistence rations in the inflated food market, starved. But a third view that may be no less tenable than others is that the catastrophe resulted from government market controls intended to assure everyone adequate food but which in fact prevented the normal channels of trade from distributing the supplies that were available, and adequate, to where there was not enough. Restrictions had in fact been imposed on grain trade across the borders of states and provinces through most of the period and a state monopoly in grain trade was established just as famine conditions were becoming severe. How much of normal internal Bengali trade was affected by efforts to control it is unclear. But for a large part of the period an objective of policy was to provide adequate supplies of food to Calcutta in the belief that the city would be vulnerable if there were a shortage. Eventually it was the people of the countryside who starved.

Whichever explanation is correct the Government bears a large burden of responsibility. The destruction of the boats was perhaps a mistake that was not justified by a realistic prospect of invasion. The extraordinary rise in the price of rice would not have been possible in India at the time given the generally developed state of transport facilities if trade had not been disrupted on the mistaken notion that welfare could be improved that way. And if the price had not risen, large numbers of people in the countryside would not have been priced out of the food market. Markets may work by themselves once established, but their development is not automatic and there are endless seductive purposes for which they can be disrupted.

AN INTERNATIONAL RESERVE

Thus the failure of the world grain markets to develop and afford the opportunity to stabilize food consumption would lead individual countries to reduce dependence upon the external market. But during the period the United States held large reserves available on favourable terms there was little incentive for other countries to accumulate their own national reserves. With the exhaustion of the US reserve, the incentives changed. If a satisfactory substitute for the US reserve fails to materialize, individual countries will be encouraged to accumulate their own national reserves. This will be costly.

Whatever the size of the reserve required to achieve a specified degree of confidence that the total regional or world deficit of any year be adequately covered, it will have to be a responsibility borne largely by some official agency without assistance from private dealers. It must be expected that private grain holding will be limited to provision of normal requirements of the customers of grain dealers. The more adequate the official reserve the less can be the expectation of profit to private speculators, and hence the less they will hold.

Recent proposals emerging from the FAO World Food Conference have set the desired magnitude of an international grain reserve at 60 million metric tons. The cost of buying that stock at 1973—74 average price of $200 per ton would be $12 billion. The annual cost of that investment at 8% interest is $960 million. To this amount should be added the administration of the reserve and the cost of storage including the value of annual losses from insects, rodents, fire and rot.[7] Despite the sentiment in favour of an international reserve system it is not clear where a billion dollars annually could be raised for the purpose. How much of their foreign aid would LDC governments be willing to sacrifice for an international grain reserve? How much would donor governments add to the aid they now provide? Is a grain reserve the project toward which the next billion dollars of aid should go, or should it go instead toward the improvement of LDC agriculture?

RESERVES AND INSTABILITY

A reserve operating policy would have two objectives: (1) to stabilize prices (or consumption); and (2) insurance, i.e. to maintain a reserve stock large enough to sustain consumption in a state of catastrophe. In so far as the first objective is served successfully the agency would behave like a commercial speculator. It would buy at low prices, sell at high, diminish the price extremes and make a profit. But this would be no more than commercial speculators would have done if the official reserve had not.

To stabilize the world price of a grain, however, an official reserve, or a private speculator for that matter, must enter an international market to buy or sell. But international markets do not exist for all grains and in particular there is none for rice. A first step would have to be the establishment of markets in those grains for which none now exist. Without international markets intervention would be limited to transactions based on country-by-country quantitative estimates of surpluses and deficits. But while this form of intervention may be suited to the insurance objective, it is full of problems for international price stabilization.

An international reserve designed to stabilize the world price of wheat would raise still further problems. If the reserve management lacked the authority to limit production, there would be a risk that production would be excessive whenever the stabilization price is set above marginal cost of production. With limited resources available to the system there would then be a breakdown of the programme. Given the authority to limit production, on the other hand, there would be the danger that the world price of wheat would be set to favour producers at the expense of consumers. Since the system would not wish to drain itself of reserves, it would be unlikely to set the price too low. Anyhow that would favour consumers only until supplies became short. If these errors are avoided and stabilization does in fact achieve a balance, lowering above-trend deviations and raising those below trend, where the source of instability is mainly the irregularity of supply, as it is in the case of food crops, it has been shown that the gains go to producers and consumers lose.[8] Wheat is a temperate-zone crop produced by countries with above-average incomes so that an international wheat stabilization reserve would thus become an international welfare transfer agency providing benefits to the rich at the expense of the poor.

The insurance objective is different from price stabilization in spite of superficial similarities. Insurance is concerned with extreme contingencies and is desired for protection in the unlikely circumstances when extreme outcomes occur and the consequences would be catastrophic. Stock management for insurance is quite different from good-practice price stabilization. In stabilizing prices the welfare gain to consumers is related to the quantity of consumption preserved and the prevented increase in prices. Benefits are continuous from the avoidance of small to large deviations. Management incentive to continue to hold back stock while market prices are high lies in the prospect that they may rise even further. If prices fail to continue their rise and stocks had not been used to prevent that much rise, a significant stabilization opportunity would have been lost. The loss in this case, incidentally, runs parallel with the lost opportunity for profit to a speculative trader whose incentives would be quite similar.

Operating a reserve stock, on the other hand, for the purpose of insurance against catastrophe, a manager ought to put less value on the opportunity cost of neglected price stabilization at moderately high price levels. His incentive to hold onto stocks at moderately high levels would be less diluted and the resulting probability of stocks remaining on hand in the rare event of more extreme price levels being reached would be greater. We have here a stabilization–insurance trade-off, the harshness of which depends upon the size of the total investment in a reserve stock. With a tight budget the possibility of price stabilization at the same time as stocks are held for insurance may become slight.[9]

The conflict between the two objectives might well be dealt with by an optimization scheme in which the technical trade-offs are brought into correspondence with the relative weights of preferences for consumption security on the one hand and producer income security on the other. Differences in the means for serving each objective are only one aspect of the conflict in need of resolution. The resolution would not permit a straightforward technical solution because of the bias in the interests of governments. Those who believe they face a risk of consumption catastrophe would prefer as large a reserve as possible while governments that believe their interests are in the maintenance of farm incomes would favour a small reserve and a large reserve-buying capacity.

The insulation of national grain markets from the rest of the world is a condition resulting from government efforts to stabilize internal grain prices. It is an obstacle to the establishment of an effective international grain reserve, and even though it may be less efficient (for its failure to pool reserves) than a unified world grain reserve, it preserves control in the hands of governments, permitting them each a separate policy tailored to local political interests of consumer groups and farmers in price levels and in the price stability–insurance trade-off. It is also feasible for governments separately to control production in the administration of a price policy for the protection of

farmer interests. Given these advantages it is not clear that governments will soon agree to alter the condition, so the odds on an effective international grain reserve cannot be very high.

SECURITY THROUGH BROADER MARKETS

The world grain deficit in 1972 was very large, in absolute quantity probably the largest in history, yet it was still less than 4% of total world grain production in that year. A deficit of that magnitude can be managed in the future without building a cumbersome and expensive international official reserve if we can arrange for the rest of the world to share its grain with deficit countries. But for sharing to work it must be widespread, and if we are to spare ourselves the burden of accumulating reserves, the system used to institutionalize sharing must be reliable.

The conclusion of the previous section is clear. A buffer of reserve stocks can do two jobs; it can smooth out temporal price instability (and geographical price discrepancies), and it can be an insurance reserve in the rarer event of crop disaster. But the two are competitive. There may be some optimal reserve policy by which the cost of further price instability is brought into equality with the gain in insurance benefit.

But now compare an overall official reserve policy, even one administered optimally, with the alternative of no official reserve and reliance instead on improved grain marketing. The operation of competitive grain markets too can be seen in relation to the two tasks of official reserves. Free markets in which speculative purchases and sales are permitted affect the ordinary seasonal and yearly movement of prices. But in addition, in the rarer event of crop disaster, a grain economy organized by free markets will spread the price effect, and distribute the transitory burden of loss via the incentives of price changes. There is a free-market solution to the problem of ordinary instability and to catastrophe. We will consider the efficiency with which each of these tasks is performed. But note first that in the market – (no-official-reserve) – policy alternative the performance of the two tasks is not competitive in the way it is in the official reserve policy. The better is ordinary stabilization accomplished by markets, the more there is security against catastrophe. The reason for this difference is that a reserve policy must be based on a fixed, limited and specifically designated stock which cannot be augmented in the short run, even if it is needed, whereas market-based stabilization depends upon a form of institutional organization designed to expand access to the entire supply of grain. The extent of access at any particular time and need is governed by the price level. An efficient market would expand the domain of access greatly in response to slight increases in price. The market route to stabilization is to increase the extent of the market by removal of market barriers and by investing in information and transport facilities to increase the quantitative responses to price changes.

There is a factual question however that needs to be answered. Would not large reserves be needed to smooth severe inter-temporal instability − to relieve crop disasters − when they do occur? And could market-price incentives ever be sufficient to generate adequate reserves for this purpose?

The ultimate feasibility of sharing without special reserves can be judged by converting a 1972-sized deficit into an estimated market-price increase by assuming a plausible demand elasticity and an integrated world market. The deficit in 1972 was about 40 million metric tons, taking into account all grains. Total production of all grains in 1975 was about 1,150 million tons, making that shortfall 3.5% of the total. If elasticity of demand were − 0.3 on average[10] over the entire world and deficit countries had the means to purchase the full amount they lacked, the price of grain would have to increase by only 11.6%.

As we well know the 1972 deficit was not absorbed by the world market that effortlessly. Even after the large US 'official' reserve was sold off at pre-shortage prices to the Russians, the remaining deficit regions in Asia, Africa and Europe pushed grain prices up to four times their 1971 levels.

Having experienced this cataclysmic price rise the world might not recognize an 11% rise as indicative of serious crop failure. If the correct elasticity of demand were only half of the assumed − 0.3 and the price increase were to be double 11%, it would still be luxurious. This increase assumes deficit countries tighten their own belts no more than the rest of the world would in the years of their worst deficit, which of course, did not happen in 1972 when prices quadrupled. And we have made no allowance for the shock-absorbing role of national reserves, private speculative holdings and normal carryovers.

But this measure of feasibility of sharing without official reserves which reveals a result so different from recent experience is, by this very contrast, also a measure of how far the critical assumption of integrated world grain markets is from current reality. Can reality be brought close enough to the state of integration needed to absorb expected scarcities with acceptable price increases?

Disintegration of world grain markets is one of the effects of farm-income protection against low farm prices induced by productivity gains at home or cheap purchases abroad. And it is worsened by the financial incapacity of deficit countries to buy grain in the world's commercial markets. Those who would sell find few willing buyers and those who would buy lack credit or finance. The need for protection is the mirror image of our primary problem, the destabilizing effect of a world-wide deficit. When a large deficit occurs its market impact is concentrated on a narrow segment of the world grain markets and consequently prices in that thin market rise inordinately. Symmetrically, surpluses would also have to be sold into a thin market and to absorb them, prices would have to fall inordinately. Indeed sometimes both problems confront different countries at the same time although in different grains or in geographically separated places. Such instability is either bad for farmers or bad for consumers and in the end it is bad for both. If thinnesses could be overcome by broadening the scope of markets, bringing into communication and effective contact both buyers and sellers, deficit and surplus countries, they could rely upon world markets for mutual gain by exchange. The irregularity of production over time would not need to impose upon a country equivalent irregularity of consumption. To an individual country the opportunity of selling on those occasions when they have a surplus and buying to make up for a deficit is equivalent to storing and holding a grain surplus until there is a deficit, without the burdens of actual storage. It is also equivalent to lending a surplus to the rest of the world in exchange for a call on repayment when in need, but without the awkwardness of in-kind credit contracts. Because deficits and surpluses in relation to trend for the world as a whole are small, these benefits can be had without anyone holding large reserves. Viewing the problem in this symmetrical way offers the key to its solution. The fact that the market problem is a symmetrical one makes it possible to deal effectively with the second cause of market disintegration, the difficulty of financing deficit countries' purchases.

Broadening markets to improve the prospect of gainful sale of food surpluses creates the basis for the repayment of external loans. A country that cannot hope to benefit from a surplus harvest must plan to repay loans to cover its deficit harvests out of export surpluses unrelated to the random shifts of food production. But these other export surpluses may not materialize. If all the random deficits create debt and the random surpluses go to waste, there must be a severe limit on the ability to finance the debt associated with deficits. But if grain markets can be broadened to absorb surpluses, we can contemplate the establishment of a successfully institutionalized grain loan facility.

The association of a loan facility and broadened grain markets arises in a second relationship. A food loan facility operating within a broad world market environment will have a valuable service to offer participants, one that will permit important budget economies in the management of consumption standards. By establishing, as a condition of participation, specified degrees of market access to other participants, such a loan institution can guarantee the conditions for its own success.

Market access need not mean unrestricted free trade in grain. Import quotas might be specified to limit the level to which grain prices would be permitted to fall. Most countries are familiar with import controls and have established policies, frequently managed in connection with their US PL480 grain import programme, for the protection of their home farm producers. Most countries have not excluded, and would not wish to exclude all grain imports to give their own farmers unlimited market benefits. Only a modest adjustment of their import policies would be required therefore to permit commercial grain imports in place of aid imports.

An international grain reserve system would of course also require participant countries to adapt to the price consequences of grain-reserve imports. For if an international reserve system were to buy grain only from major grain export countries and supply grain only to chronic deficit countries, an enormous transfer would be involved. It would be greater than the now-ended US food-aid programme for there would be no surplus available at below market cost that was the unintended consequence of the US farm price-support programme. If alternatively a reserve system were operated by buying and selling from and to any and all countries, it too would depend upon more of a free grain trade world than now exists. The change in grain trading patterns is desirable now because there is no longer a US-financed grain

reserve, not only in order to establish a no-reserve system.

Thus while the establishment of a no-reserve system of food security would require governments to arrange for grain imports through commercial channels, the changes in policies they would thereby be called upon to accept would not so much threaten farm incomes as they might present new budget strains and financial burdens for which solutions must be found. The form of assistance the international community can best provide is a system of credit that includes a means for the liquidation of debt as well as its creation, if the relief of transitory food shortages is not to remain in the realm of international charity.[11]

An international grain-loan agency intent upon encouraging integration of the world's grain economy would set its terms to encourage member countries to rely upon commercial imports to make up deficits in periods of poor harvests. Credit might be granted with the expectation of repayment over periods long enough for it to be repaid out of export earnings in times of good harvests. These credits would be limited then to amounts related to deficits measured from a country's own grain production trend. It would not provide credit to increase consumption levels above production trends, for such a food-import balance could not be paid for by sales from expected above-trend outputs. Countries with planned net imports of food would have to plan for an offsetting export surplus of other goods or services or some other means to pay for it.

To some extent commercial imports financed by a new international grain-loan agency would replace US PL480 food imports, although not to the extent to which many countries had become accustomed. For US food aid was not limited to offsetting transitory deficits and could not be repaid by exports of food commodities to the US (or to other countries) when there were better-than-normal harvests. The experience of food imports from the US however has been responsible for the establishment of some of the institutional foundations needed for the operation of a commercial exchange system. Under the terms of the US food aid programme the distribution of US food imports was accomplished through an internal grain trade system. The same channels of trade might well serve the potential export flows through which debt repayment would be derived. The enrichment of these developments ought to draw the energies of a new grain trade bank. Farmers as well as consumers might then recognize the importance of a grain bank instead of only consumers who received the limited benefits of unrequited food aid.

Measured by its loan capacity, a grain loan fund should have an ultimate standby loan capacity to finance the extremes of the range of possible, or even somewhat unlikely deficits, including an accumulation of deficits over two or perhaps more years. Unlike a physical grain reserve, however, a loan facility can be 're-stocked' without waiting for the next surplus growing season. So it is clearly less important to anticipate the worst contingencies. In any case, most of the 'capacity' would be a call right on its primary creditors. Actual authorized stand-by capacity might be a small fraction of ultimate credit capacity. Capitalization, if the fund were to raise resources in the capital markets, would be the fraction of the authorized loan fund appropriate to bear the residual risk of such business.

At present we need to be concerned about an annual deficit of 40 million metric tons. At $4 a bushel, the cost of a metric ton is $240, the total value of such a deficit is just below 10 billion dollars. Two such bad general harvests in a row would push the amount to 20 billion. There would have to be some understanding about how such funds would be raised and a procedure to be followed in the event of need, but most of this amount could be regarded as a standby obligation. For normal allocation, on the authority of fund management, one billion dollars of loan capacity, enough to finance the purchase of 4 million tons, would be the required order.

This estimate of the magnitude of resources is intended to indicate the relative feasibility of a financial bank in contrast to a stored-grain bank. The services of a financial bank might be expected to be paid for ultimately by countries who use its facilities to finance their own deficits; doing so would make it possible for them to bear the cost of the instability of their own farm system. Aid flows would not be tied to specific food commodities or related to the timing of bad weather. Most of the capital funds for the establishment of the facility might well be available in the international market on commercial terms and not compete with pure aid funds. By shifting the food salvation task to a self-financing commercial system a significant part of official aid funds devoted to food crises might be released to aid general economic development.

Finally the limits of the proposal ought to be clear. This food-financing proposal is not designed to deal at all with chronic food deficits either of particular countries or of the world as a whole. But then neither are the many proposals for international grain reserves.

NOTES

1. Sec. Henry Kissinger, in a speech, 'Strengthening the world economic structure', Bureau of Public Affairs, Department of State (13 May 1975).

2. 'Whenever we grew additional grain prices went down . . . . We ended up as losers', observes an Indian farmer quoted in the *New York Times* (28 November 1976) in a story on the recently instituted Indian grain storage programme. Now, the report continues, 'Mountainous piles of wheat and rice lie in the open . . . . The storage policy has already cost the Government $2.5 billion . . . . Indian economic writers have warned that the huge investment in food may lead to distortions in the economy'.

3. *World Wheat Statistics,* International Wheat Council (1974), Tables 12, 17, 22.

4. Examples from Indonesia illustrate the point dramatically. In February 1962 the price in Palembang, Sumatra was over six times the price in Bali. By October the price in Bali had risen three and one-half times. In February of 1966 the price in Djakarta was 178% of the price in Jogjakarta, a city 275 miles away. The price in Djakarta had by October of that year more than doubled since February. These wild price movements were not extraordinary.

5. Achtar Hameed Khan, 'A history of the food problem', Agricultural Development Council (New York: 1973).

6. Amartya Sen, 'Famines, food availability and exchange entitlements: the case of the Bengal famine', mimeo (1976).

7. MacAvoy estimates the cost of holding buffer stocks of food commodities at 7–12% of the value of the stock at its peak price. He assumes, in reaching this result, that one-half to two-thirds of the maximum stock is the average amount held and that warehousing costs are 1–2%. The annual cost of a grain reserve would then be $800 million to $1,400 million. Paul W. MacAvoy, 'Economic perspective on the politics of international commodity agreements', The Reuben G. Gustavson Memorial Lecture, University of Arizona (Tucson, Arizona: 1976).

8. Cf. D. Hueth and A. Schmitz, 'International trade in intermediate and final goods: some welfare implica-

tions of destabilized prices', *Quarterly Journal of Economics* (August 1972), pp. 351–365. A simple explanation of this result is that consumers have more to lose by stabilization of prices by their sacrifice of low-price benefits than they can gain by the avoidance of high-price losses because of the negative slope of demand.

9. The US Department of Agriculture authorization of grain sales in 1972 was largely motivated by revenue maximization, which corresponds operationally to price stabilization, and it was led thus to grasp the early market opportunities to sell out even though this implied a sacrifice of protection against an extreme contingency, which unfortunately did quickly materialize in some parts of the world.

10. Although grain itself is a diet essential, it is consumed as an intermediary good, embodied in other forms of food such as in meal for grain-fed animals. This is more true of high-income than low-income countries. The quantity of grain consumed indirectly as an embodied intermediate in an individual diet can be substituted for significantly less grain consumed directly. The ease with which consumers can make this substitution suggests that the demand for foodgrain may well be at least as elastic as -0.3% on average. In poor countries where the diet contains little grain-fed meat, the elasticity will be smaller than in rich countries. But in very poor countries where food-grain consumption is a dominant part of budgets, price-elasticity must be high because a rise in the price of food of say 10% approaches a decline in income of 10%. Even where it has been difficult to obtain satis-factory estimates of food-price elasticities, income elasticities are revealed to be reliably high. See for example H. S. Houthakker and L. D. Taylor, *Consumers Demand in the United States: Analysis and Projections* (Harvard University Press, 1970), p. 62, which finds a short-run income (total expenditure) elasticity of approximately 0.5 and a long run elasticity of 0.7.

11. In the best imaginable circumstances there will still remain considerable need for international charity. Extraordinary food shortages in very low-income countries may not be relieved by commercial imports paid for by international credit, for some countries may still not be creditworthy under these proposed conditions. The problem of food aid surely deserves more systematic attention than it has received. But it also ought to be clearly separated from the problem with which I am concerned in this paper.

World Development, 1977, Vol. 5, Nos. 5–7, pp. 623–631. Pergamon Press. Printed in Great Britain.

The New Politics of Food

LYLE P. SCHERTZ*

and

BYRON L. BERNTSON

US Department of Agriculture

Summary. – Increased pressures for political decisions regarding food have come at a time of great discontinuities in relations among nations, wide disparities of wealth and income and insulation of domestic markets. Issues relating to instability of prices, rules of the game for trade, food aid and productivity in developing countries confront political decision-makers. Important decisions are involved with respect to stocks of food, ways in which the United States handles trade with countries such as the USSR, the stability of quantities of commodities available for food aid and cooperation of the US agricultural science community in the world. The specific choices selected will significantly affect the relationships among all countries and the extent to which the new politics of food will extend into the future.

Millions in the world continue to suffer from inadequate diets. With modern communications they realize that others do not. In still other countries, such as Poland and the USSR, millions would like to add more meat and animal products to their diets. With modern communications they know that others enjoy such diets.

Again through modern communications and through price changes millions in the United States have increasingly realized that the incomes of American farmers, the budgets of American consumers, and subsidies for the US maritime interests are closely related to poverty in Northeast Brazil, drought in Europe, decisions in the Kremlin, and empty food bowls in parts of Asia as well as the productivity and size of farms in the United States. This heightened awareness and the forces underlying it have led an increasing number of citizens and officials in the United States and in other countries to press for political decisions regarding food. Therefore, I have chosen to discuss in this paper:

1. The increasing pressures for political decisions regarding food.
2. The context in which these decisions will have to be made:
   a. Great discontinuities in relations among nations;
   b. Wide disparities of wealth and income;
   c. Insulation of domestic markets.

3. Issues which are especially related to prices, distribution and production of food:
   a. Instability of prices;
   b. Rules of the game for trade, especially with the USSR;
   c. Food aid;
   d. Low productivity in developing countries.

NEW PRESSURES FOR POLITICAL DECISIONS

Many are dissatisfied with food prices and distribution of food in the world. In the United States, government agencies and economic groups which heretofore had paid little attention to food policies have become aggressive participants in the debate. Some have even argued that US food is the ultimate weapon in world politics, while others suggest that such a view is deceptive.

Many participants other than representatives of the traditional food and agriculture units of government have become attracted to international meetings focused on food.

Spokesmen for special interests in the United States have used the sales of grain to the

---

* This article draws on materials included in L. P. Schertz, 'World needs: shall the hungry be with us Shue (eds.), *Food Policy: US Responsibility in the Life and Death Choices* (New York: The Free Press, forthcoming).

USSR and the related public concerns as opportunities to press for increased government subsidies for the maritime industry and to draw attention to the effect of such sales on the US cost of living. Farm organizations established 'hot line systems' aimed at neutralizing the political influence of those critical of such sales. Internationally, the World Food Conference in 1974 established new institutions to give greater attention to food problems of developing countries and to encourage political decisions affecting prices and distribution of food.

Another set of political dimensions to food questions was added by détente policies with the USSR and the People's Republic of China. Government units in both countries conduct their international trade. Political, as well as economic considerations undoubtedly influence the timing and amount of their contracts for food imports and food exports. These considerations are part of the total political framework in which world food problems must be examined.

Domestic economies and international markets have always been affected by political decisions. The techniques for intervening in the markets are many. Buying and selling of commodities and setting trade subsidies and tariffs are examples. In the United States restraints on meat imports, marketing agreements, and the food stamp programme illustrate political decisions affecting food prices and distribution.

Political decisions about international exchange rates have also affected production and consumption of food. For example, the devaluation of the US dollar mitigated the effects on the consumers of many importing countries of the nominal dollar increases in the prices of US farm products in 1972 and subsequent years. The Indian situation exhibits the opposite effect as the value of the rupee relative to the dollar deteriorated. As a result, in early 1976 US wheat import unit values in terms of US dollars were some 200 to 220% of the 1971 levels. But in contrast in terms of rupees, they were 300% of 1971 levels.

Traditionally, the Soviets have done without when they experienced crop shortfalls. Internal adjustments have included large-scale livestock slaughter. But not in 1972. In response to large shortfalls in production they made a different political decision. To maintain food consumption and livestock production, they purchased some 30 million tons of cereals, 18 million of them from the United States.

Again in 1975, as their cereal output dropped to 140 million tons, some 80 million tons below planned production, the USSR decided

to import substantial amounts of cereals. However, in that year, in order to balance consumption needs with availabilities, livestock were also slaughtered.

International food trade has involved politics, as well as economics, over many years. National trade barriers and the overriding influence of domestic food policies on international trade have been major concerns of the General Agreement on Tariffs and Trade (GATT). The International Wheat Agreements have been criticized in many ways. However, in the 1960s they provided a legitimate framework for the United States and Canada, and to some extent Australia, in which to cooperate in making government decisions regarding international wheat trade.

In the past, such as in the mid-1960s, there has been great interest in world food problems with subsequent diminution of these concerns. Thus, it is reasonable to examine the context in which political decisions with respect to food will have to be made in the coming years. Three of them — new discontinuities among nations, increased sensitivities to wide disparities of wealth and income and the continued insulation of most domestic markets from developments in other countries — are of special importance and are discussed in the following section.

It is likely that there will continue to be an uneasy balance between supply and demand for food, even though the crisis conditions of 1974 and 1975 will not be ever-present. They have already dissipated. *Per capita* supplies of less developed countries (LDCs) will maintain an upward trend. But the gains will be modest and the masses of low-income people in these countries will experience only limited improvements in nutrition. Supplies in developed and developing countries are bound to be affected both by weather variation and energy prices and availabilities. Levels of demand for imports are highly uncertain; and, the unpredictable decisions of countries such as the USSR and China are involved. Thus, without significant build-up of stocks of grain and effective rules of the game for monopoly traders, such as the USSR, in international markets, crisis conditions similar to those of 1974 and 1975 could return from time to time.

THE SETTING FOR POLITICAL DECISIONS

New discontinuities among nations

Interest in the politics of food comes at a time of great discontinuities in relations among nations. Decisions of the Organization of Petroleum Exporting Countries (OPEC) have caused sharp changes in distribution of income among nations. Détente with the USSR and the People's Republic of China calls for political, non-market considerations by the United States in exporting food to these countries.

Intensified pressure by low-income countries for better terms of trade and distribution of goods, including food, are likely to continue. Improved transportation and communication make it increasingly unlikely that the masses in lower income countries will quietly tolerate a widening gap between rich and poor countries. The same may be true of gaps between rich and poor within low-income countries.

Leaders of developing countries saw the OPEC countries, through political decisions, exact the type of prices that they desire for other products. Many developing countries take satisfaction in the injury the OPEC inflicted on developed countries, even to the extent of quietly tolerating serious consequences of the OPEC actions on themselves. Developing countries argue that the rich, through GATT, the Organization for Economic Cooperation and Development, the International Monetary Fund, and multinational firms, have politically controlled the economics among nations and, in some cases, the economics of their countries. They object that developed country politics has limited their political and economic influence.

Increased sensitivities to wide disparities of wealth and income

One of the central questions in the new politics of food is, should wealth and income continue to have an overwhelming effect on distribution of food and, therefore, incidence of hunger in the world?

Today, people in developing nations, which include two-thirds of the world's populations, eat only one-fourth of the world's protein, mostly in the form of cereals. In countries such as India, people consume less than 400 pounds of cereals *per capita* each year. On the other hand, in developed countries, large quantities of cereals are converted to protein. Annual *per capita* grain consumption is over 1400 pounds in the USSR, over 1800 pounds in West Germany, France and the United States. People in rich countries number only one-half those in the lower income countries. However, the rich nations, with tastes for livestock products and incomes to pay for them, use practically as much cereal for livestock feed as the low-income nations use directly as food.

While population growth has obviously been a significant factor in increasing world food demand, even more striking has been the sharp recent increase in cereal consumption *per capita* in developed countries, where populations have not been growing rapidly. In the 8-year period, 1964—66 to 1972—74, *per capita* consumption of cereal grains increased by 250 pounds, or 16%, in the United States and by 330 pounds, or 30%, in the USSR. These gains were far more than half the 1972—74 total consumption of 395 pounds *per capita* in developing countries.

The USSR's decision to protect diets was felt world-wide by both rich and poor. When the Soviets purchased almost one-fifth of the total US wheat supply in the 1972/73 crop year, supplies normally available to others dropped sharply. Nations and people reacted by bidding up the price of the remaining wheat, the more aggressively because currencies of Japan and several other commercial importers of US foodstuffs were worth substantially more in terms of dollars as a result of successive devaluations.

In contrast, the limited wealth and low income of poor countries again determined how well they could compete in food purchasing. So long as total cereal production is responsive to needs, effects on the poor are minimal, especially over time. But in times of sharply increased demand or curtailed supplies, impacts can be harsh. For example, the 1972/73 Indian food grain crop dropped from 105 million to 96 million tons. In the tug-of-war between maintaining diets and saving foreign exchange, diets lost and food prices were allowed to increase. In some areas, foodgrain rations were cut in half in fair-price food shops, which serve many of the lowest income Indians. *Per capita* calorie availability dropped toward the critical levels of the mid-1960s. More recently production increases in India have permitted recovery in the *per capita* availability of food and also the building of stocks to record levels.

Short-run and long-run distinctions are important when considering effects of wealth and income on distribution of food. In the short run, the world is dealing with food already produced or about to be produced. Distribution of income among rich and poor is then a primary determinant of the distribution of food. In contrast, response of producers over time is an important consideration in the long run. For example, production in the past has been responsive to demand flowing from incomes. Thus, in the long run, low incomes of low-income nations, not the high incomes of developed countries, have been a primary determinant of low food consumption levels of the developing countries. Regardless, the sensitivities to the wide disparities of wealth and income in the world have increased. In turn, more people are asking if the incidence of hunger in the world is 'right'. Reflecting these concerns, the US Congress considered but did not pass legislation in 1976 resolving that the hungry in the world have an inalienable right to food. The resolution was similar to that approved by the World Food Congress.

Continued insulation of domestic markets

The politics of food must be contemplated in the context of continued insulation of internal markets, especially in rich countries, from the effects of changes in food production in their own country and in other countries.

Domestic prices and food supplies in most countries are insulated from changes in prices and supplies in international markets and from changes in internal production. The devices are many in number. International trade is used by many countries including the United States. Egypt, an example of an importer, holds farm prices of rice relatively low through importation of increasingly larger quantities of wheat. The European Community uses variable levies on imports to insulate internal prices from fluctuations of international prices. Argentina, Burma and Thailand use taxes on exports. In Brazil, quotas, and in some cases, embargos on exports are employed. In Canada, the Canadian Wheat Board decides whether to offer wheat for sale and at what price. Unless supplies are considered to be available in sufficient amounts that desired domestic prices can be realized, contracts are not made. Thus, their actions in terms of effect are equivalent to export quotas. The prices paid to state and collective farms in the USSR are administratively set. They were increased in 1970. They have not been changed since. Retail prices for bread and meat were increased in 1962 and have not been changed since that time.

Many countries, other than the United States, have placed the·responsibility for conducting international grain trading in one governmental unit. Thus, international transactions with these countries involve government agencies or their agents and are, therefore, significantly affected by political decisions. Similar arrangements are utilized for many other commodities. Arrangements in the European Community countries are different. However, political decisions are still involved

for most agricultural commodities. Target prices, which, in turn, influence levies on imports and subsidies for exports, are determined politically.

The US approach is unique. For many years the market was insulated with export subsidies, restrictions on land use, price supports and stockpiling of cereals. These activities to moderate price swings nationally and internationally, also caused changes in livestock production and consumption of cereals as feed for livestock.

The situation changed completely in the 1970s largely due to increased export demand. Stocks held by the government were eliminated and land once held out of production was freed for production. In general, any amount of food commodities could be purchased by foreign governments and private traders for export from the United States. Exceptions to this approach involved the export limitation on soybeans and oilseeds during July—September 1973, the cutbacks on USSR purchases in the fall of 1974, and the subsequent arrangements with the USSR for limits on their purchases. The openness of the US cereal markets to influences of international and domestic developments contrasts sharply with the conditions in the US markets for dairy products and beef.

The international grain markets also involve a small number of very large grain trading companies. These companies buy and sell grain from government trading units, as well as private traders, in the United States and in other countries where they are permitted to do so.

Thus, aside from the United States, the international cereal market includes a relatively small number of large, centralized government exporting units, centralized government importing units, and private international trading companies. This structure of the international grains market has great relevance to the politics of food. The entities of this structure provide many instruments for insulating domestic markets. But, in addition, their operations give rise to significant issues, especially with respect to how their actions can affect international and US prices. In turn, these give rise to an important issue. What should be the rules of the game for large trading units — government and private — in international commodity markets?

FOOD PRICE, DISTRIBUTION AND PRODUCTION ISSUES

Of the many food issues demanding attention, this paper focuses on four: instability of prices, rules of the game for trade, food aid, and low productivity in developing countries.

Instability of cereal prices

By maintaining large grain stockpiles, the United States has in past years been able to moderate price swings, nationally and internationally. Availability of US stocks dampened price changes in the international market while discouraging increases in domestic prices. In times of general surplus, the United States chose to stockpile grain and withhold land from production rather than accept lower domestic prices or pay larger export subsidies.

As pointed out earlier, this situation has completely changed in 1973—75. Stocks held by the government were eliminated, and land once held out of production was freed for production. In general, any amounts of food commodities could be purchased from private traders for export from the United States. With increased production in the United States and around the world, US stocks increased in 1976/77. In the absence of substantial US Government stocks, US farm prices are strongly influenced by international markets. With the domestic US market and the international market moving together, food prices will be unstable. Without stocks, this instability will exist, as weather conditions around the world change from year to year, producing changes in import needs and export supplies.

In the face of this price instability, several different types of adjustments may be made. Adjustments may occur in the feed livestock sector. The United States experienced sharply higher feed costs in 1974/75 and in turn, sharply reduced consumption of cereals as feed. This adjustment in feedgrain consumption was in marked contrast to the increased consumption of cereals in the USSR.

Thus, under a policy which does not result in the building of stocks, one outstanding political issue will be, should the United States establish export controls, taxes or subsidies? Although export taxes have been commonly employed by other countries to insulate domestic prices by reserving supplies for domestic consumption, the US Constitution apparently forbids such taxes. However, for a brief period during the 1960s, techniques were devised whereby wheat exporters on occasion 'paid' the US Government specified amounts under a balancing arrangement. On other occasions, when US prices were higher than international prices, the exporters 'received' a payment.

In a real sense, the United States already has a form of export licensing for a portion of US exports. For shipments of food under Public Law 480, the country desiring commodities approaches the US Government. The US Government, considering US market conditions and the credit needs of the applying country, decides on the amount to be financed by PL480 funds. This agreement is made public, and the recipient government proceeds to deal with the private trade in making the purchase. If such an approach were expanded to commercial sales, the review process in the US Government could be focused primarily on supply availability.

On the other hand, adjustment to prospective price instability may also take the form of political decisions to establish food stocks nationally, by importers or exporters or both, or conceivably on an international basis. The mechanics and policy framework for acquiring and managing these stocks are not easily established, due to the multiple and sometimes conflicting objectives of a stocks programme. Such programmes can operate in a host of ways: they can stabilize prices, or, by withdrawing supplies, actually increase prices; they can be used to stimulate production; or as a set-aside to meet acute shortages; they may or may not be earmarked especially for lower income countries.

There are other questions such as where should stocks be held and by whom? Stocks need to be distributed throughout the world to avoid overdependence on a small number of countries in times of shortage. US stocks alone are not an adequate answer. Moreover, significant build-ups of US stocks would surely operate, as in the past, to lull others into believing that they need not build their own reserves.

An especially crucial question for the United States is, should the private trade or the government carry stocks? Private trade will limit stocks they carry if large stocks are carried by the US Government. How much they will accumulate and carry if the government does not have any stocks is not known. It is clear, however, that for the trade to carry significant stocks requires market conditions which make such activities profitable.

Costs of stocks also argue that not just major exporters should be involved in a food reserve scheme. Food stocks are expensive to purchase initially, and they are costly to store. Rough estimates of monthly costs of storing grain stocks in the United States are 60 cents per ton, exclusive of interest costs of money invested in the commodities or any allowance for physical deterioration or losses. If interest costs are added at 8% on an assumed value of 75% of the current US market prices for grain, the annual carrying cost of 1 ton of wheat would be $21, or for 1 ton of corn, $14.

Estimates of the amount of stocks 'needed' vary and depend on objectives. One way to estimate the need is to consider the fluctuation of production in past years. Based on 1960–73 world production changes, 25 to 40 million tons of grain would be needed to meet two-thirds of the annual shortfalls.

For the United States, there are important trade-offs. As long as energy imports are high, the benefit from high export sales of agricultural products is bound to weigh heavily. On the other hand, over time, exports would be expanded if supplies to foreign customers could be assured from year to year at relatively stable prices. For dependability, an exporter of farm commodities may not only need supplies for which importers can bid but available supplies at relatively stable prices.

Eventually US interests may dovetail with an international food stocking programme. Unstable food prices concern consumers and labour unions. Farm interests, too, may become frustrated with effects of instability. Major groups of American farmers have benefited from high prices; for others, benefits have been more limited or none at all. The day could come when US farm producers as a whole would prefer cattle prices that stabilize close to $40 rather than $55 one year and $30 for another. Further, US stocks could be built inadvertently. A combination of increased production in the United States and around the world, and political and economic pressures for supporting US farm prices above market-clearing levels could result again in substantial accumulation of government-owned stocks.

*Rules of the game for international
trade in food*

GATT was designed to bring about progressive liberalization of trade – including agricultural trade – especially among Western Europe, North America, and Japan. Results for agricultural trade have been limited. The European Community is highly protected with a variable levy system on most agricultural imports. Japan retains significant control on imports and high internal food prices. However, since their food needs exceed food production, their imports have expanded, and the United States has adjusted its commodity programmes to permit a close interfacing of the international and domestic markets. But these adjustments have come largely as a result of US objectives rather than from partnership in reordering economic relations.

The role of developing countries in GATT has been severely limited. Further, the developed countries for a long time avoided dealing with a wide range of trade matters in other forums where developing countries have been prominent. But perhaps the problems of international trade in agricultural products having the most significance for the lower income countries, as well as the United States, relate to rules of the game for importing countries for buying in the United States, especially for the USSR and other state-controlled economies. These problems are especially acute for the United States because of its dominant exporter role. All countries have a stake in the US rules since they affect commercial and non-commercial supplies and prices to other importing countries.

When the United States made export payments and had substantial stocks of wheat, international prices and shares of export markets among suppliers such as the United States, Canada, and Australia reflected those known political and economic facts. In contrast, information about Soviet crop conditions, government budgets, political directions, and other relevant factors is extremely limited. The recent agricultural agreement between the USSR and the United States calls for exchange of information on crop conditions and forward estimates of crop production and trade. However, these provisions are yet to be fully realized.

Variations in Soviet cereal production are largely weather-related. Only one-third of Soviet agricultural land lies south of the 48th parallel and only 1% of it lies in areas with an annual rainfall of 28 inches or more. In contrast, almost all of the United States lies below the 48th parallel, and 60% of US arable land receives at least 28 inches of rainfall annually. Little wonder, then, that frequent and wide changes occur in Soviet cereal production. There has been an impressive upward trend of 3% annual growth since 1960, but annual variations along the trend resemble jagged teeth of a saw.

In spite of its long-term production increases, the USSR has pushed livestock production so hard that only in years of outstanding cereal production are feed supplies adequate without imports. In years of poor harvest, such as 1975, large imports are required to avoid extensive livestock liquidations.

The problem is broader than trade with the USSR. In the 1973—74 crop year, the People's Republic of China became a much larger buyer of grain with purchases totalling probably more than 9 million tons, a 50% increase over recent import levels. Moreover, China switched heavily to the US market, taking 7 million tons of the total here and becoming the largest US wheat customer for this period. And this occurred after a good weather year. Neither the present guidelines for Chinese purchases nor the true state of Chinese stocks is known outside China.

The Japanese Government and Japanese importing interests work together closely. In 1973, Japanese concerns purchased relatively large amounts of cotton and shrimp, sharply raising prices in both markets as private US traders attempted to buy from remaining supplies. The Japanese purchases of grain have been more stable, however, and Japan has been willing to indicate its import needs at an early stage.

There is an urgent need to develop understanding of the rules of the game with large countries, especially those dealing as monopolies or near monopolies. At a minimum, the US Government and the public must know developments within these countries on weather, agricultural production, stocks and prices. However, information alone would not automatically prevent wide swings in US prices. To permit any large country to make purchases of any size in US grain markets subjects the US market to possible wide fluctuations in purchases and could amount to possible manipulation of the US market by foreign political leaders.

Perhaps bilateral deals and understandings are not the long-term answer to this problem, but for the time being they are essential. In the Soviet case, for example, sales of US grain could be part of larger arrangements involving US imports of Soviet products, such as petroleum products. Arrangement also for maximum and minimum purchases to permit sharing by the USSR, as well as the United States, in adjustments to possible shortfalls in Soviet and US production need to be continued. In any case, traditional rules of the game are now unacceptable politically and economically to many people and governments. New rules will have to be instituted.

Food aid

Developing countries would benefit enormously from measures to limit the fluctuation in world food prices and from greater stability of USSR activity in international food markets. A crucial question is whether nations, including the United States, should take other steps to help developing countries attain at least minimum essential levels of food and to avoid situations whereby, in periods of depressed markets, food aid recipient countries are pressured to take too much food aid.

The upward pressure on prices and the potential to export all available cereals in excess of US domestic needs in 1973—75 brought significant changes in PL480 programmes. Quantities of 1974 food aid dropped significantly. Because of higher prices, value dropped much less. Quantities in fiscal year 1975 increased, but were still significantly below levels of earlier years.

PL480 has been a programme for US agriculture. For many years, PL480 programmes were consistent with commercial objectives for agricultural exports. They permitted charging lower prices to poor countries without undercutting prices to the richer countries. Through adjusting terms — use of the local currency, credit and commercial sales — effective prices were tailored to the customer's financial, political and security status.

With strong demand, negligible stocks and high prices, it was not advantageous to move significant amounts of food under PL480. Therefore, political support for food aid waned somewhat. In 1976, as supplies relative to demands were more plentiful and US prices were under pressure, quantities in PL480 programmes increased. The United States needs to consider the appropriateness of the amounts of commodities in PL480 programmes fluctuating in response to commercial export opportunities and US prices.

The world will need to evaluate trade-offs between food aid and other economic assistance. Most developed countries and international assistance agencies have limited but significant resources for assisting lower income countries. They have never had to closely evaluate trade-offs. In the United States, such consideration could be avoided since the funding appropriations flowed from different congressional committees to different executive departments. The international assistance agencies did not pick up food aid simply because it was in the US self-interest to finance and implement a programme of food assistance as a major adjunct to US agricultural programmes. It was mutually advantageous to have this division. Resources for international assistance could be used for items other than food, and the Department of Agriculture could carry food aid costs.

It is time for international agencies such as the World Bank to ask, should not food aid be made an integral part of economic assistance programmes? And, it is time for the lower income countries to ask, should we use aid proceeds to buy turbines or to buy grain in times of food shortage?

Food assistance can be a form of investment. As with PL480, proceeds from the sale of food provided on a concessional basis can be used for investment in irrigation facilities, locally-made machines and production facilities, much as hard-currency loans can be used to provide foreign-made machines, and perhaps with greater employment and productivity effects. These choices have not been faced simply because through PL480, food was 'priced' low and the money, once appropriated for food aid, could not be switched to other assistance activities. The variability of food prices and the availability of food under PL480 point up the conflict in this area of the interests of the developing and developed countries and the difficult and complex choices required.

Low productivity in the developing countries

The Department of Agriculture, US universities and private industry have contributed importantly to the productivity of world agriculture. The widely acclaimed international research centres have been staffed almost exclusively by US—trained personnel. Further, the US agricultural community has generated much of the basic knowledge on which these centres and other research organizations rely.

Significant changes have occurred which call for a re-examination of the prospective role of the Department and the US universities in the emerging international network of agricultural research. These changed conditions include:

1. A greater recognition by the lower income countries, as well as the United States, of the importance of improving food production in the lower income countries.

2. A greater recognition of the role of technology in bringing about increased food production.

3. An expanded role of international research institutes in contributing to world agricultural scientific know-how and technology.

4. Aggressive efforts by OPEC to enhance productivity of their agricultural sectors and related requests for substantial technical cooperation.

These developments are likely to lead to heavy demands on the US agricultural community for participation in technical cooperation programmes and for engaging in collaborative research. Effective response to these demands would require building of increased capacity. Not doing so could lead to (1) effective cooperation with OPEC countries, but inability to meet the greatest needs, namely those of the poorest countries, and (2) perhaps long-term inability to develop an effective world-wide network of science to support improved production and rural development and, in turn, increased food consumption in the low-income countries.

In deciding on the appropriate role for the United States research system, account needs to be taken of the important research being conducted throughout the world, including that of the low-income countries, and how US technology could benefit from US scientists being more effectively involved with scientists in other countries.

Such an approach would require substantial increases in funds for international research and education. Steps are already under way to bring about political decisions to appropriate expanded funds. Many advocate centralized decisions on how such funds might be utilized. However, professional collaboration in research involves many complexities. Further, the ability of a small central staff to merely execute the many decisions required with a centralized, expanded research activity is doubtful. These factors suggest that careful consideration be given to the potential inefficiencies of highly-centralized decision-making and to the potential payoffs from decentralized decision-making. Automatic allocation on a formula basis to research institutions in the United States of a significant proportion of such funds would be an important step in this direction.

SUMMARY AND CONCLUSION

Increased pressures for political decisions regarding food have come at a time of great discontinuities in relations among nations, wide disparities of wealth and income and insulation of domestic markets.

Issues relating to instability of prices, rules of the game for trade, food aid and productivity in developing countries confront political decision-makers.

Important decisions are being called for with respect to stocks of food, ways in which the United States handles trade with countries such as the USSR, the stability of quantities of commodities available for food aid and cooperation of the US agricultural science community with counterparts around the world.

In the past, interest in world food problems has changed from time to time. There was great interest in the mid-1960s with subsequent diminishing of the concerns. Thus, it is reasonable to ask, 'Is the present situation fundamentally different and will the recent politicizing be more sustained?' One cannot be sure, but there is a greater chance that it is different and the politicizing will be more sustained even though its intensity will likely vacillate from year to year. The situation will depend significantly on the extent to which stocks are held.

The crisis conditions of 1974 and 1975 will not be ever-present. They have already dissipa-ted. *Per capita* supplies of less developed countries will maintain an upward trend, but will change from year to year. However, the gains will be modest, and the masses of low-income people in these countries will experience only limited improvements in nutrition. Without substantial stocks, it is reasonable to expect an uneasy balance between supply and demand for food.

Supplies in developed and developing countries are bound to be affected both by weather variation and energy prices and availabilities. Both the availabilities of supplies for exports and the demands for imports are highly uncertain. And, the unpredictable decisions of countries such as the USSR and China are involved. Thus, without significant build-up of stocks of grain and effective rules of the game for monopoly traders such as the USSR in international markets, crisis conditions similar to those of 1974 and 1975 could return from time to time. It is in this context that political decisions on food aid and increased food production in developing countries take on increased importance.

World Development, 1977, Vol. 5, Nos. 5—7, pp. 633—639. Pergamon Press. Printed in Great Britain.

External Assistance for Food and Agricultural Development in the Third World

J. P. BHATTACHARJEE*

FAO, Rome

Summary. — Trends in the flow of investment in and external development assistance to food and agriculture in developing countries are the subject of this paper. These are discussed in the context of targets regarding agricultural production increases set both by the FAO and by the World Food Conference (1974). The paper deals specifically with external assistance commitments offered by such donors as the DAC, IBRD, OPEC, Regional Development Banks, etc., with a special emphasis on 'concessional assistance'.

INTRODUCTION

The flow of investment in agriculture in the developing countries has been a matter of continuing concern especially since the early 1960s. At the international level, the Food and Agriculture Organization of the United Nations had been voicing it for more than a decade. Underlying this concern are the two premises that the allocation of domestic resources for investment in agriculture has fallen short of the requirements for achieving the targeted development objectives and that this sector has received inadequate financial and technical assistance from external sources. While the first premise may be a matter of debate in particular countries, there is hardly any disagreement on the second. The two issues are, of course, interrelated and essentially so at the national level. However, for analysis at the aggregated global level, the paucity of data on investment in agriculture almost leaves no other choice than to concentrate on external assistance flows. The importance that the International Development Strategy attaches to resource transfers also lends meaningfulness to an analysis of the 'adequacy' of the external assistance going to agriculture in the developing world.

The background to the analysis attempted in this paper is the target of 4% annual average increase in food and agricultural production in developing countries within the framework of the overall objectives set forth in the International Development Strategy for the Second

United Nations Development Decade (the 1970s). The World Food Conference (1974) reaffirmed this as the minimum performance required for meeting 'the rapidly growing demand for food . . ., the requirements for security stocks and the need to raise the consumption by malnourished people to universally accepted standards'. The Conference recommended far-reaching policies, programmes and arrangements concerning various aspects of food production, consumption and nutrition, food security, trade, food aid and development assistance. For the purpose of this paper, it is important to note that the Conference expressed concern, among other things, 'at the inadequacy of the present level of resources, including development assistance, flowing to agriculture in these countries', and called on the government of each developing country to accord a high priority to agricultural and fisheries development with all that this implies. It also called on all governments in a position to do so, 'to substantially increase their official development assistance to agriculture in developing countries, especially the least developed and the most seriously affected countries, including capital assistance on soft terms, technical assistance, transfer of appropriate technology and programme loans for imports of essential inputs'.[1] Recognizing the

---

* The views expressed in this paper are those of the author and do not necessarily represent the views of FAO.

need for mobilizing and channelling additional external assistance to agriculture, the Conference, in one of its major achievements, called for the establishment of an International Fund for Agricultural Development, which is soon to become operational.

More than two years have passed since the World Food Conference issued its call for an increase in the flow of investment in and external development assistance to food and agriculture. What has been the response so far? This paper attempts to provide an answer to this question. It presents an analysis of changes in the flow of external assistance committed for food and agricultural development in developing countries since 1973 and an assessment of its adequacy in relation to estimated requirements. The quantitative data available for this analysis relate to official *commitment* of such assistance by donor countries and multilateral agencies. Data on a *disbursement* basis are not available; hence it is not possible to meaningfully analyze the flow of external assistance to agriculture within the framework of the net flow of resources to developing countries.

EXTERNAL FINANCIAL ASSISTANCE REQUIREMENTS FOR AGRICULTURAL DEVELOPMENT

The generally accepted purpose of external financial assistance for development is to help a country get over the twin problems of shortage of foreign exchange and inadequacy of domestic savings needed for the planned investment programme. The requirement of such assistance is country-specific and depends on the economic status, financial position and foreign trade situation of each country *vis-à-vis* its plan and programmes. For a particular sector such as agriculture, assessment of external assistance requirements has to be made in the context of the overall requirements of the economy, the policies and programmes for the sector *vis-à-vis* its state of development. Any global estimate of such requirements must, therefore, be built up by aggregating individual country estimates; and there is no short cut to this method. Furthermore, there are no universally accepted criteria for assessing these requirements.

The Indicative World Plan for Agriculture (IWP) prepared by FAO in the late 1960s, presented the first comprehensive estimates, among other things, of the investment and current input requirements for meeting the claims on agriculture in developing countries during the period 1962–85. This normative

study covered 85% of the developing countries in terms of both population and GDP, and adopted as objectives the satisfaction of the food demand, ensuring adequate supplies to meet the main dietary deficiencies, increasing employment in agriculture and meeting foreign exchange needs. In line with these objectives, feasible targets of agricultural production growth were worked out for the developing countries included in the study. These aggregated to a global growth rate of agricultural production per year of 3.7% for the period 1962–85. The policies and programmes suitable for attaining the objectives in each country were analyzed, and those considered realistic and feasible were included in the strategy. The investment and financial requirements of these were then worked out for each programme and aggregated.

The investment requirements in these countries taken as a group were thus estimated at the cumulative total of $112.5 billion (in 1962 prices) for the 23 years to 1985, in such fields as irrigation and land development, machinery and equipment, livestock, fisheries and forestry. The financial requirements for current inputs were estimated to rise from an annual outlay of $8.5 billion in 1962 to $26 billion in 1985.[2] If the requirements of countries excluded from this study are added, the estimate of total requirements for investment in agriculture in the developing world would go up to around $132.5 billion for the period 1962–85. The financial requirements for current inputs should grow at an annual rate of 5%.

Using and partially updating the IWP analysis, FAO prepared, for consideration by the World Food Conference in 1974, estimates of investment requirements for increasing food production in developing countries at a rate at least matching the projected 3.6% annual growth rate of demand during 1975–85. Nearly three-quarters of this amount would be accounted for by programmes for irrigation, drainage and development of new arable land.[3]

This global estimate was prepared by aggregating the investment needs for identifiable programmes for increasing food production, judged feasible in each country over this period. They were considered achievable provided there were 'sufficient political commitment, bold policies, realistic programming, adequate mobilization of domestic resources, acceleration of institutional change and effective implementation and administration, backed by the needed support from bilateral and multilateral sources of external assistance'.[4]

To achieve a realistic phasing, the investment

requirement for the next six-year period, 1975–80, was then worked out, taking into account also the needs of the non-food sub-sectors of agriculture. It was thus estimated that the total annual flow of investment in agriculture would have to be about doubled to reach a level of $18–20 billion over 1975–80, if the growth rate of agricultural production was to be stepped up from the trend rate of 2.6% towards 4.0% per year. It should be noted that investments in fertilizer plants and other input industries, in agro-industries, rural communications and transport and multi-purpose river basin projects were *not* included in these estimates.[5]

External financial assistance needed to support this level of investment during 1975–80 was then worked out separately for each sub-sector, taking into account the likely foreign exchange requirements, as well as the need for financing of local currency expenditures on the lines of the practice followed by the World Bank. External financial support of about $2.5 billion annually was estimated for land and water development programmes including renovation and improvement of existing irrigation facilities, equipping new land for irrigation and opening up new arable land. For crop and meat development, another $1 billion per annum was estimated as a requirement of external assistance to support such programmes as seed development, livestock inventory build up, tse-tse fly control in Africa, pig and poultry production facilities, milk, meat and other livestock processing industries. External assistance for stepping up the level of credit flows to farmers, particularly the small farmers, and for development of marketing storage and processing facilities, was estimated at an annual level of about $1.2 billion, of which $200 million would be required for setting up revolving funds for extension of production credit. In addition, $600 million would be required annually for building up research and training facilities.

The requirements of external financial support for these specific programmes add up to a total of $5.3 billion, which comes close to one-half of the identified investments for food production. The requirements for the whole of the agricultural sector would of course be higher. Taking into account the need to concentrate in the short run on investments yielding quick returns and the constraints imposed by the absorptive capacity of the developing countries, the broad requirement for external financial assistance to agriculture, as put forward to the World Food Conference, was

placed at $5–6 billion (in 1972 prices) per year during 1975–80. A significant part of this amount would be needed on concessional terms, although no specific figure was worked out. Private investment and other private flows are not included in this figure.

This estimate, it must be admitted, provides only broad orders of magnitude and further work is necessary to improve on its precision. However, it is the only available global estimate of external financial requirements for the development of food and agriculture in the Third World during the second half of this decade. While the World Food Conference did not set any quantitative target for such assistance the above estimate provided the basis for discussion and received a broad measure of support. Further, the 1975 Conference of FAO, in a resolution (9/75) on the Strategy of International Agricultural Adjustments, agreed to a figure of 'at least US$5 billion annually during the period 1975–80' for transfer to developing countries for investment in agricultural production.[6] The above estimate thus provides the normative frame for assessing the progress so far achieved in increasing the flow of external resources for agricultural development. For the sake of comparison with current prices, it will of course be necessary to adjust it in line with the rate of inflation since 1972. Inflated by the UN Unit Value Index for the export of manufactures,[7] the estimate of $5–6 billion a year in 1972 prices would amount in 1975 prices to $8 to $9.5 billion.

EXTERNAL ASSISTANCE COMMITMENTS SINCE 1973

The requirements for external financial assistance to agriculture, discussed in the last section, are in terms of annual flows of resources to developing countries during the period 1975–80. Assessment of progress in the achievement of this objective requires data on the net flow of resources to agriculture of the type that is brought out and published by the Development Assistance Committee (DAC) of OECD every year. However, there is no sectoral breakdown of the data on resource flows, nor is it feasible to net the gross flows to any sector like agriculture. Under the circumstances the best that can be done is to assess the progress achieved in increasing the commitment of external financial assistance to agriculture since the World Food Conference. This would not, admittedly, present the true picture of resource flows for a number of reasons. There is a time lag between the commitment of assistance and its disbursement. Further, in the project type of assistance – and this accounts for the bulk of the commitments – the disbursement of each commitment is spread over a number of years depending on the project period and the budgetary resources. There is also a problem of comparability of commitment data for different years because of the likely differences in the composition of projects in respect of rate and period of disbursement. However, in spite of these known difficulties, there are no other data to fall back upon. What should always be kept in mind is that the rate of commitment will have to be much higher if the flow or disbursement of external resources is to reach the required level with a time-lag.

The bulk of the development assistance to agriculture, as indeed to other sectors, is provided by countries belonging to the DAC of OECD[8] and by multilateral financing institutions such as the World Bank and the Regional Banks. Of late, OPEC has also emerged as an important source of such assistance, while the socialist countries provide a relatively small amount. External assistance committed to agriculture from these resources are compiled and analyzed by DAC and also studied by FAO.

The data on assistance to agriculture are classified by DAC according to two definitions. The *narrow* definition includes activities directly contributing to the development of agricultural production such as crop and livestock development, fisheries, forestry, irrigation and land development, supply of fertilizers and other inputs, agricultural services and storage. The *broad* definition includes, in addition, agro-industries, rural infrastructure, construction of plants for fertilizers and other inputs and projects for rural, regional and river basin development.[9] The *narrow* definition, though somewhat wider because of the inclusion, e.g. of forestry, comes closer to the components that have gone into the FAO estimate of $5–6 billion of annual assistance requirements.

Table 1 gives the data for 1973–75 on official commitment, from different sources, of external assistance to agriculture in terms of the *broad* definition. It appears that such assistance increased sharply from US$2.34 billion in 1973 to US$5.70 billion in 1975. The rate of increase was as much as 85% in 1974 but came down to 32% in 1975. In constant prices, however, the increase was much less and amounted to 52% in 1974 and 17% in 1975. It is obvious that the food crisis that started in late 1972 did lead to a spurt in the official commitment of external assistance to agriculture in 1974 and continued with some slow-down in 1975.

Around 85% of the total official assistance was committed by DAC member countries and multilateral agencies in 1973 and 1974. But in 1975 their share came down to 77%, as a result of a decline in this year of DAC bilateral assistance. Over this period OPEC countries emerged as an important source of assistance to agriculture with an 18% share in 1975. By far the most important source is constituted by the multilateral agencies comprising the World Bank, the Regional Development Banks in Asia, Africa, Latin America and the Near East, which have accounted for around one-half of the total from all sources. These, along with OPEC countries, have provided the dynamic elements of growth in the commitment of assistance. The surprising development was the decline in DAC bilateral assistance in 1975, the reasons for which are not very clear and will be referred to later.

Table 1 also shows the 'concessional assistance' committed by the important sources. This has been defined, following the OECD classification, to include all grants and those loans that have at least a 25% grant element. Such concessional assistance increased from US$1.67 billion in 1973 to US$3.30 billion in 1975. However, its share in the total decreased steadily and significantly over this period.

The last row of Table 1 gives the value of the external resources committed in 1973–75 in constant 1972 prices. It appears that in spite of a two-and-a-half times increase in 1975 over 1973 in nominal terms, the commitment in 1972 prices was only US$3.54 billion for the whole of the agriculture sector as compared to US$5–6 billion of requirements mentioned earlier for the narrowly defined food production programmes.

Another point worth noting here is that new commitments of external resources increased during this period at a faster pace for agriculture than for the total of all sectors. As a result, the share of agriculture in total commitments has increased sharply. In the case of multilateral and DAC bilateral assistance, the proportion increased from 16.1% in 1973 to 21.6% in 1975, and the figures for the former are much higher. This shows the higher priority accorded to agriculture in the lending programmes of the multilateral agencies. The question as to whether and how far this has been achieved through net additionality or diversion from other sectors is a valid one, but cannot be answered without much further work.

For the purpose of comparison with the estimated requirements for food production increase, data on commitments related to the *narrow* definition of OECD are more appropriate, as has been mentioned earlier. Such data are available for most of the major sources of external financial assistance except for the centrally planned economies and others, and are presented in Table 2, according to both the broad and the narrow definitions. The 'concessional commitments' corresponding to the criterion for Official Development Assistances are shown separately in the table. Broadly speaking, the changes discussed earlier appear to be even more pronounced in the commitment of external resources for the narrower field of food and agriculture, hereafter referred to as food production.

In general, the commitments for food production have increased at a lower rate than those under the broader definition. As a result the share in the latter of the assistance committed under the former has decreased steadily from 84% in 1973 to 64% in 1975. But for the increase in commitments for food production from OPEC countries and the multilateral agencies, there would have been a decline in 1975. Indeed, the surge in the commitment of assistance noticed in 1974 was not sustained in 1975 and perhaps disappeared in 1976.

It has been mentioned early in this paper that the World Food Conference asked for substantial increases in assistance to food and agriculture on soft terms. Progress in this respect can be assessed from the data on the commitment of concessional assistance, given in

Table 1. *Official commitments of external resources to agriculture,*[1] *1973 to 1975* (million US $)

	1973	1974	1975
DAC bilateral sources	881	1,725	1,516
Official development assistance (ODA)	809	1,557	1,485
Other official flows (OOF)	72	168	31
Multilateral agencies[2]	1,142	1,975	2,902
Grants and loans (grant element 25% and over)	725	993	1,056
Loans (grant element under 25%)	417	982	1,846
EEC (ODA)	101	143	94
OPEC bilateral sources	35	336	1,010
ODA	–	166	700
OOF	–	170	310
Centrally planned economies[3]	164	130	150
Others[4]	20	25	30
	2,343	4,334	5,702
At constant (1972) prices:[5]	(1,986)	(3,031)	(3,542)

Source: OECD and FAO estimates: presented in FAO, *State of Food and Agriculture* (1976) and updated.

Notes:

1. *Broad definition,* covering not only activities directly contributing to the development of food and agricultural production, but also including agro-industries, manufacture of modern means of production (in particular construction of fertilizer plants), rural infrastructure and composite projects of rural, regional and river basin development.

2. IBRD, IDA, IDB, AsDB, AfDB, UNDP.

3. Assumed as 8% of total economic aid commitments to developing countries from Eastern Europe and the USSR, and 15% of such commitments from China.

4. Technical cooperation among developing countries not covered elsewhere, based on very rough estimates.

5. Deflated by the UN Unit Value Index for the Export of Manufactures.

Table 2. These show a lower rate of increase of such assistance during 1973–75 than of total commitments under both the definitions. As a result, the share of concessional commitment progressively declined over this period. The implication is that the terms of lending had hardened rather than softened between 1973 and 1975.

It is not possible to analyze the components of the external resource commitment for different development programmes. Such data are not available except for the DAC bilateral sources. The scattered information that exists indicates that the technical cooperation element has tended to suffer in 1975 and also in 1976 to a large extent because of the financial crisis in UNDP. The assistance for projects of fertilizer and other inputs increased sharply 1974, particularly from DAC bilateral sources,

but has since fluctuated. The major part of the assistance, both under multilateral and bilateral assistance, has been capital assistance for investment projects or for the financing of import of items of machinery and equipment for use in investment schemes.

The actual level of external resources commitment for food production amounted in 1975 to a little over US$3.5 billion which, when deflated by the UN Unit Value Index for the export of manufactures, amounts to US$2.2 billion in 1972 prices. By 1975 the commitment of such assistance had thus reached only 42% of the US$5.3 billion level of flow, mentioned earlier. The actual flow, of course, would be much smaller. In other words, there is a long way to go before the goals discussed in the World Food Conference are achieved, particularly when it is realized that

Table 2. *Official commitments of external resources for agriculture from major sources, 1973–75, according to broad and narrow definitions and by 'concessional' nature*
(million US$)

Source	Broad definition			Narrow definition		
	1973	1974	1975	1973	1974	1975
Total official commitments to agriculture						
DAC bilateral	881	1,725	1,516	802	1,372	1,107
EEC	101	143	94	101	134	94
OPEC bilateral	35	336	1,010	19	103	635
Multilateral agencies	1,142	1,975	2,902	895	1,505	1,713
Total	2,159	4,179	5,522	1,817	3,114	3,549
In constant 1972 prices[1]	1,830	2,922	3,430	1,540	2,178	2,204
Narrow as percentage of broad	–	–	–	84	75	64
'Concessional' commitments to agriculture[2]						
DAC bilateral	809	1,557	1,485	739	1,214	1,088
EEC	101	143	94	101	134	94
OPEC bilateral	35	166	670	19	103	618
Multilateral agencies	725	993	1,056	513	675	617
Total	1,670	2,859	3,305	1,371	2,126	2,417
In constant 1972 prices:[3]	1,415	2,000	2,053	1,162	1,487	1,501
Concessional as percentage of total	77	68	60	75	68	68

Source: OECD and FAO estimates presented in FAO, *State of Food and Agriculture* (1976) and updated.
Notes:
 1. Assuming same proportion as for 1974, 1975.

 2. 'Concessional assistance' defined here to include all grants and loans with a minimum grant element of 25%.

 3. Deflated by the UN Unit Value Index for the Export of Manufactures.

there was no increase in resource commitment to food and agriculture in 1976.

ISSUES FOR FURTHER THOUGHT

This analysis brings out certain developments favouring increased external resource flow to agriculture, which do not appear to have been sustained. Without summarizing all of these, I would refer in conclusion to some pertinent issues that these developments raise.

In the first place, it is evident that there was an upsurge in new commitments of external assistance for food and agricultural development in 1974. This increase continued, though at a slower pace, in 1975, but according to available evidence has now stopped. Secondly, the level of commitment of resources for food production is, in real terms, less than half the requirements of the flow of external assistance discussed by the World Food Conference. The actual flow, for which no data are available, is of course even lower. Thirdly, the terms of lending had been hardening, primarily because of the increasingly larger share of the commitments coming from the lending of the multilateral agencies on commercial terms. The recent agreement on the replenishment of the IDA (World Bank's soft loan window) at a much higher level, may help in reversing the trend. However, much will depend on the level of increase of official development assistance commitments from the bilateral sources.

There are, of course, reasons for these developments, but they are not known. In this situation, the best that can be done is to pose certain questions for consideration by donors as well as by recipients. Is the stagnation or decline in external assistance to agriculture noticeable in 1975/76 due to slackening of the concern that was widespread during the years of the acute food crisis and at the time of the World Food Conference? Could this have been due to the improvement in the world food supplies that has taken place since late 1975? If so, attention deserves to be given to ways and means of keeping up the momentum generated in 1974. Another equally valid question is whether and how much the increasing level of commitment of new assistance to food and agriculture is constrained by the absorptive capacity of the recipient countries, especially with respect to formulation and implementation of projects? Equally relevant is the point often made by bilateral donors that their assistance is determined by the priority of the recipient countries. To the extent this is so, the question arises as to how far the developing countries are attaching priority to increased external assistance for food and agriculture development. There is also a broader question of the distribution of external assistance on a more equitable basis in favour of countries with lower levels of income, which has not been analyzed in this paper but should not be forgotten.

NOTES

1. Resolution I of the Conference, UN, *Report of the World Food Conference* (UN: New York, 1975).

2. FAO, *Provisional Indicative World Plan for Agricultural Development: Summary and Main Conclusions* (Rome: 1970), pp. 63, 64 and Appendix Table V.

3. UN World Food Conference, *The World Food Problem: Proposals for National and International Action* (Rome: 1974), Chapter 8.

4. ibid., p. 28.

5. ibid., p. 132.

6. *Guideline 10* of the Annex to the Resolution, *Report of the Conference of FAO* (Rome: 1975), p. 33 and corrigendum.

7. This is the index used by FAO for inflating/-deflating the external resource flows to agriculture. OECD has developed its own deflator for flows of the DAC countries. See *Development Cooperation: Report of DAC Chairman* (OECD: November 1975), p. 121, for a discussion of deflators.

8. The Development Assistance Committee (DAC) of the Organization for Economic Cooperation and Development (OECD) was formed in 1960 to provide a forum where donors of bilateral assistance to developing countries could consult together and exchange views on common problems. DAC now has 18 members, including EEC.

9. DAC Report, op. cit., pp. 90–91.

World Development, 1977, Vol. 5, Nos. 5–7, pp. 641–649. Pergamon Press. Printed in Great Britain.

The Role of the Developed Countries in World Agricultural Development

A. SIMANTOV*

OECD, Paris

Summary. — Although the food and agricultural problem does not have the same dimension for all developing countries, the author presents an overview of the potential role to be played by developed countries in assisting the agricultural development of developing countries. A number of actions should be taken by developed countries including stabilization of international food supplies, according of better market access and/or export earning guarantees and provision of financial and technical assistance. The allocation and coordination of foreign aid are discussed along with the means of integrating the aid component in a particular country's overall development effort. Also, significantly, the author examines why it is in the short and long-term interest of the developed countries to take positive action with regard to these problems in order to assure a stable and prosperous world economic order in the future.

WHY ARE WE CONCERNED WITH THE AGRICULTURAL AND FOOD PROBLEMS OF DEVELOPING COUNTRIES?

It is important at the outset to say that not all developing countries have a food and agricultural problem. Some of them, especially those which have important sources of income from minerals or oil, can compensate for their inability to produce the food they require through imports. But for a majority of countries, among which are the most densely populated, the increase in agricultural production is necessary for at least two reasons: to ensure better nutrition and better employment possibilities for their growing populations. For several of them, the increase in agricultural production is also a means of acquiring foreign exchange, even if in some cases their agricultural exports could imply the existence of unsatisfied demand for food at home.

By examining in the following paragraphs the nature of the food problem and the bottlenecks which prevent rapid progress, it will be possible to identify the role that the developed countries could play as well as the impact of their action.

The needs of the developing countries are increasing. It is well-known that population is increasing rapidly all over the developing world, and in some regions, in the Near East, Africa and Latin America, it is increasing at more than 3% per annum. It is only after 1985 that

growth rates are likely to stop increasing: until then at least, but also afterwards, population is expected to exercise a very great pressure on available supplies.[1]

The rapid urbanization is another factor in the greater increase of claims on market supplies than in the past. Urbanization is taking place in many developing countries at rates far exceeding those for population growth, so that a rapidly growing number of people are no longer taken care of — even very badly — by farm subsistence sector. Their needs, either effective or real, have to be taken care of by increased market supplies of food; the governments of all developing countries are very sensitive to the needs of this group of people, who are the most vocal in political terms.

The needs of the developing countries are increasing rapidly not only because the number of people is increasing but also because these people are poor. The low *per capita* consumption which prevails at present in most developing countries gives rise to fast increases in consumption whenever *per capita* incomes in-

---

* Mr. Simantov is Director for Agriculture and Food at the Organisation for Economic Co-operation and Development (OECD), Paris. He is responsible for the views expressed in this paper which do not necessarily correspond to those of the organisation to which he belongs. This paper is a revised version of a lecture delivered at Wye College, University of London on 11th November, 1976.

crease, i.e. the income elasticity coefficients for food demand are very high. This question may appear theoretical, as in many countries *per capita* incomes have tended to stagnate in recent years (e.g. Burma and Ghana), and in some cases have even declined (e.g. Bangladesh and Uruguay). But it could also be said that the inability to increase food production more rapidly than before is one of the reasons for the slow growth in *per capita* incomes in the country as a whole.

The growth in demand is likely to become stronger if the developing countries follow more egalitarian income distribution policies. The concentration of wealth and of income in many, if not most, developing countries is a too well-known phenomenon to need to be stressed here. It is generally accepted that a better income distribution pattern has a positive effect on overall growth, including in the long run the agricultural sector itself, but what is important to stress here is the effect of such a policy on food demand. It has been estimated that the growth in food demand resulting from more egalitarian income distribution can exceed, and in some cases by a large margin, the growth in demand resulting from a general growth in incomes[2] and several countries may find it difficult or impossible to finance substantially larger imports of food until domestic agriculture is capable of satisfying these needs. There is every reason to believe that an increasing number of developing countries are going to adopt such a policy, under the pressure of either ideological or political forces.

Against this growing demand, *agricultural production has been lagging behind*. During the past two decades agricultural production has been increasing at rates barely sufficient to cope with the increase in population, and only in a few cases (e.g. Mexico, Bolivia, Togo, Thailand) have domestic supplies been sufficient to ensure a marked improvement in *per capita* food availability. In some years of bad harvests, there have been famine situations such as recently in the Sahel or Ethiopia, as the level of reserves was, and still is, low or even non-existent.

It is often said that many developing countries do not have an adequate agricultural base or do not pursue the right agricultural policies, but it is also forgotten that in some cases the rates of production increase have been equal to, if not higher than, those experienced in developed countries. Agricultural production seems to be stagnating especially in the face of the rapidly growing requirements.

Is the outlook better or worse? It is difficult to give an answer to this question without noting that the easy sources of production increases have already been used in most countries; these sources include the possibility of extending the arable land at low cost, even at the expense of grasslands; the possibility of reducing the fallow land due to better rotation practices; the utilization of easily exploitable water resources; and a more intensive utilization of labour. This means that future increases in production will need to come primarily from higher yields, i.e. from a higher degree of technological application.

This raises the crucial question of the rapidity with which technology can be applied in agriculture. Economic theory but also experience show that the level of technological application in agriculture is closely related to the technological level of the socio-economic environment, i.e. of the overall economy.[3] It is certainly possible to raise agricultural production and productivity at high rates in limited sectors of a country's agriculture — the Green Revolution is there to prove it — but it is very difficult to obtain such results throughout the agricultural sector without a concomitant development of the industrial and service sectors.

In this connection it is also necessary not to lose sight of the great human, financial and institutional obstacles which hamper rapid expansion and modernization of agriculture in many of these countries.

At this point of the discussion it is important to remember that the farm population accounts for more than two-thirds of total population in developing countries and that *the farm subsistence sector predominates*. Between two-thirds and three-quarters of the farmers live in a subsistence economy. This means that developments — or the lack of developments — in this sector will in the long run have a greater determining effect on the country's economy than the transformation of the manufacturing sector. As said earlier this sector is often forgotten, or at best is thought to react in the same manner as the commercial farm sector. This raises difficult policy choices, to which reference will be made later in the discussion.

The food situation of a country, especially of a developing country, is not characterized only by the growth in demand in relation to that of production, but also by the utilization which is made of potentially available supplies. *Storage and marketing systems are particularly deficient.* It is often said that in some countries a third, or even more, of output is lost, because of inadequate harvesting and storage. The contribution which a reduction of these losses could make in the short run on the food situation of many developing countries far exceeds the contribution which could be obtained from possible increases in production.

But the problem goes beyond the question of avoiding losses: the marketing system is extremely deficient. There are several examples, notably India and in the past China, of famines in parts of a country, while other parts of the same country have an exportable surplus of food. Transportation, storage, and distribution channels are often rudimentary. It is important to keep this fact in mind, because it can set a limit to the possibility of increasing the food supplies obtained from abroad, either commercially or as aid. Port facilities and the whole infrastructure of many countries seem to be developing at rates far below those required by the growth in population and in their food — and non-food — requirements.

To these agricultural factors, it is important to add *the difficulties encountered by a large number of developing countries in the foreign trade sector, including balance-of-payments difficulties.* These difficulties stem from the inability of many of these countries to benefit from their comparative advantage, either present or potential, by increasing their exports of a number of agricultural commodities — and in some cases even by developing such new lines of exports under stable marketing conditions.

There are then the difficulties suffered by a number of developing countries as importers of food: they suffer from the wide price fluctuations in the agricultural markets and being the residual buyers they tend to be priced out of the market as long as the market is ruled by the price mechanism. For the poorest developing countries (i.e. those with less than $200 of income *per capita*), if all their cereal imports had been on a commercial basis in the last two seasons, this would have cost 40% of their total export earnings.

The balance-of-payments difficulties are due to a variety of reasons, which do not need to be discussed here: it will suffice to note that these difficulties reduce the capacity of these countries to import the food they may require and at the same time finance their economic development while maintaining a reasonable level of consumption.

In *summing up*, it is important to recall that the food and agricultural problem does not have the same dimension for all developing countries. For some it is a matter of finding better conditions for their agricultural exports; for others what is important is to be protected against wide fluctuations in the supply condi-

tions of food in the international markets; for others it is how to cope with food emergency situations; for others it is how to accelerate the growth in their food production; for others it is how to deal with the poverty — and lack of adequate nutrition — of large segments of their population in historically short periods of time; for many it is important to reduce the rates of demographic expansion. Many of these problems may affect the same country: it is then that the need for large-scale and far-reaching action becomes necessary.

VARIOUS FORMS OF ASSISTANCE

In the efforts to deal with these situations it is customary to state that foreign help, especially that granted by industrialized countries, is essential. Later on in this discussion reference will be made to the complementary nature of foreign aid and of national self-help. But it is preferable to state first that there are a number of actions which developed countries could — or should — take which can greatly ease the problems of developing countries, and which do not necessitate a large contribution by the latter. These actions concern primarily trade. They could be classified into two categories: measures to stabilize food supplies internationally and measures to allow an increase in agricultural export earnings by developing countries.

The stabilization of food supplies internationally is necessary for the sake also of developed countries, and the efforts made so far to that effect are dictated primarily by the interests of the industrialized countries: developing countries which address themselves to the international market to secure part of their food supplies stand however to gain from an improvement in the situation.

A large number of actions are — or could be — contemplated in this respect: they range from the simple constitution of emergency food reserves, to the negotiation of full-fledged commodity agreements; they take also the form of long-term purchase and sale contracts and could also involve the constitution of large-scale internationally coordinated or administered food stocks.

It is obvious that the interests of developing countries are not automatically taken care of by these actions: for example, the proliferation of bilateral long-term contracts which so far have been concluded only between industrialized countries could exacerbate the fluctuations in the residual market to which developing countries usually have recourse. It should, however, be easy to devise measures which would guarantee developing countries against such adverse effects, for example by guaranteeing the sale of a minimum quantity of grains to developing countries at a pre-determined price, without a full reciprocal obligation to buy. This is the least that developed countries could do either bilaterally or preferably in a multilateral framework: a small effort by them — and by the countries traditionally trading with them — could have a more than proportionate beneficial effect on developing countries, in particular on the poorest. These countries, for example in 1973 and 1974 imported 16 million tons of cereals, but paid about $1 billion in 1973 and $2.3 billion in 1974. It is for this reason that the attempts to stabilize international markets come also under the heading of world food security.

The only difficulty which may arise — although this seems at present a theoretical possibility — is that food supplies could be assured in international markets for periods of a few years at prices which are so low that they may tempt some developing countries to import larger quantities of food at the expense of their present agricultural production or of the effort needed to develop their domestic production. As said above this is a theoretical possibility, but it should not be discarded for the future.

Before turning to the question of better market access, it is worth stressing the significance of an adequate stocks policy. Very important discussions and negotiations are at present under way in several organizations and particularly in the International Wheat Council, the GATT and the World Food Council. Proposals vary considerably, but all recognize that the difficulties which have occurred in recent years on the cereal (and soya bean) markets are largely the result of a very low level of stocks, while during the 1960s, stocks usually were of sufficient volume to compensate largely for variations in supply and demand. Several formulae are at present under discussion: national stocks exclusively, or an international reserve as an addition to national stocks; stocks considered exclusively as reserves for meeting emergency situations, or as a market regulating instrument to be integrated in general market organisation systems, etc. Whatever the policy options which may be adopted in the last analysis, the means of implementing them or the negotiating bodies, it is essential that rapid progress be made in this field because a well-managed and coordinated stocks and reserve policy serves the interests of both developed and developing countries.

Better market access and/or export earning guarantees are another method of helping developing countries. Sales of agricultural products to industrialized countries provide about 30% of developing countries' export earnings from those markets. Contrary to what was said earlier about the action to moderate excessive fluctuations in international markets, securing for developing countries' agricultural exports better access to the markets of industrialized countries is — or would be — of primary benefit to developing countries; the industrialized countries might also benefit from potential increased purchases by developing countries thus made possible by this action. But this action by the industrialized countries does not require a complementary or simultaneous action by the beneficiary developing country, except probably to provide an assurance as to access to their supplies and to make sure that domestic policies do not prevent the country from taking advantage of this newly offered possibility. The developed countries could not invoke the argument of the absence of adequate policies by developing countries for not providing this type of assistance. The only difficulty would arise from the opposition of their own agricultural sector, which would consider that the additional imports from low-cost producers is an unjustified threat to their interests.

Several products could fall in this category: various types of meat, various fruits and vegetables, vegetable oils, sugar. Special mention should be made of the processed agricultural products because of their positive effects on the industrialization of these countries and because they provide a higher value added. It is often said that relatively few developing countries can benefit today from such an action, although the disruptive effect on the domestic market of developed countries could be large. It is however forgotten that there are many developing countries which could develop this export-oriented sector if they were given adequate long-term guarantees by the industrialized countries and if they were assisted financially and technically whenever such assistance was necessary. There are several examples in the field of processed fruit and vegetables and also of bananas of actions by multinational enterprises which show how rapidly and efficiently these new forms of production could be developed if the industrialized countries provide the markets. It should be possible to devise appropriate measures to provide compensatory adjustment to those producers in developed countries who might be unduly affected. It is often forgotten that the quantities thus imported will always be marginal compared with the total volume of production and consumption in industrialized countries.

Another argument which is also put forward against this form of assistance, is that it provides undue help to some countries only and that, within these countries, it helps an export-oriented sector which is relatively well-developed and which operates almost in isolation from the rest of the agricultural sector, especially the subsistence sector. It is also argued that this form of assistance can help perpetuate the dual-type economy which characterizes the developing countries. Some of these arguments are valid, but their effects could be minimized if the assistance in the trade field was only one form of assistance — other countries benefiting from financial or technical assistance for example — and if sufficient stimuli were given to the export-oriented agricultural sector of the beneficiary country to produce food for the domestic market if this line of production was more important to their economy. The overall beneficial results could be maximized and the possible limitations minimized, if this type of assistance was decided on and implemented in a multilateral framework. The Lomé Convention which provides a greater degree of access to European Community markets for some commodities exported by a number of developing countries and some stabilization of their export earnings, is a good example in this respect. But absence of such a multilateral framework should not be an excuse for not initiating or further developing programmes in this area.

Developing countries, exporters of agricultural products and particularly of temperate zone foods, need to be guaranteed in several respects. The need to reduce fluctuations and uncertainties in international markets has already been stressed above: a developing exporting country cannot face sharp price fluctuations especially for commodities which have long production cycles. Either price fluctuations are smoothed through appropriate arrangements or compensatory financing of export fluctuations becomes necessary. Consideration of the problems for a number of agricultural commodities, e.g. sugar, cotton, jute, tropical beverages, is being given at present by the UNCTAD integrated programme for commodities in the framework of the negotiations decided upon by the Nairobi Conference earlier this year. For other commodities, like grains, livestock products and oilseeds, the Multilateral Trade Negotiations in the GATT should provide an opportunity for improving the position of developing countries.

It is in the provision of financial and technical assistance destined to increase agricultural production that most questions arise. Contrary to what was said so far the foreign financial assistance requires, to be effective, a corresponding effort by the beneficiary country. It is often argued that the role of foreign assistance is always marginal compared to the development efforts which a country must undertake. This argument is certainly true, as long as foreign financial aid remains at levels close to those experienced at present. (In 1974 and 1975 official development assistance represented respectively 0.33 and 0.36% of GNP in developed countries with a market economy and 2.6 and 2.9% of GNP in OPEC countries.) The argument could also be invoked — with certain justification — even if the volume of assistance was substantially increased. The reason behind this argument is the recognition that the most important factors limiting the growth in agricultural production are not the lack of foreign resources but the lack of determination by developing countries to develop their agriculture and when this determination exists the difficulty of translating it into effective political, economic and agricultural policies.

To note these facts is not to say that there is no need to provide financial assistance to developing countries for the purpose of increasing food production, nor to say that it might be undesirable to increase this form of assistance if it is not matched by adequate policies by the beneficiary country. The flow of foreign financial assistance to the agricultural sector, though increasing, is so low — about $3.7 billion in 1974 or $2.00 *per capita* in developing countries excluding China — that we are far from having reached the limit of either the donating capacity of industrialized countries or the absorptive capacity of developing countries.

It is important, however, to stress these facts in order to avoid creating the impression that foreign aid is a substitute for self-help efforts or that self-help policies cannot be envisaged in the absence of foreign financial assistance. This dual impression can be a source of real danger to developing countries: it is important to avoid a situation where foreign aid, no matter what its size, reduces the need for adequate domestic policies, because unless such policies are developed the conditions for sustained growth — economic and social — will not be created. It is also important to avoid a situation in which the absence of adequate foreign aid should create a demobilizing spirit of despair in the developing countries. Examples are there to show how a country without access to substantial aid can successfully develop its economy (notably China), but examples are also available to show how foreign aid can help to accelerate the rate of economic and social progress (South Korea, Malaysia, Ivory Coast).

If a developing country has the determination to develop its agriculture, it should be possible to successfully integrate the foreign aid component in the overall effort; it might also be possible to attribute to foreign aid a high marginal value, and in some cases this aid can serve as a catalyst for far-reaching domestic policies. It is because of this potential role that foreign aid should be made available in the amounts required and under the proper conditions (long-term programming, appropriate balance between grants and loans, etc.), and geared also to the absorptive capacity of the beneficiary country. If it should be higher than the absorptive capacity would justify — a theoretical case at present — the danger may arise of its misuse and of a possible negative effect on the long-term sustainable growth of the economy.

ALLOCATION AND COORDINATION OF FOREIGN AID

As the volume of foreign financial and technical aid is limited compared to the requirements, the question arises as to its coordination, allocation and use. There is on the one hand the problem of coordination of aid so as to increase its overall effectiveness and there is on the other hand the problem of its allocation among countries as well as of its use within a beneficiary country.

The positive response of the international community to the urgent problems of development has led to the emergence of new donors and the creation of new institutions dispensing technical and financial assistance. This growing multiplicity of aid donors combined with the search for new aid relationships raises new problems for international *aid coordination.*[4] Despite the desire to channel an increasing percentage of overall aid through multilateral institutions, the fact remains that most aid provided by the industrialized countries and also by the OPEC countries is administered by regional or bilateral agencies. It becomes evident that rationalization of fragmented channels of development cooperation can improve

the effectiveness of the 'multilateral—bilateral' system, but neither developing nations nor donors seem to be prepared to see a supranational agency emerge for the administration of development assistance.

In the case of *allocation among countries* the following considerations are appropriate. If the real problem is to increase food production, should the volume and efficiency of aid be primarily aimed at maximizing production in the short run, thus favouring those countries which are probably better off than others? If the intent is to enable developing countries to participate more than in the past in the international division of labour, should aid be given in the first place to those countries with a production potential capable of increasing their exports (agricultural or not) with a view to covering their food import requirements? If, on the contrary, the purpose of aid is to favour the poorest countries, should aid donors place a slightly lower priority on the efficiency of aid? If, finally, the purpose of foreign assistance is to stimulate self-sustained growth in the longer run, it might become important to consider whether the recipient country gives a clear priority to the development of agriculture. But this course of action might mean interfering with the definition of domestic policies: a course of action difficult to follow unless it were applied with a collective consensus of the developing countries themselves.

The provision of aid is to a large extent a tool of foreign policy of the donor countries, especially for the larger countries, and it is realistic to expect that this will remain so. It would however be desirable to associate the developing countries as a group in the discussion of the allocation of aid and of its use, to make them bear an increasing responsibility in this field. Inevitably such a course of action would have beneficial effects on the formulation of more rational policies.

Similar questions arise when deciding about *the use of the assistance within a country,* i.e. whether to assist the modern agricultural sector or the one capable of rapid modernization or whether to assist the subsistence sector which occupies the bulk of the population. With an economic structure essentially based on traditional agriculture and lacking the financial resources needed for rapid development, many developing countries are faced with a difficult choice:

— either to produce as much as possible as fast as possible, to satisfy the demand of the rapidly growing urban population, concentrating on the most modern sector of agriculture.

In this case, the mass of the peasant population would be neglected, its diet would remain at the same inadequate level, and its potential contribution to overall economic development would not be utilized;

— or to try to raise productivity in subsistence agriculture, to improve the food situation for the great mass of the rural population. The food needs of the urban centres would then have to be met by mounting imports; yet the slender foreign exchange resources are insufficient to cover both the food requirements of the urban areas and capital investment needs.

It might be possible to solve this dilemma by developing a balanced strategy whereby progress in the advanced sector would have a stimulating effect on the traditional sector. Past attempts to achieve integrated development of the rural economy have not always been successful but current efforts, in particular by the World Bank, deserve attention. In any event, the aim should be to ensure that the increase in agricultural production exceeds the increase in population, not merely to prevent any deterioration in the present food situation, but to bring about some improvement.

To sum up, the answers which will be given to these sets of questions by both industrialized and developing countries will determine the course of events for a number of years. These answers will reflect the priorities attached to the solution of one problem as against the solution of another: in simple terms, they will reflect the balance of power and of interest at any given point in time. Consideration of short-term questions and the necessity for many governments, be they aid donors or recipients, to obtain rapid political successes, may retard the implementation of more basic policies upon which the long-term development of agriculture — and of the entire economy — rests.

EXAMPLES OF LIKELY ACTIONS

The aid programmes can cover a whole range of actions: water and land development, mechanization, institution building, price and credit policy, research, education, processing and distribution, production of inputs.[5] In the context of this discussion two actions merit particular attention because of their impact: education and food aid. The first is a long-term, persistent and basic requirement; the second is by definition a short-term, emergency and temporary but equally necessary action.

As regards *the role of education* it is sufficient to say that a high level of sustained growth has always occurred in countries with an adequate level of general and vocational education. One could argue about the cause and effect relationship between development and education, but it has to be noted that they are concomitant. For my part I consider that education is a prerequisite for social and economic development. Educational development was considered so far to be a rather slow process, but should it be so? I doubt it. There are examples — admittedly few — which prove the contrary; they also prove that a higher degree of education, though necessary for promoting economic growth, cannot be prevented from promoting social growth too. Not many countries today, either donors or recipients, seem to be prepared to face this consequence because they are afraid that this development might be too rapid and not gradual. But should it be so?

As regards *food aid,* it is important to stress that the 'food-aid—disposal-of-surpluses' of the 1960s belongs to the past and may never recur on the same scale as before. The suspension by the United States, in particular, of the policy of agricultural subsidies and stockpiling, will induce agricultural producers in that country, as is already the case in Canada and Australia not to step up production or sales beyond what the market can absorb at what they consider reasonable prices. As regards Western Europe, it is still too early to say whether it will enter upon a phase of deliberate over-production entailing large-scale food aid programmes.

Food aid, however, might prove necessary during fairly long transitional periods, and to cope with such a necessity food production for aid purposes should be programmed in all industrialized countries or countries with a high agricultural potential, as is already the case for some of them. This is not the place to enter into a detailed discussion of such a form of production, or to consider the problems of financing and utilization it will involve. It is, however, already possible to lay down certain principles.

For example, all the rich countries, i.e. all countries which have passed a certain level of economic development, whether they are exporters or importers of foodstuffs, should set aside for food aid programmes an agreed percentage of their food production: in particular, of cereals and milk powder. These percentages would depend on the estimated requirements which could not be satisfied through commercial channels.[6] The big question which will arise in this connection is to decide how to allocate available supplies between affluent purchasers and the hungry world. The quantities concerned would be transferred to a multilateral agency administered by all donor and receiving countries. Another feature of the scheme should consist in giving developing countries which are exporters of foodstuffs the possibility of increasing their exports to other developing countries by instituting a special fund for the purpose.

The essential aim should be to integrate in one and the same mechanism production growth, food aid and expansion of exports from developing countries, while taking steps to ensure that as the countries attain a certain level of economic development, food aid should give way to trade. It is justified to encourage the institution of ambitious food aid programmes at present but they should be progressively eliminated within a certain time.

THE RESPONSIBILITY OF THE INDUSTRIALIZED WORLD

The responsibility of aid donor countries is great, whether they provide a low or a high level of assistance, because of the implications of their action — or lack of action — on the future of the world. The pattern of development in general, and of agricultural development in particular, does not need to follow the pattern used in industrialized countries — in some cases it is essential indeed that it does not — but aid policies, if generous, can have a determining effect on the basic choices that developing countries are bound to make.

The interest of industrialized countries does not lie in the moral satisfaction of having assisted people in need; but there is a selfish justification in such an action.

As I have said on another occasion,[7] the industrialized liberal economy countries have managed, with varying degrees of success, to promote a society where man's demands — economic, social or political — have been taken into consideration and progressively satisfied. Under the impact of the incessant struggle waged by the working classes over the last century, the industrial society has come to realize that a better distribution of income and the better economic and social integration of the citizens of a given country, represent in themselves a decisive factor of general and individual economic growth.

The fear of growing pauperization has not been fulfilled, due to this capacity for adaptation of the liberal economy, but that fear is in danger of being confirmed on the international scene, when we consider the tragic situation in certain countries. Would it be Utopian to try to convince the populations of the rich countries that it is in their best economic interest to help to avoid this schism in the world? It is hard to admit the possibility of adding indefinitely to one's own wealth in an increasingly destitute world.

In the short term, increased development aid of every kind, financial, commercial, economic, might perhaps reduce somewhat the rise of individual incomes in the rich countries. Provided that such an eventuality did not set up grave social stresses which might compromise economic growth and the very power to provide aid, such a step would afford the best guarantee that two billion people at present and four billion by the end of the century will be able to enter the world economic system, to the benefit of all. Whereas any aggravation of the present situation, or even its maintenance, may in time result in the collapse of many markets, especially agricultural markets, and the break-up of the world economic order.

Such a step would give greater moral weight to demands from the liberal industrial societies for urgent reforms in the developing countries, starting with birth control. Does not the moral, humanist attitude coincide with the general economic interest, even if at times setbacks in the process of economic development, or the narrow-minded, selfish interests of certain groups, may raise some doubt even in the minds of those most favourably disposed to international aid?

The responsibility is not only for developed countries with a market economy, but for the centrally-planned countries too, and for the newly-rich oil exporters. Some of the oil exporters have already displayed a strong desire to help developing countries solve their food and agricultural problems, but the effort made so far by the international community is far too small compared with the magnitude of the task.

If the world is not capable of resolving the food problem by coordinated action, how can it face all the other dangers which threaten it: inflation, pollution, exhaustion of resources, the arms race, the moral crisis? To find the way to attenuate and if possible resolve the world food crisis would enable our societies to surmount their feeling of powerlessness, and serve to assure them that their institutions are capable of resolving the grave problems which are gathering on the horizon.

NOTES

1. For a full discussion of world trends in food supply and demand in the next 10 to 15 years see OECD, *Study of Trends in World Supply and Demand of Major Agricultural Commodities* (Paris: 1976).

2. A. Simantov, 'Food and feed: future needs', in *Agriculture in the Whirlpool of Change* (University of Guelph, 1974).

3. A. Simantov, 'The dynamics of growth and agriculture', *Zeitschrift für Nationalökonomie,* Vol. XXVII, No. 3 (1967).

4. For a full discussion of this question see the 1976 Annual Report by the Chairman of the Development Assistance Committee (DAC) of the OECD.

5. In 1974 the major components of foreign aid allocations were as follows: Land and Water Development, 914 million dollars; Construction of fertilizer plants, 352; Agro-industries, 304; Supply of fertilizers, 338; Integrated rural development, 178; Improvement of crops, livestock and fisheries, 314; Agricultural services, banks, storage, 215; Technical assistance, 367.

6. The target of 10 million tons of cereals for food aid established by the World Food Conference could be met by using slightly more than 2% of the cereals grown in North America, Oceania, Western Europe and Japan.

7. Address to the Académie d'Agriculture de France (May 1974).

World Development, 1977, Vol. 5, Nos. 5–7, pp. 651–660. Pergamon Press. Printed in Great Britain.

The World Food Situation and Collective Self-Reliance

SARTAJ AZIZ*

United Nations World Food Council

Summary. — The potential insecurity which developing countries may face in meeting their food requirements can be minimized by 'collective self-reliance' among them. The author cites import requirements and instability of production as two main reasons for the vulnerability of developing countries in the context of world food markets. Developing countries have, in some international fora, demonstrated the political will necessary to work towards collective self-reliance and based on this, several specific proposals are made in the sphere of food reserves and grain trade.

Recent developments on the food front are both encouraging as well as disquieting. As a result of failures of crops, rocketing food prices and the emergence of famines in several regions of the world in the early 1970s, food has become a politically live issue both within developed and developing countries. There is an increasing public concern regarding the growing disparities in food consumption levels between countries as well as within countries between rich and poorer people. Despite unprecedented increments in agricultural production in many developing countries, such disparities have further widened, and even though one may question the accuracy of various estimates of under- and malnourished people, it may be difficult to contest the fact that the number has gone up. It is also incontrovertible that the dependence of the developing countries on food imports has significantly increased as a result of increasing population, rising incomes and changing food habits. This in itself may not be a bad thing; after all, most developed countries of Europe (excluding France) and Japan, both in absolute as well as relative terms, import much more than even the most populous developing countries like China and India. But most developing countries do not have the resources or the export potential to sustain growing dependence on food imports, and the political implications of such dependence cannot be ignored.

A more disquieting fact has been the recent tendency of the richer countries to enter into long-term contracts between themselves, which has already pre-empted a sizeable portion of annual grain trade. The typical examples are the US and Japanese long-term agreement, or the grain deal between the US and the USSR. The inevitable result of such deals would be to further narrow the world market in grains, which is already small because of the protective policies of some of the richer countries. Under the circumstances, any fluctuation in world output in grains, as was experienced in the early 1970s, will introduce a much greater degree of volatility in the market. The poorer countries with a lack of adequate foreign exchange will naturally be least prepared to compete for scarce supplies in such a situation.

The developing countries in coming years thus face two interrelated problems: (1) how to increase their domestic output to keep their imports at a reasonably low level, and (2) to safeguard their interests in the face of fluctuations in domestic as well as international demand and supply of grains. Obviously, in both cases, they will need the support and cooperation of the richer countries — both developed and developing — but the potential insecurity that they face in meeting their food requirements can be minimized by 'collective self-reliance' among the developing countries.

* The author is Deputy Executive Director of the United Nations World Food Council, Rome, and Executive Secretary of the Preparatory Commission for the International Fund for Agricultural Development. The views expressed in this article reflect his personal opinions.

Before some concrete ideas on the subject are discussed it may be worthwhile to assess the magnitude of the problem facing the developing countries.

IMPORT REQUIREMENTS OF DEVELOPING COUNTRIES

Any estimation of import requirements must rely on projections of domestic demand and supply and these at best represent a statistical exercise. Both because of the limitations of the methodology and the data available such exercises cannot be more than broad approximations. As is well-known, because of the difficulties in assessing likely political and social situations and future price trends, most demand projections take into account mainly population and income growth. In simple projection exercises these two are often treated as exogenously determined and independent of each other. Similarly, on the supply side, it is only the quantifiable variables that are taken into consideration. No attempt is made to include political and sociological variables in a model, even though one would accept, particularly after the Chinese example, that sociological variables do have a significant influence on agricultural production. All this suggests that demand and supply projections have to be used with a great deal of caution essentially as broad indications of likely trends. Such trends can be modified significantly by political actions of the countries concerned.

The projected demand for cereals, wheat, rice and coarse grains for years 1980, 1990 and 2000 are presented in Tables 1 to 4.[1] The main conclusions that can be drawn from these projections are summarized below:

(a) In the developed countries total demand for cereals is likely to increase over the 30-year period by 72% or 1.8% per annum, from 387 million tons to 665 million tons, but the demand for coarse grains is expected to increase by about 90%, from 275 million tons to 520 million tons. In fact about 80% of the total projected increase in the demand for cereals in the developed countries is attributable to feed uses of grains.

(b) In the developing countries the total demand for cereals could, however, increase from 387 million tons to 1,015 million tons, or by 162%, if the underlying assumptions turn out to be realistic. This will imply an annual average increase of 3.3% for the 30-year period for

cereals. (The average increase will be somewhat higher if non-cereal foods were to be included.)

(c) In the centrally-planned economies consisting mainly of Eastern Europe, USSR and China, the demand for cereals is likely to increase at the slowest rate — about 70% over 30 years (or 1.8% per annum) — despite an increase of 128% in the demand for feeds. This is because the average population growth rate in China and some other centrally-planned Asian countries in this group is much slower than that in other developing countries and the proportion of grain fed to livestock in the USSR and Eastern Europe will be a somewhat smaller proportion of total consumption than in the capitalist developed countries, increasing from 50% in 1970 to 59% in the year 2000 against 73% in the capitalist developed countries.

(d) If the current consumption trends were to continue, *per capita* consumption in developed countries would increase from about 3,000 calories to 3,242 calories and protein consumption from 95 to 100 grams (see Table 5). Such increments could certainly be categorized as further 'over-consumption'. In the developing countries the average increase in consumption from 2,211 calories to 2,615 calories will be unevenly distributed between different regions, but would provide a welcome improvement if it can be achieved. It is also clear that except for the middle-income developing countries, the demand for cereals for direct consumption will not decline appreciably.

Factors which are likely to affect the supply of food in the future are much more uncertain and unpredictable, and include the physical resource base, availability of financial resources, technological progress, access to internal and international markets, and social and institutional factors. It is clear, however, that the projected increase of less than 2% per annum in the demand for cereals in the capitalist developed countries and the centrally-planned economies is lower than the average increase these two groups of countries have achieved in the preceding two decades (see Table 6). It is therefore reasonable to assume that despite some years of bad harvest, these groups of countries will be able to increase their production of cereals to meet their own long-term demand. The developed exporting countries

Table 1. *Developed market economies: demand for cereals 1970 actual, 1980, 1990 and 2000 projected*
(million tons)

	1970			1980			1990			2000		
	Food	Feed	Total*	Food	Feed	Total*	Food	Feed	Total*	Food	Feed	Total*
Wheat												
North America	15.7	8.1	26.1	16.1	9.6	28.0	16.9	11.3	30.8	16.5	13.4	32.8
Western Europe	37.4	14.2	55.9	36.2	18.3	59.2	34.6	22.1	61.6	41.0	26.7	73.7
Oceania	1.5	0.9	2.9	1.8	1.1	3.4	2.0	1.4	4.0	2.2	1.7	4.5
Others	5.5	0.7	6.7	6.6	1.1	8.5	7.8	1.3	10.1	8.9	1.6	11.6
Total	60.1	23.9	91.7	60.7	30.1	99.2	61.4	36.2	106.5	68.6	43.5	122.7
Coarse grains												
North America	3.7	140.3	157.4	4.0	169.9	192.6	4.3	206.5	233.6	4.2	251.0	282.9
Western Europe	4.9	79.4	99.0	4.7	105.0	129.0	4.4	127.1	154.9	4.5	154.0	186.8
Oceania	0.1	1.7	2.6	0.1	2.5	3.7	0.1	3.2	4.7	0.1	4.2	6.0
Others	3.3	10.9	16.4	3.9	17.3	24.7	4.6	23.3	33.1	5.0	31.5	44.3
Total	12.0	232.2	275.4	12.7	294.7	350.0	13.5	360.2	426.3	14.0	440.6	519.9
Rice												
North America	1.0	0.4	1.5	1.2	0.4	1.7	1.4	0.4	1.9	1.5	0.5	2.1
Western Europe	1.4	0.0	1.6	1.6	0.1	1.8	1.8	0.1	2.0	1.9	0.1	2.2
Oceania	0.1	–	0.1	0.1	–	0.1	0.1	–	0.1	0.1	–	0.1
Others	14.3	0.8	16.4	14.9	1.0	17.2	14.7	1.1	17.2	15.2	1.4	18.0
Total	16.8	1.2	19.6	17.7	1.4	20.8	17.9	1.7	21.2	18.7	1.9	22.4

*Includes other uses.
The totals do not necessarily add up due to rounding.

Table 2. *Developing market economies: demand for cereals 1970 actual, 1980, 1990 and 2000 projected* (million tons)

	1970			1980			1990			2000		
	Food	Feed	Total*	Food	Feed	Total*	Food	Feed	Total*	Food	Feed	Total*
Wheat												
Africa	6.5	–	7.2	9.3	–	10.5	13.1	–	14.6	22.2	–	24.2
Latin America	14.0	0.5	16.1	19.3	0.8	22.2	26.5	1.2	30.6	34.3	1.8	40.0
Near East	20.1	2.0	27.9	25.2	3.5	35.8	30.0	6.4	44.9	38.1	11.7	59.9
Far East	31.9	0.4	36.2	45.0	0.4	50.3	64.2	0.8	72.1	84.6	1.5	96.3
Total	72.7	2.9	87.6	98.9	4.7	119.0	134.1	8.4	162.4	179.6	14.9	220.9
Coarse grains												
Africa	26.8	1.3	33.0	35.8	4.0	45.9	48.9	7.2	65.0	65.9	13.0	91.7
Latin America	12.3	20.3	38.5	15.6	31.6	55.9	19.7	48.9	80.6	24.4	75.6	116.8
Near East	7.3	7.6	17.4	9.1	13.2	26.2	11.3	23.8	41.1	14.4	42.7	66.6
Far East	32.2	2.4	38.9	40.9	5.2	51.4	51.2	9.5	67.7	59.9	17.4	86.5
Total	78.7	31.5	128.1	101.6	53.9	179.6	131.4	89.3	254.6	165.0	148.8	361.9
Rice												
Africa	5.0	0.1	5.7	7.2	0.1	8.2	11.2	0.3	12.9	17.1	0.5	19.8
Latin America	9.8	0.0	11.3	13.2	0.1	15.1	17.0	0.1	19.6	22.3	0.1	25.6
Near East	4.1	–	4.4	6.2	–	6.7	9.3	–	10.0	12.2	–	13.2
Far East	132.9	1.0	150.2	181.5	2.1	206.0	243.3	3.9	277.3	312.3	7.3	360.1
Total	152.2	1.2	172.0	208.6	2.3	236.5	281.5	4.2	320.4	378.2	7.9	433.1

*Includes other uses.
The totals do not necessarily add up due to rounding.

Table 3. *Centrally-planned economies: demand for cereals 1970 actual, 1980, 1990 and 2000 projected*
(million tons)

	1970			1980			1990			2000		
	Food	Feed	Total*	Food	Feed	Total*	Food	Feed	Total*	Food	Feed	Total*
Wheat												
Asian centrally planned economies	30.3	5.5	40.2	40.1	11.1	58.0	52.3	17.6	78.5	65.9	27.9	104.8
USSR and Eastern Europe	52.6	37.1	113.1	53.5	47.7	127.6	55.3	56.3	142.4	54.7	66.3	153.0
Total	83.0	42.6	153.2	93.6	58.8	185.6	107.5	73.8	220.9	120.6	94.2	257.8
Coarse grains												
Asian centrally planned economies	34.8	7.6	47.2	42.8	23.2	72.1	51.2	36.9	97.1	58.3	58.6	130.0
USSR and Eastern Europe	17.3	77.1	115.3	15.6	94.0	132.1	12.9	111.4	149.1	15.4	132.0	174.8
Total	52.2	84.7	162.5	58.4	117.2	204.2	64.1	148.3	246.2	73.7	190.6	304.8
Rice												
Asian centrally planned economies	99.0	2.2	116.5	117.6	4.4	139.6	121.8	6.9	147.6	142.2	10.8	173.2
USSR and Eastern Europe	2.1	0.0	2.3	2.8	0.0	3.2	3.7	0.0	4.1	4.4	0.0	5.0
Total	101.1	2.2	118.9	120.4	4.5	142.8	125.5	6.9	151.7	146.6	10.8	178.1

*Includes other uses
The totals do not necessarily add up due to rounding.

Table 4. *World: demand for cereals 1970 actual, 1980, 1990 and 2000 projected* (million tons)

	1970			1980			1990			2000		
	Food	Feed	Total*	Food	Feed	Total*	Food	Feed	Total*	Food	Feed	Total*
Wheat	215.7	69.4	332.5	253.2	93.7	403.7	303.0	118.4	489.8	368.8	152.6	601.3
Coarse grains	142.8	348.4	566.0	172.8	465.8	733.7	209.0	597.8	927.1	252.8	780.1	1186.6
Rice	270.0	4.6	310.5	346.7	8.2	400.1	424.8	12.8	493.4	543.5	20.6	633.6

*Includes other uses.

Table 5. *Per capita demand for cereals*

	1970				1980				1990				2000			
	P	C	Pr	FV	P	C	Pr	FV	P	C	Pr	FV	P	C	Pr	FV
Developed market economies	724.4	3091	95.0	100.0	792.4	3146	97.3	104.81	861.0	3232	101.1	111.45	923.3	3242	100.7	114.30
North America	226.3	3318	105.5	100.0	248.7	3354	106.7	102.78	275.0	3409	109.3	106.29	296.0	3342	108.2	107.77
Western Europe	353.9	3133	93.7	100.0	375.2	3206	96.9	106.85	395.6	3311	101.5	115.77	414.5	3377	106.6	120.08
Oceania	15.4	3261	108.1	100.0	18.4	3287	109.4	102.85	21.5	3335	111.7	107.51	24.3	3368	112.8	109.12
Other developed	128.8	2554	79.1	100.0	150.0	2636	81.6	107.56	168.9	2745	85.4	118.05	188.4	2772	88.8	123.21
Developing market economies	1754.7	2211	56.1	100.0	2291.2	2333	59.4	108.33	2996.7	2481	63.7	119.90	3692.6	2615	67.4	127.67
Africa	279.2	2188	58.4	100.0	368.0	2273	61.7	108.11	497.7	2413	67.0	122.57	654.9	2476	68.9	128.09
Latin America	284.2	2528	65.0	100.0	373.8	2660	69.0	107.94	488.9	2795	73.4	117.37	619.9	2875	75.6	122.06
Near East	170.7	2495	69.3	100.0	226.7	2611	72.8	111.46	303.2	2682	75.8	123.46	380.4	2765	78.1	129.17
Far East	1016.5	2082	50.7	100.0	1317.4	2208	53.8	107.51	1699.9	2375	57.8	119.04	2029.1	2553	62.4	129.06
Centrally-planned economies	1142.0	2506	72.2	100.0	1317.4	2608	75.7	109.81	1488.2	2708	79.9	123.98	1637.4	2764	82.0	128.39
Asia c.p.e.	794.1	2174	60.4	100.0	936.3	2339	65.6	115.00	1071.8	2473	70.8	135.25	1196.6	2574	73.8	142.24
USSR and Eastern Europe	347.9	3265	99.3	100.0	381.1	3268	100.5	107.80	416.3	3312	103.3	118.12	440.8	3279	104.3	122.34
World	3621.0	2480	69.0	100.0	4401.0	2562	71.1	103.76	5345.9	2665	74.2	109.96	6253.3	2746	76.1	111.75

P – Population (millions)
C – Calories (per day)
Pr – Proteins (grams per day)
FV – Farm Value (index, 1970=100)

Table 6. *Rates of growth of food production 1952 to 1975*
(% per year)

	1952–62		1962–70		1971–75	
	Total	*Per capita*	Total	*Per capita*	Total	*Per capita*
Developed market economies	2.5	1.3	2.3	1.3	1.9	1.0
Western Europe	2.9	2.1	2.2	1.4	2.0	1.4
North America	1.9	0.1	2.2	1.0	1.7	0.8
Oceania	3.1	0.9	2.9	1.2	2.9	1.3
Eastern Europe and USSR	4.5	3.0	4.3	3.3	2.3	1.5
Total developed countries	3.1	1.8	2.9	1.9	2.0	1.1
Developing market economies	3.1	0.7	2.8	0.2	2.5	−0.2
Africa	2.2	–	2.5	–	0.7	−2.0
Far East	3.1	0.8	2.8	0.3	2.8	0.3
Latin America	3.2	0.4	3.1	0.2	2.5	−0.3
Near East	3.4	0.8	3.2	0.4	3.8	0.8
Asian centrally-planned economies	3.2	1.4	2.7	0.9	2.4	0.7
Total developing countries	3.1	0.7	2.9	0.5	2.5	0.1
World	3.1	1.1	2.9	0.9	2.2	0.3

Source: FAO

could also produce a sizeable surplus to meet the commercial demand for cereals from other countries and a marginal quantity for concessional sales to developing countries.

The projected increase of 3.3% in the demand for cereals in the developing countries is, however, considerably higher than the average increase of 2.8% in production attained by these countries in the past two decades, and 2.5% in the past five years (1970–75). The average increase of the past two decades is quite remarkable and is faster than that achieved by the developed countries. But the bulk of it was eaten up by unprecedented population growth. *The key question in the food debate is therefore whether the developing countries as a group can produce over the next 25 years an additional 600 million tons of cereals (or 550 million tons if the lower demand projections are used) over and above their current production of about 400 million tons?*

The commitment of the international community at the World Food Conference, held in November 1974, to abolish hunger and malnutrition within a decade, is based on the optimistic prospect of increasing food production in the developing countries at an annual rate of about 4% per annum. The World Food Council has already begun work on the concrete implications of this goal in terms of requirements for investment and inputs and by identifying a group of food priority countries whose food problem is more serious or whose production potential is significant, to allow adequate concentration of efforts on these countries. But there is no assurance so far that adequate financial and policy support will be forthcoming for the attainment of this goal.

If these efforts succeed only in maintaining the average annual growth of 2.8% attained in the past 20 years, the food gap of developing countries will increase to 85 million tons by 1985. This is a trend projection for a normal year. The gap would be larger in years of bad crops. In fact, the ability of developing countries to maintain and accelerate their growth rates for agricultural output could be seriously affected by inevitable fluctuations in production and prices and the resultant patterns of international trade in grains.

INSTABILITY OF PRODUCTION

Even if developing countries succeed in improving their longer-term prospects for food production towards the desired rate of 4% per annum, the problem of short-term fluctuations around the trend will continue to be a serious problem for most developing countries. It must be stressed that developing countries themselves are not more susceptible to such fluctuations than some of the richer countries.[2] Instability of output in richer countries, such as the USSR, has a much greater impact on the world market because of the size of their imports. But the economic and political capacity of developing countries to cope with the consequences of fluctuations, in their own production and in the production of richer countries, is much more limited. Unregulated free play of the 'market', so far as the world grain market is concerned, has more serious consequences for the developing countries, particularly those which have a large malnourished population. It was for this reason that the World Food Conference had recommended the establishment of an internationally coordinated system of grain reserves to minimize the adverse consequences of such instability, but so far little progress has been made towards the creation of such a system.

COLLECTIVE SELF-RELIANCE

While the developing countries must participate actively in the implementation of the plan of action adopted at the 1974 World Food Conference to solve the world food problem, the longer-term solution of this problem lies within the developing countries, provided they can find ways and means to cooperate with each other on the principle of collective self-reliance.

The Conference on Economic Cooperation Among Developing Countries held in Mexico in September 1976 paid special attention to food and agriculture and adopted several important decisions for strengthening sub-regional, regional and inter-regional cooperation and integration among developing countries. Some of these are reproduced below:[3]

> An appropriate machinery of the Group of 77, in cooperation with the Food and Agriculture Organization of the United Nations (FAO), the World Food Council, other appropriate institutions and the appropriate organizations and appropriate institutions of the developing countries, taking into account the work being done under existing programmes of the developing countries, should coordinate the preparation and evaluation of studies and make recommendations on the possibilities of:
> (a) Increase in agricultural output and food production through cooperative action on a sub-regional, regional and inter-regional basis;
> (b) Cooperative ventures between present and/or potential food-exporting developing countries, and other developing countries in a position to do so in terms of finance, technology and markets; . . .
> (f) Cooperation at the sub-regional, regional and inter-regional level for reorienting the structure of their agriculture, where appropriate, to-

wards increased production of food for consumption in developing countries.

The Ninth FAO Regional Conference for Africa held in November 1976, asked for a regional food plan 'which on its implementation would enable member states of the OAU to be self-sufficient in food in a period of 10 years'.

These pronouncements and decisions are a welcome manifestation of the political will of developing countries to cooperate with each other in increasing food production and in reducing their dependence on food imports, but these intentions have not so far been backed by concrete actions and plans to implement them. The developing countries do not so far have the requisite machinery in the form of a secretariat or brains trust which can translate political intentions into concrete plans of action, undertake consultations with developing and developed countries and create appropriate institutions to implement these programmes of action.

There is now enough experience of agricultural development in many developing countries (China, Mexico, India, Pakistan and Philippines, for example) which can be made available to other developing countries. Many of the developing countries can provide technical know-how which would be comparable to expertise provided by the richer countries. In fact experts coming under bilateral and multilateral arrangements between developing countries would certainly be cheaper than those from developed countries. Similarly, research and teaching in agricultural science, rural sociology and agricultural development can be provided by developing countries, probably more effectively than most developed countries because of the similarity of their problems. The first and relatively simpler area for cooperation is exchange of agricultural technology or training facilities. But this potential for cooperation and inter-change cannot be utilized without effective institutional and financial arrangements.

Perhaps a beginning towards these arrangements can be made with the creation of the International Fund for Agricultural Development (IFAD) and the OPEC Special Fund. IFAD is the first major international institution created for the benefit of the rural poor and would as a matter of deliberate policy promote greater cooperation among developing countries in sharing agricultural technology and expertise and in encouraging the growth of national institutions for agricultural development.

The problems involved in securing a larger measure of cooperation with respect to key inputs such as fertilizers and agricultural machinery are, however, more difficult. In these areas the developing countries will remain dependent on western technology for a considerable period of time and existing investment and trading arrangements are highly cartelized and closely guarded. But if the oil-producing countries, which have considerable cost advantages in setting up fertilizer plants, were to take the initiative and conclude longer-term arrangements with other developing countries for pooling technical know-how and for securing guaranteed markets in return for a reasonable subsidy on fertilizer sales, many far-reaching benefits could begin to flow. Similarly, developing countries could cooperate by buying agricultural machinery from each other on the basis of agreed specialization.

The problems of cooperation among developing countries in the area of food reserves and grain trade are even more complex than those that will be encountered in cooperation for increasing agricultural production. As already mentioned, the developing countries face growing insecurity in meeting their minimum food requirements and yet their capacity to counteract the consequences of this insecurity is more limited. At the same time, the developed countries which have the grain surpluses and the resources to build an international system of food security do not really need the system to safeguard their grain supplies. They would therefore be tempted to build the system only to the extent that it does not conflict with their own national objectives. The developing countries should therefore seriously consider evolving their own collective system of food security.

The first important step towards such a system should be a pooling of their national grain reserves. If each developing country were to maintain a separate reserve equal to say 15% of its annual consumption, the developing countries as a group would need reserves of 60 million tons. But if they were to 'pool' say 3 or 4% of their annual consumption, they could manage most emergencies with 12 to 16 million tons. These reserves do not have to be physically pooled, but a viable system could be built up on the following lines:

(i) Each participating developing country would earmark, over a three-year period, say, 3% of its annual grain consumption as a part of a 'Grain Cooperative for developing countries' and the total reserve of 12 million tons thus pooled will be potentially available for meeting emergency situations.

(ii) In practice each country would physically keep and finance its contribution to the reserve as its 'basic quota' and could draw on it after consultation with the Cooperative.

(iii) The Grain Cooperative would have the mandate to buy and sell grain on behalf of its members. In years of good crops, for example, member countries can either increase their contribution, and the Cooperative would be responsible for financing the storage costs of the extra contribution, or they can ask the Cooperative to sell the extra grain on their behalf.

(iv) Those member countries which buy grain regularly in the world market could use the Grain Cooperative for their purchases. This would enable the Cooperative to provide assured outlets to grain surpluses from developing countries and also provide benefits of large-scale buying to importing developing countries. In due course, the Cooperative could enter into long-term contracts with land-surplus or potentially exporting developing countries to produce food for other developing countries.

Proposals on these lines, though a product of frustration, should not reflect an 'anti-rich' attitude. They are legitimate alternatives for cooperation among developing countries and if properly implemented could help to solve one of the most serious problems facing developing countries. In the absence of adequate food reserves, the malnourished populations in these countries will suffer each time there are fluctuations in the world markets and their ability to achieve greater self-sufficiency in food will be seriously undermined if they cannot participate in the world grain market by exporting their periodical surpluses at reasonable prices.

Once concrete proposals for cooperation among developing countries for increasing their food production and for building a system of food security have been formulated, they would require political support at the highest level and would need continued financial and policy backing for effective implementation. Perhaps a Third World Economic Summit on the lines proposed by the former Prime Minister of Pakistan could give the minimum necessary impetus to these and other proposals and begin to give concrete shape to the philosophy of collective self-reliance.

The philosophy of collective self-reliance is a persuasive concept which in many ways goes beyond the concept of the New International Economic Order. Its starting point is the principle of self-reliance at the national level geared to the development of human resources, followed by a policy of greater reliance on local resources of land and other materials and greater equality of opportunity geared to basic needs of everyone. Only the adoption of these two principles at the national level will prepare the ground for a new order at the international level and for collective self-reliance among all developing countries.

All the implications including the theoretical foundations of the philosophy of collective self-reliance have yet to be fully worked out but cooperation in respect of food can provide an important starting point for its implementation.

NOTES

1. The demand projections are derived from the application of regional income elasticities to the growth of private consumption *per capita* which was projected to grow at the rates corresponding to the trend assumption for gross domestic product shown in Table 26 of the 'Assessment of the world food situation present and future', United Nations World Food Conference (E/CONF.65/3), i.e. for developed market economies the growth assumed is 3.6% per annum; for Eastern Europe and USSR, 5.3%; for developing market economies, 3.6%; and for Asian centrally-planned economies, 2.5%. Total demand was calculated by multiplying the projected *per capita* demand by total regional population assuming the United Nations medium variant, which is based on 'World population prospects, 1970–2000, as assessed in 1973', Working Paper ESA/P/W.P.53 (Population Division, United Nations, March 1975). For the more developed countries the rate of population growth 1975 to 2000 is assumed to be 0.7% per annum and for the less developed countries the growth is 2.2% per year. The projected demand under the low population growth variant for the more developed countries would be 3.9% less than under the medium variant; it would be 5.4% higher under the high population variant. For the less developed countries the figures would be 7.4% less and 6.3% more respectively. These projections were also presented in a paper prepared by the author for the 'World Food Conference of 1976' organized by Iowa State University in June 1976.

2. The instability indices for the world as a whole, calculated by FAO for cereal production in the period 1952 to 1972 is 4, indicating that normal fluctuations can occur within the limits of 8%. But within this average, the instability index in the Asian centrally-planned economies is 4, 6 to 8 in most developing countries, 10 in North America and 13 in Eastern Europe and the USSR. The overall index for developed countries is 6, compared to 3 in the developing countries, reflecting the effect of changes in agricultural policies and climatic conditions. See FAO, *The State of Food and Agriculture 1974*, p. 12.

3. Report of the Conference on Economic Cooperation among Developing Countries, No. 77/Conf./C. MEX/12 (28 September 1976), pp. 20–21.

World Development, 1977, Vol. 5, Nos. 5–7, pp. 661–664. Pergamon Press. Printed in Great Britain.

A Selected Bibliography

Prepared by

GAUTAM PINGLE

Abelson, P. H. (ed.), *Food: Politics, Economics, Nutrition and Research* (Washington, D.C.: American Association for the Advancement of Science, 1975).

Ady, P. (ed.), *Private Foreign Investment and the Developing World* (New York: Praeger Publishers, 1971).

Amin, S. and Okediji, F.O., 'Land use, agriculture and food supply and industrialization', *Population in African Development*, Vol. 2 (1971).

Austin, J. E., *Agribusiness in Latin America* (New York: Praeger, 1974).

Aziz, S., 'The Chinese approach to rural development', *World Development*, Vol. 2, No. 2 (February 1974).

Balogh, T., *The Economics of Poverty* (London: Weidenfeld and Nicolson, 1974).

Baran, P. A., *The Political Economy of Growth* (London: Penguin Books, 1973).

Barnes, P. and Casalino, L., *Who Owns the Land? A Primer on Land Reform in the USA* (Berkeley: Centre for Rural Studies, n.d.).

Barraclough, S., *Agrarian Structure in Latin America,* (Massachusetts: Lexington Heath and Co., 1974).

Bellingham, A. B., 'Wheat marketing in major exporting countries', USDA, *Foreign Agriculture* (1970/71).

Bhagwati, J. N. 'Market disruption, export market disruption, compensation and GATT reform', *World Development*, Special Issue, Vol. 4, No. 12 (December 1976).

Blakeslee, Leroy L., Heady, Earl O. and Framingham, Charles F., *World Food Production, Demand and Trade* (Ames: Iowa State University Press, 1973).

Borgstrom, G., *World Food Resources* (New York: Intext Publishers, 1973).

Breimyer, H., *Economics of the Product Markets of Agriculture* (Ames: Iowa State University Press, 1976).

Brown, P. G. and Shue, H. (eds.), *Food Policy: US Responsibility in the Life and Death Choices* (New York: The Free Press, forthcoming).

Bryson, R. A., *World Food Prospects and Climatic Change,* testimony before joint meeting of the US Senate Sub-Committees on Foreign Agricultural Policy and Agricultural Production, Marketing and Stabilization of Prices (18 October 1973).

Casley, D. J., Simaika, J. B. and Sinha, R. P., 'Instability of production and its impact on stock requirements', *Monthly Bulletin of Agricultural Economics and Statistics*, Vol. 23, No. 5 (May 1974).

Cassen, R. H., 'Population and development: a survey', *World Development*, Vol. 4, Nos. 10 and 11 (October–November 1976).

Central Intelligence Agency, *Potential Implications of Trends in World Population, Food Production and Climate* (Washington, D.C.: 1974), mimeo.

Chamber of Commerce of the United States, *The Changing Structure of US Agribusiness and its Contributions to the National Economy* (Washington, D.C.: Chamber of Commerce of the United States, 1974).

Chao, K., *Agricultural Production in Communist China, 1949–65* (Madison: The University of Wisconsin Press, 1970).

Chen, L. C. and Chowdhury, R. H., *Demographic Change and Trends of Food Production and Availabilities in Bangladesh (1960–74)* (Dacca: Ford Foundation, 1975).

Clark, C. and Haswell, M., *The Economics of Subsistence Agriculture* (London: Macmillan and Co. Ltd., 1970).

Clark, C. and Turner, J., 'World population growth and future food trends', in Recheigl Jr., Miloslav (ed.), *Man, Food and Nutrition* (Cleveland, Ohio: CRS Press, 1973).

Cochrane, W. W. and Ryan, Mary E., *American Farm Policy 1948–73* (Minneapolis: University of Minnesota Press, 1976).

Concepcion, Mercedes B., 'Emerging issues on population policy and population program assistance', *Third Bellagio Conference on Population* (New York: Rockefeller Foundation, n.d.).

Connelly, P. and Perlman, R., *The Politics of Scarcity: Resource Conflicts in International Relations* (London: Oxford University Press, 1975).

Demarco, Susan and Sechler, Susan, *The Fields Have Turned Brown: Four Essays on World Hunger* (Washington, D.C.: Agribusiness Accountability Project, 1975).

Ehrlich, Paul R. and Ehrlich, Anne H., *Population Resource Environment: Issues in Human Ecology* (San Francisco: W. H. Freeman and Company, 1972).

Etienne, G., *Studies in Indian Agriculture: The Art of the Possible* (Berkeley: University of California Press, 1968).

Etienne, G. (ed.), *China's Agricultural Development* (Geneva: Graduate Institute of International Studies, Asian Centre, 1974).

FAO, *The State of Food and Agriculture* (Rome: FAO, annually issued).

FAO, *Provisional Indicative World Plan for Agri-*

cultural Development (Rome: FAO–UN, 1970).

FAO, *Energy and Protein Requirements: Report of a Joint FAO/WHO Ad Hoc Expert Committee* (Rome: FAO, 1973).

FAO, *Population, Food Supply and Agricultural Development* (Rome: FAO, 1975).

FAO, *National Grain Policies* (Rome: FAO, 1976).

FAO, 'World food and agricultural situation – November 1976', *Monthly Bulletin of Agricultural Economics and Statistics,* Vol. 25 (November 1976).

Freedman, R. and Berelson, B., 'The record of family planning programs', *Studies in Family Planning,* Vol. 7, No. 1 (January 1976).

Frejka, T., *The Future of Population Growth* (New York: John Wiley, 1973).

George, S., *How the Other Half Dies: The Real Reasons for World Hunger* (London: Penguin, 1976).

Goldberg, R. A., *Agribusiness Management for Developing Countries – Latin America* (Cambridge, Mass.: Ballinger Publishing Co., 1974).

Gordon, K., 'Needed: world grain reserves', *The Brookings Bulletin,* Vol. 13, No. 2 (Spring–Summer 1976).

Guither, H. D. (ed.), *Who will Control US Agriculture? Policies Affecting the Organizational Structure of US Agriculture* (Urbana–Champaign: University of Illinois, Special Publication 27, 1972).

Hadler, Sandra, *Developing Country Foodgrain Projections for 1985,* World Bank Staff Working Paper No. 247 (World Bank, November 1976).

Hall, M. Francoise, 'Population control: Latin America and the United States', *International Journal of Health Services,* Vol. 3, No. 4 (Fall 1973).

Hamilton, Martha M., *The Great American Grain Robbery and Other Stories* (Washington, D.C.: Agribusiness Accountability Project, 1972).

Hardin, G., 'Living on a lifeboat', *BioScience* (October 1974).

Harlan, J. R., 'The plants and animals that nourish man', *Scientific American,* Vol. 235, No. 3 (September 1976).

Hawthorn, G., *The Sociology of Fertility* (London: Collier–Macmillan Ltd., 1970).

Heady, E. O., 'The agriculture of the US', *Scientific American,* Vol. 235, No. 3 (September 1976).

Henrichsmeyer, W., *et al.* (eds.), *Trade Negotiations and the World Food Problem* (London: Trade Policy Research Centre, 1974).

Hightower, J., *Food, Farmers Corporations, Earl Butz . . . and You* (Washington, D.C.: Agribusiness Accountability Project, 1973), mimeo.

Hildreth, R. J., Krause, K. R. and Nelson Jr., P. E., 'Organization and control of the US food and fibre sector', *American Journal of Agricultural Economics,* Vol. 55, No. 5 (December 1973).

Hopper, W. David, 'The development of agriculture in developing countries', *Scientific American,* Vol. 235, No. 3 (September 1976).

IBRD, *Population Policies and Economic Development* (Baltimore: Johns Hopkins University Press, 1974).

IBRD, *Assault on World Poverty* (Baltimore: Johns

Hopkins University Press, 1975).

IBRD, *Rural Development: Sector Policy Paper* (Washington, D.C.: Johns Hopkins University Press, 1975).

International Food Policy Research Institution, *Meeting Food Needs in the Developing World: The Location and Magnitude of the Task in the Next Decade,* Research Report No. 1 (Washington, D.C.: IFPRI, 1976).

Ishikawa, S., *Economic Development in Asian Perspective* (Tokyo: Kinokuniya Bookstore Co. Ltd., 1967).

Jacoby, Erich H. and Jacoby, Charlotte F., *Man and Land: The Fundamental Issue in Development* (London: Andre Deutsch Ltd., 1971).

Johnson, D. Gale, *World Food Problems and Prospects* (Washington: American Enterprises Institute for Public Policy Research, 1975).

Johnson, D. Gale, *Increased Stability of Grain Supplies in Developing Countries: Optimal Carry-overs and Insurance* (Chicago: University of Chicago, Agricultural Economics Research, paper no. 76: 14, 1976).

Johnson, D. Gale, 'Increased stability of grain supplies in developing countries: optimal carryovers and insurance', *World Development,* Special Issue, Vol. 4, No. 12 (December 1976).

Johnson, H. G., 'Mercantilism: past, present and future', *Manchester School of Economic and Social Studies,* Vol. XLII, No. 1 (1974).

Johnson, H. G., 'World inflation, the developing countries, and "An Integrated Programme for Commodities" ', *Banca Nazionale Del Lavoro Quarterly Review,* No. 119 (December 1976).

Jones, D., *Food and Interdependence – The Effect of Food and Agricultural Policies of the Developed Countries on the Food Problems of the Developing Countries* (London: Overseas Development Institute, 1976).

Josling, T. E., 'Agricultural policies in developed countries: a review', *Journal of Agricultural Economics* (September 1974).

Josling, T., 'Government price policies and the structure of international agricultural trade', *Journal of Agricultural Economics* (September 1977, forthcoming).

Kaldor, N., 'Inflation and recession in the world economy', *Economic Journal,* Vol. 86, No. 344 (December 1976).

Krebs, A. V., 'Of the grain trade, by the grain trade and for the grain trade', *Congressional Record,* Vol. 118, No. 160 (Washington, D.C.: 1972).

Krebs, A. V. (ed./publisher), 'Monitoring the activities of agribusiness', *The AgBiz Tiller,* various monthly issues, Issue Number 1 (August 1976).

Labys, W. C. (ed.), *Quantitative Models of Commodity Markets* (Cambridge: Ballinger Publishing Co., 1975).

Ledogar, R. J., *Hungry for Profits – US Food and Drug Multinationals in Latin America* (New York: IDOC/North America, 1975).

Lehmann, D. (ed.), *Agrarian Reform and Agrarian Reformism* (London: Faber & Faber, 1974).

Lipton, M., *Why Poor People Stay Poor – A Study of*

Urban Bias in World Development (London: Temple Smith, 1977).

McNamara, Robert S., *One Hundred Countries, Two Billion People: The Dimensions of Development* (New York: Praeger Publishers, 1973).

MacKerron, G. and Rush, H. J., 'Agriculture in the EEC – taking stock', *Food Policy,* Vol. 1, No. 4 (August 1976).

Martens, V. (ed.), *Grains and Oilseeds: Handling, Marketing, Processing,* Second Edition (Winnipeg, Manitoba: Canadian International Grain Institute, 1975).

Mauldin, W. P., Choucri, N. Notestein, F. W. and Teitelbaum, M., 'A report on Bucharest', *Studies in Family Planning,* Vol. 5, No. 12 (December 1974).

Mayer, Jean, 'The dimensions of human hunger', *Scientific American,* Vol. 235, No. 3 (September 1976).

Meadows, Donella H., Meadows, Denis L., Randers, Jorgen and Behrens, William W., *The Limits to Growth: A Report for the Club of Rome's Project on the Predicament of Mankind* (London: Potomac Associates Book, 1972).

Mellor, J. W., 'The agriculture of India', *Scientific American,* Vol. 235, No. 3 (September 1976).

Mesarovic, M. and Pestel, E., *Mankind at the Turning Point: The Second Report to the Club of Rome* (London: Hutchinson and Co. Ltd., 1975).

Moen, H. J. and Beek, K. J., *Literature Study on the Potential Irrigated Acreage in the World* (Wageningen: ILR Institute, 1974).

Moore, John R. and Padorano, Frank A., *US Investment in Latin American Food Processing* (New York: Praeger, 1967).

Moraes, D., *A Matter of People* (London: Andre Deutsh Ltd., 1974).

Myrdal, G., *Asian Drama: An Inquiry into the Poverty of Nations* (London: Allen Lane, the Penguin Press, 1968).

National Academy of Sciences, *Recommended Dietary Allowances,* Eighth Revised Edition (Washington: 1974).

Niernberger, F. F. and Schnake, L. D., *Grain Marketing in the United States – Trends and Changes, 1963–72,* CED Working Paper, Commodity Economics Division (Washington, D.C.: USDA (ERS), 1975), mimeo.

North American Congress of Latin America, 'US grain arsenal', *NACLA's Latin America and Empire Report,* Vol. IX, No. 7 (October 1975).

OECD, *Agricultural Policy in the United States* (Paris: OECD, 1974).

OECD, *Study of Trends in World Supply and Demand of Major Agricultural Commodities* (Paris: OECD, 1976).

Paddock, W. and Paddock, P., *Famine – 1975!,* (Boston: Little, Brown and Co., 1967).

Poleman, T. T., 'World food: a perspective', *Science* (9 May 1975).

Power, J. and Holenstein, *World of Hunger* (London: Temple Smith, 1976).

Regier, D. and Goolsby, O. H., *Growth in World Demand for Feed Grains Related to Meat and Livestock Product and Human Consumption of*

Grain, Foreign Agricultural Report No. 63 (Washington, D.C.: USDA, 1970), mimeo.

Revelle, R., 'The resources available for agriculture', *Scientific American,* Vol. 235, No. 3 (September 1976).

Robinson, E. A. G., 'J. M. Keynes: economist, author, statesman', *Economic Journal,* Vol. 82, No. 326 (June 1972).

Saleh, Abdullah A., 'Disincentives to agricultural production in developing countries: a policy survey', *Foreign Agricultural Supplement* (March 1975).

Sarris, A. and Taylor, L., 'Cereal stocks, food aid and food security for the poor', *World Development,* Special Issue, Vol. 4, No. 12 (December 1976).

Schumpeter, J., *Capitalism, Socialism and Democracy* (London: George Allen & Unwin Ltd., 1950).

Scrimshaw, N. S. and Young, U. R., 'The requirements of human nutrition', *Scientific American,* Vol. 235, No. 3 (September 1976).

Sen, A., *Employment, Technology and Development* (Oxford: Clarendon Press, 1975).

Shonfield, A., *Modern Capitalism – The Changing Balance of Public and Private Power* (London: Oxford University Press, 1969).

Simaika, J. B., 'Probability of success of a "stock and allocation" policy', ESS/MISC/74-1 (Rome: FAO, September 1974), mimeo.

Sinha, R. P., 'World food security', *Journal of Agricultural Economics,* Vol. 27, No. 1 (January 1976).

Sinha, R. P., 'Chinese agriculture: a quantitative look', *Journal of Development Studies,* Vol. 11, No. 3 (April 1975).

Sinha, R. P., *Food and Poverty: The Political Economy of Confrontation* (London: Croom Helm, 1976).

Spengler, J., *Population Change, Modernization and Welfare* (Englewood Cliffs, N. J.: Prentice–Hall Inc., 1974).

Stavis, B., 'How China is solving its food problem'. *Bulletin of Concerned Asian Scholars,* Vol. 7, No. 3 (July–September 1975).

Stavis, B., 'A preliminary model for grain production in China, 1974', *China Quarterly,* No. 65 (January 1976).

Sukhatme, P. V., 'The protein gap – its size and nature', *Proceedings Nutrition Society of India, No. 8* (reprinted by the FAO).

Thurgood, L., 'Agribusiness on the farm', *Financial Times,* Iran Survey (28 July 1975).

Thurgood, L. 'Food shortfall', *Financial Times,* Iran Survey (28 July 1975).

Thurston, S. P., Phillips, M. J., Haskell, J. E. and Volkin, D., *Improving the Export Capability of Grain Cooperatives* (Washington, D.C.: US Department of Agriculture, Farmer Cooperative Service Research Report 34, 1976), mimeo.

Tolley, G. S. and Zadrozny, P. A. (eds.), *Trade, Agriculture and Development* (Cambridge, Mass.: Ballinger Publishing Co., 1975).

United Nations, *Towards a New Trade Policy for Development – Report of the Secretary–General of the United Nations Conference on Trade and*

Development (New York: UN, 1964).

United Nations, *The Determinants and Consequences of Population Trends – New Summary of Findings on Interaction of Demographic, Economic and Social Factors,* Vol. I (New York: UN, 1973).

United Nations, *Selected World Demographic Indicators by Countries, 1950–2000* (New York: UN, ESA/P/WP. 55, 1975), mimeo.

UN World Food Conference, *The World Food Problem: Proposals for National and International Action* (Rome: UN–FAO, 1974), mimeo.

UN World Food Council, *International System of Food Security,* WFC/22 (Rome: WFC, 1976), mimeo.

UN World Food Council, 'Food aid targets and policies', Report of the Executive Director, 22 April 1976, (New York: UN), mimeo.

US Department of Agriculture, *World Demand Prospects for Grain in 1980 with Emphasis on Trade by the Less Developed Countries* (Washington, D.C.: Government Printing Office, 1971).

US Department of Agriculture, *The World Food Situation and Prospects to 1985* (Washington, D.C.: Government Printing Office, 1974).

US Department of Agriculture, *Statement of James J. Naive before the Sub-Committee on Special Small Business Problems;* House Select Committee on Small Business, US House of Representatives, 22 May 1974, mimeo.

US Department of Agriculture, *The Food and Fibre System – How It Works,* Agriculture Information Bulletin 383 (Washington, D.C.: 1975).

US Department of Agriculture, *The Agricultural Situation in the People's Republic of China and Other Communist Asian Countries – Review of 1975 and Outlook for 1976* (Washington, D.C.: USDA, 1976).

US General Accounting Office, *Grain Reserves: A Potential US Food Policy Tool* (Washington, D.C.: GAO, 1976).

US Senate, Committee on Agriculture and Forestry, *Russian Grain Sale* (Washington, D.C.: US Government Printing Office, 1975).

US Senate, Committee on Agriculture and Forestry, *Marketing Alternatives for Agriculture* (Washington, D.C.: US Government Printing Office, 1976).

Wagstaff, H., *World Food: A Political Task* (London: Fabian Society, 1976), Fabian Research Series 32.

Westlake, M., *World Poverty: The Growing Conflict* (London: Fabian Society, 1976), Young Fabian Pamphlet 44.

Yudelman, M., Butler, G. and Banerjee, R., *Technological Change in Agriculture and Employment in Developing Countries* (Paris: OECD, 1971).

Index